GOD'S WORD
TO A WIDOW'S HEART

DAILY HOPE TO OVERCOME PERSONAL LOSS

This gift is given by:
HIGHER GROUND
Widows Ministry
Grace Church of the Nazarene

RONDA LITTLE MARTIN

CROSSBOOKS
PUBLISHING

CrossBooks™
A Division of LifeWay
1663 Liberty Drive
Bloomington, IN 47403
www.crossbooks.com
Phone: 1-866-879-0502

Unless otherwise noted, all Scripture quotations are taken from the Holman
Christian Standard Bible®, Copyright © 1999, 2000, 2002, 2003, 2009 by Holman
Bible Publishers. Used by permission. Holman Christian Standard Bible®, Holman
CSB®, and HCSB® are federally registered trademarks of Holman Bible Publishers.

First published by CrossBooks 02/18/2014

ISBN: 978-1-4627-3474-0 (sc)
ISBN: 978-1-4627-3473-3 (hc)
ISBN: 978-1-4627-3475-7 (e)

Library of Congress Control Number: 2014901729

Printed in the United States of America.

This book is printed on acid-free paper.

Any people depicted in stock imagery provided by Thinkstock are models,
and such images are being used for illustrative purposes only.
Certain stock imagery © Thinkstock.

Because of the dynamic nature of the Internet, any web addresses or links contained
in this book may have changed since publication and may no longer be valid. The views
expressed in this work are solely those of the author and do not necessarily reflect the
views of the publisher, and the publisher hereby disclaims any responsibility for them.

DEDICATION

This book is dedicated in loving memory to Edgar (Eddie) Adolph Martin and Clinese Hargett Little. Without a doubt, my husband and my mother were the two most impressionable individuals who influenced me most. My husband showed me true, unconditional love while my mother instilled a strong faith in Jesus Christ in me. I sense their absence every single day, but I take great pleasure in knowing I will see them again and rejoice with them in heaven. Salvation through Jesus Christ is the greatest gift you can leave behind to your loved ones, and they both left me with the comfort of knowing they are in a better place than I. I love you, Eddie and Mama.

Ronda

After more than a decade of praying, seeking, and crying out to God, I finally had everything I always wanted. In 2005, I found myself in a very good place as I was living my dream as a wife and stay-at-home mom to a beautiful four-year-old boy named Samuel. I had a wonderful, godly, loving husband who adored me and who was an excellent father. We were both dedicated Christians, actively involved in our church serving God. While we had endured both struggle and disappointment in our short marriage, we had learned to turn to God and to each other to see things through to the end. I felt truly alive and blessed to be where I was.

August 5, 2005 changed everything. My husband, Eddie, went to work that morning on his motorcycle and never came home. He was killed in an accident on his way home from work that day, and all of my dreams came crashing down on top of me. My husband, best friend, and son's father was gone at the age of 37. Every part of my life began to change as I was thrust into a lifestyle and identity I did not want and for which I never asked: I became a widow.

When you become a widow, everything changes. Your family, your relationships, your finances, your security – everything changes in ways you probably don't expect and cannot control. You have a different social status, and you are forced to find a new identity now that you are no longer a wife. Just what do you do to find yourself again as you pick up the pieces of a shattered life and begin to rebuild? I found my answers by going to the Bible on a daily basis and crying out to God. As a committed Christian already strong in my faith, this was the only thing I knew to do. In retrospect, I now see it as the path God gave me to begin a journey where He would reconstruct a new life for me – one of which I neither expected nor dreamed.

While I had taught Sunday School and women's Bible studies for years, I found myself with an insatiable desire to study the Bible and hear from God. I learned that He would speak directly to me and to my problem if I would only spend time with Him as Mary did at His feet. I loved to research and often found myself digging through a concordance or commentaries to learn more on different subjects – especially on that of the widow in Scripture. This newly found hunger for the Word of God led me to complete a Master of Arts degree in Theological Studies from Liberty

Baptist Theological Seminary and Graduate School in 2009. Going to seminary was never in my original plan.

In late 2009, I attended a missions program at my church, Immanuel Baptist in Lebanon, Tennessee, where I had been a member only a short time. I began asking God where He would have me serve and to show me where my spiritual gift of teaching and my experiences might best serve Him. Since I had just completed seminary, I thought I would find the answer by going on one of the wonderful mission trip opportunities my church supported. God, however, answered in a different way.

My pastor, Rev. John Hunn, went to the pulpit during this Wednesday night missions meeting and began to announce prayer requests, as he did every week. He mentioned a new widow who had asked him the question, "Pastor John, when does it ever stop hurting?" He did not know how to respond. He explained to the congregation that he had never walked that road, and he could not give her an answer. He knew, however, that someone had walked that journey and needed to step forward to be a support to those who are hurting now. I knew what I had just prayed, and I could clearly see that my mission opportunity at this point was not to go to a foreign country but to begin to minister to other widows around me who were experiencing the same thing I had. I went forward at the end of service and told him I had walked that road, and I felt God was calling me to help others. He asked to meet with me to discuss ways to begin helping other widows.

I called my friend, Elaine Pearson, who lost her husband in August of 2006, just a year after my husband, Eddie, died. Elaine has a compassionate evangelistic heart and has been involved in mission work throughout her lifetime. We both met with Pastor John and learned the need to minister to widows was tremendous from his perspective. We both felt overwhelmed, and I recognized the need for someone with administrative skills to help.

Elaine called her friend, Carol Pharris, to join us. Carol is the most gifted administrator I have ever met, and she immediately began to orchestrate and give wise direction. Carol called her friend, Glynda Green, who is the life of the party as a socialite and encourager. We began to see that God was bringing together widows with different gifts and talents together to minister to the needs of other widows. Through much prayer and the support of Pastor John and Pastor David Freeman of First Baptist, Lebanon, we formed PHOEBE Ministries as a support group to connect widows with one another and to minister to the needs that require someone who has already walked that road and understands.

After numerous attempts to name the ministry something that would not sound somber or depressing, Carol suggested we focus on writing our mission statement and purpose statement. She believed the name would just pop out at us once we did. She had no idea how prophetic her instruction was! The four of us discussed our purpose, our mission, and I wrote those suggestions down. I went back to my group with a draft, and they continued to edit. While I was incorporating the final edits, something literally popped out at me. I found the first letter of each of the declarations of our purpose statement spelled the name, PHOEBE, as an acrostic. I immediately began to research what the Bible had to say about Phoebe, and I found her name mentioned in only one place.

Romans 16:1-2:

I commend to you our sister Phoebe, who is a servant of the church in Cenchreae. So you should welcome her in the Lord in a manner worthy of the saints, and assist her in whatever matter she may require your help. For indeed she has been a benefactor of many – and of me also.

Phoebe was most likely a widow who had committed herself to the service of the church, as is explained in 2 Timothy 5:9-10. Paul instructed the church at Rome to welcome her because she had been such a great help to the church in Cenchreae (port city for Corinth) through her service. Phoebe, however, is not mentioned as a widow; she is forever recognized for her acts of service—that is the heart of PHOEBE Ministries.

PHOEBE Ministries seeks to help widows connect with other widows for the purpose of fellowship and to provide a platform for service. Widows need the strength, friendship, and encouragement of one another as they engage in their respective journeys and begin to discover a new identity as an individual. They also need to find a place to serve, where they feel they are making a difference and contributing to society. Service is a part of healing, and we encourage participation in a local church and the local community to meet that need.

Prior to our launch in September of 2010, I began writing daily devotions via email to the dear PHOEBES who worked so diligently to help us prepare. They were originally simply meant to bring a timely word of encouragement, but I found myself continuing to write after the launch as the PHOEBES requested more devotions. Therefore, the daily devotions became a part of my ministry. I found myself giving to them what God would give me every morning in my own personal devotion time with Him. As a result, His word to me flowed also to many others who needed to hear the same words of hope and encouragement to take on another day in their widow's journey. This book is a compilation of those devotions.

To learn more about PHOEBE Ministries, visit our website: **www. phoebeministries.com**, where the daily devotions are posted from our Facebook® page. Like us on Facebook, and you can receive the daily devotions in your newsfeed every morning. May you find hope, encouragement, direction, and a new zeal for life as you turn to Him daily for the answers you need.

A Beautiful Plan

Jeremiah 18:2-6:

"Go down at once to the potter's house; there I will reveal My words to you." So I went down to the potter's house, and there he was, working away at the wheel. But the jar that he was making from the clay became flawed in the potter's hand, so he made it into another jar, as it seemed right for him to do. The word of the LORD came to me; "House of Israel, can I not treat you as this potter treats the clay? - this is the LORD's declaration. "Just like clay in the potter's hand, so are you in My hand, house of Israel."

Notice where the jar was when it became flawed — in the potter's hand! The potter was in control of the jar the whole time. When he found something that didn't pass his inspection, he reformed it. He removed the flaw by creating another jar from it.

As long as we live in this earthly body, we will have flaws. God will continue to create us into new jars that are effective for His purpose. This is why we experience changes in eras or seasons in our lives. We are still in the Master Potter's hand, and He is still working. What starts poorly can be beautiful in the end. Success depends upon realizing the vision He gives for our lives and allowing Him to fill us with passion for our purpose. As long as we are being transformed for God's purpose, we can count on a beautiful ending. Once His purpose is served, God recycles us to extend the use of His creation. He wastes nothing!

Today, know that God is the Master Potter in control of your life (Eph. 2:10). You could never make yourself the masterpiece He intends to create. You are merely clay and not a skilled artist. Submit to His leadership, and look for His purpose in creating you. Stop comparing yourself to other lumps of clay that are flawed and unfinished. Whether God is removing a flaw or recycling to extend your usefulness, He has a plan, and it is beautiful!

Have a blessed day!

A Safe Place

Psalm 12:5:

"Because of the oppression of the afflicted and the groaning of the poor, I will now rise up," says the LORD. "I will put in a safe place the one who longs for it."

God is angered when His children are oppressed. He has compassion for the poor and those in need. When He rises, His enemies scatter. Never hesitate to cry out to God in your pain. Expect Him to rise up on your behalf.

God promises to put those who long for it in a safe place. Just as a mother will remove her child from danger and place him next to her, so God will remove us from the people, places, situations, and spiritual forces that threaten us. He moves us to a safe place that is close to Him.

When a mother removes children from danger, they may not realize what she is doing. They may see the danger as adventure and think she is spoiling their fun. Just think about how many times you have seen children cry, rebel, and even kick and scream when their mother moves them to a safe place. We do the same with God at times.

If you find God moving you from one place to another, realize that He may just be taking you to a safe place. Don't fight it. Just move with Him. If your life seems to be in transition at the moment, let go of what is in the past, and embrace the place where God is taking you. His safe place may not always appear to be a fun place, but it will protect us from the Devil's schemes against us. Submit to His loving care, and rest in His presence.

Have a blessed day!

Encouragement for the Journey

Acts 14:21-22:

After they had evangelized that town and made many disciples, they returned to Lystra, to Iconium, and to Antioch, strengthening the hearts of the disciples by encouraging them to continue in the faith, and by telling them, "It is necessary to pass through many troubles on our way into the kingdom of God."

Paul strengthened disciples by encouraging them. Encouragement certainly seems to have a way of motivating us for our journey; it is an extremely valuable gift to the church. Discouragement is one of Satan's greatest weapons against us. When he knows he can't defeat us, he will try to discourage us so we will give up the fight.

This verse reveals the reason Paul needed to encourage the believers. Troubles were necessary and inevitable in their journey into God's kingdom. Troubles are necessary because we are in a battle. The Devil won't give up without a fight. Our journeys are all a part of God's plan in defeating the Devil and in overcoming evil. While Christ has already gained the victory through death in the spiritual realm, our earthly battles still remain to be fought. We need both courage and grace to overcome.

Storms damage, injure, and kill. The storms and battles we face may leave us injured, but injury does not mean defeat. We need healing and strengthening to continue.

Our victories provide us with testimonies that encourage others to face an approaching storm or battle. Any wisdom or insight we gain can be a tool to help others survive. For some, just knowing they are not alone in their journey can give them strength to go the next mile. While some have the gift of encouragement, we are all called to encourage one another and to help strengthen one another.

Dare to be an encourager to someone today. Tell someone how God has helped you through a storm or a battle, and pray for those who are encountering difficult times now. If you have fallen, reach out to someone who is standing. God gave us the gift of fellowship as a tool to encourage, strengthen, and sharpen one another.

Have a blessed day!

Enlarge Your Tent

Isaiah 54:2-3:

Enlarge the site of your tent, and let your tent curtains be stretched out; do not hold back; lengthen your ropes, and drive your pegs deep. For you will spread out to the right and to the left, and your descendants will dispossess nations and inhabit the desolate cities.

In the previous verse, God compares Israel to a barren woman, and a later verse refers to her as a widow. God promises to give her a greater blessing than the married woman, who was perfectly capable and equipped to build a family. In order to contain the blessing God planned to give this barren woman, she was to enlarge her tent so she could hold what He was about to give her.

A barren woman would have had a small tent. A married woman would have had a large tent to accommodate her family. God wanted the barren woman here to believe Him for a blessing and to prepare for it. He needed room in her life to give her more. You cannot pour more water into a glass that is full without making a mess and disturbing everything around it. If we are to hold what God has in store for us, we must make room for Him to bless us.

Just how do we enlarge our tents? We can begin by clearing out the clutter in our lives. Get rid of things, attitudes, motives, bad habits, and even people, if necessary, that you don't need. If you are currently managing your tent well, take on a new responsibility or volunteer where you can meet a need. Take on a new project or a new hobby you've been considering. Be open to new people and adventures. Start living life, rather than allowing it to pass you by. Stop waiting for something to happen before you decide to enjoy your life.

Today, find one area where you can enlarge your tent. Make a little room for God to bless you. Rejoice, barren one! Burst into song and shout because God wants to bless you with the very things you cannot do for yourself!

Have a blessed day!

Determine to Sing a New Song

Psalm 144:9:

God, I will sing a new song to you; I will play on a ten-stringed harp for You.

In this Psalm, David is crying out through praise for deliverance from his enemies. He vows to sing a new song to God in response to His deliverance. Apparently, David has learned something through this experience, and he is determined to give God the glory for it.

Where do you need to be delivered today? Cry out to God in praise. What is He teaching you through this struggle? Where has He been faithful to you already? Determine to respond to His deliverance with a new song.

Old songs may be easy to remember, but they can become monotonous with repetition. While reciting their familiar words, we often forget their meaning. We need a new reason to praise God! We need a new victory, a new testimony, a new passion to share! Determine to sing a new song to God for what you are experiencing right now. He is alive and active in your situation, and He is waiting to reveal Himself in a whole new way. He deserves a new song of praise!

Have a blessed day!

Comfort for the Waste Places

Isaiah 51:3:

For the LORD will comfort Zion; He will comfort all her waste places, and He will make her wilderness like Eden, and her desert like the garden of the LORD. Joy and gladness will be found in her, thanksgiving and melodious song.

This verse brings great comfort and hope to those who are hurting. We have all experienced hurtful situations where we need to be comforted. God promises us that comfort. Many of us have experienced waste places where it seems nothing can be salvaged from a life that was once full and vibrant. We may even have had to cut our losses and start anew in an unfamiliar place. Some of us have gone through dry places where it seems no life could grow; these are the very places God promises to comfort.

God allowed Zion (Jerusalem) to be taken into captivity. He allowed the waste places, the wilderness, and the desert places to take over what was once a blessed, vibrant, flourishing city devoted to Him. God's intention, however, was not to leave her in such a condition. He fully purposed to restore her with joy and gladness, thanksgiving and melodious song.

If you find yourself in a dry, wasteful wilderness today, look up. God does not intend to leave you there! He who has promised is faithful! Has He not done great things for you before? He still wants to show Himself strong in your barren places. A garden doesn't grow in one day. Wait for His harvest, and watch with eager expectation of good. Joy and gladness will soon come to you, and you will break forth with thanksgiving and melodious song. If you never experience the dry, lonely, barren places, you may never come to appreciate the blessing.

Have a blessed day!

From Cursed to Blessed

Jeremiah 17:5-6:

This is what the LORD says: Cursed is the man who trusts in mankind, who makes human flesh his strength and turns his heart from the LORD. He will be like a Juniper in the Arabah; he cannot see when good comes but dwells in the parched places in the wilderness, in a salt land where no one lives.

If we put trust in anyone's ability, including our own, we will be disappointed. Some things require a power greater than any earthly power to succeed. Only the divine providence of God can provide the right breakthrough at just the right time. Trusting in people, government, or self is futile.

This passage explains that such people cannot see the good that comes to them. They are focused on the wrong thing. If we look to human flesh, we will see weakness, inability, and lack. We will lose hope and fail to see the good that God is doing behind the scenes. It is as if we need bifocals and refuse to use them! If we need bifocals and try to read small or even normal print, we will become frustrated! We will miss the blessing that is right under our noses because we are focused on the wrong thing. Our blessing will be hidden from us.

The juniper in the Arabah is a parched, dwarfed bush in the desert: dry and fruitless. This is the condition of the cursed person who puts trust in the flesh: barren and unproductive. In contrast, we see the blessed person who puts his trust in God; he or she is like a tree planted by the water, which gives life—fruitful and productive, even in drought.

Today, if you feel like a dry, parched juniper, move to the water. Sink your roots deep into the life-giving source of Jesus (John 4:14), and drink from the well of His Word. Take your eyes off the flesh, whether yours or someone else's. Place your trust in the finished work of the cross, and believe in the grace of God for your situation. You will find yourself changing from cursed to blessed!

Have a blessed day!

God Surrounds You

Psalm 125:2

Jerusalem - the mountains surround her. And the LORD surrounds His people, both now and forever.

A village surrounded by mountains is much harder to attack than one on an open plain. The mountains provide an obstacle to the enemy. God gave Jerusalem a form of natural protection, but He also gave her undeniable spiritual protection. He surrounds His people like a mountainous terrain so no enemy may come in and completely devour to take what is not rightfully his.

This does not mean the enemy won't howl, threaten, or intimidate. The greatest strategy of the enemy is to create fear in you by intimidating your thought life. If he can gain control of your mind, you lose sense of God's protection and may ultimately give yourself over to the enemy. Your mind is his battlefield. This is why it is so very important to meditate on God's Word daily and to concentrate on what it says. God's Word will make you aware of His presence and enable you to resist the Devil, and God's hedge of protection becomes even stronger.

The fact that God surrounds His people does not mean that bad things won't happen. As widows, we have all encountered this. By turning to God, His presence surrounds us and begins to radiate His glory through us. When an enemy attacks, he does not remain victorious. What doesn't kill us really can make us stronger. When it does, the enemy will think twice before he attacks you in that area again. When God made Job's latter years greater than his first, the Devil didn't go back and try to do the same thing again! He knew he was defeated! When any enemy knows a mountain terrain will derail and defeat him, he won't try to take that path again. He will look for a new one or give up altogether.

Today, realize that God surrounds you. No weapon formed against you shall prosper because God is your bullet proof vest! What greater covering could we have?

Have a blessed day!

God's Declaration Over You

Isaiah 43:10:

"You are my witnesses" - the LORD's declaration - "and My servant whom I have chosen, so that you may know and believe Me and understand that I am He. No god was formed before Me, and there will be none after Me."

God has declared that we know Him and believe Him. He is intentional about having a relationship with us. He wants us to know that He is alive and active in our lives. He is working out every little detail, and His plans for us are the best! He plans to do something that only He can do, and no other god we try to substitute in His place can accomplish His great purpose for us. When He is finished, His glory will surround us, and others will recognize His distinct handiwork in our lives. He has chosen us for such a purpose, and we can count on Him to accomplish it.

We are His witnesses and His servants. We must do what He has called us to do. We know He equips us and works through us, but we have to seek Him and obey Him for His glory to appear. When everything falls apart and all our dreams or plans crumble before us, God is up to something bigger than we can imagine. We must simply submit, trust, and obey. God works through His submissive servants.

God has declared that you know Him and believe Him. Trust Him today as you submit to His plan for you. Expect Him to appear in your situation in a big way so that no other god can compare. This is His declaration over you!

Have a blessed day!

Happy Are His People

Psalm 84:5:

Happy are the people whose strength is in You, whose hearts are set on pilgrimage.

This verse tells us that those whose hearts are set to worship are happy people. This doesn't mean you have to be happy to worship; it means that when your heart is determined to worship, you will become happy as a result of your worship.

This verse also tells us that those who are determined to worship and are committed to the journey it will take, are those whose strength is in the LORD. They do not depend upon their own efforts. Their happiness does not come from what they can accomplish. Happiness comes from the LORD.

Today, set your hearts on pilgrimage and enter into worship of our heavenly Father. Place your hope in Him, alone. He is your strength. The end result is your happiness!

Have a blessed day!

Living on the Edge

2 Corinthians 5:7:

"... for we walk by faith, not by sight..."

We often ask the question, "What is God's will for my life?" We want to be in His will. We have a longing inside that needs to be satisfied, and only He can satisfy that longing. Just how do we find God's perfect will for our lives and live a life that is fulfilled?

When a need arises, we know God can meet that need, but we might wonder if it is His will to meet it. Matthew 8 tells us of a man with a serious skin disease who knew Jesus could heal him if He were willing. Like this man, we may know God can work in our lives, but is He willing? Just how do we determine God's will?

God's will is to increase our faith. He tends to bring us to the very edge of our faith, where we feel like we are hanging over a cliff. If we look down, we become terrified of the fall below. If we look to those around us, they discourage us and call us back. Yet, when we look straight ahead, we face the One who bids us, "Come." We must take one step forward, trusting that He loves us enough not to let us fall. When we do, a road rolls right out underneath our feet, allowing us to walk in places we never dreamed we'd walk! We can walk that road only by keeping our eyes on Jesus. Walking by faith is living life on the edge. It is God's will for us.

Most of us are not comfortable living on the edge—it's just too nerve wrecking! This life, however, is no place to become comfortable; it is temporary. If we are going to truly live, we must experience the edge. We may not be able to see the road before us, but we walk it by faith, one step at a time. We may not know the answers when we begin to walk, but we walk anyway, believing God will answer.

Hebrews 10:38 reminds us that the righteous are called to live by faith. That means we are called to live life on the edge. If we draw back into our comfort zones, God is not pleased with us. When we begin to walk that road that rolls out beneath us from the edge, it leads us to another edge. That is a life of increasing faith!

Today, we have a choice. We can shrink back into safety and discontentment, or we can take one step over that edge in faith. Christ bids us to come. He doesn't push us off a cliff! The safety of the mountain behind us won't satisfy. How long can we live an unsatisfied life? Dare to step where you have never stepped before, and allow God to increase your faith.

Have a blessed day!

When Nothing Makes Sense

Proverbs 3:5-6:

Trust in the LORD with all your heart, and do not rely on your own understanding; think about Him in all your ways, and He will guide you on the right paths.

Have you ever found yourself in a situation where nothing made sense? You thought you heard from God and began following in that direction, then everything began to crumble and fall apart? Mary Magdalene must have felt the same way (John 19–20). Having been freed from seven demons, she followed Jesus from town to village, watching Him perform one miracle after another. Then, she followed Him to the hard place of the cross and watched Him die. She continued to follow Him to see where He was buried, and she returned three days later to find Him missing from the tomb. How can you continue to follow a Savior who is not there?

These verses from Proverbs are for those times when nothing makes sense. Did you really hear from God, or did you follow your own flesh in hopes God would comply? Did God lead you to a place where your faith would be shattered only to leave you high and dry? Like Mary Magdalene, we don't have the full story. Something wonderful had just happened, but Mary could not comprehend it with her own eyes or her own understanding. Jesus had to reveal Himself to her. When we come to a place where nothing makes sense, we cannot rely upon our own understanding of the situation. We must trust God with all our heart, focus on Him, and rely upon Him to guide us. Our faith can never be in another person or something we want God to do for us. Our faith must be in Him—and Him alone.

Before you act, trust God. Even if you made a mistake and wandered onto the wrong path, He still has the power to guide you back to the right one. Don't dismiss all you know to be true simply because you don't know what God is doing. He is still there somewhere. This is the time to be still and know that He is God (Psalm 46:10). Accept the fact that your understanding is limited, and trust the One who knows all things. At the right time, He will reveal Himself to you, and you will see where He has been all along. You will witness His glory!

Have a blessed day!

Prescription for Discouragement

Luke 18:1-8:

He then told them a parable on the need for them to pray always and not become discouraged: There was a judge in one town who didn't fear God or respect man. And a widow in that town kept coming to him, saying, "Give me justice against my adversary." For a while he was unwilling, but later he said to himself, "Even though I don't fear God or respect man, yet because this widow keeps pestering me, I will give her justice, so she doesn't wear me out by her persistent coming." Then the LORD said, "Listen to what the unjust judge says. Will not God grant justice to His elect who cry out to Him day and night? Will He delay to help them? I tell you that He will swiftly grant them justice. Nevertheless, when the Son of Man comes, will He find that faith on earth?"

Persistence was Jesus's prescription for discouragement. When we need a move of God, we may have to be patient enough to keep asking, seeking, and knocking until we get our breakthrough. Patience is something this generation does not possess, desire, or appreciate. We are accustomed to immediate gratification where we get what we want without a fight. We live in a time of tremendous spiritual warfare, and our battles will not be won with immediate gratification. We must be patient and be willing to fight the Devil for what we want and need.

The Devil's weapon is discouragement. We must fight him with persistence and prayer. Don't give up on the things God has placed in your heart. The reward will certainly be worth the fight!

Have a blessed day!

Reaching New Widows

James 1:27:

Pure and undefiled religion before our God and Father is this: to look after orphans and widows in their distress and to keep oneself unstained by the world.

As widows, we are called to minister to other widows. Who knows what they will face better than we? As 2 Corinthians 1:4 explains, God comforts us so we will be able to comfort others who are hurting in the same way. For this reason, PHOEBE Ministries was formed, and we have been a tremendous support to other women who are facing the same journey.

Not every widow, however, finds herself in the same predicament. Many widows are older widows who have already raised their families. Some may find themselves now raising children alone. Some widows may have inherited means by which they may live a comfortable lifestyle. Others may find themselves financially devastated and needing to become employed. Some widows may know Jesus as Savior and have a strong faith upon which to lean. Others may not know Him and be completely lost in handling grief, loss, and the new identity that comes with widowhood. We are fortunate enough to have been blessed by God with a desire for life and a willingness to serve others. We must find a way to help other widows, regardless of their situations in life.

The key to surviving widowhood is the same today as it was in biblical times. The widow needs a relationship with God through Jesus Christ. Without this relationship, she can do nothing. With Him, however, she can do all things! She can have hope for tomorrow and even enjoy the days to come because of Jesus's work on the cross. How can we best deliver this message to new widows? Nothing is as powerful as the Word of God and our own testimonies! We are each a miracle of faith and a product of grace! We must find ways to be the hands and feet of Christ to new widows who are hurting.

A new widow may not yet be ready to receive ministry. She may find it difficult to even accept the term, *widow,* into her vocabulary at first. She may want to take care of business and settle the husband's estate before becoming involved in a support group, or she might need the support immediately. Just when and how to approach a new widow can be difficult to determine, and no one wants to offend. We must remember that Jesus's love through us meets needs. When we see or sense a need, be willing to reach out and meet it. Showing we care and understand may be the best approach we could possibly have.

We have all faced the newness of widowhood with different feelings and perspectives. Remember your own experience, and carefully consider how God would have you minister. While it may be a very sensitive matter, God still will lead us. He has equipped us with faith and experience. You never know when your simple act of kindness or your words may have lasting impact. Trust the Holy Spirit to work as you move forward.

Have a blessed day!

A God Like No Other

Micah 7:18:

Who is a God like You, removing iniquity and passing over rebellion for the remnant of His inheritance? He does not hold on to His anger forever, because He delights in faithful love.

How wonderful to know that God cannot stay mad at us! Some of us may stay mad for a long time, but that is a part of our human frailty. Being mad at us is not God's nature. He looks over offenses just so He can love us: that is His delight.

Any other god we may serve demands from us. If we serve money, it will demand we become a slave to it. If we serve self, we find she is never pleased. If we serve others, they will always want more from us. God, however, longs to give us Himself. He longs to give us the desires of our hearts and to make us whole. When we serve Him, we are fulfilled, rather than depleted. He frees us from the bondage that other gods have invoked upon us.

Take time to worship God today. There is no God like Him! He is faithful to us even when we are not to Him. Give Him praise today for He is worthy of our praises!

Have a blessed day!

At His Feet

Matthew 15:30-31:

...and large crowds came to Him, having with them the lame, the blind, the deformed, those unable to speak, and many others. They put them at His feet, and He healed them. So the crowd was amazed when they saw those unable to speak talking, the deformed restored, the lame walking, and the blind seeing. And they gave glory to the God of Israel.

Those who came to Jesus to be healed were those who had nowhere else to go. They were unable to do anything about their helpless conditions, and they recognized their need for a power greater than their own. Jesus displayed such power, and crowds followed Him in hope of finding an answer to their own needs.

Notice when and where these people were healed. They were placed at Jesus's feet. This symbolized His authority over them and their submission to Him. When they were placed at His feet, He healed them, and the crowds gave glory to God.

Many people today want and need healing that only Christ can give. The healing need may be physical, emotional, or spiritual. They recognize His power, and they may even ask for His healing. They are not willing, however, to submit to Him and give Him complete authority in their lives.

With authority comes responsibility. If we don't surrender authority to Him, He is not responsible for the outcome. He has no obligation to do anything for us. By surrendering completely, however, He becomes responsible for us, and He will do His very best work in our lives. Those watching will see our inability to overcome on our own and give glory to God.

What can you not do for yourself that only the power of God can do? Submit that area to Christ today. His power can enable you to talk, walk, and see like never possible in your own strength! Surrender your own way of thinking and doing things. Allow Him to do a work in you that will give glory to God and blessing for yourself. The Devil will try to convince you that God will only disappoint you and that you know better what will work for you. If your own way of doing things hasn't worked for you, you need a new strategy! Turn it over to God, and experience His healing and restoring power!

Have a blessed day!

Come and Dine

Luke 14:16-24:

Then He told him: "A man was giving a large banquet and invited many. At the time of the banquet, he sent his slave to those who were invited, 'Come, because everything is now ready.' But without exception they all began to make excuses. The first one said to him, 'I have bought a field, and I must go out and see it. I ask you to excuse me.' Another said, 'I just got married and therefore I'm unable to come.' So the slave came back and reported these things to his master. Then in anger, the master of the house told his salve, 'Go out quickly into the streets and alleys of the city, and bring in here the poor, maimed, blind, and lame!' 'Master,' the slave said, 'what you ordered has been done, and there's still room.' Then the master told the slave, 'Go into the highways and lanes and make them come in, so that my house may be filled. For I tell you, not one of those men who were invited will enjoy my banquet!'"

This man prepared a meal on good faith that his invited guests would attend. Other priorities, however, got in the way. A business venture prevented one from attending. Family matters prevented another. Similar things prevent us from dining with God today, and we find unemployment climbing and families falling apart as a result.

Those first invited were people who obviously had their needs met. When they declined to come and dine, the man issued the invitation to those who were in need. The lacking came to the table. They were the ones ready to receive the banquet. God is the source of all that we have, yet we may not be willing to dine with Him unless we are empty and hungry. Those who are full have no need for Him and do not make Him a priority. Why is it that we have to hurt before we are willing to receive the blessings of the Father? Why are we willing to settle for less when we could be filled with satisfaction?

Perhaps, our economy is in such sad shape because God has invited us to dine at His table many times, yet we have made other things a priority. If we are lacking financially, we may be more willing to turn to Him to meet our needs, rather than relying upon our income. Perhaps, if we would simply dine at His table to find satisfaction, we would stop trying to live above our means. A poor economy is certainly an invitation to come and dine at a banquet table that is filled. Don't ignore your invitation!

There seems to be an epidemic of divorce within the church. Families are falling apart. Children fall into rebellion. Spouses and even children die. The sense of "family" has been shattered for many as they search for a safe and loving place to belong. Broken families need to feast at God's banquet table.

Psalm 34:8 invites us to taste and see that the LORD is good. Make God a priority today, and dine at His table. Come and be filled with satisfaction. He has good things waiting for you if you will only seek Him first. You won't find happiness in work, career, family, or relationships. God gives us those things, and only He can sustain them. Taste what He has prepared for you today. You will be glad you did!

Have a blessed day!

Becoming a Woman of Influence

Acts 17:4:

Then some of them were persuaded and joined Paul and Silas, including a great number of God-fearing Greeks, as well as a number of the leading women (referring to Paul's ministry in Thessalonica, where he preached in the Jewish synagogue).

Verse 12:

Consequently, many of them believed, including a number of the prominent Greek women as well as men (referring to Paul's ministry in Berea, where he preached in the Jewish synagogue).

Paul took special note to mention that leading and prominent women followed the gospel of Christ. He found these women worshiping in the Jewish synagogues in Asia. Within these synagogues, he found Jews and Jewish converts who were dispersed throughout different areas. He went to the synagogues first to find people who were already seeking God. Here he found the most influential women of society.

God grants influence to those who seek Him. He calls out leaders among His people who have a heart for Him. To those, He grants the influence to lead others to Him and to portray His glory. An ordinary woman in that day would have had very little influence in society. Yet, we find the ones who did were in the synagogues seeking God. These women received the gospel and followed Christ. God sent His message of salvation back to the community through those whom others would respect.

God also changed the lives of women who were not respected. We see this in the stories of Mary Magdalene and the woman at the well. Radical conversion changed their lives from despicable and rejected women to loyal, faithful, and respectable women with a message and a story to tell. In the Scriptures above, we find God moving among those already with influence.

Whether you are a prominent woman or one who has been despised and rejected, God's plan has always been to move in your life in such a way that you can influence others for the gospel. Being a woman of influence means that you fully receive what God has for you and you are willing to share it. Your testimony of salvation, deliverance, or victory has the power to deliver others.

Share your testimony with others. If you have been a Christian for a long time, you have many testimonies of deliverance and victory to share. Pray and ask God for the boldness to share your story. He grants influence to those who reflect His glory.

Have a blessed day!

Completely His

2 Chronicles 16:9:

For the eyes of the LORD range throughout the earth to show Himself strong for those whose hearts are completely His...

This verse is a great comfort for those who are completely devoted to God. To think God is just looking for someplace where He can show Himself strong proves that God has much more for us than we can imagine! He wants to do more in our lives than we will allow at times. God will not force

His blessings upon us, but He will watch to see who really wants what He desires to give.

A heart completely devoted to God is a heart dependent upon Him. This heart does not seek to do anything in its own strength. It sets aside its own agenda so God can work His plan in that life. In this heart, God displays His glory!

Our faith can never be placed in ourselves, another human, or in something we want God to do for us. Our faith must be placed firmly in the Person of Jesus Christ and His sacrifice for us on the cross. In other words, we must depend upon grace in every area of our lives. Through grace we are saved. Through grace we are blessed. Through grace we live and move and have our being. When we receive His grace, God shows Himself strong in our lives. The simple act of belief brings His power to any hopeless situation!

Have a blessed day!

Destined for Victory

Psalm 30:1:

I will exalt You, LORD, because You have lifted me up and have not allowed my enemies to triumph over me.

Every Christian will face times when they feel defeated by the enemy. 1 Peter 5:8 warns us to be sober and alert because the Devil prowls like a roaring lion, seeking whom he may devour. The Devil, however, is no match for the Lion of Judah! Jesus Christ was lifted up on a cross so our sins could be forgiven and counted against us no more. By trusting in this sacrifice, God lifts us up from the traps the Devil has set for us and does not allow him to be victorious over us.

The roar of the enemy lion can be deafening at times. This certainly conjures images of danger, peril, and even horror. We must not allow the roar of this lion to paralyze us with fear. God will not allow Him to triumph over us. We must be alert to avoid him, and if we do fall into his trap, we can cry out to the Lion of Judah to rescue us.

God does not want to see His people defeated by the Devil's schemes. That is the whole reason He sent Jesus into this world! Exalt the LORD today. Lift His name high because He has destined us for victory through Christ!

Have a blessed day!

Distinguishable Difference

Malachi 3:18:

So you will again see the difference between the righteous and the wicked, between the one who serves God and one who does not serve Him.

Have you ever become discouraged from seeing the ungodly prevail? Have you ever served God as faithfully as you knew how, only to see one who is not as devoted relish in blessing while you remained in want? Have you ever seen those who do not serve God prosper and wonder what good serving God did in your life? If you have ever answered yes to any of these questions, this verse is for you!

God certainly intends for His people to be distinguishable from the rest! This difference comes from the presence of the Holy Spirit, which dwells in each of us upon salvation. As we begin to walk in obedience to God and grow spiritually, the Holy Spirit will anoint us with an effectiveness that speaks an internal witness to others. This anointing is a distinguishable mark that proves we belong to God and draws others to Him.

An unbeliever may be blessed or successful in an area, but he carries no anointing. A Christian who falls into sin or does not serve God quenches the anointing of the Holy Spirit and must rely upon his own strength in ministry. People can't help but notice when the anointing is present!

Today, focus on where the Holy Spirit is working in your life. Look for His anointing on you. If you don't sense it, ask for it to be revealed to you. Follow Him in complete obedience. Don't let the Devil gain a stronghold in your life to quench your effectiveness in ministry. Walk in full power and be marked as one of His own. Let others see the difference in you!

Have a blessed day!

From Lament to Dancing

Psalm 30:11:

You turned my lament into dancing; You removed my sackcloth and clothed me with gladness.

There is a time for weeping and mourning, and we all must face those difficult times. When we turn fully to God, however, we can expect Him to turn our lament into dancing. This form of dancing is merely an outward expression of joy in our hearts. When God grants us such joy, it pleases Him for us to express it.

Sackcloth was used as mourning clothes. God removes our sackcloth and gives us reason to rejoice again. He doesn't want us to walk around in our mourning clothes with our sorrowful attitudes. He wants us to reflect the love, freedom, and delight we have found through His grace. Who wants to worship a God who keeps His people in mourning? When we who have hurt find reason to rejoice, it gives hope to those whose hurt is fresh. Is there hope for the widow who has lost her spouse and her way of life? You bet there is! Hope is found in the finished work of Christ on the cross, and it has the power to change your life if you will trust it!

God will turn your sorrow to gladness if you let Him. You can choose to hang on to your hurt, but you will not progress one inch further in your walk, and you will give hope to no one. Don't be afraid to dance! In fact, I encourage you to buy some dancing shoes if you don't have any! Like the group Mary Mary sings, "Take the shackles off my feet so I can dance! I just want to praise you!"

Have a blessed day!

He Has Done Everything Well

Mark 7:37:

They were extremely astonished and said, "He has done everything well! He even makes deaf people hear, and people unable to speak, talk!"

Jesus had caused quite a stir in the land of Israel. His teachings were succinct and profound. He cast demons out of people. He made the lame to walk and the blind to see. In the preceding passage, He had just healed a deaf man and enabled him to speak clearly. According to Isaiah 35:5-6, everything He did displayed the glory of God and indicated the kingdom of God was at hand. People could not help but note that He had done everything well!

In John 5:19, Jesus explained that the Son could do nothing on His own but only what He saw the Father doing. If God is doing something, you can rest assured He is doing it well; He does nothing half-heartedly! He always works with purpose and in a way that brings Him glory.

If we want God to display His glory in our lives, then we must do what we see Him doing. We must move where we see God moving in our lives and stop trying to be something we are not. God did not call us to do everything, but He does call us to do a few things well. If we will concentrate on doing what He desires us to be doing, He will work miracles in those things He has called us to do!

What do you see God doing in your life? Move in that area. Where has He gifted you to serve? Serve in that gift. If He has not yet filled a void in your life, don't try to fill it yourself. Wait on Him to move in that area, and don't dare think God will bless you in anything that directly contradicts His Word! If we are going to be effective for His purpose, we must do only what we see Him doing, or we stand to lose our destiny and the glory He wants to reveal in us. He has done everything well, and that includes His plans for our lives. Don't settle for anything less. Today, determine to do only what you see the Father doing, and watch for His glory to be revealed in you!

Have a blessed day!

A Flourishing Olive Tree

Psalm 52:8-9:

But I am like a flourishing olive tree in the house of God; I trust in God's faithful love forever and ever. I will praise You forever for what you have done. In the presence of Your faithful people, I will put my hope in Your name, for it is good.

A flourishing olive tree in the house of God is one which bears much fruit. Think of it in contrast to the barren fig tree, which Jesus cursed. The fig tree was beautiful and dressed in foliage, but it had no fruit for Jesus when He approached it for food. As a result, Jesus cursed it, and it was dead the next day.

The psalmist compared himself to an olive tree that was fruitful and flourishing in God's love. When we are conscious of His love for us and dependent upon His grace, we are like that flourishing olive tree. If we are trying to earn God's love or approval through self-effort, our self-righteousness may cause us to look pretty but bear no fruit—like the fig tree. Jesus curses self-righteousness but gives grace to the humble, who freely receive His righteousness through faith.

When bad things happen, we can count on God's faithful love for us to see us through it. We don't have to earn His help or His blessing because we have the righteousness of Christ, who died for us. We can praise Him for the things He has already done in our lives, resting assured that His good name will watch over us. We may not understand all that is happening in our lives, but He doesn't command us to understand. He commands us to trust.

Today, put your hope in the goodness of God. He has always been good to you in the past, and He won't stop now! Praise Him for the blessings He has already given you, and trust Him to bless you where you need it now. God is good all the time!

Have a blessed day!

A Wide-Open Place

Psalm 18:19:

He brought me out to a wide-open place; He rescued me because he delighted in me.

Have you ever felt confined or limited? Have you ever felt the crush of an oppressor that seemed to want to shut you out or drain the life right out of you? Believe me, that is just what your enemy, the Devil, wants to do to you. He wants you confined and limited because you are a reflection of the grace and goodness of God, and he doesn't want that exposed. That is why he places circumstances and even people in your life that seem to crush you.

God, however, intends for His glory to shine through you. He will not allow you to be destroyed by the enemy, and He rescues you from the Devil's evil clutch. You are His delight, and He will take you to a wide-open place, where you can flourish and grow.

Our wide-open places are often right in front of us, yet we refuse to enter because we are so consumed with our confined places. To enter into the wide-open places God has for us, we must turn our eyes and our minds from the oppressing thoughts, attitudes, and desires that cause anger, frustration, and depression in us. By pouring our hearts and emotions out to God and seeking Him, we are able to make that turn from the confined place to the wide-open place and see all that God has for us. He is not trying to squash or limit us. He is bringing us to wholeness. When we receive this revelation, the Devil loses his grip on us and can no longer confine us.

See yourself as God's delightful child today. Turn from that crushing, confining frustration and look to your heavenly Father, who raves over you and has good planned for you. Look for your wide-open place and begin to grow in the grace and goodness of your LORD, Jesus Christ. You will soon find that grip loosened and your spirit free!

Have a blessed day!

Blooming Where You Are Planted

Jeremiah 17:7-8:

Blessed is the man who trusts in the LORD, whose confidence indeed is the LORD. He will be like a tree planted by water; it sends its roots out toward a stream, it doesn't fear when heat comes, and its foliage remains green. It will not worry in a year of drought or cease producing fruit.

A tree can't help what happens around it; it can only grow where it is planted. A tree planted by water has been strategically placed there by its Maker. The water nourishes the tree and gives it life. The Maker has provided for its every need to grow, bear fruit, and beautify its surroundings. So it is with you and me.

God placed us where He did for a reason. We may be experiencing difficulty, but He has provided us with everything we need to grow and bear fruit, making our surroundings a more beautiful place than if we weren't there. Sometimes, the best thing we can do is just grow where we are planted.

Growing requires trusting God. If we trust ourselves or others, we will become disappointed and begin to shrivel and die. Christ is our life source— our stream of living water. We must be firmly planted next to that life source and draw from it daily if we are to grow. He is God's provision for us. In Him we find grace to face any drought we may encounter.

In a drought, we feel the heat. It is uncomfortable, and we look for relief. Christ provides the living water needed to refresh, renew, and revive the drought of the world. As Jesus told the woman at the well, we will never thirst again if we drink from His water. We can continually produce fruit, bloom, and flourish! We become a sign of hope for a dry, thirsty world that needs relief.

Today, simply bloom where you are planted. Draw from the living water of God's Word, and trust fully in the finished work of Christ for everything you need. Beautify your world simply by being what God made you to be—fruitful!

Have a blessed day!

A Shield of Favor

Psalm 5:12:

For You, LORD, bless the righteous one. You surround him with favor like a shield.

As Christians, we must remember that God is our source of blessing. We cannot create or manipulate a blessing. As His children, however, He will withhold no good thing from us (Psalm 84:11), and every good and perfect gift is from Him (James 1:17). We can count on God to bless us.

God surrounds His children with favor. His goodness toward us is a protective shield against the enemy. When doors open for you that you don't deserve nor qualify to open from your own merits, you are operating in His favor. When people look to you for answers and seek your counsel as honest and trustworthy, you are operating in God's favor. When you are blessed to fully operate in the gift God has given you, you are operating in His favor. When your experience a disappointment from a closed door that would have brought negative repercussions down the road, you are operating in His favor.

To turn from God and follow our own path is to step outside that protective shield of favor. If we find ourselves paying the consequences of sin, God is not punishing us. We have just stepped outside His shield of favor. We must turn back to Him.

Thank God today for His blessings and His shield of favor around you. Know that He holds you in the palm of His hand, which is nail-scarred from His great love for you. We can have no greater protection or security than the blessing and favor that surround us every day as one of His own. Trust that He has your best interest at heart, and offer your heart in worship to Him. There is no safer place on earth than to be in the center of His perfect will for you.

Have a blessed day!

Don't Jump!

Matthew 4:5-7:

Then the Devil took Him to the holy city, had Him stand on the pinnacle of the temple, and said to Him, "If You are the Son of God, throw Yourself down. For it is written: He will give His angels orders concerning you, and they will support you with their hands so that you will not strike your foot against a stone." Jesus told him, "It is also written: Do not test the LORD your God."

This temptation is a very sobering temptation for Christian leaders. Notice that the Devil took Jesus to the pinnacle—the very top—of the temple. He was in an exalted place where all would look up to see Him. Here, Satan tempted Jesus to throw Himself down. In other words, "Go ahead and sin. You can get away with it because you are the leader. God has already promised He will send His angels to support you so you won't get hurt."

The Devil quoted Psalm 91:11-12 to Jesus. The implication from these verses is that if you have trusted in God as your refuge, He will protect you from the attacks of the enemy. For someone to willingly rebel against God's Word, however, is not an attack of the Devil. It is suicide! The Devil tried to get Jesus to kill His own ministry. To trust God as your refuge is to trust His care over you in doing what you know to be the right thing to do. If you have done God's will in a matter, He will protect you. If you have stepped outside that, you might get hurt or worse! The thing to remember here is that the Devil can't do anything to you without your cooperation. Don't cooperate with him!

Finally, Jesus quoted Deuteronomy 6:16 in response to the Devil's temptation. Moses reminded the people how they had tested or tempted God at a place he named Massah or Meribah. The Israelites were thirsty, and they complained against God, doubting that He was with them. When we doubt that God is with us and try to take matters into our own hands, we run the risk of jumping off the pinnacle and causing damage. Not only can we damage ourselves, but those looking up to us may be damaged in their faith, as well. Trust that God is with you, and He is taking care of every matter you have submitted to Him. Don't jump off the pinnacle! That really will hurt!

Have a blessed day!

God is For Me

Psalm 56:8-9:

You Yourself have recorded my wanderings. Put my tears in your bottle. Are they not in Your records? Then my enemies will retreat on the day when I call. This I know: God is for me.

God knows where we have been and each heartache we have suffered along the way. Can you imagine trying to put tears in a bottle? Yet, God does not forget the tears we cry when we cry out to Him. They become records of the hurts we have suffered and the pain we carry. The enemy trembles to see them collected in His hands because He knows who caused them!

Anyone who has harmed a child does not want to have to face the parent. When God collects our tears for His records, He plans to address someone with them! They are proof that His child has been hurt, and He will hold someone accountable!

Pay careful attention to the very last part of that Scripture, and memorize it today. Meditate on these words on a regular basis. Whenever the Devil tries to tell you a situation is hopeless, repeat this phrase to him, "This I know: God is for me!"

If you have cried out to God in the midst of your pain, know that your tears are His record. He will use them against the enemy. Always remember that He is for you, and He will work things out for your good. When the enemy tries to attack you with fear, dread, depression, discouragement, anger, or any other negative emotion, stand on what you know to be true from God's Word. Feelings come and go, but God's truth remains the same. He is for you! Just fix that point in your mind and repeat it throughout the day! If God is for us, then who can be against us? (Rom. 8:31)

Have a blessed day!

God Protects the Widow's Territory

Proverbs 15:25:

The LORD destroys the house of the proud, but He protects the widow's territory.

This verse reflects a widow who is dependent upon God. While the proud man boasts of all he has accomplished and wants the world to see all he has, the widow has no one to protect her or to provide for her. She is dependent upon God for all she has.

The proud man does not realize that God has allowed and enabled him to gain all he has. God detests pride and will not tolerate it in His people. If we will not humble ourselves, He will humble us. This verse explains that God will tear down the house of the proud man. If he thinks he has built it on his own, God takes it away.

The widow in Scripture is often a symbol of complete humility. We see that God protects the boundary or the territory of the widow because of her humble position. God is able and willing to speak to and work through the humble because He is glorified. The proud man would try to steal that glory.

No one wants to be a widow; it happens not by choice. When we accept our position in life and continue to serve God, we become a witness to His grace. God is able to speak to us and work through us in ways we never dreamed possible. Moreover, He protects our territory. We don't lose ground with God. We gain!

May we be women who remain humble before our God and who allow Him to speak to us and work through us. May we be living examples of His grace and goodness. May we be humble women He can trust.

Have a blessed day!

How Big Is Your God?

Isaiah 45:20:

"Come, gather together, and draw near, you fugitives of the nations. Those who carry their wooden idols, and pray to a god who cannot save, have no knowledge."

How big is your God? Do you serve the God who created everything in heaven and earth and has power and dominion over every little thing, or do you serve a god who is powerless, unwilling, and has no interest in your situation? Dare to increase your faith to believe that God is bigger than your problem, bigger than your predicament, and bigger than your pain.

Through the finished work of Christ, you have access to the all-powerful God of the universe who loves you so much He gave His only Son to die for you. If He would do such a great thing as that, would He not give you lesser things? Would He not provide for your every need and comfort your pain? Indeed, we must decrease in our own eyes so that He might increase (John 3:30). In this, we find our joy complete.

If you are going through a difficult time, realize that this is an opportunity to increase your faith. Our entire Christian walk is designed with opportunities to increase our faith and to gain a better revelation of who Christ is. Discipleship is a process of making ourselves smaller and Christ bigger. Where you cannot provide for yourself, He can. Don't concentrate on your limitations. Realize He is bigger and can do it. Where you are weak, He is strong. Where you have no more answers, realize He knows it all. Where you hurt and cannot stop hurting, realize He is comfort. Your answer lies in the power of Christ. Magnify Him in your life today!

Have a blessed day!

God's Eternal Love

Psalm 136:1-4:

Give thanks to the LORD, for He is good. His love is eternal. Give thanks to the God of gods. His love is eternal. Give thanks to the LORD of LORDs. His love is eternal. He alone does great wonders. His love is eternal.

There are 28 verses in this chapter, and they all end the same. God's love is truly eternal. It has no end. Repetition is often used as a teaching tool because you will retain what you hear over and over. In fact, some of us never learn without it! This Psalm tells the story of a mighty, faithful God who created the world, delivered His people from danger, and provided for His people. Throughout the entire passage, one constant message rings with certainty: God's love is eternal, and we can depend upon it in our darkest days.

During hard times, we may think God's hand is against us. That is never the case! He may thwart our plans that set us up for disaster, but He is never against us (Rom. 8:31). His love for us is eternal, and we will experience it in the next life to an even greater capacity than we can understand now. Regardless of where you find yourself, realize that God's love for you never ceases. Run to Him and rest in His embrace.

In the good times, we feel His love—it is easy to rejoice. We have reason to praise in every situation because of His great love for us. Today, take some time to consider the eternal love God has for you, and respond to Him with praise. He is truly a God like no other, and He is worthy of all our praise!

Have a blessed day!

A Heritage of Faithful Love

Psalm 103:17-18:

But from eternity to eternity the LORD's faithful love is toward those who fear Him, and His righteousness toward the grandchildren of those who keep His covenant, who remember to observe His instructions.

Your relationship with God can affect your grandchildren. God's favor upon you can filter through generations to continue to operate within your lineage. This truth should make us want to cultivate as close and as intimate a relationship with Him as we can. In fact, a strong relationship with God is the best gift you can give your family. This is a heritage that can bond a family like glue, inspiring generations to come.

This verse describes God's love as a faithful love toward those who fear Him. We see little faithfulness in this world anymore. Marriages fail because one or both partners are unfaithful. Friends stab one another in the back. Employers focus upon who can do the most for them in the moment. Faithfulness can be hard to comprehend. Yet, God's love is faithful—loyal and committed—to those who fear Him. Even when you have failed Him in some area, He will be faithful to you. If one of your family members has veered off the right path, God is still faithful. Continue to lift that family member in prayer, knowing that God's righteousness is toward that wayward child or grandchild.

Today you have an opportunity to cultivate your relationship with God. Never underestimate the power and effectiveness of worship on your life. Be faithful to God in this area, and watch how faithful He is to you. Find a place to serve Him in church, and watch how He will bless your life through it.

Have a blessed day!

A Royal Wedding

Psalm 45:13-15:

In her chamber, the royal daughter is all glorious, her clothing embroidered with gold. In colorful garments she is led to the king; after her, the virgins, her companions, are brought to you. They are led in with gladness and rejoicing; they enter the king's palace.

This Psalm describes a royal wedding and is a reflection of the wedding that will one day take place between Jesus and His bride. The bride does not wear white, which is a symbol of purity. Instead, she wears colorful garments, embroidered with gold. Colorful garments were a symbol of the family's wealth and their pride in her. Gold represents deity, a sign that this bride will serve a king as her husband.

One day we will wear a colorful wedding dress, embroidered with gold as we marry the King of Kings! Regardless of how impure our lives have been on earth, we bear the righteousness of Christ as Christians. The Father is proud to call us His own!

As we enter the King's palace, we will be led forth with gladness and rejoicing. All the tears, sorrows, and hardships of this life will be over as we claim a new life as the royal bride. We will definitely have reason to celebrate!

Today, picture yourself clothed in colorful garments, embroidered with gold. It is your destiny in Christ. You were created to serve Him at His side forever, and this is one wedding you will not want to miss! Rejoice with gladness as you make yourself ready!

Have a blessed day!

A Knight in Shining Armor

Psalm 91:14-15

Because he is lovingly devoted to Me, I will deliver him; I will exalt him because he knows My name. When he calls out to Me, I will answer him; I will be with him in trouble. I will rescue him and give him honor.

These are promises straight from God's mouth to those who love Him. He promises to deliver. You can deliver someone only if she is in trouble. He promises to exalt. You can exalt someone only if she is first lowly. He promises to answer those who call out to Him. He promises to be with us during trouble. He promises to rescue and to give honor. This could only mean that you must first be in danger and without honor.

These promises cover any devastating thing that could threaten us. If trouble or tragedy comes our way, He is our deliverer. If we find ourselves in need of provision and call out to Him, He promises to answer. When we fall deeply into sin, whether by deceit or by premeditation, He will rescue us and restore us to a place of honor in His kingdom. That sounds like a knight in shining armor if ever I've heard of one!

If you find yourself to be a damsel in distress today, know that you have someone waiting to rescue you. His name is Jesus. These are the things He does for those who love Him. How could you not love such a knight in shining armor, who died so you might have a right standing with the Father, live eternally, and be blessed with every spiritual blessing? He is more than just a knight. He is the Prince of Peace, and you are His greatest desire!

Have a blessed day!

Beautiful with Jewelry

Song of Songs 1:10-11:

Your cheeks are beautiful with jewelry, your neck with its necklace. We will make gold jewelry for you, accented with silver.

What a man! This is how Jesus adores His bride. He is so in love with her that He wants to give her the very best and adorn her with His finest. I believe my love for jewelry and all that sparkles and shines is simply God's priming me for heaven!

You, dear one, are His bride. He is not only your Savior, He is in love with you. He wants only the best for you, and He is in the process now of fashioning gold jewelry for you, accented with silver. Keep in mind that gold and silver are refined in fire. They are the valuable results of a refining process. He does the jewelry making and presents us with the treasure.

Every trial you endure should produce a beautiful adornment for you. The greater the process, the more valuable and attractive the necklace it will create. Learn to treasure the trials you survive. They serve as a part of your dress for Christ.

Even if you feel the hardships of life have worn you down, realize that Jesus sees you in beautiful jewelry. He sees every token of affection He has given you. Wear them well. Don't let bitterness or anger rob you of the beautiful jewels He is fashioning just for you. Get excited about what He is doing in your life now. You will soon wear the treasure of it when He reveals His glory in the midst of it!

Have a blessed day!

Date Night

Titus 3:4-7:

But when the goodness and love for man appeared from God our Savior, He saved us - not by works of righteousness that we had done but according to His mercy, through the washing of regeneration and renewal by the Holy Spirit. This Spirit He poured out on us abundantly through Jesus Christ our Savior, so that having been justified by His grace, we may become heirs with the hope of eternal life.

Out of God's goodness, He sent Jesus to die for us. When we encounter bad situations or difficult times, it can be tempting to doubt God's goodness. He may seem like a cruel taskmaster. The truth, however, is that goodness is God's nature. He longs to express His goodness to His children, and He began with the cross. It is a symbol to us that any difficult or heartbreaking circumstance in our lives can be redeemed because of God's goodness toward us.

God saved us because of what Christ did on the cross for us. For those of us who are born again, He sees us through the righteousness of Christ. We are justified by HIS blood alone. God, however, did not stop there. He knew we would need more than a bath of righteousness. We need to be renewed and made whole so we can live the abundant life to which we are called. Therefore, He gave us the Holy Spirit through Jesus Christ that continually renews us and transforms us into a new creation in Christ.

God gives us the Holy Spirit in abundance! Many people mistakenly think the abundant life is a life of wealth and physical prosperity. These are merely by-products. While God is the source of our wealth and our health, what He gives us in abundance is the Holy Spirit, who guides us and renews us to become what God has purposed for us to be.

The Spirit led life is the life of abundance. The Holy Spirit is a Person who greatly desires to communicate with you on a daily basis, and He has much to say. His mission is to speak to you as you read the Word of God and seek His kingdom first (Matt. 6:33). He will transform your thinking from the perspective of the world to the perspective of Christ. What would Jesus do? The Holy Spirit will tell you.

Today, ask God to refresh you with abundance by making you aware of the Holy Spirit's presence in your life. Listen to Him, and meditate on His Word to you. Let His peace overtake you, and simply flow in what He leads you to do. Communication with Him will become addicting as He renews your way of thinking. You will begin to see life anew and operate in ways you never imagined possible!

The Holy Spirit is a gentleman and will never demand your company or violate your will. You must invite Him to dine with you. Spend time with the Holy Spirit, and give date night a whole new meaning!

Have a blessed day!

The Blanket

Psalm 36:10:

Spread Your faithful love over those who know You, and Your righteousness over the upright in heart.

David wrote these words as He appealed to the very heart of God. He saw God's love as a blanket that warmed and soothed the soul. Indeed, there are times when we are left cold and hurting from the struggles of this world, and we need to feel God's love spread over us like a warm blanket on a chilly night, allowing us to rest in the comfort of His care.

David depicts God's righteousness as a blanket in this verse, too. We have no righteousness in ourselves, but God spreads His righteous over those who are in Christ. We can rest in comfort, knowing that His righteousness covers all of our mistakes, failures, iniquities, and transgressions.

Self-righteous people are often cold and hard hearted. They feel like they have had to work for everything they have, and they have not felt the comfort of the warm blanket of love and the righteousness of Christ that we know as grace. Their hard work has hardened them. Grace, however, warms the heart and changes the person to live a peaceful and joy-filled life. May we all trade in our flimsy, self-righteous garments for the warm blanket of grace. Wrapped in its delicately woven threads, we find rest in His great love for us.

Have a blessed day!

My Delight is in Her

Isaiah 62:1-5:

I will not keep silent because of Zion, and I will not keep still because of Jerusalem until her righteousness shines like bright light, and her salvation like a flaming torch. Nations will see your righteousness, and all kings your glory. You will be called by a new name that the LORD's mouth will announce. You will be a glorious crown in the LORD's hand,

and a royal diadem in the palm of your God. You will no longer be called Deserted, and your land will not be called Desolate; instead, you will be called My Delight is in Her, and your land Married; for the LORD delights in you and your land will be married. For as a young man marries a virgin, so your sons will marry you; and as a bridegroom rejoices over his bride, so your God will rejoice over you.

God's will is not to keep us isolated and alone. He desires to display us as a shining light to a dark world. Our righteousness, however, is not our own. The only righteousness we have is in Christ. God wants Christ to shine through us so much that we become a crown in His hand.

Notice that this shining, radiant, glorious crown was once deserted and desolate. God brings her from such lonely areas of darkness and renews her through the righteousness of Christ. His intention is for the world to see how the love of Christ has changed her life. She is now married, and the LORD delights in her!

The most precious and costly gemstones are found deep within dark, cold, and often isolated mines. They are often so costly because of the difficulty it takes to bring them to the surface where they can be used. I find it fascinating to see what beauty grows beneath such dark surfaces of the earth! Jewelry makers dress these fine gems in the most beautiful gold and silver settings so people will buy them and treasure them.

We are like those precious gemstones in cold, dark, isolated places. Only God knows what kind of a jewel our lives can become when filled with the righteousness of Christ. He dresses us in His finest by transforming our lives with His power as we trust Him. The best part is that He delights in us! We become His precious treasure!

When God seems to be silent in your life, realize that He will not keep silent forever. Once He has adorned you with the beauty of Christ's righteousness, He will speak through you! You are His statement!

Have a blessed day!

Pleasant and Friend

Ruth 1:1-7:

During the time of the judges, there was a famine in the land. A man left Bethlehem in Judah with his wife and two sons to live in the land of Moab for a while. The man's name was Elimelech, and his wife's name was Naomi. The names of his two sons were Mahlon and Chilion. They were Ephrathites from Bethlehem in Judah. They entered the land of Moab and settled there. Naomi's husband Elimelech died, and she was left with her two sons. Her sons took Moabite women as their wives: one was named Orpah and the second was named Ruth. After they lived in Moab about 10 years, both Mahlon and Chilion also died, and Naomi was left without her two children and without her husband.

The move to Moab was a costly one. They may have fled the famine in Israel in hopes of survival, but the men lost their lives, anyway. I can't help but wonder if they had waited, would they have seen God's provision in Israel? Famine may have been difficult, but God's presence still resided in Israel. They chose to find relief outside of the presence of God. Taking matters into our own hands always brings consequences.

The meanings of the men's names are quite interesting. Elimelech means *God of the king.* Old Testament names always give insight into the character and destiny of the people. Scripture also reveals where God, Himself, gave names to people. Elimelech's name refers to the one the king worships. God desired to display Himself through Elimelech. When Elimelech took matters into his own hands and went into a pagan land that was forbidden to worship in God's temple, God brought judgment upon him. The true God of the king will not share His glory with another. He is the source of life and of blessing.

Mahlon means *sick* and Chilion means *pining, destruction, consumption, failing.* The outlook doesn't seem favorable for either! Perhaps, Mahlon received his name because of an ailment from birth. Chilion seemed doomed from the beginning. These names may also indicate the nature of their spiritual condition. Either way, sick and sicker did not survive. The answers to their problems were not found in Moab, either.

The meanings of the names of the women are also interesting. Naomi means *pleasant.* She must have been a warm, delightful person. Orpah's name implies the idea of being *stiff-necked*. It is easy to understand why she chose to remain in her own land and serve her own gods. She was obviously not open to receive the God of Israel, and her experiences with those who worshiped Him seemed sorrowful. Ruth means *friend.* In the end, Pleasant was left with a Friend; later God would bring redemption.

Never underestimate the power of being pleasant and being a friend. God can take those qualities and multiply them into something wonderful. He can give you new life through them!

Have a blessed day!

The Sorrow of Settling

Ruth 1:7-14:

She left the place where she had been living, accompanied by her two daughters-in-law, and traveled along the road leading back to the land of Judah. She said to them, "Each of you go back to your mother's home. May the LORD show faithful love to you as you have shown to the dead and to me. May the LORD enable each of you to find security in the house of your new husband." She kissed them and they wept loudly. "No," they said to her. "We will go with you to your people." But Naomi replied, "Return home, my daughters. Why do you want to go with me? Am I able to have any more sons who could become your husbands? Return home, my daughters. Go on, for I am too old to have another husband. Even if I thought there was still hope for me to have a husband tonight and to bear sons, would you be willing to wait for them to grow up? Would you restrain yourselves from remarrying? No, my daughters, my life is much too bitter for you to share, because the LORD's hand has turned against me." Again they wept loudly, and Orpah kissed her mother-in-law, but Ruth clung to her.

As we learned yesterday, Ruth means friend. Naomi may have lost a husband and two sons, but she certainly gained a friend in Ruth. Orpah and Ruth represent two kinds of followers. They both have needs and are willing to look to God. One, however, will turn away when it looks like all hope is lost in ever getting that need or desire met. They follow as long as they expect God to move on their behalf. When they don't see Him move, they go back to their old ways thinking that Christianity just didn't "work" for them. Their focus is strictly upon receiving. They never know the joy that giving their all to Christ can bring.

Ruth represents the follower who is willing to commit completely to God's plan, regardless of whether or not her own personal desires are met. Ruth abandoned all other gods to follow Naomi and worship her God. Perhaps, Ruth's own gods had failed her enough and she determined to find new life by following a God who brought her the love and company of a pleasant mother-in-law. Ruth didn't have much, but she gave all of herself to Naomi and to Naomi's God. She cared more about giving than receiving.

Knowing the end of the story, my heart aches for Orpah. I don't know what kind of life she found by going back to her homeland and to her former gods, but it could never compare to what Ruth found. Orpah settled for less than God's best for her.

Receiving the very best God has for us may mean that we must travel roads that are uncomfortable and undesirable, but God will always make the destination well worth the journey! Don't settle for less than God's best for you. If He has called you to give up something or has taken something away, follow Him to completion. He has a greater plan for you. Devote yourself to His purpose. He will not leave you deserted or in despair. Redemption awaits!

Have a blessed day!

Hesed

Ruth 1:16-17:

But Ruth replied:

Do not persuade me to leave you or go back and not follow you. For wherever you go, I will go, and wherever you live, I will live; your people will be my people, and your God will be my God. Where you die, I will die, and there I will be buried. May the LORD do this to me and even more, if anything but death separates you and me.

We often hear this read or sung at weddings. When Ruth said it, however, it had nothing to do with a wedding. She simply described her dedication to Naomi. Her commitment and actions eventually led to a beautiful marriage, which brought redemption and restoration to both Ruth and Naomi.

With Ruth's loyalty and commitment to Naomi, we begin to see the essence of the Book. Ruth made a covenant with Naomi here that illustrates the Hebrew word, *hesed* meaning lovingkindness or mercy. This word implies loyalty, regardless of circumstances. God loves His people with a *hesed*-type of love that we don't often fully understand. Ruth gave up any hope she had of a husband or a life for herself among her own people in order to follow Naomi and to serve her God. She promised never to leave her or forsake her, and, thus, pledged a *hesed*-type of love to Naomi. This is the same type of love required for a marriage to work. You have to be loyal and committed, regardless of any circumstances.

This is the way God loves us. He will never leave us nor forsake us, regardless of how bad our situation becomes. Even when it looks like there is no hope, He still loves us with a lovingkindness that brings a much needed hope.

Breathe in the lovingkindness of God's *hesed* love for you today. He is moved by loyalty because He is loyal. Determine to live for Him today and to serve Him forever. His love is worth anything you can lose on this earth.

Have a blessed day!

Divine Providence Unfolding

Ruth 2:1-3:

Now Naomi had a relative on her husband's side named Boaz. He was a prominent man of noble character from Elimelech's family. Ruth the Moabitess asked Naomi, "Will you let me go into the fields and gather fallen grain behind someone who allows me to? Naomi answered her, "Go ahead, my daughter." So Ruth left and entered the field to gather grain behind the harvesters. She happened to be in the portion of land belonging to Boaz, who was from Elimelech's family.

The Mosaic law allowed widows, orphans, and other poor people to follow behind the harvesters to pick up any left-over grain. This was their "welfare system" of that day. Since women could not work outside the home for income, it was often their only means of survival.

In these few verses, we begin to see God's divine providence unfold. Neither Ruth nor Naomi realized that their answer to inheritance lay in Ruth's gleaning in the fields. Ruth was willing work, and Naomi agreed. God graciously and divinely placed Ruth right where she needed to be while she was completely unaware of His working in her life.

That is how God is—He is often at work in our lives when we cannot see a single thing He is doing. He moves us into places of opportunity and into positions of grace without our knowing or seeing it. This is why we should proceed with the task at hand in faith that God has already gone ahead and prepared His answer for us. We don't always know everything He is doing nor the divine purpose in it all. Sometimes, we just have to accept our situations and move forward with faith. That is exactly what Ruth did.

Move forward with faith today. Don't be content to just sit back and moan about your problems. This will only keep you unfulfilled. Step forth in the opportunity God places in front of you, and watch where He leads. He is at work in your life in ways you never imagined. He is a God of grace and purpose, and you are His blessed child.

Have a blessed day!

Faith that Moves Forward

Ruth 2:4-6:

Later, when Boaz arrived from Bethlehem, he said to the harvesters, "The LORD be with you." "The LORD bless you," they replied. Boaz asked his servant who was in charge of the harvesters, "Whose young woman is this?" The servant answered, "She is the young Moabite woman who returned with Naomi from the land of Moab. She asked, 'Will you let me gather fallen grain among the bundles behind the harvesters?' She came and has remained from early morning until now, except that she rested a little in the shelter."

Boaz took notice of Ruth. She was different in both appearance and in character. His servant in charge of the harvesters described her as a hard worker. Notice that she is not called by name here. She is described as *the Moabite woman who returned with Naomi.* She was a foreigner, an outsider, and a pagan. She was a prime target for abuse, but her relationship with Naomi brought her acceptance in Boaz's field. The servant here almost seems to be encouraging Boaz to allow her to remain. Boaz, however, did not need encouraging. He had already decided to take care of her.

At this point, Ruth still did not realize that she was in the field of a kinsman-redeemer or that she would soon be married to the wealthy landowner. She had simply chosen to give her all to the task at hand, though it be a lowly one. God was at work in her life, but she still had no idea how.

Faith moves forward, even when it does not see how God is working. We can sit back and grumble and complain about our sad situations all day long and never move one inch forward out of them, or we can accept the task at hand and give it our all. When God is ready to reveal Himself in our lives, we see His glory and realize He was there all the time.

Ruth chose to move forward; she even asked for the opportunity. God placed her right where she needed to be, and a wealthy kinsman-redeemer took notice of her. There are no coincidences in life. There is only the divine providence of God that unfolds as we move forward in faith.

Move forward in your faith today. Allow the divine providence of God to unfold in your life. Boaz was there all the time—it was just a matter of Ruth's getting to his field. God has a place of answer for you, and it is found in looking forward, rather than back.

Have a blessed day!

A Lily Among Thorns

There is a difference between the thorns and the crosses we have to bear in this life. We don't ask for thorns. They come without our permission. They are unfair, and they can make us bitter. Crosses are things we choose to bear out of love. I did not choose for my husband to die, and neither did you. We did not choose their illnesses nor their accidents. These are thorns we bear. Christ, however, chose to bear the cross for us.

Song of Songs 2:2:

Like a lily among thorns, so is my darling among the young women.

This is such a touching verse. Here, the Beloved sees His bride as a lily among the thorns. The first verse of that chapter refers to the bride as the rose of Sharon, the lily of the valleys. She is the bright spot that blooms in the midst of sharp, prickly daggers that defy you to touch her. While the thorns bid one to stay away, her beauty draws Him to her.

I cannot think of a more fitting verse for us today. Thorns may have infested our lives and brought pain, but God is drawn to the beauty surrounded by those thorns. This reminds me of roses, my favorite flower. Roses bear such beautiful blooms, but they also bear thorns. I can't help but think it is God's way of preserving the bloom.

As women are receiving roses today from their Valentines, keep in mind that you are God's rose or lily to the world. Your beauty shines among the thorns. If you don't receive roses, go out and buy some just to remind yourself how God sees you today. It may even help you appreciate the thorns.

Have a blessed day!

Love Meets Needs

Ruth 2:8-12:

Then Boaz said to Ruth, "Listen, my daughter. Don't go and gather grain in another field, and don't leave this one, but stay here close to my young women. See which field they are harvesting, and follow them. Haven't I ordered the young men not to touch you? When you are thirsty, go and drink from the jars the young men have filled." She bowed with her face to the ground and said to him, "Why are you so kind to notice me, although I am a foreigner?" Boaz answered her, "Everything you have done for your mother-in-law since your husband's death has been fully reported to me: how you left your father and mother, and the land of your birth, and how you came to a people you didn't previously know. May the LORD reward you for what you have done, and may you receive

a full reward from the LORD God of Israel, under whose wings you have come for refuge."

Boaz not only noticed Ruth; he began to care for her needs. Love meets needs. If a woman wonders if a man really loves her, all she has to do is to consider his actions toward her needs. If he is considerate of her and taking care of her, there is love in his heart for her. If he is taking from her and making demands, his heart is focused upon himself.

Boaz had heard of Ruth's reputation before he ever met her. Her character went before her and gave her an honorable name. She is a perfect illustration of the common phrase, "Your reputation precedes you." Boaz knew she could be trusted because of the loyalty she had pledged to Naomi. He knew her desperate condition as a foreign widow and how she had sought refuge in the God of Israel. He also had a respect for her as a widow because he knew how God provided for widows and cared for them under the law. He was a man Ruth could trust.

Trust is a critical ingredient in any relationship. Once trust is destroyed, the relationship is destroyed. When trust is strong, the relationship is strong. Boaz was a man of God who had Ruth's best interest at heart. This was not a man to take for granted. He was a provision from God.

Boaz's comment to Ruth is most interesting. "May the LORD reward you for what you have done, and may you receive a full reward from the LORD God of Israel, under whose wings you have come for refuge." God fully planned to reward Ruth, and He would do it through Boaz, who had just spoken the word over her! Boaz spoke God's best for Ruth. He was God's best provision for her, although he may not have known it at the time.

You may be someone's blessing and not realize it. You may be the instrument God wants to use to free someone or to grant wholeness again. You may be the answer to someone's prayer. Keep in mind that Ruth brought tremendous blessing to Boaz! This was a relationship of mutual benefit. Loving someone will move you to meet a need.

Have a blessed day!

Filled with Abundance

Ruth 2:13-18:

"My Lord," she said, "you have been so kind to me, for you have comforted and encouraged your slave, although I am not like one of your female servants." At mealtime Boaz told her, "Come over here and have some bread and dip it in the vinegar sauce." So she sat beside the harvesters, and he offered her roasted grain. She ate and was satisfied and had some left over. When she got up to gather grain, Boaz ordered his young men, "Be sure to let her gather grain among the bundles, and don't humiliate her. Pull out some stalks from the bundles for her and leave them for her to gather. Don't rebuke her." So Ruth gathered grain in the field until evening. She beat out what she had gathered and it was about 26 quarts of barley. She picked up the grain and went into the city, where her mother-in-law saw what she had gleaned. Then she brought out what she had left over from her meal and gave it to her.

Ruth responded to Boaz's kindness with humility. She recognized her lowly state among the Hebrew women and did not equate herself to one of his slaves. She was a poor destitute who came for the left-overs. Yet, he treated her as if she were a first-class citizen and provided for her. We see a vague familiarity with the prodigal son who returned to the father after having eaten with the pigs. Both Ruth and the prodigal received grace in their humility.

Boaz went a little further than just providing for Ruth. He invited her to lunch. He wanted to get to know her better. He obviously was concerned about her personally. The law allowed for her provision, but Boaz offered grace—an invitation to know him personally. He is a picture of Jesus.

Ruth found abundance in the presence of Boaz. She ate until she was filled and had some left over! A personal relationship with Jesus will always fill us to overflowing so we have something to share with others! Jesus doesn't just give abundance; He *IS* abundance!

Boaz also provided a place of rest for Ruth. He ordered his workers not to touch her. She was safe in his field. He provided abundantly for her by instructing his men to leave some choice grain for her. They were not to rebuke her for taking it.

The law allowed for Ruth to be in Boaz's field, but his grace gave her what the law never could - relationship and abundance! The law may show us the standard and how we fall short of God's commands, but Jesus's sacrifice on the cross gives a relationship with the Father and abundance to meet our need!

Accept Jesus's invitation to dine today. Allow Him to get personal with you, and enjoy His fellowship. Let Him fill you to the point where you are overflowing and just have to share it with others! Expect Him to give you choice grain, not leftovers. You are undeserving, but His grace extends to you personally. Seize the opportunity to be filled with abundance!

Have a blessed day!

The Brightness of a Shadow

Ruth 2:19:

Then her mother-in-law said to her, "Where did you gather barley today, and where did you work? May the LORD bless the man who noticed you." Ruth told her mother-in-law about the men she had worked with and said, "The name of the man I worked with today is Boaz."

Naomi immediately recognized that someone had noticed Ruth. He had sent her away full. She pronounced a blessing upon him before she even knew his name.

Boaz is known as the husband of Ruth, the kinsman-redeemer, the father of Obed, and the grandfather of Jesse the father of David. His name was also given to one of the pillars in Solomon's temple.

Boaz was the great-great-grandfather of Solomon. When Solomon built his illustrious temple, he hired a craftsman named Hiram to construct two pillars for the portico of the sanctuary. He named the pillar on the left Boaz. Interestingly enough, Hiram was the son of a widow.

The kindness Boaz showed to a widow is remembered as a pillar of the temple. It is one of the major functions of the church. Remember **James 1:27: Pure and undefiled religion before our God and Father is this: to** look after orphans and widows in their distress and to keep oneself unstained by the world.

The same Holy Spirit that inspired Solomon to build the temple also inspired James to write the New Testament book for the church. While the pillar on the left of the sanctuary was named Boaz, the pillar on the right was named Jachin which means *he will establish* and comes from a word meaning *to establish or erect, to be faithful.* This is reflective of someone who is undefiled by the world. The commands of pure religion mentioned in James 1:27 were the pillars of the temple!

Boaz's name was forever honored as a pillar of the temple because he practiced true religion. As widows, we can rest assured that God blesses those who bless us! Ultimately, Jesus is our Boaz. He is our kinsman-redeemer. He provides for our every need and issues an invitation for us to know Him more intimately. He is also the cornerstone of the church. Boaz is merely a shadow of Jesus. When a shadow shines as brightly as Boaz, the brightness of the real kinsman-redeemer is unfathomable!

Have a blessed day!

Restoration of Hope

Ruth 2:20-23:

Then Naomi said to her daughter-in-law, "May he be blessed by the LORD, who has not forsaken his kindness to the living or the dead." Naomi continued, "The man is a close relative. He is one of our family redeemers." Ruth the Moabitess said, "He also told me, "Stay with my young men until they have finished all of my harvest." So Naomi said to her daughter-in-law Ruth, "My daughter, it is good for you to work with his young women, so that nothing will happen to you in another field." Ruth stayed close to Boaz's young women and gathered grain until the barley and the wheat harvests were finished. And she lived with her mother-in-law.

When Naomi heard about Boaz, she knew God was at work in her life and in Ruth's. Boaz had the ability and the right to redeem their inheritance and to continue the lineage of the dead. The question was whether or not he was willing. She knew Ruth was in the right field and that God had placed her there. She did not know at this point how it would all work out. She just knew God was at work, and her hope was restored.

Many times before God gives us the breakthrough we need, He restores our hope for the situation. Knowing that He is with us and that He is at work gives us hope that our need will be fulfilled. We may not know just how things will happen, but we know God is doing something on our behalf. She who was bitter with God for allowing her pain now found hope in the grace bestowed to Ruth!

Naomi knew Ruth would be safe in Boaz's field. Not only had Boaz promised her safety, God was blessing her through Boaz. Naomi knew to remain with the blessing. There was no need to check out someone else's field to see if there was a better deal around.

Know that God has not forgotten you nor forsaken you. He is at work in your life, leading you to places where His purpose can be fulfilled. He will lead you to people who can bless you. He will direct you to positions where you can find meaning in life. When you feel His presence, don't abandon it to look for something else. Allow Him to bless you and provide for your every need while you accomplish the task at hand He has given you. This will lead you to greater things.

Have a blessed day!

A Strange Proposal

Ruth 3:1-7:

Ruth's mother-in-law Naomi said to her, "My daughter, shouldn't I find security for you, so that you will be taken care of? Now isn't Boaz our relative? Haven't you been working with his young women? This evening he will be winnowing barley on the threshing floor. Wash, put on perfumed oil, and wear your best clothes. Go down to the threshing floor, but don't let the man know you are there until he has finished eating and drinking. When he lies down, notice the place where he's lying, go in and uncover his feet, and lie down. Then he will explain to you what you should do." So, Ruth said to her, "I will do everything you say." She went down to the threshing floor and did everything her

mother-in-law had instructed her. After Boaz ate, drank, and was in good spirits, he went to lie down at the end of the pile of barley. Then she went in secretly, uncovered his feet, and lay down.

Naomi had committed herself to a life of widowhood, but she felt responsible for finding a husband for Ruth. According to Levrite law, only a kinsman-redeemer could gain back the family inheritance and have children for the dead man's lineage to continue. Boaz fit the bill, and he had already shown kindness to Ruth by allowing her to glean in his fields and assuring her protection and her provision. He had also issued an invitation for her to know him personally by inviting her to dine with him.

Naomi's instructions to Ruth may seem strange to our culture. Her instructions, however, followed an ancient Near Eastern custom of a marriage proposal. Typically, the man would approach the woman and spread his blanket over her to indicate he desired to protect her or provide for her. Boaz had already shown a desire to protect and provide for Ruth. According to Levrite law, Ruth had every right to ask for marriage since he was a kinsman-redeemer. By proposing marriage to Boaz, she displayed a desire to obtain marriage and inheritance according to the law. For Ruth, this was an honorable act.

Ruth approached Boaz after he had been winnowing barley on the threshing floor, where the wheat was separated from the chaff. Here they kept what was valuable and threw away what was not. Ruth, a Moabitess, appealed to the law for her future. She had not tried to find a husband by her own means. Her actions indicate a woman of virtue and value. She was a woman worth keeping.

Boaz was at least a generation older than Ruth. Naomi knew he was an honorable man and he would likely not pursue Ruth for marriage because of the age difference. She also knew Boaz would do the right thing. He would instruct Ruth further.

Remember that Boaz is a representation in the Old Testament of Christ. We find our future, our protection, and our provision in Christ. As widows, we can to go Him with our private matters and ask Him to cover us with His blanket. We can lay everything at His feet and trust that He will instruct us in the way we should go. We are of great value to Him, and He will not throw us away! Boaz was Ruth's security. Christ is ours.

Have a blessed day!

Commit or Submit?

Ruth 3:14-18:

So she lay down at his feet until morning but got up while it was still dark. Then Boaz said, "Don't let it be known that a woman came to the threshing floor." And he told Ruth, "Bring the shawl you're wearing and hold it out." When she held it out, he shoveled six measures of barley into her shawl and she went into the city. She went to her mother-in-law, Naomi, who asked her, "How did it go, my daughter?" Then Ruth told her everything the man had done for her. She said, "He gave me these six measures of barley, because he said, 'Don't go back to your mother-in-law empty-handed.'" "Wait, my daughter," she said, "until you find out how things go, for he won't rest unless he resolves this today."

Boaz didn't want anyone to know a woman had come to the threshing floor. He cared about protecting Ruth's reputation and about the matter he intended to settle for her. He did not want to risk the closest redeemer learning about her request before he approached him. Boaz had Ruth's best interest at heart. He even sent a provision of food back with her so Naomi would know he was taking care of the matter.

Ruth had previously committed herself to Boaz. She gleaned only in his fields upon his advice and Naomi's instruction. She was blessed where she was, and she was content to stay there while receiving his protection and provision. She was a hard worker and a woman of noble character.

When Ruth approached Boaz on the threshing floor, she submitted herself to him. Referring to herself as his slave, Ruth gave herself to Boaz as property. She was subject to him for whatever he desired. His will would become hers. Boaz was not a man to take advantage of this situation, as he could have. He chose to do the honorable thing by the law and take Ruth as his wife, rather than as a concubine. When she submitted herself to him, he felt the responsibility of the kinsman-redeemer and sought to restore her inheritance.

When we commit to something or someone, we pledge or obligate ourselves to serve or perform. While a commitment may stem from the heart, it is displayed in works. If we submit to something or someone, we yield or surrender ourselves to the authority of another. Submission allows us to be subjected to something. We become dependent upon the works or acts of another. To commit is much easier than to submit. We need only to look at ourselves and our own hearts in making a commitment. To submit to someone, we must be able to trust the heart of the other person toward us.

God is moved by our submission, not our commitment. If we have submitted a matter to Him, we are trusting Him to work it out for our good. We trust the outcome He will bring. He does not want to violate that trust. He is moved to act on our behalf. If we have only committed to Him, we are still working or trying to earn what we desire. He will let us keep on working until we see we can never earn it. To be dependent upon His grace means that we fully submit to Him and allow Him to work in our lives. To trust our own works is much easier than to trust what God has in store for us. Our submission to God takes a realization that our own works are not enough and a recognition that God's abundant love for us provides more than we could ever imagine.

Submission has become a dirty word in our society for women. Not every woman is called to submit to every man. That is not biblical at all! A woman is called to submit to her husband and to the authorities God has placed over her. Those should be men in whom she can trust. When a woman submits, the responsibility is felt by the authority placed over her, and it calls him to action. As Naomi told Ruth, "He won't rest until he resolves this today."

It is important we notice the first part of Naomi's instruction to Ruth after she visited with Boaz on the threshing floor. Her words are, "Wait, my daughter...." These are hard words for the commitment-minded woman. She wants to see results. She wants an answer now, and she is personally willing to do something about it. The submitted woman, however, must wait for her authority to move on the matter. We have trouble submitting when we don't want to wait.

Submit and wait before the LORD today. These may seem like hard words by which to live, but they are actions that move God. What we all need is a move of God in our lives. Turn your commitment into submission, rest before Him, and wait for Him to do what He has promised to do for you. He is your redeemer, and your inheritance awaits!

Have a blessed day!

Making it Legal

Ruth 4:1-4:

Boaz went to the gate of the town and sat down there. Soon, the family-redeemer Boaz had spoken about came by. Boaz called him by name and said, "Come over here and sit down. Then Boaz took 10 men of the city's elders and said, "Sit here." And they sat down. He said to the redeemer, "Naomi, who has returned from the land of Moab, is selling a piece of land that belonged to our brother Elimelech. I thought I should inform you: Buy it back in the presence of those seated here in the presence of the elders of my people. If you want to redeem it, do so. But if you do not want to redeem it, tell me, so that I will know, because there isn't anyone other than you to redeem it, and I am next after you." "I want to redeem it," he answered.

The city gate was where everyone gathered to conduct business. If you wanted to find anyone, you would begin your search there. Boaz found the nearest kinsman redeemer at the city gate. He also took 10 elders of the town with him. This was required to conduct any type of legal transaction, such as the selling of property. Boaz was ready to initiate conversation with the nearest kinsman redeemer with the 10 witnesses already in place so there could be no doubt of the details of the matter. He actually put the man on the spot to find out his intentions up front, before he had time to plan any type of scheme.

Since Naomi was a woman, she could not engage in legal transactions. A kinsman had to do that for her. Boaz represented her interest. Boaz wanted an answer immediately. If the nearest kinsman-redeemer did not choose to buy the land, he would do so at that moment.

Upon hearing the news, the nearest kinsman wanted to redeem it. This seemed like a golden opportunity to buy land not previously known for sale. He had everything in place to do it immediately. Why not seize the opportunity?

There was just one more thing. One requirement might determine whether or not this kinsman would take the valuable property or be willing to throw it away as chaff. Ten witnesses were ready to verify it. We will take a look at that one thing tomorrow.

Have a blessed day!

One More Thing

Ruth 4:5-8:

Then Boaz said, "On the day you buy the land from Naomi, you will also acquire Ruth the Moabitess, the wife of the deceased man, to perpetuate the man's name on his property." The redeemer replied, "I can't redeem it myself, or I will ruin my own inheritance. Take my right of redemption, because I can't redeem it." At an earlier period in Israel, a man removed his sandal and gave it to the other party in order to make any matter legally binding concerning the right of redemption or the exchange of property. This was the method of legally binding a transaction in Israel.

One more thing should be considered. If the redeemer purchased the property from Naomi, he would also acquire Ruth, the Moabitess, as his wife and would be bound by law to raise children in the dead man's name. The transaction entailed much more than just acquiring property; it created a whole new family! The nearest kinsman redeemer spoke correctly. He could not redeem it.

The nearest kinsman-redeemer is representative of the law, the standard by which men are to live. The law has absolutely no power, however, to redeem; it is incapable of taking a woman of pagan, despicable origin, and making her an acceptable wife in which to cultivate a new family line. To do such would tarnish and violate the standard itself.

Boaz, however, is representative of Christ. He voluntarily swore to take the unclean woman and make her his own. He would create a lineage through her. Within this lineage, a Savior would be born who would make a much greater sacrifice and acquire a tarnished bride. Through His purchase, the bride will become radiant!

The nearest kinsman redeemer saw chaff and a loss to his inheritance. Boaz saw value and worth. The law saw sinful man; Christ saw a radiant Bride!

The nearest kinsman redeemer did nothing wrong. He simply did not offer grace, which is undeserved. We cannot offer what we don't have. The law has no grace to grant. Boaz, however, granted grace. He went above and beyond what was required for Ruth and Naomi. The law exposes our sin before man and God. That is what it was designed to do. Jesus, however, purchased us with His own blood! He granted us grace and redeemed us from our destitute condition!

Boaz was also rich! Ruth would live a life of abundance as his wife. In Christ, we partake of all the riches of His glory! He came that we might have life and have it more abundantly! The road from pagan slave to abundant bride is red with Christ's blood and paved with His grace!

Have a blessed day!

Missed Orpah-tunity

Ruth 4:9-10:

Boaz said to the elders and all the people, "You are witnesses today that I am buying from Naomi everything that belonged to Elimelech, Chilion, and Mahlon. I will also acquire Ruth the Moabitess, Mahlon's widow, as my wife, to perpetuate the deceased man's name on his property, so that his name will not disappear among his relatives or from the gate of his home. You are witnesses today."

Orpah had an inheritance waiting for her that she never received! She decided to return to the comforts and gods of her homeland to start a new life, the easiest of the two roads before her. Ruth, however, chose the difficult road. She left everything behind and dared to walk into unfamiliar territory with an unfamiliar people to whom she was considered a pagan and an outcast. When she did, she walked right into the abundance of her God-ordained destiny by marrying the richest man in town!

Notice that Boaz not only purchased Elimilech's and Mahlon's property; he also purchased Chilion's property. God gave Ruth the inheritance that should have been Orpah's. This reminds me of the parable of the slave owner who gave differing measures of talents to his slaves before departing for a journey. When he returned, he found two had used their talents while one had buried his in fear of losing it altogether. The angry slave owner took the talent away from the foolish slave and gave it to the one who had gained the greatest return (Matt. 25:14-30). God's greatest blessings are reserved for those who are willing to go the distance with

Him and put to work what He has given you to do. He blesses those who act on their faith.

Perhaps, Orpah did not follow Naomi for fear of failure. Granted, failure is a part of life, and we all experience it if we ever succeed at anything. Maybe she just didn't want to leave the comforts of her homeland. We will live only mediocre lives if we insist on remaining comfortable. The blessing of our destiny awaits only when we act on faith. Faith is the pathway between our God-given desires and our destiny. We walk it one step at a time. If we never begin the journey, we will never reach the destination.

Like Orpah, you may have experienced the pain of losing a spouse. You do not, however, have to experience the loss of inheritance as she did. Take a look at what God has placed in your hand. What gifts has He given you that can be used for His kingdom? What desires and passions has He placed in your heart? Begin to act in faith and use what God has given you. Take advantage of the opportunities He places before you to glean from His fields. If you don't know quite how or where to use your talents, pray and ask for His wisdom to direct you. Pray for God to reveal this to you.

Ruth's story proves that there is new life after widowhood. God can begin anew with us and take us to places we never imagined. It is not too late for any of us. Choose the Ruth-life and act on your faith today. Leave the Orpah-life behind, and believe God for a glorious inheritance!

Have a blessed day!

Love and Fruitfulness

Ruth 4:11a:

The elders and all the people who were at the gate said, "We are witnesses. May the LORD make the woman who is entering your house like Rachel and Leah, who together built the house of Israel...."

The people of Israel would watch the power and grace unfold in the lives of Boaz and Ruth and know that God was moving in the land. They pronounced a threefold blessing upon the household of Boaz. We will take a look at the first this morning and the other two in the days to come.

First, they asked that Ruth be like Rachel and Leah, who together built the house of Israel. If you've ever closely studied the house of Jacob (aka Israel), you know that it was anything but peaceful. There was strife, jealousy, favoritism, competition, violence, deceit, and much scheming. As dysfunctional as it was, however, God still raised up the twelve tribes of Israel from it to create His chosen nation.

Rachel and Leah were sisters who were never satisfied. They each wanted what the other had and schemed and competed to get it. So, why would the elders want Ruth to be like both of them? If she was like both of them combined, she would be full, possessing fully what the other lacked. She would have the heart of her husband and be fruitful at the same time.

Many women have desired the love of a man and never found the love they desperately needed. You cannot make a man love you. God places that in a man's heart. If you have to do something to earn love, it really isn't love. You can never work hard enough to deserve love. This was Leah's plight. Jacob was obligated to her, but he did not love her. She is a symbol of the law.

If you have God's love, however, you truly have all you need. Many of us, however, are unsatisfied with that. Rachel had all she would ever need in the arms of Jacob, who loved her with all his heart. He worked 14 years for her! Whether or not she ever had a son would not have changed his heart toward her. While she may not have deserved it, Jacob really loved Rachel. She is an example of grace.

In Ruth, we find a proclamation of both the law and grace. Her descendant would fulfill both. Jesus is the only one who has ever lived who fulfilled the law, and His sacrifice offers us grace. The law without grace leaves us hopeless and unfulfilled. Grace, without the law, is unnecessary.

The elders had no idea the depth and meaning of what they prophesied over Ruth that day, but God did. May we live under grace—but conscious of the law so that we, too, may have a household of love and fruitfulness. To live like Leah means that we constantly work to try to deserve something we can never achieve. To live like Rachel means we never appreciate the love we have. But, to live like Ruth means we are complete, fulfilled in every way with love and fruitfulness. May the rest of our journey be like Ruth's!

Have a blessed day!

Bridging the Gap

Ruth 4:11b:

May you be powerful in Ephrathah and famous in Bethlehem.

Ephrathah or Ephrath was the ancient name of the town of Bethlehem. Abraham, Isaac, and Jacob all knew the town by the name Ephrath. This is where Jacob buried Rachel. Ephrathah means *fruitfulness.* Bethlehem means *house of bread.*

The elders proclaimed that Boaz would be powerful in Ephrathah (fruitfulness). Boaz was already an established leader in the community and respected by the older citizens. This seemed to increase his standing with the older generation and illustrate the acceptance of the outcast Moabitess as one of their own.

The elders also proclaimed Boaz would be famous in Bethlehem (house of bread). Bethlehem was the new name for the town by which the younger generation and generations to follow would more easily recognize. Boaz seems to bridge two generations by strengthening the older and leading the younger with hope, grace, and new life through the redemption of Ruth. Likewise, Christ bridged the gap between earth and heaven, between the law and grace, between God and people.

Do you remember the pillars that Solomon built for the temple? He named one of them Boaz. This redemption is a picture of what Christ did on the cross for us. He died to redeem pagan, sinful, undeserving, outcast humanity, but He didn't stop with the death. Christ takes us as His bride and gives us all the inheritance of a princess becoming a rightful queen— a far cry from which we came!

Jesus was born in a town first known as fruitfulness that became the house of bread. In Him, we find both. In Him, we are fruitful and abundant. In Him, we have the bread of life that nourishes those who are hungry. In Him, we find redemption and inheritance we do not deserve but obtain through grace. Only in Him can we find the life worth living!

Have a blessed day

A Blessed Family Line

Ruth 4:12:

May your house become like the house of Perez, the son Tamar bore to Judah, because of the offspring the LORD will give you by this young woman.

Tamar was a widow who was not as fortunate as Ruth. Her father-in-law, Judah, did not want to rightfully redeem her and raise up a family line through her because he thought she was cursed. He lost two sons that were married to her, and he did not want to lose a third. He tricked her into waiting until the third son grew up, then he refused to give the son to her. Tamar craftily seduced him and shamed him into giving her a family, himself. As a result, she gave birth to twin sons named Perez and Zerah.

Tamar must have had a difficult delivery of the twins. Zerah stuck his hand out first, and a midwife tied a scarlet thread around his wrist. Then, he drew his hand back in. Perez was born first, then Zerah. The two struggled to see who would receive the title of firstborn. Perez means *a breach* or *a breaking forth;* this describes his birth. Perez is an ancestor of Boaz, David, and Jesus.

Perez's descendants were numerous. The elders desired a long, prosperous, and fruitful lineage for Boaz and Ruth. That is exactly what they received.

Tamar manipulated her redemption. Ruth submitted to receive hers. We have the same choice daily. We can try to manipulate what we think is rightfully ours, or we can submit ourselves to God. Ruth received everything Tamar did and more! If God has promised it, we can count on it! We don't have to manipulate the way Tamar did.

God is still faithful, even when we resort to undesirable tactics. The greater blessing, however, is found when we fully submit to Him. He will not deny us as Judah did Tamar. He is our Redeemer. Boaz is only a shadow of what Christ is to us today! He is our Savior and Fulfillment. He is our inheritance. He is our Groom and coming King!

Have a blessed day!

Satan's Destruction, God's Masterpiece

Ruth 4:13-17:

Boaz took Ruth and she became his wife. When he was intimate with her, the LORD enabled her to conceive, and she gave birth to a son. Then the women said to Naomi, "Praise be the LORD, who has not left you without a family redeemer today. May his name be famous in Israel. He will renew your life and sustain you in your old age. Indeed, your daughter-in-law, who loves you and is better to you than seven sons, has given birth to him." Naomi took the child, placed him on her lap, and took care of him. The neighbor women said, "A son has been born to Naomi," and they named him Obed. He was the father of Jesse, the father of David.

I love happy endings to a good story! You can't get any happier than this! She who was born pleasant and became bitter rejoiced in the end. Naomi endured tragedy, heartache, and loss to see redemption and the goodness of the LORD!

What about your own story? Have you endured with faith in God long enough to see your own life move from being pleasant to bitter to redeemed and restored? I must admit, I'm still hanging in there, myself.

Boaz and Ruth married and had a son who represented much promise to Naomi. He was the assurance that her family line would continue, and he would care for her in her old age. His birth brought about praise from the local women. His life was welcomed into this world with great joy! He represented life, promise, and the presence of God. How appropriate that Obed means *serving.* His birth served much anticipation and fulfillment. His life would be one meant to serve a family line the Devil tried to destroy.

What has Satan taken from you? Where has he worked to destroy you? That area must hold some promise in God's kingdom, or it wouldn't be so important for the Devil to destroy! Trust God to work to take that evil and turn it into something wonderful and beneficial for you in the light of His divine purpose. He loves to give us what He has destined for us! Satan can't take that from us!

Let the words of David comfort you today:

Psalm 27:13-14:

I am certain that I will see the LORD's goodness in the land of the living. Wait for the LORD; be courageous and let your heart be strong. Wait for the LORD.

Have a blessed day!

Widowhood with a Purpose

Ruth 4:18-22:

Now this is the geneaology of Perez:

Perez fathered Hezron. Hezron fathered Ram, who fathered Amminadab. Amminadab fathered Nahshon, who fathered Salmon. Salmon fathered Boaz, who fathered Obed. And Obed fathered Jesse, who fathered David.

Perez was a twin conceived from a widow's manipulation. He struggled with his brother in the womb to see who would be born first. It was as if he knew the lineage of the firstborn would be blessed.

Satan never wanted Tamar to have a family lineage; it was dangerous to him. Perhaps, Satan even tried to bring forth the wrong twin first because he knew what was coming from the line of Perez. Perez was a son of Judah, which means *praise.* Any offspring from praise was a threat to the Devil.

God had an important plan for the lineage of Perez, although he would never know it in his lifetime. He made sure Perez brought forth Hezron and that Hezron produced Ram. His plan for Ram was to bring forth Amminadab so Nahshon could be born. Nahshon was to father Salmon so Boaz would be born. He used Boaz to father Obed so Jesse could father David—a destined king of Israel.

God had a plan to bring every one of us to this earth because we are all a part of His great purpose. He used us to bring forth our children, who all have a destiny in Him. We may never know just how crucial our lineage is to God's plan in this lifetime. For some reason, however, He made sure we got here.

The lineage of Christ contains two widows. God planned their widowhood for His greater purpose. While it may seem hard to accept the fact, He planned our widowhood, too. We can become bitter about it and linger in self-pity, or we can accept it and embrace the new life God has planned for us. We still have purpose in Him. Who knows what we may yet produce that can add value to His kingdom?

The story of Ruth is one of redemption. She was an undeserving pagan who chose to follow God and submit her lowly state to Him by leaving her family and her gods behind. God brought her to a state of grace and used her in the lineage of His own Son! Hers is a story of hope that God has a plan greater than our struggles. When all is lost, we find everything in Christ, who has already paid the price for our redemption.

Boaz is a type or shadow of Jesus Christ. What he did for Ruth is a glimpse of what Christ can do in our lives. The same grace that gave Ruth an inheritance is ours today. He is the kinsman-redeemer who gives us hope and a future.

Have a blessed day!

The Power of Grace

Ephesians 2:1-5:

And you were dead in your trespasses and sins in which you previously walked according to this worldly age, according to the ruler of the atmospheric domain, the spirit now working in the disobedient. We too all previously lived among them in our fleshly desires, carrying out the inclinations of our flesh and thoughts, and by nature we were children under wrath, as the others were also. But God, who is abundant in mercy, because of His great love that He had for us, made us alive with the Messiah even though we were dead in trespasses. By grace you are saved!

Our salvation is completely from God. We can do nothing to get it right on our own. Unless His Spirit moves on us, we have no hope. We've done nothing to deserve His mercy and everything to deserve His wrath. By His grace, He moves on us in our dead condition and brings us to life in the Messiah. We cannot make a change on our own. God must work in us.

The ruler of this atmospheric domain is Satan. When we are born into this world, his influence is all around us. We will succumb to his power as a natural response from our human nature because he controls human nature. This path leads to death and eternal separation from God in hell. To respond in a manner contrary to the human nature, we must be moved by a greater spirit. We have no ability in our human nature to do what is godly. Unless God's Spirit moves on us to draw us to Him, we remain dead in our trespasses. God's love for us makes us alive in Christ through grace. We do not come to Jesus on our own. We are drawn to Him by grace, where we can either respond to Him or reject Him. Grace was never our idea.

Do you have a difficult person in your life who is controlled by the ruler of the atmospheric domain? Pray for God's Spirit to move on that person. He or she will never change, and you can do nothing to change him or her. The grace of God, however, has tremendous power to change a life. Thank Him for His powerful love, mercy, and grace today.

Have a blessed day!

MARCH 2

Walk Free by Grace

Romans 1:7:

To all who are in Rome, loved by God, called as saints. Grace to you and peace from God our Father and the Lord Jesus Christ.

Paul began his letter to the believers in Rome with a warm greeting. He reminded them that they are loved by God and called as saints. This would be very different than the approach a Jewish leader would make toward them. The Jews would consider them pagan, unworthy of consideration from God, and unchosen by merit of their race. To the Jewish religion, they could become converts only after participating in certain rituals but never receiving full acceptance into worship. As Gentile believers, they would always have to worship outside the temple. They would never be holy enough to be fully accepted by Jews or by God.

Paul continued his loving acceptance of the Romans with a proclamation of grace and peace to them. By expressing grace, he reminded them that although they were once unworthy to stand before God, they now have a right standing with Him through Jesus Christ. Through grace, their sins are forgiven. The Jewish leaders were offended by grace because it negated their self-righteousness and religious works. Through grace, anyone could stand before God in peace without going through all the rituals of the law. Grace made the unholy Gentile holy before God, and that just didn't set well with those who had worked all their lives to gain what they thought was a rightful place in the kingdom of God. To them, grace was unfair and offensive. But, to the Gentiles who knew they were sinners and outcasts, grace was a warm and endearing force that drew them to God.

Grace does not approve sin. Grace enables us to overcome the sin. When we truly realize that we are sinful and deserve punishment, grace reminds us that Jesus has already suffered the punishment for our sins, and God still loves us. There is nothing we can do to atone for that sin, so we must continue our Christian walk in grace and peace, knowing that we are loved and called by God for His purpose. Sin condemns. We will have to either justify it or admit it and receive grace. As long as we justify it, we will have to continue to defend ourselves from its condemnation. Only by grace can we receive forgiveness and be able to walk free from it. If we justify sin or deny it, we will continue to walk in condemnation and feel the need to earn an acceptance that cannot be earned.

Know that you are dearly loved by God and called as His saint today. Christ has already suffered the punishment for your sins on the cross. Grace to you and peace from God our Father in the LORD Jesus Christ. You are not condemned. You are highly favored and deeply loved by God. Walk free from any sin that hinders you or condemns you today. You don't have to prove anything to anyone. Admit your failures, realize grace, and leave that sin behind. You have a great purpose in Christ, and God wants you to fulfill it!

Have a blessed day!

Created, Saved, and Living by Grace

Acts 17:28-29:

For in Him we live and move and exist, as even some of your own poets have said, "For we are also His offspring." Being God's offspring, then,

we shouldn't think that the divine nature is like gold or silver or stone, an image fashioned by human art and imagination.

These verses remind us of the holiness of God. He is wholly other and separate from us. He gives us the very breath we breathe and enables our movement. We can do nothing without Him, and we belong to Him. He is not like gold, silver, or stone that can be crafted into things for us to admire. We are His handiwork.

Many times we are guilty of trying to fashion a god to suit us. We get a picture of what we would like for God to be for us, and we try to present Him as such to others. When our god fails us and does not become what we created him to be, we get hurt or angry. We must remember that we cannot mold or create God to suit us. He has created us to suit Him for His purpose.

Our created gods have no power. Only the God who created us gives us our very life. He wants to live and move through us. We are the ones who should be molded.

Verses 30-31:

Therefore, having overlooked the times of ignorance, God now commands all people everywhere to repent, because He has set a day on which He is going to judge the world in righteousness by the Man He has appointed. He has provided proof of this to everyone by raising Him from the dead.

God will judge everyone by the righteousness of Christ. We cannot create righteousness on our own. We receive righteousness through grace from the One who created us. Our works could never be enough. Jesus is the standard, and His righteousness is granted to us, not earned.

We cannot create a god to please us, nor can we obtain righteousness through our works. We must submit in full assurance that the One who created us has a wonderful design for our lives and that when He looks at us, we reflect the righteousness of Christ. Created by grace, saved by grace, living by grace—this was God's design all along.

Have a blessed day!

Access God's Grace through Faith

Romans 4:16-18:

This is why the promise is by faith, so that it may be according to grace, to guarantee it to all the descendants—not only to those who are of the law, but also to those who are of Abraham's faith. He is the father of us all in God's sight. As it is written: I have made you the father of many nations. He believed in God, who gives life to the dead and calls things into existence that do not exist. Against hope, with hope he believed, so that he became the father of many nations, according to what had been spoken: So will your descendants be.

Abraham was a man under grace. The law had not yet been given. God's promise and covenant with Abraham was one of grace, as is ours. While Abraham and Sarah became impatient and tried to take matters into their own hands at one time by producing a son with Hagar, their efforts did not bring them the blessing of God's promise. They had to wait for it. If God has promised us something, we must wait for His grace to perform it, as well.

Grace is accessed through faith. We simply believe God at His word and allow Him to do it. We cannot hurry or manipulate the process to operate in our own timing. God often gives our faith an opportunity to grow by allowing us to wait upon His promise. God's timing always reveals His glory and diminishes ours.

What has God promised you? Realize today that it will come by His grace through faith. You cannot work to earn it nor manipulate it to hurry. Simply take God at His Word, and rest in the assurance the He can and will perform that which He has promised. Grace through faith glorifies God, but we partake in its divine blessing. Hallelujah!

Have a blessed day!

God's Promise Comes through Grace

Romans 4:19-21:

He considered his own body to be already dead (since he was about a hundred years old), and the deadness of Sarah's womb, without weakening in the faith. He did not waver in unbelief at God's promise, but was strengthened in his faith and gave glory to God, because he was fully convinced that what He had promised He was also able to perform.

As Abraham's reliance in self decreased, his faith that God would do as He said increased. When it was totally apparent to Abraham and everyone else that he had no ability in and of himself to bear a child, God moved on his behalf and gave him a son. The glory of God literally shone through the child born to Sarah by Abraham because everyone knew it was impossible for them. What is impossible with us is possible with God!

Romans 4:22-25:

Therefore, it was credited to him for righteousness. Now it was credited to him was not written for Abraham alone, but also for us. It will be credited to us who believe in Him who raised Jesus our Lord from the dead. He was delivered up for our trespasses and raised for our justification.

Because Abraham believed in God's word, it was credited to him for righteousness. This passage explains that it was written for us as well. We are credited with righteousness by believing in the finished work of Christ. Our works mean nothing; His grace is everything! By His grace through faith, we have a personal relationship with Christ, which gives us access to the throne of grace with the Father. We may come boldly to that throne of grace and ask anything, knowing that He sees the righteousness of Christ and not our works.

Boldly go before God's throne of grace today for whatever need you may have. The cross gives us access to the throne, and grace embraces us at the throne. God's promises to you come through grace, and you can do nothing to earn them. God credits righteousness—the righteousness of Christ through faith—to your account when you appeal to Him. By grace you stand before Him, by grace you are saved, and by grace you receive your promise.

Have a blessed day!

Righteousness from Grace through Faith

Romans 9:30-32:

What should we say then? Gentiles, who did not pursue righteousness, have obtained righteousness—namely the righteousness that comes from faith. But Israel, pursuing the law for righteousness, has not achieved the law. Why is that? They did not pursue it by faith, but as if it were by works.

Israel attempted to earn righteousness by obeying the law. The law, however, was never given for righteousness sake. It was given to expose our unrighteousness. Gentiles obtained righteousness by pursuing faith in the finished work of Christ. By faith, they received righteousness. Through faith came the grace of God for forgiveness of sin. Works cannot forgive nor remove sin because they stem from ourselves. Only God can forgive us and remove our sin because our sin violates His commands. Therefore, He must be the One to forgive the sin. This requires grace, which cannot be earned. Our works cover nothing. His grace covers everything!

In our Christian walk, we often think that because we have obeyed in this area or that, we deserve to be blessed. While God does honor obedience, He does not bless us simply because we are good. Our own righteousness is still as filthy rags in His sight. He blesses us simply because He loves us.

Christians often become jealous of others that have been blessed. Like the elder brother in the parable of the Prodigal Son, they think they have earned the blessing the prodigal received because of their good works. The prodigal, however, simply turned back to his father after a season of sin, and his father rejoiced to have the son back again. His blessing was a sign of his goodness that he still welcomed the prodigal as a son. Works were never a factor. Faith, grace, and forgiveness brought restoration to this relationship.

The Pharisees had the elder brother mentality. They had worked all these years to establish what was right and what was wrong in the people's eyes. Then, Jesus came in and began to forgive, heal, restore, and bless people who had sinned. How dare He violate the Pharisees' standard! They failed to realize that Jesus was the standard, and they were the violators.

If you have blown it as a Christian, you are in good company! Don't worry about what the elder brothers will say. They must discover grace to overcome their own shortcomings. Place your faith in the finished work of Christ, and enjoy the blessing of a restored relationship with the Father as He rejoices over you!

Have a blessed day!

Blessed to Display His Grace

Ephesians 2:4-10:

But God, who is abundant in mercy, because of His great love that He had for us, made us alive with the Messiah even though we were dead in trespasses. By grace you are saved! He also raised us up with Him and seated us with Him in the heavens, in Christ Jesus so that in the coming ages He might display the immeasurable riches of His grace in His kindness to us in Christ Jesus. For by grace you are saved through faith, and this is not from yourselves; it is God's gift—not from works, so that no one can boast. For we are His creation—created in Christ Jesus for good works, which God prepared ahead of time so that we should walk in them.

God desires to display His grace through us! He wants others to see the riches of His grace in His kindness to us through the finished work of Christ on the cross. When God blesses us, it is to point others to Christ. We cannot boast in what Christ did on the cross. He took our sins upon Himself so that we might not have to suffer what we deserved. The cross humbles us by giving us a picture of what we truly deserve. Because Christ took our punishment in full, we receive grace to walk in newness of life. If God only blesses those who are good, then those who are good could boast in their works. The world does not need our works. The world needs the finished work of Christ on the cross!

Our works do not gain us access to salvation or to God's blessing. God saves us and blesses us so we can do the works He has prepared for us to do. We often place the cart before the horse in this matter. We can do no good works for God unless and until He blesses us with HIS grace. When

He does for us what we cannot do for ourselves, we have a testimony of HIS grace to share.

You get what you expect. If you have faith for the worst, you will receive according to your faith. God always gives us His best. He proved that by giving us His only Son to die for us. Just think back to the many blessings you have received and see God granting you His very best in each situation. How could you improve on the very best God has to offer?

Expect God to grow your faith in the years ahead. That means you can expect to experience His grace. Hallelujah! May God be glorified!

Have a blessed day!

Grace and Discouragement

Ephesians 3:7-13:

I was made a servant of this gospel by the gift of God's grace that was given to me by the working of His power. This grace was given to me— the least of all the saints!—to proclaim to the Gentiles the incalculable riches of the Messiah, and to shed light for all about the administration of the mystery hidden for ages in God who created all things. This is so that God's multi-faceted wisdom may now be made known through the church to the rulers and authorities in the heavens. This is according to the purpose of the ages, which He made in the Messiah, Jesus our Lord, in whom we have boldness, access, and confidence through faith in Him. So then I ask you not to be discouraged over my afflictions on your behalf, for they are your glory.

Paul had amazing insight into his own grace and afflictions. Without a doubt, he realized his purpose and that God, Himself, had made him a servant of the gospel by grace. In his own strength and knowledge, he would have continued to persecute followers of Christ and felt justified to do so. God, however, intervened and gave him a revelation of the truth. God's truth changed him—that's what grace is designed to do. Grace reveals our destructive behavior to us and gives us the ability to adjust our behavior while accepting us, rather than punishing us. Grace is favor we could never deserve.

Paul realized his purpose was to share the gospel to the Gentiles, but they were not his only audience. God's plan was also to send a message to the spiritual beings. God uses us to speak to them. He displays His power and His glory through us to speak to rulers and authorities in heavenly places. This is exactly what He did with Job. We have an earthly audience and a heavenly audience, and the message God always sends is rooted in the power of Christ.

If you are a Christian, you have the righteousness of Christ. You do not have to earn your position with God. You do not have to earn the right to be blessed. You are given grace through faith in the work done for you on the cross. Christ gives us access to the very throne room of God, where we may approach boldly and ask for whatever we need. As God sees Christ, He also sees you because of your faith in Him.

This fact alone should encourage us. When everything falls apart and things seem to look their worst, you have access to the throne room of God Almighty! When the enemy sends multiple distractions and difficulties your way, you have an advocate with the Father who works on your behalf! Whatever the Devil has sent your way to cause harm, God has the power to use it for your good and His glory! God loves to take the Devil's own stick and beat him with it! That is exactly what He did with the cross!

Your current afflictions are destined to be your glory if you will walk in the grace given you through faith in Christ. Now is time to unloose the chains of discouragement and run the race of grace. Allow the power of Christ to be revealed in you!

Have a blessed day!

Grace and Truth

John 1:16-18:

Indeed, we have all received grace after grace from His fullness, for although the law was given through Moses, grace and truth came through Jesus Christ. No one has ever seen God. The One and Only Son—the One who is at the Father's side—He has revealed Him.

God's grace has given us all more than we truly deserve, and His mercy has prevented us from receiving the full measure of wrath we deserve. Everyone is a beneficiary of grace. In fact, we don't deserve to have ever heard the gospel, but God has seen fit to make sure we have access to it.

The law came through Moses; it was designed to expose sin. No one other than Jesus has ever been able to fulfill the law because breaking even one part of it in thought or deed violates the entire law and makes man guilty before God. While the law exposes sin, it has no power whatsoever to save man or to cause him to change.

Only the finished work of the sacrifice of Christ on the cross has the power to save. He took our place so that His righteousness might be imputed to us. This is an act of grace—our only hope of salvation. Grace, however, has a counterpart known as truth.

The truth is that we are all sinners, and sin separates us from God. The truth reveals that God is love, and He sent His only Son to die for us so we could experience grace and live in fellowship with Him. The truth is also that God freely gives this grace to all who believe. The truth also reveals that His grace has the power to transform believers' lives to live victoriously through the power of the Holy Spirit.

If we think God gives grace only to those who deserve it, we miss the whole point of grace. If we think we can fall so far that grace cannot help us, we don't understand the Father's heart. If we take God's grace for granted and use it as a license to sin, we place ourselves above the law and, therefore, become judged by it. God gives grace to those who realize their sinful condition and turn to Him. Understanding the truth but failing to accept grace places us under the law, where we cannot stand. Grace and truth work together in the Christian walk. Both came through Jesus Christ.

No one has ever seen God, but Jesus revealed the Father through His life. He came in grace and in truth so we might see the beauty of the Father and truly know His heart for us. The truth is that God loves you, and He has already done for you what you could not do for yourself.

In whatever situation you may find yourself today, accept the truth in it. Recognize where you have failed, where you have done the right thing, and the things that are out of your control that need the Father's touch. Confess this before the Father and submit it fully to Him, realizing that His grace can work beyond your wildest dreams to work everything for good!

He is full of grace and truth, and His answer to you is found in the cross. Grace and truth keep on giving!

Have a blessed day!

Faith, Grace, and Hope

There are three things by which the Christian must live daily: faith, grace, and hope. We must have faith in Christ as our Savior and that God has a purpose for our lives and is working it out in us for our benefit and His glory. His grace enables us to face the challenges this life holds. We hope in the glory that is to be revealed in us by the Father. Where these three abide, God is at work.

Romans 5:1-2:

Therefore, since we have been declared righteous by faith, we have peace with God through our Lord Jesus Christ. Also, through Him, we have obtained access by faith into this grace in which we stand, and we rejoice in the hope of the glory of God.

When we are actively walking in faith, hope, and grace, God is in control of our lives. On our own, we are dirty, filthy, and unworthy of anything from the Father. He won't even look upon us because of our sin. Faith in Christ, however, gives us the righteousness that God accepts. Through this righteousness, and nothing of our own merit, we may receive grace from the Father. This grace provides us with everything we need to live according to our calling. Grace fulfills every longing and empowers us to fulfill God's purpose. We hope in the glory that God reveals in us when His purpose is complete. Otherwise, we are on our own, subject to the Devil's control and his tactics of manipulation, intimidation, and domination. In his control, there is no peace, only destruction.

We stand in grace. When we start thinking that we have to earn God's favor in some way, we begin to fall. We must come back to Him in full repentance and faith, depending upon the righteousness of Christ. Everything we have is an act of grace from the Father. Any trial He calls us to face comes complete with His measure of grace. We stand in that grace, rather than falling from the pressure. When we walk outside that grace into an area of sin, we fall subject to Satanic influence and into the path of destruction. While the Devil cannot destroy our salvation, he can certainly do a number to our witness, our credibility, and our joy. We must turn from sin and to God.

Finally, where God is at work, we have hope in the glory of viewing the finished product! As the old saying goes, God is not finished with us yet, but when He is, we will be a work that reveals the precision of His handiwork. We must hope in what will be, according to the grace of God by the faith that works in us.

Have a blessed day!

Grace, Mercy, and Peace

2 John 3:

Grace, mercy, and peace will be with us from God the Father and from Jesus Christ, the Son of the Father, in truth and love.

This verse offers us great promises from God the Father and from Jesus Christ the Son. Grace, mercy, and peace are ours in truth and love. God's plan for our lives will be guided by these things. He gives us grace, mercy, and peace to walk where He has called us to walk. He calls us to these places in truth and in love.

I have found it hard to accept the fact that widowhood is God's will for my life. At times it seems like harsh punishment, but punishment is associated with condemnation. God does not condemn us. He calls us in love to walk where He has destined us for His purpose, and He gives us grace, mercy, and truth to find our way.

Condemnation is a tool of the Devil, as is its close sister, guilt. Both will prevent you from realizing God's best for your life and will keep you working to try to overcome them. Grace, mercy, and peace will open you to receive every good thing from God that He has for you on your journey as He works all things together for your good and His glory.

Today, throw away any feelings of condemnation or guilt the Devil tries to force on you. Embrace the grace, mercy, and peace that God provides for your journey. His glory is yet to be revealed in this place. Grace, mercy, and peace will guide you to it!

Have a blessed day!

Stand in Grace, Rejoice in Hope

Romans 5:1-2:

Therefore, since we have been declared righteous by faith, we have peace with God through our Lord Jesus Christ. Also through Him, we have obtained access by faith into this grace in which we stand, and we rejoice in the hope of the glory of God.

Our works, or lack of them, do not declare us righteous with the Father. Faith in the finished work of the cross declares us righteous. If we look at what we have done, we will feel unworthy, unloved, and unable to stand before a holy God. We could never do enough to earn a right standing or a blessing from Him. If He always gave us what we deserve, we would deserve hell.

We don't stand before God by our own merit. We stand before Him by faith in the righteousness of Christ. This same faith gives us access to the grace of God. With this grace, all things are possible (Phil. 4:13)! There is no hurdle or sin we can't overcome by His grace. While we might endure suffering for a little while, His grace gives us hope to rejoice that the glory of God will be revealed through our suffering, and we will be blessed in the midst of it.

When all seems lost, never underestimate the grace of God in your life. You have a hope that does not disappoint. Come boldly before the throne of God in the righteousness of Christ to make your plea. Regardless of what you have done, what Christ has done has given you access to grace. Rejoice in the hope of the glory of God in your negative situations. His grace is greater than your failures, and His glory is greater than your guilt.

Have a blessed day!

Strong in Grace

2 Timothy 2:1:

You, therefore, my child, be strong in the grace that is in Christ Jesus.

At first glance of this verse, we may think Paul is instructing us to be strong in granting grace. While we should certainly be gracious people, this verse has a much stronger meaning than that. To be strong in the grace that is in Christ Jesus is to be strong in the grace He has for us.

Those who don't realize their need for grace never fully understand grace. Grace is not deserving of anything but being granted everything! When you get a blessing you know you do not deserve, you have realized grace. Many of us, however, often feel we deserve the blessings we receive and that we have somehow earned them.

To be strong in the grace that is in Christ Jesus is to be full of humility, realizing that our standing with the Father has nothing to do with our good works—it has everything to do with the righteousness of Christ. When God looks at us, He sees us through the lens of Christ's righteousness. We are loved, blessed, and highly favored because of the righteousness of Christ. When we get a full revelation of this, we become strong in the grace that is in Christ Jesus.

Being strong in the grace that is in Christ Jesus allows us to come boldly before God's throne. We can ask Him for anything because we are aware that grace has granted us a right relationship with Him through Jesus. Being strong in grace means we no longer live with a feeling of guilt or condemnation because we realize and accept the grace God has granted us.

Today, accept the grace God has already granted you through Jesus Christ. Now is the time to free ourselves of the guilt and condemnation the Devil has laid upon us. We are righteous because Christ has made us righteous, and we have an audience with the God of the Universe! He is our loving, heavenly Father, and He longs to bless us with good things.

Have a blessed day!

Gold, Silver, and Grace

Isaiah 60:17:

I will bring gold instead of bronze; I will bring silver instead of iron, bronze instead of wood, and iron instead of stones. I will appoint peace as your guard and righteousness as your ruler.

Jewelry makers are increasingly making more jewelry with iron and bronze, rather than silver and gold. With the prices of silver and gold skyrocketing, people cannot afford to buy the real thing anymore and must settle for something less in a more affordable price range. While bronze is similar to gold in appearance, it lacks the shine and luster of gold. Iron is a strong metal, but it is dull compared to the sparkle of silver.

Bronze, iron, wood, and stones are all excellent material for tools. We work with tools. Gold and silver, however, are more suitable for adornment. While God has suited us for good works in Christ, He adorns us with His grace.

When God reveals His glory in a situation, He adorns it with grace. The foolish man who gives his wife an iron for Christmas expects her to work with it. An iron is a tool and not a token of affection. The wise man who gives his wife fine jewels or gold and silver expects her to wear his expression of affection to her as a symbol of beauty. God's glory brings the very best to our hopeless situations with all the glamour, glitz, sparkle, and shine of the finest of precious things! Furthermore, He brings peace to the chaos, and the righteousness of Christ rules over it!

In Scripture, bronze is a symbol of judgment while gold is a symbol of deity. God will judge our works, but He adorns us with grace as His children! Never settle for bronze or iron when gold is your inheritance! We serve a God who longs to adorn us with the best from His grace. Why would we want to settle for anything less?

Have a blessed day!

Equal Through Grace

Philemon 1:6:

I pray that your participation in the faith may become effective through knowing every good thing that is in us for the glory of Christ.

In this verse, Paul edified and encouraged Philemon, a fellow Christian and wealthy businessman who hosted a church in his home. Paul prayed for good things to happen to Philemon. When good happens to us, our faith becomes effective and Christ is glorified. Paul's very reason for writing to Philemon had the opportunity for such good and for Christ to be glorified.

Verses 8-12:

For this reason, although I have great boldness in Christ to command you to do what is right, I appeal, instead, on the basis of love. I, Paul, as an elderly man and now also as a prisoner of Christ Jesus, appeal to you for my child, whom I fathered while in chains—Onesimus. Once he was useless to you, but now he is useful to both you and me. I am sending him—a part of myself—back to you.

Philemon had a runaway slave named Onesimus. While Philemon could have suffered financial harm, it was not without purpose. Indeed, the things that appear to cause us harm are used for our good and for God's glory! Onesimus's escape landed him in the presence of Paul, where he heard the gospel for himself and became the recipient of grace. Now a Christian, Paul sent Onesimus back to Philemon to make things right. As a runaway slave, he could be beaten or even put to death. Therefore, Paul appealed to Philemon's good nature in his letter.

Please understand that Paul is not endorsing slavery. He encourages doing the right thing so we may be free from any condemnation or accusation against us. Paul wanted things to be right between Philemon and Onesimus and between Philemon and himself.

Verses 15-18:

For perhaps this is why he was separated from you for a brief time, so that you might get him back permanently, no longer as a slave, but more than a slave—as a dearly loved brother. This is especially so to me, but even more to you, both in the flesh and in the Lord. So if you consider

me a partner, accept him as you would me. And if he has wronged you in any way, or owes you anything, charge that to my account.

Paul asked Philemon to accept Onesimus back as a brother and to free him of any debt he might owe. Indeed, beating him or killing him would be an inappropriate way to treat a brother in Christ since Jesus took our beating on the cross. Grace had made them equal.

May we realize today that grace has made us equal as brothers and sisters in Christ. May we receive each other as such and proclaim the gospel of grace to those who have not yet laid hold of it and are still enslaved to sin. May the bad things that happen to us become good in the light of grace. For these things, Christ died.

Have a blessed day!

Cling to Grace

Isaiah 64:

All of us have become like something unclean, and all our righteous acts are like a polluted garment; all of us wither like a leaf, and our iniquities carry us away like the wind.

This verse bears a striking resemblance to Romans 3:23, "For all have sinned and fall short of the glory of God." It reveals just how despicable we are in the presence of God. Our only hope of standing before Him is in Christ, who made the ultimate sacrifice so we could partake of His righteousness. Apart from Him, we have no hope and will wither away like a leaf, carried away by the wind. In Him, however, we have everlasting hope that will help us overcome and live a victorious life.

We must remember that we cannot be victorious on our own. We cannot face the hurdles and attacks the Devil throws at us on our own. We need the righteousness of Christ, His Holy Spirit, and the fellowship of other believers to get through this thing we know as life. We need grace to do for us what we cannot do for ourselves—to live a righteous life.

If you find yourself struggling with habitual sin today, lean on grace. See yourself as the righteousness of Christ, and receive grace to lay that sin aside. If you have fallen, look to Christ and find strength to rise again. Remember that Jesus died because we cannot live perfect lives. Take His garment of righteousness, and throw yours away. Know that God sees you robed in the righteousness of Christ, and His love and favor are forever upon you. Continue to work out your salvation with fear and trembling, knowing that you are covered by the blood of Christ, which has the power to transform you. You don't have to work to earn God's favor or His grace. You simply have to cling to it.

Have a blessed day!

Grace for the Testy

Isaiah 55:6-7:

Seek the LORD while He may be found; call to Him while He is near. Let the wicked one abandon his way, and the sinful one his thoughts; let him return to the LORD, so He may have compassion on him, and to our God, for He will freely forgive.

I remember times growing up when I didn't want to go home because I knew I would be punished. One time I even told my mother, "Go ahead and spank me now! I can't stand all this waiting!" There are just times when we know we have done wrong, and punishment is expected and appropriate.

For this reason, many fail to turn to God. If they do, He will punish them for the sin they enjoy. He will require a change they are not ready to make. When the sin turns sour and no longer gives them satisfaction, they are afraid that if they turn to God, He will be harsh with them. The opposite, in fact, is true. When we turn to God from our sin, He has compassion on us and freely forgives us!

While God freely forgives us, often the church folk don't! If we are going to be conformed to the image of Christ, we must remember that He is full of grace. Just as He has extended grace to us, we are to extend grace to others.

Leaning on God's grace means that we depend upon His love for us, faults and all. If God loves us despite our faults, we should also love others and accept them with their faults. This often requires some learning and testing. That is why God places testy people in our lives that drive us insane! They are His tool to teach us grace.

I once had a testy person in my life who almost drove me nuts! I hated being around her at first and really thought she was a bit odd. While I never said a word, she sensed I thought she was nuts, and I realized it was something she could just read in me. Over the years, I have been very patient and gracious with her because I knew it was the right and polite thing to do. She is still quite the chatterbox while I am much more reserved, but I can honestly say we have a real appreciation for each other. She has become a tremendous blessing to me, and I have a greater respect for her now because of how she has blessed me. Our relationship grew over time, with patience, grace, and respect. That is what God gives us and what we are to give others. Quick judgments will ruin relationships.

Seek the LORD today because He can still be found. Turn to Him for the grace and the answer you need. Make an effort to extend grace to the testy people in your life, realizing they need the same measure of grace you do. Blessings await!

Have a blessed day!

Grace in His Kindness

Ephesians 2:6-7:

He also raised us up with Him and seated us with Him in the heavens, in Christ Jesus so that in the coming ages He might display the immeasurable riches of his grace in His kindness to us in Christ Jesus.

So many people think God is punishing them for their sins when they go through difficult times. Others believe that God doesn't really love them. For some reason, they are just unlovable. According to this verse, however, God has seated those in Christ with Him in the heavens just so He can display His grace to them by showering them with His kindness.! This doesn't sound like a God who is punishing or is unloving at all!

The Devil is a liar! If you have been saved by the blood of Jesus Christ, God has already forgiven your sins, and He poured out His full wrath of judgment upon Christ at the cross. He is not mad at you and is not punishing you! God loves you so much that He gave His only Son to die for you so you might live for Him! Jesus came to bring life to you. God's plan is to display His grace through you by showering you with His kindness so the Devil and his adversaries will be exposed.

There is a dual audience in these verses. God displays His grace in you for others to see His immeasurable love. God also wants the evil rulers in the heavenly realms to see His blessings on His children! If the Devil can make you think God is punishing you or that He doesn't love you, he can destroy your faith. You access His grace through faith. Through faith, we expose the lies of the Devil.

Today, be determined to destroy the works of the Devil in your own life through faith. God loves you and desires to lavish you with His grace through kindness in Christ Jesus. Believe God for good things, and stop expecting the worst. God desires to give you His very best. Take hold of it through faith!

Have a blessed day!

Grace to Wait

Isaiah 33:2:

LORD, be gracious to us! We wait for You. Be our strength every morning, and our salvation in time of trouble.

This verse just seems to describe my life. I find myself constantly in need of God's grace and waiting for Him to move. This process never seems to end. When God finally does move in a needed area, I find myself in need of Him again. Living in grace, waiting for God, and seeking daily strength to endure trouble is a walk of faith.

Just a few verses away, however, we find hope.

Verse 6:

There will be times of security for you—a storehouse of salvation, wisdom, and knowledge. The fear of the LORD is Zion's treasure.

Times of spiritual battle can be physically, mentally, and emotionally draining, but God promises a season of rest. During our times of struggle, we are building a storehouse of things we have learned that become a treasure to us. I am longing for the day when all my struggles and trials have produced a valuable storehouse of treasure to enjoy! The fear of the LORD is the beginning of such treasure, yet He bids us come to Him through grace.

If life seems difficult right now, be confident that a season of rest is coming. Wait for it as you seek God's strength daily. There is no telling what treasures your storehouse will hold when you are able to enter!

Have a blessed day!

Grace and Glory

Psalm 84:11:

For the LORD God is a sun and shield. The LORD gives grace and glory; He does not withhold the good from those who live with integrity.

God warms and protects. He gives grace and glory. There seems to be a connection with grace and glory.

Titus 2:11-13:

For the grace of God has appeared, with salvation for all people, instructing us to deny godlessness and worldly lusts and to live in a sensible, righteous, and godly way in the present age, while we wait for the blessed hope and the appearing of the glory of our great God and Savior, Jesus Christ.

God gives us grace to live and endure until He is ready to reveal His glory. His grace enables us to live with integrity. His grace helps us work out the bugs in our Christian walk. His grace draws us to Him. When someone has wronged us, we often want to withdraw from them. God, however, draws us to Himself by His goodness. He does not withhold Himself or His glory when we are honest with Him. He just continues to work in us and reveal Himself.

God gives us grace before He gives His glory! We could not handle the glory without first having been saturated in His grace. Our response to His grace is what determines the glory that is revealed. If we reject God's grace, His glory fades, leaving us to try to do things in our own strength. When we walk in His grace, however, His glory is revealed through our weaknesses. He shines through us!

We must learn to walk in grace. The more we realize how God has forgiven our failures, the more we can forgive others. His grace is liberating and refreshing. When we realize His grace, we can be assured His glory will follow!

Have a blessed day!

Acting on Grace

1 Peter 1:13:

Therefore, get your minds ready for action, being self-disciplined, and set your hope completely on the grace to be brought to you at the revelation of Jesus Christ.

We are to get our minds ready to act on grace! The grace is our hope, and it comes through the revelation of Jesus Christ in every situation we face. He has promised never to leave us. Since His presence is with us, we can count on His grace.

So, how do we act on grace? We walk in it. We take the opportunities that are presented to us, regardless of how unworthy we may feel. We accept the challenges given to us, knowing God is at work with us.

God often opens doors for us we would dare not open. He may direct us through a window we never saw. When He brings a new offering of grace before you, there will be something inside of you that wants to do it, but fear may prevent you from going forward. That is why we are to be self-disciplined with our hope set completely on grace. If we look to our own abilities, we may lose heart. Grace, however, propels us forward to new levels.

Be ready to act upon God's grace to you today. Set your hope on a revelation of Jesus Christ in your frustrating situations. God's plan is to move you forward, not to make you comfortable.

Have a blessed day!

Grace to Guard Your Heart

Proverbs 4:23:

Guard your heart above all else, for it is the source of life.

In Scripture, the word for heart refers to the mind, will, and emotions. Our mind, will, and emotions are the source of life. What we think affects our actions. Our actions reflect our feelings.

Life is to be lived. Allowing wrong thinking into our mind will cause a domino effect that damages our heart. We will fail to enjoy all the wonderful things with which God has blessed us simply because we are focusing on the wrong thing. Guard your heart. Don't allow wrong thinking to steal your life away.

I often play the *What if* … game. *What if* this happens? What will I do? *What if* that happens? How will I overcome? *What if* God's grace has already taken care of it all, and you are worrying for nothing? We need to update the *What if...* game to include God's grace. When we do, we will gain a new perspective with peace.

Through the finished work of Jesus on the cross, we walk under a cloud of grace. God's grace can change any negative thing in our lives. Guarding our hearts means that we focus and rely upon the grace of God and keep all other thoughts and beliefs away. You are highly favored and deeply loved by God. Never lose sight of that!

Regardless of what may hit you today, remember that you are covered by grace. Clear your head of all the problems and difficulties you have to face. God loves you, and He is working for you.

Have a blessed day!

From Grace to Thanksgiving to God's Glory

2 Corinthians 4:15:

For all this is because of you, so that grace, extended through more and more people, may cause thanksgiving to overflow to God's glory.

Here we find the key to seeing God's glory revealed in our lives. When we realize God's grace in our own lives and extend that grace to others, it produces a domino effect. Grace starts pouring into lives, causing thanksgiving in the hearts of those who receive grace. Thanksgiving then overflows to reflect God's glory. Grace is not to be hoarded; it is to be shared.

Most of us have heard the saying that we are the only Bible some people will ever read. I have to admit that I am a very poor substitute for God's Word, which has the power to enrich us daily. Unbelievers, however, may be attracted to God's Word or turned off to God's Word by what they see in us. If we are a channel by which grace freely flows, that grace works in conjunction with the power of the Holy Spirit to convict people of their sins. When they see this grace in light of their sins, they have thankful hearts which overflow to God's glory. A truly convicted heart will always be thankful for grace!

Determine today to be a channel through which God's grace can flow. Extend the grace He has lavished on you to others, especially to those who desperately need to know Christ. The more grace you extend, the greater the chances of seeing God's glory revealed in your life through a thankful heart.

Have a blessed day!

When Grace Does Not Apply

Galatians 6:7:

Don't be deceived: God is not mocked. For whatever a man sows he will also reap...

I am a firm believer in grace, and my understanding of grace has broadened as I've studied the subject further. Grace, however, must never be taken for granted and used for an excuse for outright rebellion. God grants us grace when we repent, meaning we turn from our sin and change our minds about the direction we were heading. In this case, God forgives. When a person, however, determines to willfully sin and turns from God's Word, knowing fully that he is wrong, he mocks God's grace. Grace was never meant to justify sin! It was meant to deliver us from it.

Outright rebellion disagrees with God, has the arrogance to think it knows better, and attempts to get away with sin. Hiding that sin from others does not hide it from God. While one's eternal destiny will not change for the true Christian, God's spiritual law of reaping and sowing still applies. Do not expect Him to bless or glorify anything you do in outright rebellion! Sowing to the flesh reaps corruption, which comes in the form of shame, disrespect, and reproach. This is a direct contrast to the glory of God, which brings honor, respect, and rejoicing from those who witness its revelation.

Our purpose is to glorify God. We were created for His glory, and nothing satisfies us like seeing His glory revealed in our lives. Don't let rebellion and the lust of your flesh rob you of seeing the glory of God in your life. Waiting for His promises and standing firm in the Word in the midst of trials and temptations test and prove your faith. Faith pleases God; He will reveal His glory in those who please Him and diligently seek Him!

Have a blessed day!

Gifts and Varied Grace

1 Peter 4:10:

Based on the gift they have received, everyone should use it to serve others, as good managers of the varied grace of God.

God has gifted every Christian with a way to serve Him. This gift is given to serve others, and we are to use is as good managers. Using this gift is an investment in God's kingdom. He takes it and multiplies it for His purpose and His glory.

According to this verse, God's grace is varied. Grace gifts are not the same from one person to the next. You can't judge your performance based upon what someone else does or does not do. The grace God has given you is for the purpose He has called you. You should never consider yourself a failure or that you cannot be effective in God's kingdom because of what you see someone else accomplish. Your gift is valuable in your hand. Learn to use it with care and diligence.

God has also given us the privilege to worship. We can do that freely today without fear of persecution. Manage that privilege carefully. His grace is upon us for the moment; we should not take it for granted. Take time to worship God in His house. This is your service to Him.

Have a blessed day!

Prosperity and God's Favor

Psalm 30:3-12:

For His anger lasts only a moment, but His favor, a lifetime. Weeping may spend the night, but there is joy in the morning. When I was secure, I said, "I will never be shaken." LORD, when You showed Your favor, You made me stand like a strong mountain; when You hid Your face, I was terrified. LORD, I called to You; I sought favor from my LORD: "What gain is there in my death, in my descending to the Pit? Will the dust praise You? Will it proclaim Your truth? LORD, listen and be gracious to me;

LORD, be my helper." You turned my lament into dancing; You removed my sackcloth and clothed me with gladness, so that I can sing to You and not be silent. LORD my God, I will praise You forever.

When God shows His favor, it is for the purpose of praising Him. David is the psalmist, and he mentions seeking the LORD's favor by crying out to God in his distress. We don't cry out to God when things are going well. We cry out when we are in trouble or danger. David exclaims that God turned his lament into dancing. If you lament something, you grieve over it with regret. David saw his deplorable condition and regretted his sin. When he cried out to God over it, God turned his lament into dancing.

Now is the time to seek God's favor by repenting in deep remorse over sin. When we finally realize that our sad state is the result of sin, we are on the right track. Right now, Republicans and Democrats foolishly blame each other. We are all to blame in this country for our economic state. We want to live in rebellion and be prosperous at the same time. God is our source. To reject Him, deny Him, and think we are going to prosper ourselves is foolish. If we want to receive His favor, we must repent and turn from our wicked ways. We can never do this collectively as a country unless we first do it individually.

When Solomon finished building the temple and his royal palace with great success, God spoke to him:

2 Chronicles 7:12-15:

Then the LORD appeared to Solomon at night and said to Him: I have heard your prayer and have chosen this place for Myself as a temple of sacrifice. If I close the sky so there is no rain, or if I command the grasshopper to consume the land, or if I send pestilence on My people, and My people who are called by My name humble themselves, pray and seek My face, and turn from their evil ways, then I will hear from heaven, forgive their sin, and heal their land. My eyes will now be open and My ears attentive to prayer from this place.

God is the source of all prosperity. We can't just come to Him and ask for silver and gold on our own terms. We have no rightful standing with Him until we submit to the authority of Christ. God warns what will happen if His people turn from Him and choose to live in sin. His favor comes after true repentance.

Make today a day of humbling yourself and seeking God's face. Turn from your self-efforts and submit to His authority. He is attentive to your prayer, and He longs to give you His favor so you might praise Him.

Have a blessed day!

Favor for Rain

I Kings 18:43-46:

Then he said to his servant, "Go up and look toward the sea." So he went up, looked, and said, "There's nothing." Seven times Elijah said, "Go back." On the seventh time, he reported, "There's a cloud as small as a man's hand coming from the sea." Then Elijah said, "Go and tell Ahab, 'Get your chariot ready and go down so the rain doesn't stop you.'" In a little while, the sky grew dark with clouds and wind, and there was a downpour. So Ahab got in his chariot and went to Jezreel. The power of the LORD was on Elijah, and he tucked his mantle under his belt and ran ahead of Ahab to the entrance of Jezreel.

This story took place after Elijah slaughtered the prophets of Baal in the Wadi Kishon after God accepted his sacrifice on Mt. Carmel. Baal means *lord, husband, and owner.* He was the Phoenician male god who gave rain so the land would be fertile and produce a harvest. He was worshiped as a provider. King Ahab was married to Jezebel, whose father was king of the Phoenicians. She was, therefore, very loyal to Baal. While Baal worship was common in Israel due to the Canaanites, Ahab made the mistake of building a temple to Baal in Samaria and sanctioning Baal worship as a national religion, alongside worship of the God of Israel. Many Israelites worshiped Baal in order to gain favor in the courts with Jezebel.

The sad thing is that Israel did not need Jezebel's favor or Baal's. In fact, Elijah proved that Baal was ineffective as a god. When the Israelites saw this, they immediately turned and worshiped their true God. With this false god removed, Elijah knew the blessing of rain was coming to refresh a dry, parched land.

You do not need anyone's favor other than God's to meet whatever need exists in your life today. Tear down the high places of false worship and slaughter any thought or belief that tells you that you need to gain favor from anyone else in order for your need to be met. James 1:17 tells us that every good and perfect gift is from God. His favor is all you need, and you have it in Christ Jesus! Believe today that He wants to meet your need and bring life to that dry, parched place where you see no growth or harvest whatsoever. You cannot meet that need on your own. God wants to bless you there. Christ came so that we might have life and have it in abundance! Trust Him to give you the downpour of rain you need. Even if you don't see it right away, rest assured it is coming! When you see that small cloud, run and get ready! Your drought is over!

Have a blessed day!

Favor through Relationship

Genesis 6:5-9:

When the LORD saw that man's wickedness was widespread on the earth and that every scheme his mind thought of was nothing but evil all the time, the LORD regretted that He had made man on the earth, and He was grieved in His heart. Then the LORD said, "I will wipe off the face of the earth: man, whom I created, together with the animals, creatures that crawl, and birds of the sky—for I regret that I made them." Noah, however found favor in the eyes of the LORD. These are the family records of Noah. Noah was a righteous man, blameless among his contemporaries; Noah walked with God.

When God looked upon the earth, he saw so much wickedness in the hearts of men that He grieved and regretted creating man. God created man for the purpose of fellowship. Only one man had a relationship with God, and that was Noah. Noah was righteous and blameless among his contemporaries. To be righteous is to be morally upright. To be blameless means that no one can find fault in you or rightfully accuse you. This means that Noah was different from those around him. People of that day were morally corrupt and willfully engaging in evil. Noah, however, chose to do what was right and walked with God.

God favors those who walk with Him. To walk with Him, you must first have a relationship with Him. The only way to have a relationship with God is through Christ. Therefore, God's favor is not upon the unbeliever or the ungodly. They can expect to see His judgment.

The world sees prosperity as a sign of success. What Christians should seek is not prosperity but to cultivate their relationship with God. We are to seek His kingdom first, and all other things will be added to us (Matt. 6:33).

Today, seek God's kingdom first through a relationship with Christ. Once this is firmly established, all other things are yours in Christ. God favors those who choose Him first. With His favor, you have everything! Without it, you have nothing!

Have a blessed day!

God's Favor for Strategy and Purpose

Genesis 6: 13-19:

Then God said to Noah, "I have decided to put an end to all flesh, for the earth is filled with violence because of them; therefore I am going to destroy them along with the earth. Make yourself an ark of gopher wood. Make rooms in the ark, and cover it with pitch inside and outside. This is how you are to make it: The ark will be 450 feet long, 75 feet wide, and 45 feet high. You are to make a roof, finishing the sides of the ark to within 18 inches of the roof. You are to put a door in the side of the ark. Make it with lower, middle, and upper decks. Understand that I am bringing a deluge—floodwaters on the earth to destroy all flesh under heaven with the breath of life in it. Everything on earth will die. But I will establish My covenant with you, and you will enter the ark with your sons, your wife, and your sons' wives. You are also to bring into the ark two of every living thing of all flesh, male and female, to keep them alive with you.

Matthew 24:37-38 tells us that the days just prior to the second coming will be much like the days of Noah. This Scripture plainly tells us that Noah found favor in the eyes of God. God gave Noah a very detailed and specific strategy to survive His judgment. This strategy would not only save Noah and his family, it would provide a plan to repopulate the earth. God's favor contained great purpose.

What we need to face the difficult times in which we live is God's strategy to overcome. The first part of His strategy always includes a relationship with Him through Jesus Christ. To learn the rest, we must walk in close fellowship with Him. Just as He spoke to Noah, He will speak to us. He will show us the way in which we are to walk. The key to finding favor with God is walking in fellowship with Him.

Today, take time to converse with God. Keep your relationship with Him intact. Invite Him to join you in your day, and listen to what He has to say. You will find favor, strategy, and purpose to overcome life's trials.

Have a blessed day!

Glory and the Favor of God

Exodus 33:17-18:

The LORD answered Moses, "I will do this very thing you have asked, for you have found favor in My sight, and I know you by name." Then Moses said, "Please let me see Your glory."

Moses found favor in God's sight because they had a close, intimate, personal relationship. Moses talked with God daily and brought Him into his daily affairs. He would not go into the Promised Land nor lead the people of Israel there unless God went with him. He did not want the blessing unless He had the presence of the Blesser. That was the heart God favored.

Too many people want God's blessing, but when He grants it, they tend to forget Him and go their merry way. We see that in the example of the lepers that Jesus healed. Only one came back to thank Him. Moses would not go one step further without the presence of God. He wanted to see the glory of God manifested before him. He wanted proof that God was there.

Seeing the glory of God causes you to realize that you didn't just make something happen. God worked through you and brought His result. God's glory is awe inspiring, and everyone around you can recognize it. You get to see this side of God only if you have a close, intimate relationship with Him. This experience changes you, and once you have experienced it, any blessing without His presence is a lesser thing.

Experiencing the glory of God is experiencing His favor, and we all desperately need it. We have to yearn for it enough to become closely acquainted with Him and to walk and talk with Him on a regular basis. Close fellowship will display his glory.

We have probably all seen or known women who married for money. They didn't necessarily want the man as much as they wanted what that man could do for them. When the money ran out, so did they. God wants those who will dare to love Him for who He is and not just what He can provide. He wants a real, genuine relationship with us that is life-giving. If we seek Him only for the blessing He can provide, we are no better than a gold digger!

Today, seek to know God on a personal basis. Invite Him into your daily activities. If you already have that close walk, ask Him to show you His glory. Find out just where and how He is working in your life and join Him. There is no greater blessing on earth!

Have a blessed day!

Favor That Turns Back Trouble

Psalm 7:15-16:

He dug a pit and hollowed it out, but fell into the hole he had made. His trouble comes back on his own head, and his violence falls on the top of his head.

While this verse is found in Psalms, it reminds me of the evil Haman in the story Book of Esther. Haman set a trap to kill the Hebrews, particularly Mordecai, who refused to bow to him. In his plot to seek revenge, his own pride led him to be exposed. As a result, he was hung on the very gallows he built for Mordecai. He could not see how God was working behind the scenes to reverse his evil scheme.

God is still at work behind the evil schemes the Devil plots to destroy our destiny. Often, when it looks like all is lost and the Devil is reveling in his twisted glory, God moves in an unexpected way to upset the cart of poisoned apples. With Esther, God worked through the favor she had as queen and her appeal for mercy from the king. The king favored Esther more than he favored Haman. Haman did not know that Esther was a Hebrew or that his plot would directly affect the king's household.

As a child of God, you have great favor with the King of Kings! Any plot of the enemy to destroy your destiny or interfere with your purpose will directly affect His household, and He will turn the trouble back on the Devil in your life, too. Make your appeal to God, and trust Him to work on your behalf. He is a just, holy, and compassionate God, and He is greater than any evil plot of the enemy over you! In fact, He has even promised us that no weapon formed against us shall prevail (Isa. 54:17). Since His word will not return to Him empty (Isa. 55:11), state God's Word over your situation today. Proclaim God's will over the unjust or unfair places in your life, and trust Him to cause the Devil to fall into his own hole. You have favor with the King; the Devil doesn't!

Have a blessed day!

Hope in Christ

1 Peter 3:14-15:

But even if you should suffer for righteousness, you are blessed. Do not fear what they fear or be disturbed, but set apart the Messiah as LORD in your hearts, and always be ready to give a defense to anyone who asks you for a reason for the hope that is in you.

Everyone goes through times of suffering, including Christians. Suffering is a part of life and a part of growing. How we react to suffering may determine how long our season lasts and what we will gain from it. Turning to Christ and releasing our anger, worries, and fears is the best thing we can do. We can't control what happens anyway. When we make Christ LORD, we simply give Him control of our lives. He, in turn, begins to stir our lives toward a safe harbor. We can rest in hope with Him as Captain.

To make Christ LORD of our lives means admitting our failures and assuming responsibility for our mistakes. We turn from our old way of thinking and begin to follow Christ, learning from Him and applying His teaching to our daily walk. This is why we need to go to His word every day to hear a fresh message from Him. If Christ is LORD of your life, you are blessed, and you have no reason to fear the things of this world. If Christ is the LORD of your life, you have hope. In Him we find resurrection, joy, and the strength to defeat the enemy!

Always be ready to explain why you have hope and can live each day with the constant expectation of good. Many people are looking for reason to hope, and you have found it! It is not about you; it is about Him and what He can do. Someone else needs to know.

Have a blessed day!

Real Hope for Real Problems

Romans 5:1-5:

Therefore, since we have been declared righteous by faith, we have peace with God through our Lord Jesus Christ. Also through Him, we have obtained access by faith into this grace in which we stand, and we rejoice in the hope of the glory of God. And not only that, but we also rejoice in our afflictions, because we know that affliction produces endurance, endurance produces proven character, and proven character produces hope. This hope does not disappoint because God's love has been poured out in our hearts through the Holy Spirit who was given to us.

Isn't it great to know we've been declared righteous through faith in Christ? God gives us His righteousness, along with the peace to stand in His presence and receive His grace. This is all a gift of God. We rejoice in the hope of the glory of God to be revealed as the result of His grace in our lives.

Not only can we rejoice in God's goodness, His grace gives us reason to also rejoice in our afflictions. God does not afflict His people, but He may allow us to go through difficult times just so His grace may be evident in our lives and a witness of His goodness. When the Devil hits us with affliction, God uses that affliction to produce endurance in us. He then uses endurance to produce proven character. Our proven character will produce hope, which the Devil tries to steal from us.

Therefore, whenever the Devil hits us with affliction, God can use his own weapon against him to produce the very thing he tries to steal away! The remarkable thing, however, is that hope produced from proven character does not disappoint us as false hope from the Devil will. Hope from proven character has seen the goodness of God and realizes His love for us. This is a hope rooted, established, and blooming in the person of Jesus Christ and His finished work on the cross.

Take time today to remember the completed work of the cross and what it means for us. Through it, we receive the righteousness of Christ that enables us to fully enjoy God's grace in good times and through bad. The resurrection is a symbol of hope that reminds us of the new life we have through grace.

Have a blessed day!

Our Hope and Our Victory

John 20:18:

Mary Magdalene went and announced to the disciples, "I have seen the Lord!" And she told them what He had said to her.

Mary Magdalene had the privilege of being the first eye witness to see Jesus after His resurrection. She was actively seeking Him out of her love for Him, and Jesus made sure she found what she needed. That is our Savior! Whatever our need may be, we find it in seeking Him.

The fact that God raised Him from the dead is evidence our sins have been forgiven. God forgave the sins and allowed Jesus to live again. The price was paid in full, and Jesus was restored to God's favor, which came in glory and wholeness. When we are forgiven of our sins, we are free to live life anew in wholeness, as well.

Jesus's death paid for our sins, but His resurrection gives us hope and power to live again. For whatever problem you face today, the resurrection is hope. He is our hope and our victory!

Have a blessed day!

Hope or False Expectations

Matthew 21:1-10:

When they approached Jerusalem and came to Bethpage at the Mount of Olives, Jesus then sent two disciples, telling them, "Go into the village ahead of you. At once you will find a donkey tied there, and a colt with her. Untie them and bring them to Me. If anyone says anything to you, you should say that the LORD needs them, and immediately he will send them." This took place so that what was spoken through the prophet might be fulfilled: Tell Daughter Zion, "See, your King is coming to you, gentle, and mounted on a donkey, even on a colt, the foal of a beast of burden." The disciples went and did just as Jesus directed them. They brought the donkey and the colt; then they laid their robes on them, and He sat on them. A very large crowd spread their robes on the road; others were cutting branches from the trees and spreading them on the road. Then the crowds who went ahead of Him and those who followed kept shouting: Hosanna to the Son of David! Blessed is He who comes in the name of the LORD! Hosanna in the highest heaven! When He entered Jerusalem, the whole city was shaken saying, "Who is this?" And the crowds kept saying, "This is the prophet Jesus from Nazareth in Galilee!"

This entry into Jerusalem caused quite a commotion! There was nothing quiet about this incident. Jesus entered the city just as prophesied in Zechariah 9:9. Any Jew who knew the Scriptures should have recognized the significance of this event and realized it was the Messiah. Riding on a donkey symbolized His royalty and His humility. The colt He rode had never before been mounted. Indeed, the journey He was making was unprecedented!

Quite a large crowd formed around Him. They were ready to make Him their King. Hosanna means *save now*. They expected Him to perform for them. They expected Him to save them from the clutches of political tyranny. They did not realize they needed to be saved from their own sin. They were ready to make Him king if He would put them in control of their own land.

Jesus did not enter Jerusalem that day to give them political freedom. He never promised them such a thing. They had placed their hope in selfish ambition and false expectations. As a result, they abandoned their true hope because they failed to recognize Him for who He truly was—Messiah, the Anointed One.

Today, lay all your hopes and dreams aside, and just accept Christ as King. Let His presence reign in your life. He still performs miracles, and He still answers prayer. He may yet answer according to your preference, but dare to desire Him first. God does not act by popular demand. He acts according to His nature and His purpose. His nature is love, and His purpose is to draw you to Him in relationship. That was what He accomplished on the cross while the crowd who once praised Him deserted Him.

If you have been hurt by false expectations, ask God to give you real hope today. Place your faith in Him as a person and not in what you want Him to do for you. He is greater than anything else you could desire!

Have a blessed day!

To Hope, Trust, and Never Be Disgraced

Psalm 25:1-3:

LORD, I turn my hope to You. My God, I trust in You. Do not let me be disgraced; do not let my enemies gloat over me. Not one person who waits for You will be disgraced; those who act treacherously without cause will be disgraced.

Three words in this prayer leap off the page—hope, trust, disgraced. They are closely connected and reveal much of what was in David's heart. Upon examining them, you are likely to find your own heart exposed here, as well.

David turned his hope to God. David learned that other people and things would disappoint him, and he chose to turn his hope to the One who was always faithful. Our hope can never be in what we want to happen. Our hope must be firmly placed in the One who makes all things work together for the good of those who love Him (Rom. 8:28). When everything for which we have hoped comes crumbling down around us, we can look up with hopeful expectation that God is for us and not against us. As Romans 4:18 explains, against hope, with hope Abraham believed and received God's promises.

David's next statement is a declaration of his faith: "My God, I trust in You." Whatever happened, David trusted God. He knew God had a power greater than his own, and he would have to let God handle the matter. Hope requires trust, and trust requires submission. Wherever you have a trust problem, you will have a submission problem and vice versa. To trust God with a matter means we must take our hands off of it and submit it to God's control and discretion. Too often, we want His power, but we want to tell Him how to use it. To trust Him means we trust His discretion, His timing, and His methods. To give Him responsibility of the matter means we must also give Him full authority in the matter.

Finally, we see David feared being disgraced. He feared ridicule from his enemies. In Christ, we never have to worry about being disgraced. His finished work on the cross has defeated all of His enemies, and God raised Him from the dead. Since our enemies are the same as His, they are already defeated! While we may suffer times of embarrassment, we are never without the grace of God, who works all things together for our good. As God, He always gets the last word on a matter!

Today, place your hope in the One who loved you so much He sent His only Son to die for you. Dare to trust Him with every tender place of your heart, and submit those precious areas to Him. Never fear being disgraced. Release your most precious desires to Him, knowing that all grace abounds to you in Christ. Not one person who waits on God will be disgraced!

Have a blessed day!

Return to Hope

Job 42:2:

I know that You can do anything and no plan of Yours can be thwarted.

Job had a realization of just how big his God really is! The only way we can ever see this is to fully realize our own limitations and to trust in His greater power. Sometimes, God brings us to the end of ourselves so we may encounter a new beginning with Him. There is absolutely nothing He can't do, and His plan for you will succeed, regardless of how much you try to trade it for your own plan!

I love **verse 5:**

I had heard rumors about You, but now my eyes have seen You.

We can go to church and learn about God. We can listen to the testimonies of others who have experienced victories in their lives. We can read the Bible from cover to cover, but it is all rumors until we experience His presence and His power in our own lives. Knowing about someone and knowing someone personally in relationship are two different things. Job encountered the presence of the Almighty God in the middle of his lowly situation, and life changed for Job.

Verse 6:

Therefore I take back my words and repent in dust and ashes.

Job had become hopeless. He thought there was nothing that could help his pitiful situation. Even those closest to him had turned away. God paid him a little visit to remind Him of Who He was, and Job realized just who was really in charge of his life. Hope began to rise.

Verse 12-13:

So the LORD blessed the latter part of Job's life more than the earlier. He owned 14,000 sheep, 6,000 camels, 1,000 yoke of oxen, and 1,000 female donkeys. He also had seven sons and three daughters.

Job didn't have the proper view of things when he looked down at his own circumstances and abilities. God called Him to look up and get a better view of Him. When our options seem limited, our perspective needs to extend beyond ourselves. God can do anything, and His plans for us will not be thwarted! Return to hope in a God who can do all things and knows how to meet the needs of every living creature, including yours.

Have a blessed day!

Hope Unashamed

Psalm 119:114-116:

You are my shelter and my shield; I put my hope in Your word. Depart from me, you evil ones, so that I may obey my God's commands. Sustain me as You promised, and I will live; do not let me be ashamed of my hope.

When God gives us a word, it will always encourage us, motivate us, and give us peace. The Devil will come quickly to try to destroy this word in us. He often tells us that we haven't really heard from God. We've just made up something to try to make us feel better. He will even try to convince us that God is not interested in that certain area of our lives, and we had better take care of that matter ourselves. He uses such weapons as discouragement, critical attacks, doubt, impatience, and distractions to try to convince us to lose hope in God.

Here we find the psalmist in the midst of an attack from the enemy as he seeks God as his shelter and shield. He fully realizes he is in the midst of a spiritual battle. Our spiritual battles may also take the form of physical battles at times. We must realize that in both, God is our shelter and our shield.

The psalmist places his hope fully in the word of God. It is tried, true, and trustworthy. If God has said it, He will do it! Stand upon His word and claim it boldly! The psalmist instructs the evil ones to depart from him so he may obey God's commands. The Devil will always try to talk you out of obedience. If God has given you an instruction, the Devil will try to prevent you from doing it because the blessing at the other end of that obedience is a threat to him. He often floods our hearts with fear to persuade us to take another route. As Jonah quickly learned, God can redirect our course. Better to obey up front than to end up in the belly of a whale with regret and longing for another chance to get it right! If necessary, however, God will give us another chance. We just waste time and effort in the process.

The psalmist pleads to God to act on his behalf so that he is not ashamed of his hope. He has put all of his hope in the Word of God, and he knows he is risking looking like a fool in front of his enemies. Total dependence upon God may devour our pride, but it will not put us to shame! God exalts the humble, but He humbles the proud.

To place all of your hope in God, you must first humble yourself. Pride does not want to risk looking like a fool and will often take matters into his own hands. Trust God to sustain the word He has placed in you. God does not tease with a carrot then take it away and laugh at you. He is faithful to what He has promised. Trust Him. Take Him at His word, and stand in obedience to His instruction.

What word has God given you? Determine today to trust in it completely. If He hasn't given you a word yet for your situation, ask Him for one. He promises wisdom to those who ask. You can always trust the Father's heart toward you. Even when things seem to go the opposite of what you thought God would do, His heart is still toward you. He will never let you be ashamed of trusting in Him!

Have a blessed day!

The Hope of His Calling

Ephesians 1:18:

I pray that the eyes of your heart may be enlightened so you may know what is the hope of His calling, what are the glorious riches of His inheritance among the saints, and what is the immeasurable greatness of His power to us who believe, according to the working of His vast strength.

Whether I want to admit it or not, I am called to this place of widowhood. Perhaps it may be only for a season, or perhaps it may last for the rest of my earthly life. According to this verse, however, there is hope in His calling that leads to the glorious riches of His inheritance. In this place, I can expect to see the immeasurable greatness of His power shown to us who believe.

God does not intend for us to live defeated lives. He tells us plainly that we are more than conquerors in Christ. Living the victorious life, however, requires a fight. You don't gain victory over your enemy without engaging in battle. These battles are designed to strengthen us in Christ. His power working in us gives us the strength we need to prevail. We cannot do it in our own strength.

The key to strength is complete dependence upon Christ and the finished work of the cross. He has already won our victory! Because of His victory, we have hope in the glorious riches of His inheritance!

The best place to fight is at the feet of Jesus. When we are vulnerable and pliable before Him and eager to learn from Him, He will fill us with power through the Holy Spirit. Whether through prayer, Bible study, service, or praise, He will speak to us as we diligently seek Him. He will make our paths clear and give us the strength we need to do what He has called us to do. Yes, there is hope for the widow. There is a glorious inheritance to be gained if we will only believe and be willing to allow Christ to work His vast strength in us. Through that strength, He can work miracles!

You have an opportunity to worship today. Take advantage of it, and listen to what the Lord has for you. This is but one more weapon He wants to add to your arsenal against the enemy. Allow Him to strengthen you for the miracle He has already prepared.

Have a blessed day!

Our Restoring God

Joel 2:25:

I will repay you for the years that the swarming locust ate, the young locust, the destroying locust—My great army that I sent against you.

Our God is a restoring God. If He allowed something to tear apart your land or your household, He will rebuild it for His purpose. There is nothing of value that can be taken from you that God cannot restore in your life.

Locusts were sent to destroy crops. With failed crops, the Israelites went hungry and could not plan for their future. No matter how hard they worked, the locust would devour the harvest. They were left exhausted, devastated, and depleted. They had no hope in themselves or in what they could do in their own strength. Their very survival depended upon a move of God in their lives. God became jealous for His land and spared His people (Joel 2:1). For this reason, He promised to restore their land.

If God sends a great army of locust into our lives, it is to change our perspectives, our priorities, and even our purpose. The best thing we can do is to give Him our full attention and surrender.

Anything He does in our lives is for the purpose of drawing us closer to Him. He does not destroy or allow destruction because He is mad at us. He is not controlled by His emotions. If He allows loss, destruction, or devastation into a life, He has a plan to rebuild and restore for those who turn to Him and are considered His.

To encounter restoration, we may have to give up the dream of what once was. We may have to allow God to give us new dreams. When God repays us for the years the locusts have eaten in our lives, life may look very differently than it did before the locusts came. Restoration requires complete dependence upon God and surrendering to His terms. This is where many people have a problem. They want God to rebuild and restore, but they want it on their own terms. They want God to work in one area while He is busy rebuilding in another. We must pay attention to what God is doing in our lives at the moment. Otherwise, we will miss an important element that will lead us where we want to be. God restores in His timing and according to His plan.

Believe God for restoration today. Know that He is working in your life, even if you can't see it. Let go of the past, and cling to Him. Trust that what He is doing in your life is something so great you don't want to miss it. Pay attention to what He is doing right now. Who knows where the next step will lead?

Have a blessed day!

God's Restoration

Zephaniah 3:20:

At that time I will bring you back, yes, at that time I will gather you. I will make your name famous and praiseworthy among all the peoples of the earth when I restore your fortunes before your eyes. Yahweh has spoken.

God predicted a time when He would restore the fortunes of Israel after they had encountered His judgment and returned to Him in repentance. God is a restoring God. When He restores, He does a work that is so amazing, others can't help but notice and recognize His handiwork.

This verse should give us all great hope. Through whatever loss, tragedy, difficulty, or storm we have experienced, God does not leave His people devastated. Turning to Him brings His restoration. His desire is to build us up into His purpose so we may display His glory. His intention is not to leave us destroyed and depleted.

If you feel tired, run down, and empty today, ask God to restore you. Just as He creates beautiful artwork in the sky from time to time, He can restore you to a beauty and luster you could never create on your own. Turn your heart toward Him, and watch to see what He restores before your very eyes!

Have a blessed day!

The LORD Redeems His Servants

Psalm 34:22:

The LORD redeems the life of His servants, and all who take refuge in Him will not be punished.

If we have blown it in life in some way, it can seem difficult to turn to God from fear of punishment. If we failed so miserably, will He not surely punish us before we can be accepted back into His grace? Will we not have to pay for our sins in some way before God will ever bless us again?

Nothing could be further from the truth. In fact, Peter learned this lesson after denying Christ three times. After trying to go back to his old way of life by fishing, he found he couldn't do it on his own. When Jesus blessed him with the huge catch of fish, he immediately recognized his source and jumped in the water to swim back to shore. He was determined to get to Jesus as fast as he could, and Jesus lovingly restored him to ministry. The next sermon he preached led 3,000 to salvation! Now, that is restoration if ever it could be! Jesus bought Peter's life back on the cross, and he was able to preach like he'd never dared dream.

In a severe loss, just where else can you turn? Only one source has the power to take you through such a difficult time with any assurance of victory, and that is in Christ. The word, *redeem*, is most commonly used in Scripture in reference to a widow. God's plan throughout Scripture is to care for widows. You don't find a single incident in Scripture of a widow's being punished. You always find God honoring and caring for the widow.

The Hebrew word for redeems in this verse is *padah*, meaning *to sever or ransom; to release or preserve.* God ransoms His servants from the grip of the enemy who tries to punish. He releases them from the hands of the cruel taskmasters who keep them under control through guilt and condemnation. By turning to God, we receive grace through the finished work of Christ on the cross to live a blessed life again! Hallelujah!

Please notice one more thing. God redeems the life of His servants. Are you serving Him in areas where you know you are called to serve? Have you given up serving Him because you think you are too unworthy? If God would use Peter, who denied Him three times at His most critical moment, would He not surely use you? No one has sinned so far that the grace of God cannot cover it! That is why we sing, "There is Power in the Blood!" God works through us when we serve Him out of a loving heart in response to His grace and not because we think we have to earn His grace.

Worship God by serving Him today out of love for what He has already done for you in Christ. When God sees you, He sees you through the lens of the cross. You can come boldly before His throne and seek the redemption you need without fear of being punished. Christ has already taken your punishment! Find a place to serve God out of a loving heart, and watch to see how He redeems you through it.

Have a blessed day!

Personal Restoration

1 Peter 5:10:

Now the God of all grace, who called you to His eternal glory in Christ Jesus, will personally restore, establish, strengthen, and support you after you have suffered a little.

God's grace called us to share in the eternal glory of Christ Jesus. His finished work on the cross enables us to share in His glorious inheritance. As a part of His righteous inheritance, God restored all things to Christ. Likewise, after we have suffered through trials of various kinds, God personally restores us so that we might share in the same inheritance as His beloved Son!

When God restores us, He leaves His mark on it. He personally makes sure we recover all that was taken from us. We see this explicitly displayed in the life of Job. God is a personal God who cares for each of us individually. He is no respecter of persons. What He did for Job, He will do for us, too. What I find so amazing and comforting is that God's restoration is personal and specific for us. He literally calls us out and does a work especially for us and in us that cannot be hindered by anyone.

When God restores you, He leaves His anointing! God told Moses to lay down his staff. When he did, it became a snake. God told him to pick it up. When he did, it became a staff again. God gave Moses back His staff, but it had a new power it did not have before! When God gives you back something you lost or laid down for Him, He gives it back with anointing and power!

This anointing is resurrection power. The reason God allows us to suffer loss, endure storms, and fight battles is that we might be restored with power. This power has the ability to affect others because it brings forth a testimony of God's grace. He calls us by His grace. He sees us through our trials with grace, and He restores us to testify of His grace.

For whatever you are facing today, you need only a greater revelation of God's grace and how much He loves you. He is working all things out for your good and His glory. Your suffering has a time limit. After that, He will personally restore, establish, strengthen, and support you as you walk forth in a new anointing and power! Amen!

Have a blessed day!

Strength that Revives and Restores

Psalm 80:17-19:

Let Your hand be with the man at Your right hand, with the son of man You have made strong for Yourself. Then we will not turn away from You; revive us, and we will call on Your name. Restore us, LORD God of Hosts; look on us with favor, and we will be saved.

Jesus sits at the Father's right hand today. He is the One whom God has made strong for us. No one else could be the perfect sacrifice for our sins. God has given Christ the authority to rule and reign with Him, and we are in Christ.

When we go through trials, we are to look to Christ for strength. He still sits at the right hand of the Father making intercession for us. He is cheering for us and working on our behalf. Not only did He pay for our sins, He took the place at the right hand of the Father so He could grant us victory in life. Look to Him, trust Him, and cling to Him.

The psalmist cried out for restoration. When we have been hurt or have suffered loss, we need to be restored. Only God can restore and revive us. The Devil comes to steal, to kill, and to destroy, and any alternative he offers is destined to bring our demise. In Christ, however, we find the strength to overcome. We find new meaning and purpose. We find new blessings and new life.

The LORD God of Hosts in Scripture is usually a picture of God's coming in judgment against the enemy. Here, however, we see Him as a God who restores and revives His weary people. Know that when God restores and revives His people, it is a statement of judgment over the enemy. It is a reminder to him that Christ still sits at the right hand of the Father, and He intervenes on behalf of His people. The Devil cannot have what belongs to Christ.

Are you weary today? Do you need to be restored and revived? God made Jesus to be strong for you. Look to Him and draw from His strength. He will restore and revive you, pronouncing judgment over your enemy. This is the assurance we have in Christ. Where we are weak, He is strong!

Have a blessed day!

Rest for Restoration

Isaiah 62:12:

And they will be called the Holy People, the LORD's Redeemed; and you will be called Cared For, A City not Deserted.

You cannot appreciate the value of redemption unless you realize your need to be redeemed. You will not appreciate being cared for unless you have been deserted and left to fend for yourself. This verse displays the beauty of restoration. When God restores, His hand is evident upon His people as He shows He cares for them.

When God restores, He displays His love. We all need a fresh revelation of God's love for us. When we realize just how much He loves us, we can rest in His promises. We can depend upon His grace. In that resting, our faith is renewed and restoration begins. We find this in being still and knowing God is God.

After Ruth presented herself to Boaz on the threshing floor, she waited for Boaz to do what he promised to do. She could not redeem herself. She trusted the one to whom she had submitted her life. Boaz did not take that submission likely. Submission motivates those in authority to move on our behalf. Submission requires trusting and resting.

Today, trust and rest in the love God has for you. Watch how your faith is renewed and your perspective changes. Let a restoration process begin in your life that gives you a new zeal for life. God really does want the very best for you!

Have a blessed day!

From Remembrance to Restoration

1 Samuel 7:14:

The cities from Ekron to Gath, which they had taken from Israel, were restored; Israel even rescued their surrounding territories from Philistine control. There was also peace between Israel and the Amorites.

When we set up stones of remembrance and honor to show how God has helped us in our journey, we exalt God higher in our lives than our problems. We make Him greater. When Samuel did this, God turned His hand against the Philistines and restored the land they had taken from Israel.

When we turn to God, we can expect the Devil to attack us. He wants to destroy everything God plans to do in our lives because our witness and testimony are a threat to him. In this passage, God restored the cities from Ekron to Gath that the Philistines had taken from Israel. Ekron means *winding; crooked way.* Gath means *the treading out of grapes; winepress.* When you turn to God from a crooked way, you have turned from the Devil's influence and begin receiving the blessings of God. This is when the Devil begins to steal from you. He doesn't want you to know what is yours in Christ. Gath is the place where you begin to harvest the fruits of your labor. The treading out of grapes made wine. New wine is symbolic of new life in Christ. From Ekron to Gath is a place of growth in a Christian's life. God restored that place to Israel when Samuel set up a stone of remembrance and made God greater than Israel's enemy, the Philistines.

God honors growth in the Christian life. While it may be a painful and difficult journey, God will restore everything the enemy has stolen from you in that journey when you remember how He has been your help and learn to trust in Him. Sometimes, we have to let a dream go before God can fulfill it. When it looks like the Devil has won, simply trusting God to be your help is all it takes for your restoration to begin. What God restores, the Devil can't take away! He will restore seven times what was taken from you!

This verse also tells us that there was peace between Israel and the Amorites. Amorites means *publicity; prominence.* When you remember how God is your help and exalt Him above your problems, there will be peace in your publicity. What others say about you will be good. The benefits of allowing God to be your help are tremendous!

God restores His people when they remember what He has done for them. When we remember what Christ has done for us on the cross by taking of His body and His blood, it restores our faith. Restoration is the blessing of remembering God. Don't postpone setting up those stones of remembrance. Your restoration and your victory await!

Have a blessed day!

The Prayer that Brings Restoration

Job 42:10:

After Job had prayed for his friends, the LORD restored his prosperity and doubled his previous possessions.

Job went through tremendous loss and hardship at no fault of his own. You would think those close to him would offer him comfort, but they did just the opposite. They were unkind to him and even tried to convince him his troubles were his own fault. His wife even tried to convince him to curse God and die. In her eyes, he would be better off dead than to continue in his misery. If ever a man needed love, comfort, and encouragement, it was Job, but he did not find it.

Job came to the realization that God was God, regardless of his circumstances. God has the power and authority to do as He wills with anyone of us. Our works do not make us righteous or undeserving of anything God brings our way. If God takes us through difficult times, He can deliver us from difficult times. He is a sovereign and just God. Job came to realize that no plan of God could be thwarted. He is just and fair, and He loves us.

God dealt directly with those who were unkind to Job. He led them to make a sacrifice before Job for forgiveness. Job was to pray for his friends. In this setting, Job acted as intercessor for the sins his friends did against him. He is a symbol of a high priest.

When people have hurt us deliberately, it can be hard to offer a prayer of intercession for them. We might prefer justice to mercy, which is what we are asking when we pray. Notice what happened after Job prayed. God restored his prosperity and doubled his previous possessions! Asking for mercy for those who have hurt us brings our restoration.

Has someone hurt you? Has someone accused you wrongly? Has someone abandoned you in your widowhood? Pray for them. Ask God to have mercy upon them. Your restoration is at hand.

Have a blessed day!

Restored to Dream

Psalm 126:1:

When the LORD restored the fortunes of Zion, we were like those who dream.

God is a restoring God. After we have suffered loss of any kind, we need more than healing. We need to be restored to life. Restoration is what gives us the desire to live again.

Throughout her history, Israel repeated a cycle of behavior that led her from favor to the need for mercy. She began with a right standing with God as an act of His grace, took it for granted, fell into sin and the consequent judgment, then cried out for mercy and deliverance from her enemy. God reached out in His mercy and drew her back to Him, where He restored what the enemy had taken. This is depicted throughout the Book of Judges. When God restored life to Israel, she was able to dream again.

Proverbs 29:18 tells us that without a vision, people perish. The Holman Christian Standard Bible states, "Without revelation people run wild..." If you have no dream or goal to reach, you will never reach it. You will cast off any form of restraint or discipline and live for the moment, or you will shrink into depression and waste away. You have nothing for which to live if you cannot dream.

Whether we have suffered loss or failure as a Christian, we need restoration to be able to dream again. We need to let God direct our dreams instead of taking them into our own hands. Ask God to restore you and to give you a dream. This is how we partake in the abundant life of the riches in Christ Jesus. He died so that we might have life and have it more abundantly! Reach for restoration, and dare to dream!

Have a blessed day!

Threats to Restoration

Nehemiah 4:14:

After I made an inspection, I stood up and said to the nobles, the officials, and the rest of the people, "Don't be afraid of them. Remember the great and awe-inspiring LORD and fight for your countrymen, your sons and daughters, your wives and homes."

We must remember that anytime God is ordering a restoration in our lives, the enemy will attack. Neighboring rulers were afraid that if Jerusalem was rebuilt, they would become a threat. Surrounding countries felt safer since Jerusalem lay in waste, and they wanted to make sure it stayed that way.

Sadly, we may have neighbors who feel the same way about us when they see God doing a restoring work in our lives. As long as we are devastated and demolished, they have a certain control over us. If we ever gain victory in any area, however, that control is threatened. They will discourage us, intimidate us, threaten us, and do everything they can to try to prevent God's work from being accomplished. This is spiritual warfare, and we must fight to make sure God's work is accomplished.

Flesh and blood may not be standing in your way. Perhaps your own fears or worries hinder you. Many of our greatest spiritual battles are fought in the mind alone. They are, nonetheless, spiritual battles. We must keep working to rebuild where God has instructed and to fight where the enemy is threatening.

While Jerusalem's enemies claimed it could never be done, Nehemiah kept working and rebuilt the wall in only 52 days. Not only could it be done, it was done quickly! When the Devil sees he can't prevent a godly work from happening in your life, his next tactic is to delay it. If he can delay it, he can discourage you into thinking it won't happen. If you begin to believe him, your faith is damaged, and the work may be halted altogether. God responds to faith. We must remember to keep working, keep fighting, and believe until the restoration project is completed. Then, God is glorified, and the Devil is defeated!

God restores His people, but it often comes with a fight. This is why we must keep our eyes on Jesus and stop worrying about what the world is saying to us. If we keep our eyes on Him, He will give us the wisdom we need to face the world.

Have a blessed day!

From Suffering to Glory

Romans 8:16-17:

The Spirit Himself testifies together with our spirit that we are God's children, and if children, also heirs—heirs of God and co-heirs with Christ—seeing that we suffer with him so that we may also be glorified with Him.

God does not take our suffering lightly. Whether we are suffering the consequences of our own sin or being persecuted for righteousness, God wants to bring glory to our suffering. When we submit the matter fully to Him and seek His guidance, we can expect God to bring glory to the situation.

Sometimes we have to be reminded that we are a child of God. That is exactly what the Holy Spirit does. He reminds us Whose we are, and this grace enables us to overcome sin. By reminding us that we belong to God, the Holy Spirit gives hope and encouragement to endure difficult days. As God's children, we are co-heirs with Christ of the glory God bestows upon His own. Nothing can replace the favor of God on a life. While Christ suffered extreme pain on the cross, God's glory resurrected Him from the dead. As His children, if we share in His suffering, we will also share in His glory. God is in the resurrection business, and He brings new life to dead situations every day!

If you have found yourself suffering in some way, know that you are a child of God if you are in Christ. God will reveal His glory in your situation. He will not let you continue in your suffering forever. After a little while, He will establish and restore you, according to His promise in 1 Peter 5:10. Rejoice, Oh child of God! Suffering is not the end. His glory is!

Have a blessed day!

God's Glory Revealed

Isaiah 40:3-5:

A voice crying out: Prepare the way of the LORD in the wilderness; make a straight highway for our God in the desert. Every valley will be lifted up, and every mountain and hill will be leveled; the uneven ground will become smooth, and the rough places a plain. And the glory of the LORD will appear, and all humanity will see it together, for the mouth of the LORD has spoken.

Don't you just love how God works? Just before this passage, God comforted a people who had returned from their sins. He pardoned them from their iniquity and announced their time of servitude had ended. This is a picture of grace—unmerited favor.

Then, this proclamation of approaching glory resounds! God begins to prepare a way where there has been no way before. He moves heaven and earth to make sure His plan succeeds. What no one else could do, He does and displays His glory to all. Hallelujah! There is hope for our wilderness, our valleys, and the mountains that stand in our way. He even conquers the rough places that discourage us every day and makes them a smooth plain.

God intends to reveal His glory in us, and everyone will see it. We can look forward to this with excitement and expectation! Why on earth would we want to settle for anything less or serve any other god?

May we all experience God's glory revealed in us. This is the reason we were created and the source of our fulfillment. There is no other god like our God.

Have a blessed day!

He Also Glorified

Romans 8:30:

And those He predestined, He also called; and those He called, He also justified; and those He justified, He also glorified.

Here we see God's purpose for us unveiled. God chose us, called us, justified us through His Son, and His ultimate intent was to shine His glory upon us. We are not a finished work until we reflect His glory. This is true in every trial or hardship we face. Since God has called each of us to something, His goal is to reveal His glory in us through it.

The Greek word for glorified in this verse is *doxazo*, which means *full of glory, to honor or magnify.* God honors the places where we are called to walk according to His Son. He grants us the grace we need for every situation in order to glorify Him. This is why praising God in the midst of trying circumstances is so important. God honors those who honor Him, and we are called to reflect His glory.

We must also remember that the reverse is true, as well. If God has not called us to a situation, He will not honor it. God will not lead us into sin to glorify His name, and we cannot expect Him to glorify our rebellion. We cannot manipulate His glory for our own selfish purposes!

I desperately want God to be glorified in the places where I hurt, and I know you do, too. To know that this is His ultimate goal for every hardship we face comforts me. If we rely upon God through the sacrifice of His Son and walk in obedience toward Him, He will bring glory to the pain we've had to endure. He will honor and deem credible our testimony, and others will find hope in it. Hallelujah! What a Savior.

Have a blessed day!

Splendid and Majestic

Psalm 111:3:

All that He does is splendid and majestic; His righteousness endures forever.

Have you ever been through a season in life where everything just seemed dismal, discouraging, or distressed? We can certainly find ourselves in situations that don't make sense to us. We may even cry out for deliverance and ask God to take this bad circumstance from us. We must remember that everything God does is splendid and majestic. When He allows us to endure something hard, it can be because it is a part of His glorious plan for us.

That does not mean that anything we do is splendid and majestic. God does not lead us into sin, and our sin never glorifies God. When we repent and turn to Him, He can make something wonderful out of our mess. As **Ephesians 2:10** explains, **"For we are His creation, created in Christ Jesus for good works, which God prepared ahead of time."** We are a work in progress, and the end result is promised to be beautiful!

Realize today that whatever chaos you encounter will become splendid and majestic in His hands. Submit it to Him. He will not get frustrated with you and turn against you. His righteousness endures forever. He will be good to you; He will do the right thing by you; and He will do something splendid and majestic in your life. After all, He is God!

Have a blessed day!

Face to Face with Glory

John 20:15-16:

"Woman," Jesus said to her, "Why are you crying? Who is it you are looking for?" Supposing He was the gardener, she replied, "Sir, if you've removed Him, tell me where you've put Him, and I will take Him away." Jesus said, "Mary." Turning around, she said to Him in Hebrew, "Rabbouni!"—which means "Teacher."

Mary Magdalene was a woman who loved Jesus and followed Him at all costs. She followed Him from town and village, listening to Him teach and watching Him perform miracles. She had received her own miracle from Jesus when He set her free from seven demons, which would certainly explain her love for Him. She followed Him to the hard place of the cross and watched Him die. Afterwards, she just kept following Him in her grief. She followed Him to see where He was buried, and three days later, she followed to anoint His body with spices. When she could not find His body, she panicked.

Mary returned to the tomb that day to serve a dead Jesus. While her motive in serving may have been love, her mentality was looking for a dead body. Jesus was alive! Jesus revealed Himself to her that day by calling her by name. Until that point, she did not recognize Him.

Moses asked to see God's glory, and God allowed Him to view Him from behind. He told Moses that no one could see His face and live, so He hid Moses in the cleft of a rock and allowed him to see where He had been (Exodus 33:18-23). Mary, however, viewed Jesus in His glory face to face! At that moment, everything made sense to Mary. All of His teaching, miracles, and promises merged with the hard place of the cross, and Mary witnessed resurrection power in all of His glory. Everything she had learned was true, and every promise was fulfilled at that moment. She went to the tomb to anoint Jesus, but He was now alive and ready to anoint her!

Mary's response to Jesus is one we should note. By calling Him "Rabbouni," she was addressing Him as her personal, Master Teacher. Mary was able to see the glory of God revealed in Jesus because she had a teachable spirit. She was open to learn from the Master, Himself, and He showed her things He did not show others right away. She was the first to share this news. He still appeared to other followers, but He appeared to her first.

When Jesus appears to be nowhere in our situation, keep seeking Him for He is alive. Like Mary, the only way we will ever recognize Him is if He chooses to reveal Himself to us. In doing so, He will call us by name, too. He will speak to us in a way that is direct, personal, and undeniable in order that we may see He is alive and working in us in a way we never dreamed. He will enable us to see our own purpose enveloped in His. At that moment, we will witness the power of His glory, and we will be able to spread the news like wildfire.

Have a blessed day!

The Glory of a Completed Work

Exodus 24:16:

The glory of the Lord settled on Mount Sinai, and the cloud covered it for six days. On the seventh day He called to Moses from the cloud.

The glory of the Lord is so great that one cannot help but notice. Here we see the glory of the Lord settled in the form of a cloud on Mount Sinai while the children of Israel were in the wilderness. God's glory cannot be confined, concealed, or confused. For six days this cloud of glory settled on the mountain, representing the time it took God to create the earth. On the seventh day, God rested. Here, we find God calling to Moses on the seventh day. His work was completed, and He wished to reveal His glory and His purpose to Moses personally.

God is at work in your life creating something that will glorify Him. When He has completed it, He will call you forth to reveal His perfect plan and purpose to you. At that time, you will radiate with His glory because He will be the one who has done a great work in you.

If you find yourself in a wilderness where you know you have followed God's leading, He will reveal His glory to you at the appropriate time. Allow Him to complete His work in you, knowing that what He is doing is far greater than anything you could ever dream or imagine. There is no greater experience on earth than to walk in purpose and to display the glory of God!

Have a blessed day!

His Riches in Glory

Philippians 4:18-19:

But I have received everything in full, and I have an abundance. I am fully supplied, having received from Epaphroditus what you provided—a fragrant offering, a welcome sacrifice, pleasing to God. And my God will supply all your needs according to His riches in glory in Christ Jesus.

Paul had received a much-appreciated offering from the Philippians that more than met his need. As a result, he knew that God would, in turn, meet their needs according to His riches in glory. When we reach out to meet someone else's need, God makes sure our needs are met. He uses us as ministers in the process.

Giving to get in return is never the right motive to give. That would be considered an investment. We give to others out of compassion and generosity, knowing they have no way to repay us. We don't want to see others hurting when we can do something about it, and we are moved to action. That is what Christ did for us and what He expects us to do for others.

Simply put, love meets needs. God saw our needy position before Him and knew we had no means to pay the price for redemption, so He sent His only Son to pay the price for us. He loved us and met our need from His own generous supply. Since He loved us enough to meet our greatest need, will He surely not meet lesser needs? All the riches in glory to meet absolutely every need we have are found in Christ Jesus.

We cannot always meet every need we see. There may be times when we desperately wish we could do something about the situation, but we just don't have the means. God always has an answer. We can trust those matters to Him in prayer and wait in faith for Him to respond.

You may not be able to meet your own need at the moment, but God may give you the means to help someone else. Where is He calling you to love? Know that when you respond in love and meet someone else's need, God will meet yours! Your response to love is an indication of your faith, and it pleases Him.

Have a blessed day!

Would God Be Glorified?

1 Corinthians 10:23:

Everything is permissible, but not everything is helpful. Everything is permissible, but not everything builds up.

Verse 31:

Therefore, whether you eat or drink, or whatever you do, do everything for God's glory.

God has given us a tremendous amount of liberty in Christ. We can literally eat anything and everything we want, and it will not affect our salvation one bit. We are still God's children. If we eat anything and everything, however, it will affect our bodies. We must learn to ask ourselves, "Would God be glorified if I eat this?" God is not glorified if we are unhealthy, overweight, or miserable. God is glorified in our victories through Him and when we fulfill the plans He has for us.

God does not force His will on any of us. He gives us free will to choose. If we want His glory to shine through us, we must choose to honor Him. If the sky is the limit in our choices, will we choose Jesus, or will we choose to honor our own fleshly desires?

Do you want to see God's glory manifested in your life today? Think about the choices you made yesterday. God usually doesn't just zap us with His glory. He unveils it over time as we walk with Him in fellowship and obedience. To see God's glory revealed in us tomorrow, we must carefully consider the choices we make today. Everything is permissible, but not everything is best for us. Determine to glorify God in your decisions today, and watch with eager expectation of what He will do tomorrow!

Have a blessed day!

God's Glory, the Devil's Shame

Psalm 85:8-9:

I will listen to what God will say; surely the LORD will declare peace to His people, His godly ones, and not let them go back to foolish ways. His salvation is very near those who fear Him, so that glory may dwell in our land.

God desires for us to reflect His glory. In contrast, the Devil desires the opposite, which is shame. Wherever God is working to bring His glory, the Devil has a counter attack in place that will bring us shame.

This Psalm instructs us to listen to God. The Devil will always tempt us to return to evil ways. This is the time to listen to the wisdom that cries aloud in the streets (Prov. 1) and to follow the way we know to be sure and true. While the Devil will try to convince you that you will lose, fail, or miss out on something by doing the right thing, God will always make sure those who fear His name are blessed.

God will declare peace to His people. This means that He will make them whole, and whatever is missing from their lives that tempt them to fall into sin will be restored. The Devil is an illegitimate provider. He will always attempt to make you fill a legitimate need in an illegitimate way. By doing so, he spreads shame, which is a reflection of his influence. When God restores a life, He brings His glory to it so others will follow.

Determine today not to return to destructive habits that have led you to pay serious consequences. Trust God to meet whatever legitimate need you may have, knowing that He will bring glory to your life. If you find yourself in a position where the temptation is strong, realize that God's glory must be close at hand! Submit to God, resist the Devil, flee, and watch for God's salvation (James 4:7).

Have a blessed day!

Destined for Victory

Psalm 30:1:

I will exalt You, LORD, because You have lifted me up and have not allowed my enemies to triumph over me.

Every Christian will face times when they feel defeated by the enemy. Jesus Christ was lifted up on a cross so our sins could be forgiven and counted against us no more. By trusting in this sacrifice, God lifts us up from the traps the Devil has set for us and does not allow him to be victorious over us.

David knew that God had prevented his enemies from defeating him, and he exalted God for it. Like David, we would do well to realize who has helped us in every victory we've encountered and praise Him for working on our behalf. He has worked for us before, and He will work for us again.

He intends for us to be victorious over the Devil and to bring Him glory in the process.

God does not want to see His people defeated by the Devil's schemes. That is the whole reason He sent Jesus into this world! Exalt the LORD today. Lift His name high because He has destined us for victory through Christ!

Have a blessed day!

Suddenly, Life Changes

Acts 2:2:

Suddenly, a sound like that of a violent rushing wind came from heaven, and it filled the whole house where they were staying. (The coming of the Holy Spirit at Pentecost)

Acts 9:3:

As he traveled and was nearing Damascus, a light from heaven suddenly flashed around him. (Jesus appeared to Saul on the road to Damascus, changing his life forever.)

Acts 16:26:

Suddenly, there was such a violent earthquake that the foundations of the jail were shaken, and immediately all the doors were opened, and everyone's chains came loose. (God freed Paul and Silas from prison.)

God doesn't usually give us a timeframe in which He will work. He just shows up suddenly, and we see where He has been at work all along. He often hides His intricate handiwork from us. Then, suddenly, He reveals Himself to us in ways we never expected! This is exactly what happened to Mary Magdalene at the tomb. When we trust a matter to God and simply seek Jesus, He suddenly appears, and we are made whole—revived, refreshed, renewed, restored.

Don't think for one minute that God is not at work in your life. He may not be working quickly, but He may appear suddenly! We also see this in the story of the 10 virgins. The groom was a long time in coming, but He came at an hour no one expected. Suddenly, five virgins were ready to receive the Bridegroom, and five were out seeking oil for their lamps. Waiting for Jesus yields excellent returns when He comes suddenly!

Have a blessed day!

You Have Made Me Rejoice

Psalm 92:4:

For You have made me rejoice, LORD, by what You have done; I will shout for joy because of the works of Your hands.

While we may not always be able to see it, we can know with certainty that God's hand is always at work. What He is doing is good, and we can trust Him completely. God is both good and faithful, and He will not betray His faithfulness to us.

If you have ever questioned, "What are You doing in my life, LORD," it is a good indication that you have sensed God's hand at work but did not understand what He was doing. In such times, you can rejoice because God has not left you to find your way on your own. He is bringing everything necessary into your life to make sure you can fulfill the purpose for which He created you. He is continually working to thwart the plans of the enemy over you. If God is at work, He is doing something good, and you should be excited! His work in your life will bring you joy.

Can you sense His hand in your life today? If so, rejoice! God is doing something good in your life. Do you know God is leading you somewhere but are not quite sure where you are going? Rejoice! What He is doing in you and through you is good. Stop expecting the worst, and begin to walk in God's best. Don't give up simply because you still have questions with no answers. Trust the God who is always faithful, always loving, always merciful, and always working in your best interest. Rejoice that you still have purpose in Him!

Have a blessed day!

To Live By Faith

Romans 1:16-17:

For I am not ashamed of the gospel, because it is God's power for salvation to everyone who believes, first to the Jew, and also to the Greek. For in it God's righteousness is revealed from faith to faith, just as it is written: The righteous will live by faith.

The gospel is the message of the cross. Because Jesus died for us, we may share in His righteousness. This righteousness is revealed from faith to faith.

Every time we encounter a new problem, hardship, trial, or obstacle, we engage a new faith adventure. Because of the righteousness of Christ, God works on our behalf to help us overcome. He reveals more of Himself to us in each faith adventure so we see more of Christ and less of ourselves.

Faith becomes a way of life for the Christian. When God sees us, He sees us through the lens of the cross. Therefore, when we look to Him, we can never expect Him to move on our behalf because of our own efforts. We must look to Him through the lens of the cross, as well. Because of what Jesus did for us, we have grace to overcome every obstacle the Devil puts in our way. Faith in the finished work of the cross becomes our new way of life.

Faith must have an object. Without an object, faith is blind belief without any substance to back it. The object of our faith is Jesus Christ, whose very life was a substitute for us.

Because of what Christ did for you on the cross, you can trust God to help you today. Look to God through the lens of the cross, and be assured of your help. Know that He is for you and not against you. God raised Jesus from the dead as a sign He had forgiven all your sins. Know that your sins are forgiven today, and expect God to answer you and work on your behalf. He reveals Himself to us every time we turn to Him; this faith is the manner in which we are called to live.

Have a blessed day!

According to Your Faith

Matthew 9:29:

He touched their eyes and said, "According to your faith will it be done to you."

Jesus always responded to faith. He didn't heal everyone as He traveled through Galilee. He healed those who came to Him in faith. To have faith requires we admit our own inadequacies and are willing to be completely dependent upon Him.

Faith is work. When we are forced to wait, it is so tempting to take matters into our own hands. Even in situations where we know there is nothing we can do, we frantically look for something we can do to ease the situation or to make us busy so we will feel productive. Faith must have a stubborn determination to survive.

The Devil's greatest weapon against us while our faith is developing is discouragement. When we look at our situations, rather than to Christ, we make ourselves a clear target for the enemy's arrow. This is why faith is described as a shield: "In every situation take the shield of faith, and with it you will be able to extinguish the flaming arrows of the evil one" (Eph. 6:16).

If we are ever going to fulfill our destiny in Christ, faith is required. To have faith means we must engage in spiritual warfare. Faith develops in the midst of combat, and it is not for the weak or faint of heart. The violent take it by force!

Engage in your battle today. Use your shield of faith. Remember that God is for you and not against you. Whatever God has begun in you, He will be faithful to complete it. According to your faith, it will be done to you. Believe much, receive much. Believe little, receive little. This is your choice and mine. I think I'll take the big piece!

Have a blessed day!

Desire, Hope, and Faith

To hope is to desire with expectation of fulfillment. Expectation accompanies the desire. The greater the desire, the greater the need is for expectation. God-given desires cannot be denied or ignored. They demand expectation. Therefore, hope arises when God gives us a desire. The desires He gives us are directly related to the destiny He has for us. They are a part of our calling in Him.

Hebrews 11:1:

Now faith is the reality of what is hoped for, the proof of what is not seen.

Faith leads hope into reality; it is the pathway between God-given desire and destiny. Faith is our journey. The reason many of us never grasp what God has for us at times is that we are unwilling to embark upon the journey until something catapults us into it. As Jonah discovered, faith can hurl us overboard into stormy waters. We will choose to remain comfortable and not go there if we don't absolutely have to go. The question remains as to how long we can stay in our comfort zones before a storm drives us out of them. Then, we are forced to walk the road or swim the sea of faith.

Hebrews 11:6:

Now without faith it is impossible to please God, for the one who draws near to Him must believe that He exists and rewards those who seek Him.

God is pleased to send the storm that drives us into faith. Faith proves that we trust Him and believe Him while we hope He will come through for us. Faith displays our weaknesses and drives out self-reliance. It operates on total dependence upon God and can take no credit for what is achieved. Faith pleases God because it brings Him glory.

Faith requires an object—it cannot operate independently. That object must be One who can bring that desire or hope into fruition. Faith believes that the other party will deliver on its end. When we come to God with a need or a legitimate desire, we must believe that He will reward us. The key is to seek God in the midst of that desire.

What does God want to accomplish by fulfilling a certain desire? How would God be glorified? What testimony would we have if that desire were fulfilled? How would the fulfillment further His kingdom? Where is

He working in the midst of that desire? What does He want us to learn from it? When the desire becomes God-focused instead of self-focused, we are on the road of faith. That is when we begin moving toward Him instead of toward what we think will satisfy us. That movement of faith is what God rewards because it pleases Him.

Today, as you continue your own journey as a widow, realize that you cannot embark upon this road without hope or faith. Whatever God has for you will begin with a desire that sparks a ray of hope. Give that desire back to God and begin to move toward Him in faith. This will lead you to His best!

Have a blessed day!

Expect the Best

Philippians 4:8-9:

Finally brothers, whatever is true, whatever is honorable, whatever is just, whatever is pure, whatever is lovely, whatever is commendable—if there is any moral excellence and if there is any praise—dwell on these things. Do what you have learned and received and heard and seen in me, and the God of peace will be with you.

When we dwell on the worst of things, the worst is what we come to expect. Paul teaches us here to dwell on the good things. When we think the best of people and circumstances, we will come to expect the best. Expecting the worst creates stress, while expecting the best gives us peace. Furthermore, God wants us to expect the best from Him. Sometimes I'm guilty of expecting the worst from Him and forgetting all the remarkably great things He has done in my life. Why do we tend to expect the worst when God has given His best? Is this just me?

Paul's instruction is to do what we know is right. We can rely upon the things God has taught us from His Word. When we do, God is with us in a special way. He grants us peace in our troubling circumstances. When we take things into our own hands and compromise God's Word, we create more trouble for ourselves. If we have done what we know is right, we can trust God with the results.

Today, concentrate on the true, honorable, just, pure, lovely, commendable things in your troubling situations. Expect God to work the best possible outcome on your behalf. Do the right thing, and rest in His peace. He is truly for us and not against us.

Have a blessed day!

Everything is Possible

Mark 9:23:

Then Jesus said to him, "If you can? Everything is possible to the one who believes."

The disciples saw the boy and realized these demons where stronger than they were. They falsely assumed the demons were also stronger than God. We are guilty of the same thing at times. When we are faced with huge problems or trials, we often look at them with the realization that these demons are greater than we are, and we are right in that assumption. No problem, trial, need, tragedy, or even desire, however, is greater than Christ. When we assume the problem must be too big for God to handle simply because it is too big for us, we are falsely assuming God is made in our image when the opposite is true. We are made in His image. An image of something is not as great as the real thing. We must have faith in the real thing to handle the things that we, the image, cannot.

Everything is possible for the one who believes His God is greater than the problem. Everything is possible for the person who recognizes we are made in God's image and that He is greater. God cannot be measured by our standards. We are measured by His.

Everything is possible for the one who is willing to submit to God's standard and seek Him. By prayer and fasting we seek the face of God and desire to know His will. As Jesus told the disciples, "This kind can come out by nothing but prayer and fasting!" (Mark 9:29) Everything is possible for the one who is totally devoted to knowing and living the Word of God.

For whatever difficulty you are facing today, know that everything is possible for those who believe. You must activate your faith. Believe in His greatness, and seek His face. Nothing is too big or too outrageous for Him!

Have a blessed day!

Faith in the Person of Jesus

Ephesians 1:15-16:

This is why, since I heard about your faith in the Lord Jesus and your love for all the saints, I never stop giving thanks for you as I remember you in my prayers.

Faith must have an object, and that object is Jesus Christ. If our faith is in our desired answer, we will find ourselves wavering. Our faith must be in the Person of Jesus Christ, who loved us enough to die for us! If he loved us enough to give His very life for us, will He surely not be willing to give us a lesser thing if we need it? The only reason He doesn't answer our prayer the way we may want at times is because He has something better. Our faith must be firmly rooted in Him.

Paul was thankful for other Christians who placed their faith in Christ. This meant they were rooted and grounded in love. I'm thankful, as well, for a group of women who trust Jesus. These are women you can trust to love you, to understand you, and to encourage you along the way. May we be women who have placed our faith in Jesus as a Person and not just in the thing we desire Him to do for us.

Have a blessed day!

Let Faith Arise

Matthew 15:21-28:

When Jesus left there, He withdrew to the area of Tyre and Sidon. Just then a Canaanite woman from that region came and kept crying out, "Have mercy on me, Lord, Son of David! My daughter is cruelly tormented by a demon." Yet He did not say a word to her. So His disciples approached Him and urged Him, "Send her away because she cries out after us." He replied, "I was sent only to the lost sheep of the house of Israel." But she came, knelt before Him, and said, "Lord, help me!" He answered, "It isn't right to take the children's bread and throw it to their dogs." "Yes, Lord," she said, "yet even the dogs eat the crumbs that fall from their masters' table!" Then Jesus replied to her, "Woman, your faith is great. Let it be done for you as you want." And from that moment her daughter was cured.

In this passage, Jesus seems a bit unkind to this woman. Perhaps, He was using her as a visual teaching tool for His disciples, or maybe He was drawing faith out of her. Either way, we see an illustration of faith depicted here that teaches us all a lesson.

This Canaanite woman approached Jesus for healing for her demon-possessed daughter. No doctor could help her. Obviously, she had heard of Jesus and recognized His power as one that could grant wholeness to her daughter. What good mother wouldn't do everything she could to save her child? If Jesus had the power to help her, she would certainly approach Him.

The first thing we see of her faith is that she cried out for mercy. She recognized herself as a sinful woman with no right to ask for anything. In hopes that Jesus would not condemn or deny her, she cried out for mercy.

Jesus did not respond. Perhaps, we have all been there. We are in desperate need of something and realize we could never earn it, so we cry out for mercy. Yet, Jesus does not respond with our needed answer. He seems silent. This can be very frustrating, and many may give up at this point. Turning elsewhere, however, indicates there was never true faith in the beginning. Some people still falsely believe they can find an answer outside of Christ.

The disciples apparently didn't think she deserved an audience with Jesus, either. They urged Jesus to send her away. They did not want to identify with her need, and they were annoyed by her presence. Our needs have that negative effect on people—it tends to drag them down. Some may even believe we deserve the hardship we face and want to leave us in it. Sadly, we find many people like this in the church. The *good* people have yet to realize they are undeserving of their own good fortune and look down on others.

Jesus's response to her seems one that would satisfy the disciples. He was sent only to Israel, and she should not think He would do anything for her as an undeserving Canaanite. While this response could have offended her and caused her to spout off in an effort to discredit Him, we see something else. She knelt before Him and asked again for His help. She bowed in full submission to His authority and in worship.

Jesus's next response to her seems outright insulting. He compared her to a dog, indicating again how undeserving she was of His favor in light of her nationality. She could have really become offended at this point, but she didn't. She used His own argument to make a point. Even dogs eat the crumbs from the master's table.

At this point, faith took another turn. She accepted the insult and appealed again to mercy. She did not try to equate herself with Jesus. She knew she would never gain social acceptance. She also knew, however, that she didn't need that. All she needed was a crumb of His power for her daughter to be healed.

Many people who followed Jesus wanted to receive His power. They wanted position in His kingdom. They thought they deserved it and followed Him in expectation of receiving a reward for their works. Works follow the deserving and earn the prize for which they are intended. Works build status and grant position. Faith, however, follows the undeserving and rises from need. This stems from the hope that a crumb will fall and grant the fulfillment desired. Faith does not try to equate itself with Jesus; it realizes its place and bows in submission and worship.

Jesus recognized her great faith and granted her request. Faith moves God; works move people. There are times in our lives when people cannot grant us what we need. Only a touch of grace from the Father will improve our conditions, relieve our pains, or fulfill our longings. Faith must arise.

Today, look at the situations in your life where you need a touch from God. Have you been relying upon works in those areas? Do you see yourself as deserving of an answer? If so, re-evaluate. God does not owe you one thing. His purpose is not to make you His equal or to make you happy. Recognize your lowly state, and submit to Him in worship. All you need is one crumb of His grace to fall. Faith presses through until grace fulfills!

Have a blessed day!

Faith that Heals

Mark 10:51-52:

Then Jesus answered him, "What do you want Me to do for you?" "Rabbouni," the blind man told Him, "I want to see!" "Go your way," Jesus told him. "Your faith has healed you." Immediately he could see and began to follow Him on the road.

Here we find much more than just the healing of the blind man. We find how faith operates. This blind man was crying out for mercy along the road Jesus was traveling when Jesus stopped to help him. Jesus called for him and asked the blind man what he wanted Him to do. The blind man actually displayed two desires to Jesus when addressed.

The obvious desire is the one he clearly stated. The blind man wanted to see. Jesus assured him that his faith had healed him and told the man to go on his way. What he did next revealed his second desire. He followed Jesus.

Notice how the blind man addressed Jesus. He called Him, "Rabbouni," which means *Master Teacher.* Actually this word has a personal connotation which more accurately defines the meaning as *My Master Teacher!* The blind man wanted to follow Jesus and learn from Him, but He could not see how to follow. Once he could see, he began to follow Jesus on the road instead of going on his own way. His faith was not in his healing. His faith was in the person of Jesus. As Jesus told him, this faith healed him.

What do you want Jesus to do for you today? If you had that very thing, would you continue to follow Jesus with it, or would you go your own way and use it for your pleasure? Your faith will follow your greatest desire.

If your faith is in the thing you desire, you will follow it. If your faith is in Jesus, you will follow Him once your desire is granted. Faith in Jesus has the power to work miracles. Faith in anything less is wishful thinking.

Place your faith in Rabbouni, and determine to follow Him, regardless of whether or not you get what you want. This kind of faith will heal you and transform you. This kind of faith pleases God. This kind of faith will bring an anointing to your life like you never dreamed possible!

Have a blessed day!

Crazy Faith

Luke 17:26-30:

Just as it was in the days of Noah, so it will be in the days of the Son of Man: people went on eating, drinking, marrying and giving in marriage until the day Noah boarded the ark, and the flood came and destroyed them all. It will be the same as it was in the days of Lot: people went on eating, drinking, buying, selling, planting, building. But on the day Lot left Sodom, fire and sulfur rained from heaven and destroyed them all. It will be like that on the day the Son of Man is revealed.

Both Noah and Lot lived in very wicked times. These were times so wicked that God decided to bring judgment upon the people by destroying them completely. Before He did, however, He gave many warnings. The Day of Judgment should not have taken them by surprise, but it did. In each case, they totally rejected the word of the Lord and continued to plan for their futures in the midst of their wickedness. God cut off their future by sending His judgment. They did not realize that they had no future outside of God. The warnings which once seemed crazy in the midst of their evil desires eventually proved to be wisdom and compassion calling them out of evil and into safety. No one listened.

God planned a way of escape for His men. Neither Noah nor Lot was destroyed by His judgment. God took them out before His judgment fell. For us to have a close relationship with God in times of judgment is vitally important because it will lead us to safety when the world falls apart. Unbelievers may think we are crazy, but God's judgment is nothing to trivialize or ignore. To be considered crazy by men is better than to be considered wicked by God.

As Christians, the Son of Man has already been revealed to us by the Holy Spirit. He is our escape. Warning signs are all around us, and God's Word declares a day of His judgment when Christ will come again. We can do nothing about the judgment that is coming on this world, but we can cling to the One who has already provided a way out for us. If you don't know Him, now is the time for you to establish a relationship with Him by surrendering your life to Him. You have no future without Him.

The people of Noah's day and Lot's day did not heed the many warnings, and judgment fell upon them suddenly. They could not discern the difference between wisdom and ignorance. So it will be when Christ comes again. When judgment falls, it is too late. Run to His saving arms while He is still calling, and continue to point others to Him. He is the only safe place, and our security must be established in Him. Let unbelievers think what they may. *Crazy* faith is saving faith.

Have a blessed day!

Moving Mountains

Do you have mountains in your life you just can't seem to overcome? What is standing in the gap between where you are and where you want to be? I dare think that most of us have some type of mountain like this that just seems bigger than we are, and it may be a defining factor in our destiny. We can't do that thing we desire because …. We'd love to reach a particular goal, but ….

What makes a mountain move? We should all know by now that our own strength certainly doesn't move mountains. The mountain holds no glory for us. Two passages of Scripture reveal the keys for us.

Matthew 17:20-21:

"Because of your little faith," He told them. "For I assure you: If you have faith the size of a mustard seed, you will tell this mountain, 'Move from here to there,' and it will move. Nothing will be impossible for you. (However, this kind does not come out except by prayer and fasting.)"

Jesus assures us here that even a tiny amount of faith can move a mountain. Some things, however, require prayer and fasting. This is simply time when we deny ourselves what the flesh craves in order to hear from God. The flesh wants an answer and to be satisfied now. When we refuse to try to meet a need that only God can meet and allow ourselves to feel the hunger and lack of that need, we participate in a type of fast. Prayer and fasting direct our attention toward God as the provider of that need. This enables us to hear from God on that particular matter and to receive direction or wisdom.

Zechariah 4:6-7:

So he answered me, "This is the word of the LORD to Zerubbabel: 'Not by strength or by might, but by My Spirit,' says the LORD of Hosts. 'What are you, great mountain? Before Zerubbabel you will become a plain. And he will bring out the capstone accompanied by shouts of: Grace, grace to it!'"

We don't move mountains. Grace does. Our mountain may even be one that we created from sin, but grace has the power to move it. We don't deserve for that mountain to be moved on our behalf, but grace steps in by the Spirit of the LORD and moves the mountain. God is glorified, and we are changed!

God is described in this passage as the LORD of Hosts. This title is used when God acts like a warrior bringing judgment. In spiritual warfare, God comes to our rescue against our enemies in the heavenly realms. When the LORD of Hosts appears, His intention is to wipe out that particular enemy forever and bring it into full submission under His reign. That particular mountain is gone for good! God is setting up a new reign in our lives when the LORD of Hosts appears!

Faith the size of a mustard seed and grace move the mightiest mountains. Faith depends upon the love of God. The more we realize God's unmerited favor in our lives and come to receive His love for us, the more faith arises in us. The more faith we have in God, the more grace He pours into our lives. As Jesus said, "Nothing will be impossible for you."

Have a blessed day!

Real Faith, Real Power, Real Fruit

Matthew 21:18-21:

Early in the morning, as He was returning to the city, He was hungry. Seeing a lone fig tree by the road, He went up to it and found nothing on it except leaves. And He said to it, "May no fruit ever come from you again!" At once the fig tree withered. When the disciples saw it, they were amazed and said, "How did the fig tree wither so quickly?" Jesus answered them, "I assure you: if you have faith and do not doubt, you will not only do what was done to the fig tree, but even if you tell this mountain, 'Be lifted up and thrown into the sea,' it will be done. And if you believe, you will receive whatever you ask for in prayer."

Jesus was hungry, and He saw the hope of fruit in the distance. Fruit would have satisfied His hunger and have been sweet to the taste. When He approached the tree, however, it was barren of fruit. Although it had beautiful foliage and looked promising, it was fruitless. Jesus cursed the tree, and it never bore fruit again; it withered immediately.

Jesus was teaching by illustration. The fig tree was a symbol of Israel in Scripture. The fig tree was beautiful in appearance and very promising to the eye. The tree seemed to hold much hope, but it was barren. It was a pretty picture with no substance.

The Christian life may also appear as this fig tree. We can be a pretty picture with no substance. We may go to church every Sunday and associate with the *good* people or even belong to the *right* political party and send our children to private Christian schools where they are isolated from the *bad* kids in the world. If we produce no fruit, however, all we are is a pretty picture with no substance. We look promising and hopeful, but we have as much trouble handling our problems as the world does. Without fruit, we are as selfish and self-centered as any unbeliever. If we produce no fruit, we offer no real hope to anyone.

Please don't misunderstand what I am saying. I am not knocking going to church, belonging to any political party, or private Christian schools. These are all good things, but our association with them is not what makes us fruit producers. They may make us look good or acceptable in certain Christian circles, but those things will not produce fruit in our lives any more than a cow can produce honey! The only thing that will produce fruit in our lives is the Holy Spirit. He dwells in us once we surrender our lives to Christ. The key word here is surrender.

To surrender means *to relinquish possession or control of to another because of demand or compulsion.* To let go and let God is to surrender. This produces fruit in our lives. To surrender anything requires faith.

The last part of this passage deals with the matter of faith. Jesus assured His disciples that if they had faith, they could do the same thing to the fig tree that He did. He was not encouraging us to kill fig trees in this illustration. If we have faith, we will be as a tree bearing much fruit. Barren trees will wither in comparison. People will be drawn to the tree that bears fruit. Those with no substance will die out because they have nothing to offer.

To make you grow takes three things: sun, rain, and manure. In your Christian walk, God will shine upon you, send storms upon you, and He will even throw some raw sewage on you to make you grow! We can expect it. How we handle these things shows the world what it is like to be a Christian. In surviving the sun, the rain, and the manure, you have something to offer others. To survive it, you must surrender to it. Your faith rises up in the midst, and the Holy Spirit produces fruit from it.

According to Jesus, faith can move mountains into the sea for us. If we believe, we receive whatever we ask in prayer. To have this kind of faith, however, we must relinquish control. We must surrender to the One who has all power—even enough to move mountains. We will never move them in our own strength. Just as the chief priests and scribes had no real power in the temple, neither do we when we try to do things by ourselves.

Why do we try to maintain control anyway? Our nature is to seek and maintain control, which has no real power. Faith has power. Our faith cannot be focused on establishments or in our own abilities. We must be rooted in Christ to have real faith. Real faith produces real power and yields real fruit.

The Jewish religious system had no real faith; it operated on tradition. Israel placed its faith in this religious system, not on the promised Messiah. This system had no power and produced no fruit—it was as worthless as the barren fig tree. We are women who have certainly encountered sunshine, storms, and manure. Surrender to the One who has the power to move your mountains and answer your requests. There are others who are hungry, and through Christ you can offer them hope.

Have a blessed day!

The Fight of Faith

1 Timothy 6:12:

Fight the good fight for the faith; take hold of eternal life, to which you were called and have made a good confession before many witnesses.

Let us never forget that faith is a fight. I can't help but think we lose battles to unbelief simply because we are unwilling to fight. We need others who are willing to fight with us to defeat the onslaught of discouragement, doubt, and depression the enemy will send our way. We must learn to fight with one hand while lifting another up with the other. Such a warrior is a valuable asset to God's kingdom, and God will work wonders through His mighty warriors to prove Himself strong to the many witnesses who are watching.

Such warriors are known as prayer warriors—and women make the best champions! The fight of faith is not for the weak. Dare to be a strong woman of faith. Needy women are a dime a dozen in this world, and they will always be needy. We can never fix all their problems. Dare to be a strong prayer warrior. We will see miracles because of faith. We will be able to lead someone to believe because we have experienced miracles firsthand for ourselves.

Today, I challenge you to think of strong women in your life upon whom you can count to help you fight a battle of faith. If you don't have anyone, find someone. Now is the time we overcome the places where the Devil has reaped havoc in our lives and regain the territory that is rightfully ours. We won't do that by whining and complaining about our problems. We will gain that victory through the fight of faith.

Have a blessed day!

When Faith Works

Hebrews 10:38:

But My righteous one will live by faith; and if he draws back, My soul has no pleasure in him.

In Christ, we are the righteous. We must live daily by faith. When we lack faith, we are forgetting the Father's love for us, and He is not pleased in that. We need to focus on Him and spend more time in His lap.

Gal. 2:20-21:

… and I no longer live, but Christ lives in me. The life I now live in the flesh, I live by faith in the Son of God, who loved me and gave Himself for me. I do not set aside the grace of God; for if righteousness comes through the law, then Christ died for nothing.

Paul realized that his flesh would fail, but Christ in Him would not. All that is in Christ is applied to us by grace. Paul placed his faith in the love God had for him and the finished work of Christ on the cross. It didn't matter what others thought or what accusations were made against him. Indeed, there were many, and it even cost him his life.

Romans 8:1-2:

Therefore, no condemnation now exists for those in Christ Jesus, because the Spirit's law of life in Christ Jesus has set you free from the law of sin and of death.

We are all condemned before the law. We may even be condemned by others. In Christ, however, there is no condemnation because He has paid the full price for our sins. He draws us to Him by His grace—His unmerited favor. His kindness leads us to repentance, according to Romans 2:4. We are made new in His presence by His overwhelming love for us. Indeed, faith works when we realize just how much God loves us.

Take time to sit in the Father's lap today, and may faith arise in you. He will not condemn you; He longs to fill your imperfect heart with His perfect love.

Have a blessed day!

God's Faithful Love

Psalm 89:33

But I will not withdraw My faithful love from him or betray my faithfulness.

Regardless of how difficult things may be in life, we can always count on God's faithful love! He will not abandon us when we fail. While we may feel the rod of correction, He is faithful to love us and to continue in relationship with us as our heavenly Father. He cannot help but be faithful to us because that is His nature. Faithfulness is an attribute of God.

We may face times when we know correction is coming. We may feel as if a particular hardship is of our own making. While this may be true, we can still count on God's love toward us. Just as a parent still loves a child who has misbehaved, so God loves us. He may be seeking to change our behavior, but He is certainly not seeking to disown us or to reject us. We can turn to Him in those times and receive mercy. We can still experience His blessing when we have failed. Hallelujah!

Where have you blown it? Turn it over to God, and experience His faithful love toward you. Where do you feel rejected? Turn to God in that area, and immediately feel His acceptance. All discipline is designed to turn you to God and not away from Him. The Devil condemns and tries to make you think God cannot love you or use you anymore because of your failure. In reality, God is waiting for you to turn to Him so He can revive, refresh, restore, and renew you for His greater purpose. That is the Devil's worst nightmare, and he will do anything to try to prevent you from walking closer with God and to direct you to rebellion. Dare to defeat the Devil and turn to your faithful and loving Father. He will be good to you and bless you beyond your wildest imagination! You belong to Him as His child, and He cannot help but love you!

Have a blessed day!

Led by Faithful Love

Exodus 15:13:

You will lead the people You have redeemed with Your faithful love; You will guide them to Your holy dwelling with Your strength.

Job 10:12:

You gave me life and faithful love, and your care has guarded my life.

Psalm 5:7:

But I enter Your house by the abundance of Your faithful love; I bow down toward Your holy temple in reverential awe of You.

Psalm 13:5:

But I have trusted in your faithful love; my heart will rejoice in Your deliverance.

In all four of these verses, we see the faithfulness of God followed by one word—love. We cannot separate God's faithfulness from His love toward us. They are eternally connected. He is faithful to us because of His great love toward us.

This faithful love leads us, cares for us, draws us to worship, and delivers us. God's love is a constant that does not change, and we can trust it completely. This kind of love may be difficult to grasp because we see few examples like it in this world. Others may be faithful to us as long as we give them what they want or meet certain conditions. God's faithful love, however, is always faithful, always true, and never changes. His faithful love changes us!

What is it you need today? Whether you are in need of guidance, caring compassion, a place to focus your affection, or deliverance from life's struggles, you can count on God's faithful love to meet that need. His faithful love has the power to transform you, and it has been at work doing that very thing since you first came to know Christ. If you don't know Him, know that He still loves you. All you need to do is receive His faithful love and surrender to His call.

Have a blessed day!

Faithful and True

Hebrews 10:23:

Let us hold on to the confession of hope without wavering, for He who promised is faithful.

As long as our hope is firmly planted in Christ, we can expect God to hold true to His promises—He is faithful. Even when we can't see any sign that our hope is being fulfilled, He is still faithful. We must remember that God is always at work behind the scenes of our drama. He will allow us to see what we need to see at just the right time. In the meantime, we can rest in the assurance that if He has promised something, He will be faithful to perform it.

Revelation 19:11

Then I saw heaven opened, and there was a white horse! Its rider is called Faithful and True, and in righteousness He judges and makes war.

When Jesus returns, He will be called Faithful and True. He will judge and make war on this world and conquer over evil through His righteousness. He is faithful to those who are His, and we can count on His provision and His protection. He can never be unfaithful or untrue. After all, He died for you. Would He surely not be completely faithful to the bride for whom He died? Hold on to your confession of hope today, and trust the Faithful One to come through for you!

Have a blessed day!

Great is Thy Faithfulness

Lamentations 3:22-24:

Because of the LORD's faithful love, we do not perish, for His mercies never end. They are new every morning; great is Your faithfulness! I say: The LORD is my portion, therefore I will put my hope in Him.

These verses are so beautiful that Thomas Obediah Chisolm wrote a poem about them in the 1800's. Chisolm sent the poem to William Runyan of Moody Bible Institute, who set the poem to music. Today we know the song as the classic hymn, *Great is Thy Faithfulness.* The written word has ministered to millions through the work of Chilsom and Runyan, who simply expressed their gratitude for God's faithfulness. The verses capture a heart that has come to realize and appreciate the handiwork of God and His faithful love.

Whether we realize it or not, the same faithful love that inspired Jeremiah to write the book of Lamentations and Chisolm and Runyan to write *Great is Thy Faithfulness* flows abundantly toward us today. Because of God's faithful love for us, we do not perish. We are able to complete the purpose to for which He created us. His mercies never end because forgiveness is ours through the blood of Christ. His mercies are new every morning as we wake to realize He has given us another day and is ready and willing to lead us into His blessing.

God does not have to speak to us. Yet, day after day, He nudges us through His Holy Spirit to draw us even closer to Him. He speaks through His Word as we read it daily. He is faithful to us even when we are not faithful to Him.

When we consider how great God's faithful love is toward us, why would we want to trust anything else? Everything else pales in comparison. Nothing else is as trustworthy or as powerful as God's love. To put our hope in Him embraces His love and submits to His authority. What better place to be, and what a privilege we have to be able to trust in such faithfulness!

Don't look at your problems today. Look to God's faithfulness. If hurt, lack, or difficulty knocks on your door, greet them with a chorus of *Great is Thy Faithfulness.* You will serve what you magnify. Choose to minimize your troubles, and magnify God's faithfulness to you. He will continue to be faithful in an even greater way.

Have a blessed day!

God is Faithful

1 Corinthians 1:9:

God is faithful; by Him you were called into fellowship with His Son, Jesus Christ our Lord.

The first three words of this verse give us reason to praise God for all eternity. God is faithful! While there may be times we are not faithful to Him, He is always faithful to us. Our very relationship with Him was not our idea; it was His from the beginning. He called us into fellowship with Christ, and we responded. He knows every weakness and inability we have, yet He is faithful in relationship to us. As Almighty God, He can be nothing less.

God's faithfulness to us does not mean that He grants us every request. Because He is faithful to us, He may deny something that He knows will harm us in the long run. Because He is faithful to our relationship with Christ, He will not allow us to walk in ways that will damage that relationship. Because He is faithful to the calling He has placed in us, He will not tolerate anything that jeopardizes that calling. God's faithfulness is not to satisfy our desire; it is to develop our relationship with Him in Christ.

If it seems like God has failed you in some area, consider how that area affects your relationship with Christ. Know beyond the shadow of a doubt that God is faithful, and work from that premise. Your disappointment is certain to be a blessing in disguise when seen from the right perspective. God cannot and will not fail you! His nature and His purpose don't allow it. If you need a new view, try climbing to the top of that pity party mountain you are hiding behind, and ask God to reveal His faithfulness in that situation to you. Rejoice in His faithfulness to you. You are never more secure than when you are in the center of His perfect will.

Have a blessed day!

God's Faithfulness is a Protective Shield

Psalm 91:4:

He will cover you with His feathers; you will take refuge under His wings. His faithfulness will be a protective shield.

I must have read this verse 100 times, yet it spoke something new to me this time. I usually hear this verse depicted from the perspective of the mother bird providing a refuge for her babies with her wings. This morning, however, the word *faithfulness* speaks.

God is faithful, even when we are not. His faithfulness provides a protective shield for us against all kinds of dangers, especially in the spiritual realm. Just as a structured teacher provides a protective boundary for the students, so God's faithfulness provides a protective boundary for us. The beautiful thing about this is we don't have to do anything for God to be faithful. Faithfulness is a part of His nature—we can count on it.

We can feel secure today because of God's faithfulness to us. He is leading us in a direction for a purpose, and He will see that purpose fulfilled in us. Rejoice that He who began a good work in us will be faithful to complete it (Phil 1:6)!

Have a blessed day!

Always Faithful, Loving, Merciful, and Forgiving

Psalm 103:11-14:

For as high as the heavens are above the earth, so great is His faithful love toward those who fear Him. As far as the east is from the west, so far has He removed our transgressions from us. As a father has compassion on his children, so the LORD has compassion on those who fear Him. For He knows what we are made of, remembering that we are dust.

If anything should make us rejoice, it is in knowing that we serve a loving, faithful, and forgiving God. He will never cease to be faithful to us, even when we have failed Him! He removes our transgressions, meaning that He takes them away from us. When He looks at us, He doesn't see our sin. He sees the righteousness of Christ.

God separates us from our sin. In His eyes, we are not the sin that we commit. That may be difficult for us to comprehend. When someone wrongs us, we may have trouble forgetting the wrong when we see him or her. If a person has a reputation for a particular type of sin, we may be reminded of that sin when we encounter that person. God, however, sees us as an individual. He has removed that sin from our lives, and He sees us through the lens of righteousness in Christ. When He looks at us, He has compassion in His heart for us, knowing full well that we are mere humans created from dust and mired with sin.

Sin does not keep us from the faithfulness of God. He remains faithful because that is His nature. Sin does not keep us from the love of God. He is love—our sin does not change who He is. Our sin does not prevent Him from forgiving. He has already made Christ a sacrifice to remove our transgressions. While we may still reap the consequences of our sin, that does not change our state as His children. We belong to Him, and He will never abandon us, deny us, reject us, or stop loving us. He loves us despite our faults.

Rejoice today, knowing you are loved completely by God. Be assured He will always be faithful, loving, merciful, and forgiving. You do not have to perform to earn His favor or His blessing. You already have it. Enjoy being His beloved child.

Have a blessed day!

Faithfulness that Conquers Unbelief

Romans 3:3-4:

What then? If some did not believe, will their unbelief cancel God's faithfulness? Absolutely not! God must be true, but everyone is a liar, as it us written: That You may be justified in Your words and triumph when You judge.

How comforting and humbling it is to know that God's faithfulness surpasses my unbelief! He does not rely upon my belief to be faithful to me. Hallelujah! In places where I have struggled to believe God for something, He is still faithful to His promises. Just because we don't believe something does not mean it is not true—especially if it comes from God!

If God has said it, we can count it as truth. Let every man be known a liar, but God's words are true! Because of His faithfulness, He is a just, righteous, and triumphant judge. We can count on God to do what He says He will do!

The Bible is filled with promises from God. When we pray those promises, we can count on God to be true to His word. Make a practice of praying Scripture daily. When you do, you will not only see those promises fulfilled, you will recognize where God has filled them in the past. His faithfulness is woven throughout Scripture, and it will come to life for you as you begin to speak it out loud in prayer. His word, when spoken, has power! Speak the good things of God's Word into your life, and don't let the Devil's negative thoughts dominate in your attitude. Give allegiance to God when you speak. He is always faithful—even when you struggle to believe Him.

Have a blessed day!

Good and Faithful

Psalm 118:1:

Give thanks to the LORD, for He is good; His faithful love endures forever.

When things go wrong, we can count on the goodness of God. Goodness is His nature. In everything, He will be good to us. He cannot be anything else. He draws us near to Him just so He can lavish the goodness of His nature upon us.

I'm so thankful for God's faithful love to me. Even when I'm not faithful, He is still faithful to me. He keeps His Word, and we can count on Him to love us through our darkest failures. He is always good and always faithful.

God's faithful love endures forever. The Hebrew word for endure here is *amad* which means *to stand*. God is not shaken or moved by our tragedies or our failures. He stands firm in His love for us. When He doesn't let us have our way at times, He sees the beginning from the end and is only preventing our own self-destruction. The hurt He allows in our lives serves to increase our faith and make us dependent upon Him so He can be strong in the midst of our weakness, where His glory is revealed.

Rejection and disappointment are facts of life. We will face them at some point. When we do, we often question God's goodness and His love for us. If God truly loves us, how could He let such a hurtful thing happen to us? These are the times we must trust. Because God is good and His love endures forever, He will use even our heartaches to bless us and shine with His glory. He works good into those hard places and loves us through them. Rejection is direction; it tells us to go another way. Disappointment indicates disillusion—something is not as we thought it would be.

Wherever you are hurting today, know that God loves you. His plans for you are good, and He is lovingly drawing you back into His purpose. You can always trust His goodness and His love for you. His love will always stand for you, and nothing can separate you from that love. Give thanks to the LORD for His good and faithful love toward you.

Have a blessed day!

He Who Calls You is Faithful

1 Thessalonians 5:24:

He who calls you is faithful, who also will do it.

What has God called you to do? You can count on Him to be faithful to you as you walk forth in obedience to His call. Too many of us get into trouble when we try to do something God has not called us to do. We must learn to say, "No," to those things and "Yes" to the things we know He has called us to do.

I know this lesson well because I've taken the test so many times I've learned the right answers simply by getting them wrong previously! God has called me to teach, and when I do, He flows through me faithfully, as He has promised. Many people try to pin the gift of administration on me, but I stink at it! Every time I try to move in this area, I need help to dig me out of a mess.

God has first called us to Himself through Christ. He is faithful to that relationship and to help us grow in Christ. God also works through the family unit. Wherever He has placed you within the family unit, He is faithful to you in that role. If you are a wife, He is faithful as you submit to your husband and carry out your obligations as a wife. If you are a widow, He is faithful to lead you and sustain you in that journey. If you are a mother, He is faithful to guide you as you raise your children. If you try to abandon the role where He has placed you, His faithfulness reveals itself in drawing you back to the place where you should be. He who calls you is faithful to the place where He has called you.

Finally, God has given every believer a special gift to serve Him. He is faithful to that gift, whether you serve in the church or in the culture to lead others to Christ. He will do what He has planned to do in you. God has an investment in you. He paid a huge price for you through the blood of His Son. He never lets anyone go to waste. We waste our time and resources chasing things that we were never meant to chase. Find the place where God has called you, and trust His faithfulness to help you serve in that area. Watch to see how He will bless and flourish you. He who calls you is faithful!

Have a blessed day!

Our Faithful Creator

1 Peter 4:19:

So those who suffer according to God's will should, in doing good, entrust themselves to a faithful Creator.

There will be times in this life when we will suffer from doing what is right. Someone may receive a promotion from deceitful means that should have rightfully been ours. Someone of poor character may receive the very blessing for which we prayed. Someone we considered to be a friend may deliberately hurt us or betray us. Some may outright ridicule us for our faith or badger us for a stand we take based upon our belief in God's Word. At these times, we are to trust our faithful Creator.

God is recognized here as the faithful Creator to remind us that He made us with a purpose in mind. We can count on God to be faithful to equip us, sustain us, and bless us according to that purpose. If a certain promotion was not in His plan for us, we must trust that He has something better in mind that will work in our lives according to His plan. When we see others manipulate a blessing who clearly do not deserve to be blessed, we must realize that God is not withholding any good and perfect gift from us. What we thought was a blessing just might not be the good or perfect thing we thought it was! When God blesses, He adds no trouble to it. Some *blessings* come packed with trouble. They are delivered via STS: Satan's Temptation Service! Such blessings are a trap that will divert us from God's perfect plan for us. Trust Him when we see these things happening.

Whatever void or lack you are facing today, trust your faithful Creator to provide for you in that area. If your suffering is a part of His will for you, He will use that suffering for His glory and your benefit in some way. The greater the suffering, the greater the glory! He who called you to this situation or place in life is faithful! Trust your faithful Creator to shine His purpose in you.

Have a blessed day!

Yahweh: The Faithful God

Deuteronomy 7:9:

Know that Yahweh your God is God, the faithful God who keeps His gracious covenant loyalty for a thousand generations with those who love Him and keep His commands.

The God we serve is greater than our imaginations can fathom! We can count on Him to keep His promises and His covenant of grace toward us! Scripture is full of promises and provisions for widows. In both the Old Testament and the New Testament, we see how God provides and cares for the widow. He also judges those who treat her unfairly. While the widow is a symbol of humility because of her lowly state, God treats her with esteem and honor. He is faithful to every word, and He waits to see if we will believe Him.

Wherever God has called you to walk, He is faithful to equip you to walk. He does not leave you to walk alone. Not only will He walk beside you, He will send others your way to walk with you. He will never send you out on a limb and abandon you! If He has made a promise to you, count on Him to deliver! He is faithful!

Understand that you may waver in your faith, but God doesn't. His faithfulness to us does not depend upon our faith. Where we are strong in our faith, He is faithful. Where we are weak in our faith, He is faithful. His strength is made perfect in our weakness, according to 2 Corinthians 12:9. His faithfulness enables our faith to grow and to see the fulfillment of His promises!

Wherever your faith seems weak today, rest in God's faithfulness. He can be nothing but faithful because that is His nature. Trust every care to Him, look for His promises, and know that He is working all things together for your good (Rom. 8:28). He is God, and He is faithful.

Have a blessed day!

If You Are Willing

Mark 1:40-42:

Then a man with a serious skin disease came to Him and, on his knees, begged Him: "If You are willing, You can make me clean." Moved with compassion, Jesus reached out His hand and touched him. "I am willing," He told him. "Be made clean." Immediately the disease left him, and he was healed.

This leper was desperate as he approached Jesus. He was an outcast from society, and he was forbidden to touch anyone. When people came near, he was to cry, "Unclean, unclean," so others would know to stay away from him. Imagine the rejection and hatred he must have felt from the world. He must have felt cursed and completely alone.

God did not intend for us to live in isolation. We were created for relationship and fellowship with one another. Lepers were doomed to live lives of solitude as their skin rotted away. This leper knew Jesus had the power to save him, but would He? Would Jesus even consider a person as lowly as he was? No other human being had the power to help him, and he certainly couldn't help himself. If he were to have any hope of healing or happiness again, it would have to be an act of grace to rescue him.

Perhaps, this is why he came to Jesus on his knees. He bowed to him asking for mercy. While his faith had been stripped to the bone, there was still one little glimmer of hope that survived long enough to beg for mercy.

Jesus was moved with compassion. He did not try to distance Himself from the man. Many people today distance themselves from those who are hurting. Seeing someone's pain makes them uncomfortable. They would rather ignore it and hope the person just goes away. Jesus, however, faced him and dared to touch him. His desire was for the man to be made whole and to have an abundant life again. He was willing for this leper to be made whole, and His will for us as well is to be made whole.

We all know Jesus has the power to heal, to restore, to prosper, and to fulfill. We may even have seen Him do this for others. But will He do it for us? That was the question this man had.

This man was desperate enough to come out of hiding and to bow before Jesus for mercy. Had he never asked Jesus or been willing to approach Him, he would have died isolated, lonely, and forsaken. One glimmer of hope in the Jesus's power gave him the courage to submit himself to the Master.

Whatever need you may have today, Jesus is willing for you to be made whole. Be willing to bow before Him in complete submission and ask for His mercy. He is moved with compassion over the things that hurt you. One touch of His hand can change everything! Seek His touch today for whatever need you may have. He came that we might have life and have it more abundantly. Be willing to boldly ask for that abundance. He is willing to do it for you.

Have a blessed day!

Just Keep Asking

Matthew 7:7-8:

Keep asking, and it will be given to you. Keep searching, and you will find. Keep knocking, and the door will be opened to you. For everyone who asks receives, and the one who searches finds, and to the one who knocks, the door will be opened.

When read in this translation, these verses tell us to not give up. We have to ask until we receive an answer, search until we find, and knock until a door is opened. If we have nothing, we are to keep praying. I can't help but wonder how many devoted Christians give up before the answer comes. I've certainly been guilty.

There are some things God reveals only to those who are willing to seek. God does not reveal all of Himself to everyone. He waits to see who will come after Him. Those who are truly hungry and are willing to go deeper in His Word will discover much more of His nature than those who are content to learn of Him only on Sunday morning through the pastor.

This is another reason why God sends change. If we are comfortable, we have no need to seek Him further. Change alters our comfort level so that we are willing to cry out to Him and seek an answer. Through the seeking, we learn more about our heavenly Father and draw closer in relationship with Him.

Today, if you still have no answer to a prayer you've presented to God, consider it an invitation to draw closer to Him. Continue to ask, seek, and knock. Listen to the things He may show you in the process. Hope is a necessity. It is okay to hope for something good to happen. In fact, we should hope and wait in expectation for God to answer. We should look for even a glimmer of His presence in every situation to see where He might be at work.

If you are encountering change, it is another opportunity to draw closer to God. Ask, seek, and knock until you find what you need, then rejoice as the woman who cleaned her whole house to find her lost coin did (Luke 15:8-9). When she found that lost coin, she received a double blessing. She had her coin back, and her house was clean! I would rejoice at that!

Have a blessed day!

How Great is Our God

2 Chronicles 6:18:

But will God indeed live on earth with man? Even heaven, the highest heaven, cannot contain You, much less this temple I have built.

Solomon prayed this in his prayer of dedication for the temple he built for God. While this temple is still considered to be the most splendorous of all temples on earth, Solomon knew that it could not contain the entire glory of God. Our minds can simply just not imagine the greatness of our God.

Perhaps, Solomon knew that his temple was made of earthy things that could be destroyed, as this temple eventually was when Babylon invaded it. God's glory and majesty are eternal, and no earthly temple can properly display His greatness. According to Solomon's wisdom, not even heaven can contain our God. Why on earth would we want to settle for worshiping another god? The God of all creation loves us, sent His only Son to die for us so we might have relationship with Him, and wants the very best for us. If we belong to Him, He is currently working all things together for our good. If He is as great as Solomon describes Him to be, why do we not expect more of Him?

How great is your God today? Have faith to believe He is greater than any negative situation you face. If the highest heaven cannot contain Him, your little situation certainly can't restrict Him!

Concentrate on His greatness, even though your mind cannot fully comprehend it. Worship Him today for the glory and the majesty which belongs only to Him. You belong to Him, and He loves you more than you can possibly imagine. Begin to see your problems dissipate as you behold His greatness!

Have a blessed day!

Before You Call

Isaiah 65:24:

Even before they call, I will answer; while they are still speaking, I will hear.

God knows exactly what we need long before we pray for it. In fact, He often brings us to situations that lead us to pray for exactly the thing He is trying to give us. We often have to first realize our need for it. Otherwise, we will not appreciate it as we should.

God also knows the emptiness of our hearts and how we long to be filled. Before we cry out to Him, we often try to fill that void with other things. God is ready to answer the heart that cries out to Him. Many times, He is just waiting for us to pray so He can answer.

Does it seem like God is waiting a long time to answer your prayer? Perhaps, He is waiting for you. Have you voiced your concern to God? Have you completely surrendered to His will, or are you still imposing your own conditions? Are you looking for the answer to appear in a particular form? Perhaps, God has already given you the answer, but you haven't recognized it. Ask God to open your eyes to His full provision. He is not a genie in a bottle or lamp waiting to grant you three wishes. He is your heavenly Father who is molding you into the likeness of His Son. Submit to His majesty, and watch to see how He has already been answering your prayers.

Have a blessed day!

Scandalous Faith

1 Corinthians 1:23:

... but we preach Christ crucified, a stumbling block to the Jews and foolishness to the Gentiles.

The Greek word for stumbling block is *skandalon*, from which we derive the word *scandal*. A scandal brings public disgrace and vicious gossip. The

Jews saw Jesus as a stumbling block, a scandal that would bring them disgrace. Therefore, they made Him a *skandalon* by crucifying Him. The disgrace they brought to Him ultimately came right back to them when He rose from the dead, proving to be who He said He was!

One of the Greek meanings of the word *skandalon* greatly impresses me— *the movable stick or trigger of a trap.* This reminds me of how we use bait to catch an animal. How many of you have ever felt like you had a carrot placed in front of you, only to have it jerked away and leaving you in a place where you felt trapped or disappointed? The Devil is a master at using such a trap. He wants to lure you away from your purpose and disappoint you so you will lose faith in Christ. If you fall into the trap of placing your faith in anything other than Christ, Himself, you will find this carrot jerked away from you. Furthermore, you will find yourself disgraced! You cannot place your faith in what you want God to do for you. Your faith must be in Him, or you will be hurt by the real *skandalon*. God will allow you to be tested by this so your faith will prove genuine. If you survive the *skandalon*, you have great faith! You have a faith that pleases God. Watch out for a wave of His power to flow.

The Jews saw Jesus as a *skandalon* because they were serving the god of self-righteousness. Pride is the offspring of self-righteousness. Pride will always lead you to a place of disgrace, but humility will land you in a position of grace. If you ever feel a carrot has been jerked out from under you, turn your eyes completely to Jesus. Surrender to Him in the situation. This is the expression of true faith.

Have a blessed day!

Power for Persistent Women

If you want something badly enough, you will do whatever it takes to get it. When we give up easily, it usually means we didn't really want that thing. This explains why we work harder at some jobs than others and why we work harder at some relationships than others. There are those we want badly, and we will do whatever necessary to obtain it or to keep it alive. Others, we will let go and spend our energy on things more pressing or desirable.

If God has placed a desire in your heart, He will give you the longing to see it to fulfillment. You may, however, have to press through in prayer to ever see it materialize. If God has given the desire, you can't let it go with any satisfaction. You will be compelled to keep asking, keep seeking, and keep knocking.

Hebrews 11:6:

Now without faith it is impossible to please God, for the one who draws near to Him must believe that He exists and rewards those who seek Him.

This has been one of the Scriptures I have held closely since my husband's death. Since I believe in God, I must also believe in His Word—that He rewards me when I pray diligently over a matter. I know He exists. I must also know in my heart that He will answer.

James 1:6-8:

But let him ask in faith without doubting. For the doubter is like the surging sea, driven and tossed by the wind. That person should not expect to receive anything from the Lord. An indecisive man is unstable in all his ways.

God convicted me of always expecting the worst—from myself, from my child, and from God. He showed me that He always gives me His best, and I should expect nothing less. We should expect His best when we pray. If we expect the worst, we are like that doubter who is unstable in all his ways.

Let's expect the best from God. That is exactly what He did when He sent Jesus into the world. He gave us nothing less than His only Son—perfect and sinless in every way. Our best may be as filthy rags in His sight, but He does not give us filthy rags in return. He gives us grace through His Son. His grace is perfect and sufficient for all our needs, our longings, and our desires. May we all press through in prayer until he moves in our lives with the very best from His riches in glory through grace in Christ Jesus. Amen, Amen!

Have a blessed day!

From Promise to Fulfillment

Isaiah 48:3:

I declared the past events long ago; they came out of My mouth; I proclaimed them. Suddenly I acted, and they occurred.

Has God ever given you a promise then waited a while before it came to pass? He often does this with me. It seems he chooses to wait a LONG time for some of them, too! Rest assured that if God has proclaimed it, He will surely act upon it!

God often tells us of things that will happen before they do. He promised through His prophets that Jesus would be born. There are 400 plus years between the Old Testament and New Testament to prove that He doesn't get in a hurry to bring about what He has declared.

Isaiah 48:4-5:

Because I know that you are stubborn, and your neck is iron and your forehead bronze, therefore I declared to you long ago; I announced it to you before it occurred, so you could not claim: My idol caused them; my carved image and cast idol control them.

In this passage, God is speaking to Israel. Notice how He describes them. They are stubborn with a neck as iron and a forehead as bronze. He then continues to let Israel know they could never attribute His works to that of an idol. The idol is Israel, herself. When God gives us a promise and waits for its fulfillment, He is letting us know that it is something we can never do in our own strength. As hard as we may try, it will not come to pass by our own means. We can never take credit for it. The idol portrayed here is the idol of self. His promises are designed to wean us from self-sufficiency.

Isaiah 48:10-11:

Look, I have refined you, but not as silver; I have tested you in the furnace of affliction. I will act for My own sake, indeed My own, for how can I be defiled? I will not give My glory to another.

The time between a promise and fulfillment often involves testing. We may even feel like we've failed the test. That is simply God bringing our impurities to the surface so they can leave. Once we see all the ugliness, weakness, and frailty within ourselves, we realize we could never earn or take glory for what God wants to do in our lives. God fulfills His promise to us so that He may be glorified and His work in us revealed. When He fulfills a promise, He, alone, is glorified.

If you are still waiting for a promise to be fulfilled, the best thing you can do is to submit to the process. Allow all the impurities in your life to surface, and don't even try to do things yourself to hurry it along! Abraham made this mistake, and it cost him. Mistakes will cost you, too. The best thing you can do is to submit and rest, knowing that God will perform that which He has promised. Give Him the glory and the honor today by proclaiming your victory in faith as praise to Him.

Have a blessed day!

Waiting Expectantly

Luke 3:15:

Now the people were waiting expectantly and all of them were debating in their minds whether John might be the Messiah.

The chief priests and elders did not follow John in baptism. They saw no need for repentance. They were in a position of control within the temple, and they assumed God was pleased with things because it pleased them to be in control. We make a grave mistake in missing God when we think that what pleases us must please God. We are not one and the same. He is holy; we are not. He is sovereign; we are not. He is the Creator; we are the creature. We are made in His image; He is not made in ours. To find what pleases Him, we must seek Him.

Those who followed John and heard his call for repentance were those who were expecting Messiah to come. They had heard of the promise since childhood and dared to believe they might actually experience it in their lifetimes. The religious leaders were not expecting Him. They did not trust God's promise, and they sought to control things in a way that made them comfortable.

When we fail to relinquish control to God, we don't trust Him. We may be afraid of being disappointed again, or we may not trust that God has our best interest at heart. We believe that if we are going to be happy, we must be in control to make sure things go well for us.

Secondly, those who waited expectantly received revelation. They wondered if John might be the Messiah. He pointed them in the right direction in **verses 16-17: John answered them all, "I baptize you with water, but One is coming who is more powerful than I. I am not worthy to untie the strap of His sandals. He will baptize you with the Holy Spirit and fire. His winnowing shovel is in His hand to clear His threshing floor and gather the heat into His barn, but the chaff He will burn up with fire that never goes out."**

While John was not the Messiah, he prepared them to recognize the One who was coming. Those who were not expecting the Messiah to appear never recognized Him. They killed Him!

If we are not waiting expectantly for God to move in our lives, we will kill what He has for us by trying to maintain control. We will not be able to recognize the promise being fulfilled in front of us because it will threaten our reign. What threatens us or challenges us is often God's promise being fulfilled. Will we recognize it and embrace it, or will we resent it and treat it with indignation? The answer may very well depend upon whether or not we are waiting expectantly for God to move, looking for even a glimmer of His presence in everything we encounter.

Today, I dare you to wait expectantly for God to act upon the things for which you have been praying. Look for His answer in everything you encounter. As you do, you will find His presence to lead you in the direction you need to go.

Have a blessed day!

Integrity to Wait

Psalm 25:21:

May integrity and what is right watch over me, for I wait for You.

During seasons of testing, the Devil will approach us with the very thing we desire. All we have to do is bow to him or cooperate with him to get it. This often includes compromising our integrity or doing something we clearly know is wrong. We may get what we want, but our respect and effectiveness for ministry are damaged.

Integrity and doing what we know is right work as safeguards to protect us. Guilt and condemnation cannot harm us when we have maintained integrity and respect. God's ultimate provision is much better than the Devil's quick and convenient compromise. When we give in to his temptations, we are always settling for less than the best God has for us and less than what our hearts truly desire.

The Devil's provision for you will bite in the long run. Like a vicious viper, it will leave you injured and damaged. It can even kill your ministry altogether.

Waiting for God to move is always your safest and best solution, even if the wait seems unbearable. As 2 Corinthians 2:9 declares, His grace is sufficient for us in these times because His strength is made perfect in our weakness. Wait for God's hand to move on your behalf. When He answers a prayer, glory and honor come with it.

Have a blessed day!

Waiting Quietly

Lamentations 3:22-26:

Because of the LORD's faithful love, we do not perish, for His mercies never end. They are new every morning; great is Your faithfulness! I say: The LORD is my portion, therefore I will put my hope in Him. The LORD is good to those who wait for Him, to the person who seeks Him. It is good to wait quietly for deliverance from the LORD.

Waiting requires patience. Waiting requires trust. Waiting puts faith into action. Taking our hands off a matter and allowing God to work symbolizes our trust in Him as the authority over the matter. It gives Him the responsibility for the outcome.

One basic principle of management deals with the whole issue of authority and responsibility: He who has the authority also has the responsibility. The two go hand-in-hand; you cannot have one without the other. Whoever has authority in a matter must be responsible for the result. You cannot give someone a responsibility without the authority to carry it out. That is what we try to do to God many times. We want Him to be responsible for our deliverances, but we want to be in charge of how, when, and where it happens. Failure to properly delegate is a sure sign a plan will fail altogether!

According to these verses in Lamentations, God acts on our behalf out of His great love for us. We can trust Him to act in our best interest. We fail Him miserably, but He has new mercies for us every day. All we have to do is simply lay our burdens before Him. He understands our weaknesses, and He is faithful to us, regardless. His nature is to be faithful, even when we are not.

We can place our hope in Him because He has the power to save. Whatever need may lie before us, He has the ability to answer. He has the power to fulfill, and He desires to do so. With Him, we have hope. He is good to those who wait for Him, and He wants us to seek Him. He wants us to want Him first. Then, all the other things we need will fall into place.

The last verse tells us it is good to wait quietly for deliverance from the LORD. If we worry and are in a panic, we are not waiting quietly. If we grumble and complain, we are not waiting quietly. If we are trying to manipulate things by our own means, we are not waiting quietly. We must settle the matter in our own minds that He is in charge, and He is handling the situation. We must relinquish control of our emotions to Him. This will enable us to wait quietly.

Something amazing happens when we fully surrender: it brings God to move. Once He has full authority, He is then responsible for us. If we don't have the authority, there is nothing we can do. If we have truly submitted to His authority, He is the only one who has the power to make a difference in our lives. This is the power of the surrendered life!

Wait quietly before the LORD today. Surrender to Him, and place your hope in Him. His mercies are new every morning. He is good to those who wait for Him and seek Him. May God be good to us today!

Have a blessed day!

As Long as It Takes for These Things

Hebrews 6:13-15:

For when God made a promise to Abraham, since He had no one greater to swear by, He swore by Himself: I will most certainly bless you, and I will greatly multiply you. And so, after waiting patiently, Abraham obtained the promise.

In the Old Testament, a covenant was established between a greater person and a weaker beneficiary. The greater party made the oath that bound the covenant by swearing by an even greater party to make the covenant trustworthy. Since God had no greater authority, He swore by Himself, promising to bless and multiply Abraham. Unless He honored this covenant, He could not be trusted.

His promise was to bless Abraham and to greatly multiply him. This must have seemed overwhelming to a couple who was unable to have children and longed for an heir. To have such a covenant and promise certainly changed their lives and direction. Abraham had already learned he could do nothing to change his situation or his longing. What God promised, He would do in Abraham's life.

The last sentence is where I always become frustrated. After waiting patiently, Abraham obtained the promise. Just how long do we have to wait? I've learned the answer is as long as it takes. As long as it takes for God to do whatever He intends to do in you and through you is as long as you will have to wait. As long as it takes for you to be in the right place at the right time for God to be glorified is your answer.

Abraham's promise took 25 years just to see the first fruits appear when Isaac was born. Why did it take so long? During our wait, we come to seek the Giver, rather than the gift. We come to rely upon His presence and to depend upon His goodness. Abraham surely waited in expectancy month after month, year after year, wondering if God would ever fulfill His promise. At some point, he must have stopped looking for the gift and rested in the Giver, knowing with full assurance that He who swore by Himself had the power to deliver.

Luke 12:31 tells us to seek His kingdom, and these things will be provided for us. Abraham's longing was one of these things. Whatever longing may consume our hearts is one of these things. By seeking His kingdom first, these things become ours. What we must remember is that the greatest thing in His kingdom is God Himself. When He becomes the most important thing in our lives and in our hearts, He freely gives us these things.

The truth is that God is still greatly multiplying Abraham, so the blessing continues. When God makes a promise, He delivers beyond our wildest imaginations! Don't lose hope in the God who has promised to bless you and greatly multiply you. Simply seek the Giver, rather than the gift, and watch these things happen in your life.

Have a blessed day!

The Beauty of Patience

Psalm 40:1-3:

I waited patiently for the LORD, and He turned to me and heard my cry for help. He brought me up from a desolate pit, out of the muddy clay, and set my feet on a rock, making my steps secure. He put a new song in my mouth, a hymn of praise to our God. Many will see and fear, and put their trust in the LORD.

We all long for God to do the things these verses describe. I know I've often needed God to bring me out of a pit and make my steps secure upon a rock. Notice, however, that these things came to David after he waited patiently for the LORD. The blessings David described here came as a process and had purpose. God's delays are designed to bring Him glory.

We may be tired and weary of waiting, but delay does not mean denial. God always makes the answer worth the wait. There are times when God chooses to display His glory in us. When this happens, the world will see how helpless we were in our own ability and how powerful God is in bringing the answer. Many will see our situation and put their trust in God. He will use our longings and empty places to bring glory to His name and to draw others to Christ through us. We must trust and submit to His purpose.

If I have to endure hardships and trials, I want them to be worth something. If I have to wait, I want the blessing that is worth the wait. I know you do, too. Determine today to wait patiently for the LORD and to encourage yourself in His Word while you wait. Whatever He is up to in our lives is too beautiful to miss!

Have a blessed day!

The One Who Waits for Him

Isaiah 64:4:

From ancient times no one has heard, no one has listened, no eye has seen any God except You, who acts on behalf of the one who waits for Him.

There is only one God who acts on behalf of His children, and it is the living God we serve! It is the God of Abraham, Isaac, and Jacob. It is the God who raised Jesus, His only begotten Son, from the dead. He is the LORD, the LORD who protects, the LORD who heals, and He still acts on behalf of those who wait for Him.

If you wait for someone, you believe that person is coming. You have faith he or she will be there soon. If you doubt the person is really coming, you will leave to go your own way or about your own business. God acts on behalf of those who wait for Him and do not turn away to do things for themselves. He is looking for those who will not go one step further until they know His presence is with them. If you are going to see God move in your life, you must wait for Him, knowing He is working on your behalf. Believe He will do what He says He will do!

We all have a need to see God move in our lives. Stress is a sure sign we are not sure He is coming, and we are beginning to take responsibility upon ourselves. We cannot control everything, and we must depend upon *Jehovah Jireh* (The LORD who Provides), *Jehovah Rapha* (The LORD who Heals), *Jehovah Nissi* (The LORD who Protects), and *Jehovah Shalom* (The LORD who Gives Peace). We must remember that He is also *Jehovah Shammah* (The Lord who Hears), meaning He is there with us in the midst of every situation we face! Waiting for Him does not mean He is absent.

We wait to see the results of His work in our lives and for Him to reveal Himself to us in a whole new way.

Rest assured today that God is with you. He is working on your behalf, and He desires for you to know Him more fully. Wait for a revelation of Him, and do not take matters into your own hands. He acts on behalf of the one who waits for Him.

Have a blessed day!

At the Appointed Time

Habakkuk 2:2-4:

The LORD answered me: Write down this vision; clearly inscribe it on tablets so one may easily read it. For the vision is yet for the appointed time; it testifies about the end and will not lie. Though it delays, wait for it, since it will certainly come and not be late. Look, his ego is inflated; he is without integrity. But the righteous one will live by his faith.

Rest assured that God sees your distress, and He hears your cry. While it may seem there is no foreseeable way out of your difficulty, God has appointed an end to your misery. There are just times when we have to endure until that appointed time comes. According to this passage, the end is worth the wait.

The last sentence gives us the key to enduring these tough times: we live by faith. Faith is much more than positive thinking. In fact, positive thinking alone will get you nowhere. Faith must have an object. Faith must be rooted in the person of God the Father. As the words of a song illustrate, when you can't see His hand and trust His heart.

God appointed our seasons of suffering for a purpose. That is exactly what is happening in the book of Habakkuk. When His purpose is fulfilled, He moves us into a new season, where we are relieved from the suffering and renewed by His blessing, His favor, and His presence.

While God may appoint seasons of suffering, He does not deny us His presence during those times. Those are times we must seek Him in order to survive. They are the times when we may best learn to hear from Him and recognize His footsteps. Indeed, they are the times when we are most open to receive from Him.

Our seasons of suffering prepare us for the blessings that lie ahead. At the appointed time, they will come. We get into trouble when we try to rush it. There is no express delivery with God! Paying extra will just cost you more in the long run!

Have a blessed day!

Your Appointed Time

Psalm 102:13-14:

You will arise and have compassion on Zion, for it is time to show favor to her—the appointed time has come. For Your servants take delight in its stones and favor its dust.

This Psalm depicts a time when Jerusalem lay in waste. Her enemies had invaded, ransacked her beautiful dwelling, and ridiculed and mocked her in the process. She was left to deal with the ruins of a sinful past. God's servants in Jerusalem recognized that it was still a holy place, and they loved even the stones left from the rubble of a once glorious city. They favored the dust that remained from a place that once reflected the blessing and the glory of God.

In many ways, these faithful servants resemble the woman that was willing to wait for the crumbs that fell from the Master's table in Matthew 15:27-28. This Canaanite woman realized she was not a Jew and was not entitled to any favor from the God of the Jews. Yet, she knew He had the power to save her demon-possessed daughter, and she was willing to beg for crumbs of that power, if needed, for her daughter to be saved. He was her only hope. These servants knew God once favored their city, and He might, perhaps, favor her again. If God once favored their stones of rubble and its dust to make it a glorious city for Himself, perhaps, He would once again look upon them with favor and do the same.

Have you ever felt like all you have are stones and dust? Perhaps, every dream you had has crumbled before you. Maybe you have been ransacked by the enemy and are paying dire consequences for sin. Your loss has been so devastating that you don't know how to dream anymore. Don't forsake the holy things of God. Don't dismiss the small things while waiting for bigger things. A stone, a speck of dust, or a crumb may seem insignificant, but your love for even the slightest touch of God's favor reveals your faith. Look for traces of Him in everything you do. If you hunger for even a glimpse of His glory, He will arise to show His favor toward you. This is your appointed time!

Have a blessed day!

Waiting for Your Red Carpet Moment

1 Samuel 18:28-30:

Saul realized that the LORD was with David and that his daughter Michal loved him, and he became even more afraid of David. As a result, Saul was David's enemy from then on. Every time the Philistine commanders came out to fight, David was more successful than all of Saul's officers. So his name became very famous.

God gave David what Saul wanted: success and fame. Perhaps, that is because David gave God what He wanted: obedience. David had a heart that was loyal to God. Saul was loyal to himself. In the past, Saul had partially carried out God's commands in battle. When tempted or pressed to the limit of his abilities, however, Saul chose to please self over God.

Saul feared the Philistines would overtake him because his army deserted him, and he offered the burnt sacrifices that only the priest was allowed to make. He tried to force the hand of God to grant him favor. Instead, he angered God, and God permanently withdrew his favor from Saul (1 Sam. 13).

God told Saul to completely destroy the Amalekites and all their belongings. While Saul destroyed the people, he allowed his troops to convince him to keep some of their possessions. Saul justified this by agreeing to sacrifice a part of it to the LORD. This is like a thief justifying a bank robbery by tithing on his stolen goods! God does not care about the sacrifice. What He desires is complete obedience (1 Sam. 15).

Saul tried several times to place David in harm's way of the Philistines. That way, he would get their natural enemy to do his dirty work for him. God, however, gave David victory every time. When Saul saw that God was with David, he went after David himself. This forced David to live on the run, hiding in caves. What a discouraging time for someone who already had been anointed to be king!

There are times when God desires to do a work, but the Devil doesn't want to see that work happen. He desires the glory of it for himself. He will try to eliminate us from the picture altogether. God, however, will allow evil to come into full force then turn it over to its own devices. Remember that Saul fell on his own sword (1 Sam. 31).

If God has given you a desire or a vision, rest assured that He will bring it to pass. God's will is a threat to the enemy, who wants the glory all for himself. You may have to hide and lay low for a while before you see God's promise manifest before you. Don't be discouraged. Continue to obey God completely. When His favor rests upon you, you can expect there will be others who won't like it and seek to limit you or destroy you altogether. God will let their own schemes devour them. The enemy's schemes ultimately create a red carpet for you to walk straight to your throne.

Be encouraged today. Where God's favor exists, His protection and promise are secure. Your wait only allows evil to destroy itself. That is surely something worth waiting for!

Have a blessed day!

Why Do I Wait?

Psalm 39:7:

Now, LORD, what do I wait for? My hope is in You!

Has an answer to prayer ever just seemed to linger? Have you ever had to wait for God to move and really not know just what you wanted to happen? That seems to describe my life right now. My hope is that God will move in certain areas, but I really don't know what that would mean. I only know I need Him to move.

David wrote this Psalm describing the fleeting nature of life. He described himself as a foreigner and a sojourner in verse 12. David realized this was not his real home. He longed for happiness in this life before he died. If he had to stay here for a certain length of time, he merely asked to be cheered until he reached his heavenly home.

David didn't know what life would bring him or what challenges he still had to face. He simply resolved to put his hope in the LORD. We should do the same. We all know life can change suddenly. If we are hoping in anything other than Christ, we will be disappointed.

Let's not forget the meaning of the word *hope* either. It means the eager expectation of good. We can eagerly expect God to be good to us in this life.

Acts 17:28:

For in Him we live and move and exist, as even some of your own poets have said, "For we are also His offspring."

Greek poets recognized the followers of Christ as God's offspring. We are made God's offspring through Jesus Christ. He guides our lives with His very hand. He governs our entire existence. He is at work in our lives, even when we can't see it. He has not forgotten us nor forsaken us. We can eagerly expect Him to be good to us and to work all things together for our good.

What are you waiting for today? You are waiting for God to show His goodness to you in an unexpected way. This is what it means to have hope in Him. We are His beloved children in Christ. He longs to be good to us. We can count on it.

Have a blessed day!

Work or Wait?

James 2:26:

For just as the body without the spirit is dead, so also faith without works is dead.

Clearly, you must act on the things God has told you to do. When you see a need in front of you and have the ability to meet that need, you are called to do it. There are times we are called to do more than just pray. God may be using us to meet someone else's need.

James 5:7-10:

Therefore, brothers, be patient until the Lord's coming. See how the farmer waits for the precious fruit of the earth and is patient with it until it receives the early and the late rains. You also must be patient. Strengthen your hearts, because the Lord's coming is near. Brothers, do not complain about one another, so that you will not be judged. Look, the judge stands at the door! Brothers, take the prophets who spoke in the Lord's name as an example of suffering and patience. See, we count as blessed those who have endured. You have heard of Job's endurance and have seen the outcome from the Lord: the Lord is very compassionate and merciful.

This passage instructs us to wait and endure. Only God can give rain, so we must wait for it. Only God can work in a person's heart. We must be patient in our dealings with others. We cannot change them. Where we get into trouble is when we try to do what only God can do. The working of faith is waiting for God to move where only He can instead of taking things into our own hands to create the result we desire. Here, waiting and trusting is a work itself.

We act upon what God has told us to do, trusting Him for the outcome. We don't act in areas where He has authority. We wait patiently for His answer. To know the difference, we need the Holy Spirit living and active on the inside of us.

Have a blessed day!

JUNE 13

As Waters that Cover the Sea

Habakkuk 2:14:

For the earth will be filled with the knowledge of the LORD's glory as the waters cover the sea.

Don't ever let anyone convince you that God is not working in this world or in yours. There may be times when it just seems like injustice is ruling or that evil is winning, but God has promised that knowledge of His glory will fill the earth. God is still at work, and everyone will recognize His handiwork when He is finished.

If you have come to the end of your rope in a situation, it is a good thing. That means God can take the reins. If you have no more strength to try, you can rely upon God's strength to carry you. If your resources are dry, you can depend upon God's resources. God gets the glory when man can take credit for nothing. When man can do absolutely nothing about his hopeless situation and still finds victory, you know God has intervened.

Don't give up hope today. Just put your hope in God. You may not be able to change one thing about your difficulty, but God can do anything. Ask Him for the miracle you need, and give Him praise for the glory He will reveal in the midst of it all. There is more water on this earth than there is land. Knowledge of God's glory will be as the waters that cover the sea—so vast you can't ignore it! Victory rides on the power of complete surrender to Christ. Let knowledge of His glory fill the earth!

Have a blessed day!

Lifted Gates and Open Doors

Psalm 24:7, 9:

Lift up your heads, you gates! Rise up, ancient doors! Then the King of glory will come in.

The most wonderful thing we can encounter in this life is God's glory. We live in a time of such chaos, pain, and destruction that we desperately need to see God's glory revealed in our lives. We need to know that He is alive, active, and intricately working in every aspect of our lives. When He moves in us, we are able to behold His glory and see where He has been using each heartache, hardship, blessing, and gifting all along.

These two verses are identical. The repetition emphasizes the fact that God is saying something very important here that He does not want us to miss. Just what is so important about gates and doors?

Gates and doors are entry points. We open them to give access and close them to deny access. For the King of glory to come into our lives, all of our gates and doors must be open to receive Him.

In these verses, the heads of the gates seem to be looking down. Perhaps, they are loose but still intact enough to keep the gates closed. Ancient doors indicate doors that have been shut for a long time and may take effort to open in human strength. This should make all of us think about places in our lives where we have been closed to receiving the glory of God.

Notice that the gates and doors are commanded to open by themselves. When the glory of God is approaching, it will command gates and doors that have been long closed to open and rise up so He may come in! Where in your life is God making you open to receive from Him?

Perhaps, you've recently seen a door open for you that you never thought would open. Watch for the glory of God. Maybe, you were never open to consider a particular thing because your mind was set on something else, and those dreams fell apart. God just made you open to receive from Him! Watch for His glory. You may be on the verge of experiencing a miracle.

Have a blessed day!

Supply Until Blessing

1 Kings 17:14:

… for this is what the LORD God of Israel says; "The flour jar will not become empty and the oil jug will not run dry until the day the LORD sends rain on the surface of the land."

This verse is from the story of the widow at Zarephath that cared for Elijah during the famine in Israel while he was running from Jezebel. The widow's supplies were about to run out, and she was ready to prepare the last meal so she and her son could die. When she was at the end of her own resources, God sent Elijah to her. She fed him with what she thought was the last of her flour and oil, and her supplies just kept multiplying.

Notice that her flour jar and oil jug were not to run dry until God sent rain to the land. There was a destined time for her own resources to run dry, but they would supply her until God blessed the land again. God cared for her during famine because she obeyed the word given to her by the man of God. She chose to receive His grace, rather than to ignore it.

Receiving God's grace will keep our resources flowing until an appointed time. At that time, we are to walk in His blessing, where an abundance of rain will begin to nourish a dry land. If God has brought you to a famine or a dry place, He will keep your supply going. If, however, He has brought you through a dry spell and is beginning to send rain, you cannot depend upon your former supply. You must embrace the blessing of rain He pours on you.

We need to recognize where we have been and where we are going. God will not leave you in a dry place forever. If He is leading you out, embrace the rain. Don't stay in the comfort zone of your previous supply because it will soon end.

Interestingly, God uses a widow in this story. She has no husband to rely upon. She must hear from God herself. As Psalm 38:5 says, God is a father to the fatherless and a defender or champion of widows. A widow represents humility in Scripture. Here, she was totally dependent upon God for her livelihood. That is right where He wants us to be. During famine, God blessed her supply. During rain, however, God promised to bless her land.

Where are you today? Are you in a dry place where your supplies seem thin, or are you moving into a time of blessing where you are able to be productive? Both require receiving God's grace and giving of yourself to meet the needs of another. What has He given you?

What do you still need? Trusting God during famine enables you to move in faith during a time of blessing. He won't keep you in famine; you are destined to move forward.

Have a blessed day!

God's Wait

Isaiah 30:18:

Therefore the LORD is waiting to show you mercy, and is rising up to show you compassion, for the LORD is a just God. Happy are all who wait patiently for Him.

In this verse, I see two parties waiting. First, God waits to show us mercy. Secondly, happy are those who wait patiently for Him. Could it be that much of our waiting is due to the fact that God is waiting for us?

God waits to show us mercy, favor that we do not deserve. We receive mercy when we turn to God in repentance from a contrite spirit. At this point, He rises to show us compassion, not judgment. The thought of God rising to act on my behalf is awe-inspiring. God moves from a position of rest to a stance of action just to show us compassion in the places where we have hurt. Happy are all who wait patiently for God to move; He does not disappoint a single one of us!

If you are waiting for God to move in your life, check to see if He might be waiting for you to move toward Him. You don't have to be afraid. He will rise with compassion in the very place where you hurt.

Have a blessed day!

Suffering with a Purpose

Isaiah 53:3-4:

He was despised and rejected by men, a man of sorrows and familiar with suffering. Like one from whom men hide their faces he was despised, and we esteemed Him not. Surely He took up our infirmities and carried our sorrows, yet we considered Him stricken by God, smitten by Him and afflicted.

These verses prophesy the suffering Jesus would endure. The amazing thing about that is the fact that He knew it before He came, yet He came anyway. Many of us, if not most of us, would forfeit extreme blessings if we knew the trouble in advance we would have to endure. I'm convinced that is why God doesn't ask our permission on certain things.

Pain and suffering were part of God's plan for Jesus. Why would we think we would be exempt from it if He did not spare His own Son from it? Through our suffering He identifies with us. He knows what it is like to be despised and rejected. He knows what it is like to hurt and to suffer. He can sympathize with our pain because He, too, experienced it. We can trust Him and pour our hearts out to Him because He understands.

Suffering, however, was not the only part of God's plan for Jesus. The world killed Him, but God raised Him from the dead! Another part of God's plan for Christ was to reveal His glory through Him.

Philippians 2:10:

… so at the name of Jesus every knee should bow—of those who are in heaven and on earth—and every tongue should confess that Jesus Christ is Lord to the glory of God the Father.

1 Peter 5:6:

Humble yourselves, therefore, under God's mighty hand, that He may lift you up in due time.

We are to humble ourselves to God in the midst of suffering, and seek His face. We are to learn from Him during those times. He will teach us and mold us, making us into a vessel He can use for His glory. In due time, He will exalt us and display us to the world as something beautiful. A widow is a symbol of humility in Scripture. God wants to make something beautiful of us!

1 Peter 5:6:

And the God of all grace, who called you to His eternal glory in Christ, after you have suffered a little while, will Himself restore you and make you strong, firm and steadfast.

Suffering may be a part of God's plan for your life, but He doesn't plan to keep you there. Suffering alone does not bring Him glory. The greater the suffering, the greater the glory to be revealed! When you look at the suffering you face, realize that as bad as it hurts now, it will be that great when God's glory is revealed in you. You have a huge blessing coming your way. God is not finished with you yet.

Have a blessed day!

Thanking God for Adversity

1 Thessalonians 5:18:

Give thanks in everything, for this is God's will for you in Christ Jesus.

To thank God for the many blessings He has bestowed upon us is easy, but can we really say we can thank God for everything in our lives? Can we honestly thank Him for all the heartaches, trials, hardships, and adversity we face? Most of us just want Him to take those things away. We don't want them at all, let alone actually thank God for them.

Paul witnessed many miracles from God and was used mightily to spread the gospel throughout the world. In fact, He wrote more books of the New Testament than any other person, and I can't think of a greater honor God would bestow on a mere human. We must not forget, however, that Paul also endured extreme hardship, shipwrecks, beatings, imprisonments, thorns, and even execution. He did not live a life of comfort and ease at all. He was victorious over his hardships, and that is what God promises us. To witness His glory and power in our lives, we must face some adversity. This adversity is as much a part of God's will for us as is the promise of victory that comes with each battle we face.

We often long to move in the power of God we see in others, but we don't want the road they have traveled to get it. Our own roads have enough adversity, but with adversity comes the promise of victory that only we who have traveled the road can encounter. We are not qualified or equipped to handle another person's trials. God gives us only what He knows we can handle. He gives us the appropriate victories we can handle, too.

With this, we can truly begin to thank God for our trials. Even if we have not yet seen victory in our situation, we can thank God that His blessing will equal the hardship we've endured. Thank you, Lord: I know I have a HUGE blessing on the way.

Have a blessed day!

The God of Endurance and Encouragement

Romans 15:4-6:

For whatever was written before was written for our instruction, so that through our endurance and through the encouragement of the Scriptures we may have hope. Now may the God of endurance and encouragement grant you agreement with one another, according to Christ Jesus, so that you may glorify the God and Father of our Lord Jesus Christ with a united mind and voice.

To become discouraged when others don't agree with us or criticize us is so easy. Unity is very important in the body of Christ for the Holy Spirit to move and for God to be glorified. Here, Paul instructs us to stay in the Scriptures. What God has to say is more important than what others think. To know what God has to say about us or about any other matter, we must stay in His Word. God's Word gives us hope to endure the opinions of man.

Notice how Paul prayed for the God of endurance and encouragement to grant them agreement with one another. God can grant us the patience we need to deal with others and the encouragement to complete His mission. Indeed, often endurance and encouragement are just what we need to cope with fellow believers!

Often to criticize the leadership of others is so easy. I have a friend who has recently quit a leadership position because of criticism from those close to him. Those who are criticizing want to lead but will soon find themselves with no one following. People will follow those who build others up; they will not follow those who tear others down.

David faced this same situation at Ziklag, and he encouraged himself in the Lord while seeking direction. Men were ready to kill him and criticized his leadership after finding their homes destroyed and families kidnapped. David didn't address his accusers. He went directly to God for answers (1 Sam. 30). When facing criticism, we should do the same.

Today, make it a point to encourage someone you see who is struggling. Criticism is a cheap shot: be a support to someone, rather than a thorn in his or her side. If you are feeling the stings of criticism, go directly to Scripture and seek God on the matter. May the God of endurance and encouragement grant you agreement with one another in Christ Jesus, and may He be glorified.

Have a blessed day!

JUNE 20

A Waiting Audience

Romans 8:19:

For the creation eagerly waits with anticipation for God's sons to be revealed.

We all love to see a movie with a great ending that brings a happy resolution to all of the mishaps of a complicated and intriguing plot. We often watch intensely while trying to predict the end when, suddenly, a twist enters the scene that changes all of the dynamics and heightens our suspense. To leave the movie before the end would only frustrate our minds and leave us longing for answers. In a similar way the world and every created thing waits to see God's glory revealed in His children.

Can you fathom that? The whole world is waiting to see God's glory revealed in you! Everyone is watching to see if there is any sense, rhyme, or reason to the mishaps, failures, and tragedies of life. The difference between the children of God and the rest of the world is in this one twist that entered creation some 2,000 years ago and died on a cross so we might have the relationship with God as sons. That one twist changes the ending for us, but does it change anything else? If it does, all creation longs to see it.

God reveals His glory through His children. If you have not yet seen the glory of God manifested in your situation, surrender it to God, and watch for it. Stop trying to create your own ending. Let God write the final chapter. He created the first with the end in mind. Why do we think we are better writers than He? As Psalm 46:10 instructs, be still and know that He is God. You cannot create your own glory. Whatever you create will stink to high heaven in comparison to the glory that God wants and waits to reveal in you.

You may be anxious to see the ending to your trial. Know that all creation longs to see it, too. You cannot rush perfection. God's glory is worth every second you have to wait. Whether you realize it or not, there is a huge audience cheering you to victory that wants and needs to see God's glory revealed in you. God will not disappoint you or His audience. Let Him show off in your life, and bow before your Maker in gratitude for the glorious things He has planned for you.

Have a blessed day!

Learn to be Content

Philippians 4:11:

I don't say this out of need, for I have learned to be content in whatever circumstances I am.

Paul spoke from true Christian maturity here. For those of us who have lived a while and endured some hardships along the way, we know that circumstances are temporary. Those who lack today may be filled tomorrow, and those who rejoice in the present may experience sorrow in the near future. Change is imminent.

Frustration arises when we try to keep what is meant to be temporary on a permanent basis. We can rarely go back to the way things were. We must make the best of what we face in the present, submit the future to God, and trust Him to carry us through the unpleasant things around us. We cannot live in perpetual ease. If we wait until things are perfect to be happy, we will never be happy.

Notice that Paul learned to be content. This did not come naturally for him. He paid attention to life's lessons and learned the ways of God in his life. He learned from his successes and failures. When you have a close relationship with God, you have everything you need. That relationship will bless you beyond your imagination and sustain you through difficulty. That relationship will open doors you could never open on your own and close doors to dangers you never knew existed. When you know God is on your side and He loves you with an unfailing love, you can rest in any situation, knowing that He is seeing you through it. You can be content in God.

To be content is to rest and not be anxious. We live in very uncertain times, and it can be challenging not to worry over the future. Knowing that God is with you and for you will enable you to face the future with contentment. You may have to let go of some temporary things, but He will establish you in what is permanent: His unfailing love.

Stop trying to figure things out, and learn to be content today. If you can't be happy where you are, you won't be happy where you are going, either. There will always be something that is not perfect, but your God is perfect. Rest in Him, and enjoy life.

Have a blessed day!

Satisfied and Filled

Psalm 107:9:

For He satisfied the thirsty and filled the hungry with good things.

God satisfies. I have been guilty of believing God would meet my need but not really believing He would give me what I truly desired. If that desire is not fully met, however, we are still left hungry to some degree. God wants to satisfy our thirst and fill our hunger with good things, and we can count on Him to do that. He does not want us to settle for less when His power is limitless to meet our every need. We settle when we think God cannot or will not, and we attempt to meet that need on our own.

The word here for satisfied means *filled to satisfaction, having enough or plenty.* God wants to fill us to overflowing while we are just hoping He will meet the minimum requirement. We must remember that He is the one who gives us the thirst and the hunger in the first place. He will give us a hunger for the very thing for which He wants to bless us and use that hunger to draw us to Himself.

Don't be discouraged by your thirst and hunger. Seek God in whatever area you feel you are lacking. He can fill that area with good things if you will let Him, rather than trying to satisfy it on your own. Your best efforts can never satisfy you the way His grace can! He did not let 5,000 men leave hungry when they gathered to hear Him preach on the mount, and He won't let you go away hungry, either!

Have a blessed day!

Be Filled with God's Best

Psalm 81:9-10:

There must not be a strange god among you; you must not bow down to a foreign god. I am Yaweh your God, who brought you up from the land of Egypt. Open your mouth wide, and I will fill it.

Do you trust God to fill your hunger? If we are depending upon anything else or anyone else to fill that void inside us, we are serving a foreign god. God demands His rightful place in our lives, and He will not meet that need through any other god. He will let us go hungry until we turn to Him just to show us that our false god cannot satisfy. When we turn to Him in complete dependence, however, He promises to fill us with the very best!

Verse 16:

But He would feed Israel with the best wheat. "I would satisfy you with honey from the rock."

A lesser god will give us a lesser provision. God promises us the best. If we persist in going our own way and serving another god, we prove that we don't really trust Him to meet that need. In fact, a sure indication that we are serving another god is that we do not trust God to meet a need. When we serve another god, however, God cannot trust us with that provision. This is a destructive cycle that can only be breached through belief that God will hear us and answer our request (Heb. 11:6).

If you have depleted all your resources and still don't have the answer you need, you are in a good place to open your mouth wide and be filled with the very best wheat and honey from the rock. You are in place to receive from God and be satisfied. Put away any strange gods and surrender in complete faith to the God who brought you out of your own Egypt and still has much more to give you.

Have a blessed day!

Satisfied with His Goodness

Jeremiah 31:13-14:

Then the virgin will rejoice with dancing, while young and old men rejoice together. I will turn their mourning into joy, give them consolation, and bring happiness out of grief. I will give the priests their fill with abundance, and My people will be satisfied with My goodness. This is the LORD's declaration.

Storms, like grief, are not meant to last forever. They have a season. God promises to bring rejoicing to our lives by turning our mourning into joy.

God satisfies us with His goodness. He is not some terrible judge just waiting to punish us. We live in a fallen world where evil happens, sickness hinders, and death destroys. If we belong to Him, He floods us with His goodness as a comfort and a consolation for the trials we have endured. That is why we, as Christians, have hope. He uses even the storms and losses in our lives for His purpose and our benefit. He doesn't waste anything! His grace propels us forward into a glorious testimony of His existence and work in such a fallen world.

If you are hurting or grieving today, realize that it is only for a season. God has promised to turn your mourning into joy and to satisfy you with His goodness. Turn to Him and not from Him. What God declares, He will surely deliver! Praise Him today for the place He is taking you. Rejoice in Him over the plan He has for you. Trust Him to complete the good work He has begun in you. Your situation is not over until you see God's glory reflected in it. You have a testimony in the making and a story worth telling.

Have a blessed day!

God's Goodness Now

Psalm 73:1-3:

God is indeed good to Israel, to the pure in heart. But as for me, my feet almost slipped; my steps nearly went astray. For I envied the arrogant; I saw the prosperity of the wicked.

In this passage, we see someone who envied what another had. When we see the prosperity of another and fail to appreciate the goodness God has brought into our own lives, we become dissatisfied. Satan robs us of contentment and the full realization of God's goodness. Comparison never leads to anything positive.

Looking at someone else's blessing can be misleading. Perhaps it seems as if God has just graciously blessed her, but do we ever stop to think of the trials she faced to get to that blessing? The lives we live are filled with roads and paths of blessing and testing. Often, one foot falls on a blessing while the other foot lands on a test. Never envy what someone else has without considering what it took to get there, and that may not be obvious. Becoming content and accepting where we are in life will enable us to appreciate the goodness God brings to our life now.

I'm so glad the writer of this Psalm almost slipped without completely succumbing to envy. He reveals to us the answer to overcoming this vicious deceiver. We must remember that God is good to all, and when we focus upon God's goodness in our own lives, we can overcome the Devil's snare. Jealousy is an ugly monster, and no one enjoys being around her.

Today, spend some time counting your blessings. Thank God for the many ways He has been good to you. Tell someone about the goodness God has shown you. Learning to appreciate where you are now is the first step in moving forward to the next blessing God has in store.

Have a blessed day!

Satisfied by His Faithful Love

Psalm 90:14:

Satisfy us in the morning with Your faithful love so that we may shout for joy and be glad all our days.

I cherish my daily devotional time in the morning. This is a time when I can just slip away with God and hear from Him through His Word. This morning devotional time sets the whole course of my day, and I often meditate on it throughout the day.

As I read this verse, it not only reminds me of the importance of devotional time each morning with God, it confirms the fact that our joy can only be found in His faithful love toward us. When we are satisfied in His love is when we are able to shout for joy and be glad—even in the midst of difficult circumstances.

If you are struggling with doubt, depression, or discouragement today, your source of joy is in knowing just how much God loves you. If the burdens of trials are overwhelming you, your load is lightened by a greater revelation of His love for you. Whatever problem or lack you are facing is diminished when you are satisfied by God's faithful love.

Know with all certainty today that God loves you more than your feeble mind can imagine. He wants to help you through your struggle and bless you so you can live the life He has purposed for you to live in Christ Jesus. He is for you and not against you. When we turn to Him in brokenness, He makes us whole with new life in Him. Trust His love for you and know that His plans are to prosper you and not to harm you. This kind of love can give us all reason to shout for joy and be glad all our days.

Have a blessed day!

Remembering God's Benefits

Psalm 103:1-5:

My soul, praise the LORD, and all that is within me, praise His holy name. My soul, praise the LORD, and do not forget all His benefits. He forgives all your sin; He heals all your diseases. He redeems your life from the Pit; He crowns you with faithful love and compassion. He satisfies you with goodness; your youth is renewed like the eagle.

Should you ever be down or discouraged, this is the Psalm for you to read. Take note of all God's benefits. When we realize just how much He does for us, we have no reason to be sad or depressed. We have every reason in the world to praise Him, and that is exactly what will lift the depression and discouragement from us.

God forgives all our sin—this releases us from all guilt and condemnation. He heals all our diseases—this includes weariness of the soul. God's plan is for us to operate as whole individuals. While we may be suffering from symptoms at the moment, He is leading us toward wholeness. He redeems our life from the Pit. We have no need for despair. He rescues us from the things that threaten to destroy us. All we need to do is call upon Him. He crowns us with faithful love and compassion. To crown us places authority on our heads. We wear His love and compassion as crowns of authority against an enemy who would try to convince us we are alone and unloved in this world. He satisfies us with goodness. God draws us to Himself with His goodness. He is for us and not against us, and He longs to give us good gifts according to our faith.

The last benefit mentioned declares our youth renewed like the eagles. Eagles have the ability to fly higher than any other bird, and they can fly above the storms of life, where they are unharmed. God gives us the same ability when we turn to Him and dare believe His Word is true. We can fly high above the storms of our lives and remain unharmed when we trust in Him.

Praise God today for His many benefits. Don't concentrate on your loss or lack. Recall His many benefits and determine to soar above the storms. You have nothing to lose and everything to gain!

Have a blessed day!

The Presence of God

Psalm 132:1-5:

LORD, remember David and all the hardships he endured, and how he swore an oath to the LORD, making a vow to the Mighty One of Jacob: "I will not enter my house or get into my bed. I will not allow my eyes to sleep or my eyelids to slumber until I find a place for the LORD, a dwelling for the Mighty One of Jacob."

David was a man determined to live with the presence of God. He longed to build a temple where the LORD could dwell and know that he was right in the center of that will. There he was blessed; there David felt fully at home. He could not rest inside until he knew God had a place to dwell with him. That is why he had the Ark of the Covenant brought to him. He wanted to be in God's house and with God's presence. There he felt safe, loved, blessed, and whole.

Do we have that same desire and determination? Are we at complete unrest until God's presence can be seen and felt in us? With His presence come His blessings.

Today, simply seek God and rely upon His love for you. Under the new covenant, we are His temple. We do not need the Ark of the Covenant to have His presence because we are now under a covenant of grace, where He dwells in us through the Holy Spirit. When we can fully accept and believe that God is concerned about every area of our lives and that He wants the very best for us, we can begin to feel His presence. We can rest in His grace. Sometimes it just takes internal wrestling and struggling to come to that point, when all we really need to do is submit, believe, and receive.

Have a blessed day!

God Suffers with You

Isaiah 63:9:

In all their suffering, He suffered, and the Angel of His Presence saved them because of His love and compassion; He lifted them up and carried them all the days of the past.

When you suffer, God suffers. His perfect will is not for any of us to suffer or hurt. He can, however, take our hurts and use them for our benefit and His glory. God's attitude toward us is one of love and compassion. He is our Father, and He loves us with the love of a Father. He does not find joy in seeing us suffer, nor does His ultimate plan for us end with suffering. If we find ourselves suffering, God will either send the Angel of His Presence to save us, or He will enable us to endure with a reward at the end. He never sends us through painful experiences just to see us hurt.

Suffering is a part of the fallen nature. We will suffer because we live in a fallen world. While poor choices can cause us to pay consequences, we should never assume that painful experiences are always the result of divine punishment. Anything God allows us to endure is always for the purpose of drawing us closer to Him. The closer we come to Him, the more He will reveal to us. The more revelation we receive, the more blessed we are. God's ultimate intention is to bless us, even though some blessings might begin with pain or heartache.

Job's friends mistakenly thought that all health and prosperity were signs of a blessed life by God. If Job were experiencing problems in those areas, God must be punishing Him for something. They never took into consideration the fact that we have an enemy who readily attacks us where God has blessed us. God displayed Job's faithfulness by allowing the Devil to attack him. Neither Job nor his friends were ever given an explanation of this. God does not owe us an explanation. He loves us with an unfailing love, and we can always trust His love for us. When nothing seems to make sense in your life, cling to the fact that God loves you, and trust in His unwavering love for you. This is the key to surviving enemy attack.

If you are suffering today, know that God suffers with you. Seek Him and praise Him. Your victory is found in His Presence, and He dwells in the praises of His people. You can always trust His unfailing love for you, and that is something for which you can praise Him. Watch your situation turn around when you fight the enemy with the weapon of praise.

Have a blessed day!

Something of Value

Psalm 105:37:

Then He brought Israel out with silver and gold, and no one among His tribes stumbled.

When God brought the children of Israel out of bondage from Egypt, He brought them out with silver and gold. They had something valuable from their experience to sustain them in their freedom. They were not yet in their promised land, but they were on their way. No one stumbled. The KJV states this as "there was none feeble among His tribes." Everyone that God brought out of bondage was healthy enough to make the journey.

For those of us who have ever felt between two places, this verse brings encouragement. God does not want us enslaved by the Devil's schemes, and He has sent His Son to pay the price for our freedom. While we embark upon our journey to our own promised lands, we can be assured that God has given us something of value to sustain us until we reach our destination. While we may feel like we can't take another day or make one more step, we will not stumble on this journey.

What have you gained from your experience in bondage? At least, you have a testimony worth sharing. That testimony has the power to increase God's kingdom. Never take it for granted. Anything God gave you on your way out of bondage has the power to increase. How you use it will depend upon what it increases. The children of Israel used it to create a golden calf. Will you use your spoils of bondage to increase God's kingdom or to increase the influence of other gods?

The place between bondage and our promised land may be wilderness terrain, but God assures us the ability to make the journey. Will we grumble and complain or believe that if He brought us out, He will surely take us in? Only a few entered the Promised Land, along with those who were born in the wilderness. The memory of Egypt hindered them from fully believing.

Today, God has given you something of value, and you are able to make the journey to which He has called you. You have a choice to increase His kingdom or to increase the influence of lesser kingdoms in your life. If you increase lesser kingdoms, it will hinder your faith to believe in His. Don't die in the wilderness before you reach your promised land. Use whatever He has given you of value for His glory, and believe that He who has called you is faithful. Without Him you can do nothing but with Him, you can do all things. Believe, and be willing to fight the enemy to take hold of what God has for you.

Have a blessed day!

Service is Opportunity

Luke 12:35:

Be ready for service and have your lamps lit.

Jesus gave this instruction to His followers. He continued in verse 36 to teach that we must be like people waiting for their master to return from the wedding banquet so that when he comes and knocks, they can open the door for him at once. We are to be ready to seize the opportunity when it arises to welcome the Master into our lives.

Service is opportunity. We must be ready to serve at a moment's notice so when the opportunity to serve comes along, we will be able to seize it at once. In service, we find Jesus working in us and through us. In service, we also find unexpected blessings abound! We must change our way of thinking about opportunity as something that benefits us and begin to see it as a service we can offer to others. God honors the heart which truly desires to serve out of love for Him.

This verse also instructs us to have our lamps lit. Psalm 119:105 tells us that God's Word is a lamp for our feet and a light for our path. We must have God's Word illuminated in our hearts and our minds in order to serve. The best way to do this is to meditate on a part of His Word every day. The more it is in us, the lighter our path will become.

Be ready to serve at a moment's notice by filling your mind with the Word of God. This will open up new doors for you that you never imagined!

Begin to see serving God and others as an opportunity and not a chore. You will be amazed at how fulfilled your life can become!

Have a blessed day!

Serving in Love

Galatians 5:13:

For you are called to freedom, brothers; only don't use this freedom as an opportunity for the flesh, but serve one another through love.

In the verses preceding this one, Paul handled a dispute on circumcision. He explained that in Christ, we are no longer bound by the commands of the law to give us a right standing with God. This included the practice of circumcision. We have entered a new covenant of grace, whereby we are forgiven of our sins through the shed blood of Jesus Christ. In this new covenant of grace, we are free from the law.

We are not to use this new freedom on the flesh. When we fully realize the love God poured out upon us on the cross, our hearts are drawn to Him. We acknowledge the love God has for us and, in turn, love others by the power of grace. When we see fully just how much we need His grace, we are able to understand how much others need it, too! We serve others out of the love God has lavishly shown us.

You may be called to serve someone who is hard to love. While you might not have loving feelings for that person, you can serve simply in a response of love to God for what He has done for you. When you serve others, it is really not them you are serving. You are serving God by allowing yourself to be a vessel through which His love can flow to them.

Love meets needs. We may not always be able to see someone's need, but God does. Out of His great love for another, He may choose you to meet a need no one else can see. The amazing thing about this is that you are blessed in the process!

Today, meditate on the freedom you have in Christ through the covenant of grace. You are free from the law! Hallelujah! Let that freedom stir up a passion that can come only from receiving the love God has for you.

Then, serve God out of a heart of love by making yourself available to others. You don't have to serve God to make Him love you. He loves you already! Serve Him by extending His love to those who have yet to realize this amazing grace!

Have a blessed day!

Serving with the Right Motive

1 Corinthians 15:57-58:

But thanks be to God, who gives us the victory through our Lord Jesus Christ! Therefore, my dear brothers, be steadfast, immovable, always excelling in the Lord's work, knowing that your labor in the Lord is not in vain.

Wherever God has called us to work for Him, He gives us victory through Christ. We are simply to labor in what He has called us to do, knowing that the end result is in His care. We cannot measure our own success. We must do what God has called us to do and allow Him to give us success.

God sees every move you make for Him. He knows every labor of love in which you engage, and He does not take it for granted. In fact, He gives you the desire to do it because He has a purpose in it. Where God will take it or what He will produce from it is in His hands. If you do what you do to hear your own praise, you will become frustrated and disappointed. God is busy accomplishing His purpose through us, and His purpose is not to glorify us. His purpose is to draw us closer to Him and to reach others through us. If our motive lies completely in response to the love of Christ, we will never be disappointed in serving others.

I've often heard people complain about working hard for the church or other areas of the community and never receiving the recognition they think they deserve. The fact they think they deserve some type of recognition proves they were serving with the wrong motive. Your labor in the Lord is never in vain. Your labor to hear your own praise will bring you offense, discontentment, and strife. As Christians, we must become steadfast, immovable, and excellent in the Lord's work, knowing He will make our efforts productive for His purposes and not our own.

What has God put in your heart to do today? Do it for Him and for no other reason. Respond to His great love for you. Nothing in life will make you happier than knowing you are doing what He has called you to do and are living a productive life in Christ. He gives you the victory through Christ!

Have a blessed day!

Sharpening Your Ax

Ecclesiastes 10:10:

If the ax is dull, and one does not sharpen its edge, then one must exert more strength; however, the advantage of wisdom is that it brings success.

Why would one not want to stop to sharpen the ax? Some people think you will lose momentum. Indeed it can be cumbersome and time consuming to stop and sharpen the ax, even though a sharper ax would help you cut wood faster. To continue using a dull ax requires more human strength. Some people would rather exert a little more strength and keep the momentum than to stop to sharpen the ax.

Whether you stop to sharpen the ax or continue with a dull ax depends upon what you value most. If strength and precision are important, you will stop to sharpen your ax. If time is important to you, you will continue using more strength. Are you more concerned with trying to get something right or with trying to meet a deadline?

As I think about this scenario, it reminds me of my late husband. There is no doubt he would have stopped to sharpen his ax. He was precise in everything he did, and time meant nothing to him. He wanted to make sure what he did was right and the best he could do. I, on the other hand, live by the clock. As long as I got the wood chopped on time, nothing else mattered. I'm not a perfectionist, and most of what I do can be greatly improved! I thrive on meeting deadlines, and much of my former working career was based upon deadlines.

In our Christian walk, we need to take time to sharpen our axes. We do that by studying God's Word and remaining in fellowship with His people, who hold us accountable. If we continue with a dull ax, our walk will become dull and ineffective. We will lose credibility, and our witness will become tainted. The sharper our ax, the more productive we will become if we use the ax. A sharp ax that is never used is as ineffective as a dull ax that can't cut. Wisdom is in knowing when to cut and when to sharpen.

Take time to sharpen your ax today, and put it to use. Cut away anything that stands between you and God. Cut away baggage that is hindering your Christian walk. Ask God to make you productive for Him, and watch to see what wonderful opportunities He will bring your way!

Have a blessed day!

A Servant's Role

Mark 10:42-44:

You know that those who are regarded as rulers of the Gentiles dominate them, and their men of high positions exercise power over them. But it must not be like that among you. On the contrary, whoever wants to become great among you must be your servant, and whoever wants to be among you must be a slave to all.

So many times people in the church don't want to associate with sinners. Somehow, we think being around them will make us dirty. We look down on the acts of the sinner and don't want anything to do with them. We forget that sinners sin because that is their nature; there is nothing unnatural about it. We also forget that if it were not for grace and the fact that someone loved us enough to share Jesus, we would share that same nature.

We are called to make disciples. God uses the raw material of a sinner to transform him into a disciple that reflects the image of Christ. We are called to wash feet. That means we may have to get our hands dirty. Our job is to help make someone else clean, to do a slave's job. At one time, we were unacceptable, too. Someone had to love us enough to point us to Christ so we could be accepted before the Father.

I see kids every day who are dirty, ill-behaved, and socially inappropriate. Many of them come from difficult home environments. If we merely look at the appearance and the behavior, we may be repulsed. Only a heart that can love children and minister to their needs can reach them and begin to change what is wrong. This change comes from the inside and permeates out. Demanding change on the outside only will never penetrate to create the permanent change that is needed. Unless we love them and show them something different than what they see at home, their behavior will only become worse.

Many times, a child's poor behavior stems from lack. This is true of an adult, as well. We have the source that can fill any lack—His name is Jesus. Our job is to point the way to Him. If we can fill the lack, we are called to do so, if we can't, we are called to show the way. We may have to walk with them a while to direct them, but that is our purpose. Seeing a life changed is worth every step we take with them!

Have a blessed day!

Preparation

Ephesians 2:10:

For we are His creation—created in Christ Jesus for good works, which God prepared ahead of time so that we should walk in them.

Please focus on the word *prepared*. God created us for a specific purpose. His plan is for us to do good works. He has already prepared these works for us to walk in them. Since He has already prepared those works for us, is He not also preparing us to walk in them?

I often hear this saying: "God doesn't call the qualified. He qualifies the called." This statement has often been used to imply that we don't have to worry about things like education, especially in the ministry. Education is simply preparation, an equipping to work in a particular area. If God calls you to an area of service, whether in ministry or the workforce, He will NOT send you out without first preparing you. If He is directing you toward an education, by all means, become educated. A rocket scientist cannot build a rocket successfully without being trained to build rockets. If God has called you to build rockets, become educated in rocket science; if He has called you to Christian ministry, get a biblical education.

Wherever God plans for us to walk tomorrow, He is preparing us today. Wherever we find ourselves walking today, He prepared us yesterday. In fact, He is always preparing us for the next step. Trials are often just preparation for the next big blessing God has waiting. If you are wondering what God has in store for your future, just take a look at what He is teaching you today. How is He currently molding your life? What new things has He given you? What old things has He required you leave behind? What He is doing today will lead you into tomorrow.

Today, please pay attention to what God is teaching you. In fact, take time to write down any truths He has placed in your heart or changes He is requiring in your life. Write down those things that you keep hearing over and over; God is speaking to you through them. The lessons you learn today will equip you to walk in the good works He has already prepared for you. You don't want to miss any of them.

Have a blessed day!

Just Keep Running

Hebrews 12:1-2:

Therefore, since we also have such a large cloud of witnesses surrounding us, let us lay aside every weight and the sin that so easily ensnares us, and run with endurance the race that lies before us, keeping our eyes on Jesus, the source and perfector of our faith, who for the joy that lay before Him endured a cross and despised the shame, and has sat down at the right hand of God's throne.

Thankfully, God prepares us for the races we must endure. Not only does He build strength in us to endure the race, He also gives us desire and motivation for the prize! We must begin the race with the finish line in mind.

Jesus is the finish line. Since we are to finish what He has called us to do, we must keep our eyes on Him. We become quickly discouraged and want to give up if we look at ourselves or those around us. Discouragement is one of the Devil's greatest tools against us, and we fall easily to it. We must remember to keep our eyes on Jesus. He is the source of our strength and the provider of our prize. What we see in others or in ourselves really doesn't matter. Jesus has called us to the race, and He will help us endure to the end. We are not measured by what others do. Receiving our prize depends upon how well we keep our eyes on Him and continuing the race.

Rest assured today that God will not send you into a race without first preparing you. You can do what He has called you to do. Fix your eyes on the prize, and just keep running! It may hurt for a while, but you can overcome it. The finish line is just ahead.

Have a blessed day!

Our Greatest Mission Field

Psalm 78:4:

We must not hide them from their children, but must tell a future generation the praises of the LORD, His might, and the wonderful works He has performed.

Do our children and grandchildren know the wonderful things God has done for us in the past? Do they know how He has answered prayer for us? Do they know God's faithfulness to us in fulfilling promises? If they don't, how will they ever know to trust Him?

According to the latest research, young people fall out of church during their early twenties because they don't see the relevance of worshiping God. To them, God makes no difference in a person's life. As a result, many of them seek their significance in other things and leave God out of the picture completely. Some may make an effort to acknowledge God but fail to give Him priority. What our children and grandchildren see from our testimonies may very well be what steers their direction once they are no longer under our care or authority.

Several times I've told my son, Samuel, how God blessed us with him. He was our miracle baby after suffering three miscarriages. In fact, that is how he got his name. My husband and I prayed and asked God for a child and dedicated that child to God, much as Hannah did. We knew if the baby was a boy, we would have to name him Samuel, which means *God has heard my cry.* Looking back, however, God has answered many prayers for me that I'm not sure I've ever shared.

When God blesses us, it is for a purpose. He creates a testimony in us that is to be shared. His work in us is designed to lead others to follow Him. That includes our children and grandchildren. As Christians, their heritage is to follow Christ by learning from our example. What kind of heritage are we leaving if they don't know what God has done for us?

Tell the stories of your life to your children and grandchildren. In fact, writing them down in a keepsake journal could be an excellent way to pass down your testimonies to them. You don't have to travel to a distant country to be an effective missionary. Your family and friends need to know what God has done for you. Home is your greatest mission field.

Have a blessed day!

Partners of the Gospel

1 Corinthians 9:19-23:

For although I am free from all people, I have made myself a slave to all, in order to win more people. To the Jews I became like a Jew, to win Jews; to those under the law, like one under the law—though I myself am not under the law—to win those under the law. To those who are outside the law, like one outside the law—not being outside God's law, but under the law of Christ—to win those outside the law. To the weak I became weak, in order to win the weak. I have become all things to all people, so that by all means I may save some. Now I do all this because of the gospel, that I may become a partner in its benefits.

Paul made every effort to relate to people on their level. He was willing to identify with them in their environments and situations without compromising his own faith. His mission was clear—to win the lost to Christ.

I see too many Christians today who only want to associate with their own kind. They want to identify with groups with which they can benefit. Paul, however, chose to become all things to all people so he could become a partner in the benefits of the gospel, God's grace gifts. Paul chose to be a partner in extending grace.

Choose to be a partner in the gospel of grace today. Perhaps, you should reach out to another PHOEBE (widow) or someone new you just met. You may have a family member or a neighbor who is going through a rough time. The need for grace abounds all around us. Become the hands and feet of Christ to someone who needs Him. You will find yourself benefiting from the very grace you extend!

Have a blessed day!

Responding to the Nudges

John 16:13:

When the Spirit of truth comes, He will guide you into all the truth. For He will not speak on His own, but He will speak whatever He hears. He will also declare to you what is to come.

If you are a Christian, God has given you the gift of His Holy Spirit to indwell you and to lead you into the way He wants you to go. You can expect to hear from God through the Holy Spirit. This is what my friend and fellow PHOEBE, Carol Pharris, calls, "nudges from the Holy Spirit." These nudges - that inner voice that speaks to you - tell you to move in God-honoring ways. You just know inside what you are to do.

This inner voice will never contradict the written Word of God. Any voice that tries to convince you to violate a Scriptural command is not a nudge from the Holy Spirit. That voice is the Devil trying to push you off a cliff! Declare God's Word by speaking what it says to be true, and resist the Devil. You will soon find him fleeing with fright. By declaring God's Word in your situation, you speak God's authority into it. There is extreme power in His authority, and the Devil has to submit.

What is God nudging you to do today? Do you need to call a friend? Is there a matter that needs your attention, perhaps one that has failed to be a priority because of time restraints? Are there little details that have gone neglected because your life has been too rushed lately? If you answered, "Yes," to all of the above, as I just did, it's time you listened to the Holy

Spirit's nudges. The more you respond to those nudges, the more you will recognize them in the future and be blessed as a result.

Have a blessed day!

Servant, Manager, and Heir

1 Corinthians 4:1:

A person should consider us in this way: as servants of Christ and managers of God's mysteries.

It is easy to picture ourselves as a servant. We see servants in action every day. We can relate to Christ as a servant because He made Himself an example. As Christians, our calling involves serving Christ and serving others in some way. But, just what does it mean to be a manager of God's mysteries?

The word, *manager*, here is translated *steward* in other versions of the Bible. A steward managed the affairs of the master's household. While the steward held no property of his own, he was highly trusted to manage the estate for the master. He knew the master well and thoroughly understood how the master wanted his house managed. He also had full authority to run the house while the master was away. In fact, the steward was second in authority only to the master.

God's mysteries is a reference to the gospel. God sent His Son to die as a sacrifice for us so that we might stand before a holy God and have relationship with Him as His own child. As His child, we are heirs to His glory in Christ.

As a Christian, we are considered a highly trusted steward of the mysteries of God, which makes us an heir as His child. We will inherit the kingdom for which we are caring through Christ Jesus, God's Son. We are both a steward and an heir.

With that thought in mind, carefully consider how you are managing the gospel of Christ. Are you stingy with it, or are you making Him known to those who desperately need Him? Are you diminishing the kingdom or multiplying it? Are you carefully heeding every word the Master has proclaimed to us, or have you even taken time to get to know the word by which He will one day judge you? You are a highly trusted steward of the Master's business and will one day inherit His kingdom. How well are you managing what He has given you?

Have a blessed day!

Sowing Seed for Harvest

Luke 8:11-15:

This is the meaning of the parable. The seed is the Word of God. The seeds along the path are those who have heard. Then the Devil comes and takes away the word from their hearts, so that they may not believe and be saved. And the seeds on the rock are those who, when they hear, welcome the word with joy. Having no root, these believe for a while and depart in a time of testing. As for the seed that fell among thorns, these are the ones who, when they have heard, go on their way and are choked with worries, riches, and pleasures of life, and produce no mature fruit. But the seed in the good ground—these are the ones who, having heard the word with an honest and good heart, hold on to it and by enduring bear fruit.

The seed mentioned in this passage is the Word of God. This seed needs to be able to take root and grow before it produces a harvest. If anything or anyone is allowed to steal the seed before it can take root, the harvest is forfeited. The Devil will try to prevent that harvest from manifesting in our lives.

The harvest is a threat to the enemy because it testifies of the glory of God. Those who receive the seed with an honest and good heart (right motive), hold on to it, and endure are the ones who reap the harvest. To have an honest and good heart means you don't try to use the Word incorrectly to produce results the way you want them. To hold on to the Word means you keep reminding yourself of it. When things go wrong or storms hit, you hold on to what you know to be true. To endure means that you withstand whatever the Devil throws at you to try to choke out that Word or to get you to lose hope.

Reaping a harvest requires times of uncertainty, difficulty, struggle, lack, or even attack. It is through such things our character is formed. This new character lays hold of the harvest and is the enemy's greatest nightmare! To lay hold of the harvest means you have become changed in the process and are now more equipped to make disciples, as you were called to do. You have taken another step in becoming transformed from glory to glory in the sanctification process, and your harvest shines forth the glory of God. The Devil is a jealous creature who does not want to see this happen.

Luke 8:8:

Still other seed fell on good ground; when it sprang up, it produced a crop: 100 times what was sown ….

When we take the word in but do not act upon it, we are eating that seed and not allowing it to grow. To reap a harvest, we must sow the seed of God's Word by acting upon what it says and applying it to our daily lives. When we've been hurt, we may find it difficult to forgive, when we experience lack, to give, or when it just doesn't seem convenient, to obey. These examples require mercy and grace on our part, and they are the very things we need from God to both survive and thrive in this life. Whatever we sow, however, will produce 100 times more than what we gave! We can never out-give God because of His great love for us. Grab hold of some seed and sow it today. Your time of harvest awaits.

Have a blessed day!

A Heart Worth Anointing

1 Samuel 16:11-12:

Samuel asked him, "Are these all the sons you have?" "There is still the youngest," he answered, "but right now he's tending the sheep." Samuel told Jesse, "Send for him. We won't sit down to eat until he gets here." So Jesse sent for him. He had beautiful eyes and a healthy, handsome appearance. Then the LORD said, "Anoint him, for he is the one."

Because of Saul's rebellion, defiance, and his desire to please men, God rejected him. Saul had become a stench to God, so God sought a man after

His own heart as king. God chose a king for Himself from the sons of Jesse, and He instructed Samuel to go and anoint Him as king.

As Samuel began to examine Jesse's sons, he found the first to be quite impressive in appearance, just as he had found Saul to be. God, however, rejected him. He told Samuel not to look at the outward appearance or his height. God could see much deeper than Samuel could. God did not like something in his heart, but it was not outwardly noticeable.

God rejected all seven of Jesse's sons in attendance at the sacrifice. Poor Samuel must have wondered if He had heard from God correctly. He asked Jesse if he had anymore sons, and one remained. He was the unlikely candidate. He was in the field tending sheep while his brothers were seeking a blessing. God chose the son who was actively serving and caring for the flock. This was the kind of heart He required to lead His people. Those who were merely seeking a blessing for themselves would fail Him and the people miserably, as had Saul.

We must be careful not to judge others or even ourselves by appearances. God does not bless us or anoint us based upon any brownie points we earn. He looks for hearts that are devoted to Him and are actively serving Him out of love. These are the lives He can trust to anoint with the leadership and care of others. We must remember that God's kingdom is not all about what we can get or what we think we deserve. It is about God's plan and fulfilling His purpose. To be anointed by God is to be engaged in His purpose and disengaged with our own.

Notice that David was very handsome, too. He did not depend upon His handsome appearance, however, to gain favor with man. He had a heart turned toward God, and his appearance was merely a bonus for him. God chose him based upon his heart.

If God were to look at our hearts today, what would He find? Would He find one worth anointing, or would He find one that is self-absorbed? Would He find one who seeks Him or the blessings He can provide? Would He find one that merely looks pretty sitting in church or one actively tending the flocks? Dare to be a woman totally devoted to God and serving Him out of a loving heart. If your heart just isn't where it should be, ask God to change it and give you one worth anointing. From the farm to the palace is a long way, but only God's chosen make the journey.

Have a blessed day!

The Outpouring

Joel 2:28-29:

After this I will pour out My Spirit on all humanity; then your sons and your daughters will prophesy, your old men will have dreams, and your young men will see visions. I will even pour out My Spirit on the male and female slaves in those days.

Joel warns about a day of God's wrath and His call for repentance. God becomes jealous for His people and begins to bless them. After this, He pours out His Spirit on His people, giving them power to proclaim His name. While we saw a glimpse of this at Pentecost, most Bible scholars believe there is yet a day when we will see this type of outpouring again. Just what does it mean for God to pour out His Spirit?

When we become a Christian, the Holy Spirit comes to dwell in us. He teaches us, guides us, and transforms us as we walk the Christian life. Before Christ ascended into heaven, God's Spirit spoke only through the prophets. Now, His Holy Spirit comes to live in us, and all Christians can hear from God. In these verses, however, the Holy Spirit seems to be doing something more. He is igniting them with power. He is anointing them to proclaim His Word like never before because of His impending wrath. He is using His people to give fair warning to the nations of His coming.

Every Christian scholar or great teacher I know believes we are living in the last days before the coming of Christ and the wrath of judgment that He will bring to this world. If that is true, and I believe it is, we should expect to see God's blessing upon His people and an outpouring of power upon God's people to proclaim the gospel to all nations.

Everyone is included in this outpouring! Neither age nor gender is a deterrent. You have the power of God upon you. The fact that you are a woman should not stop you. God promised to extend this outpouring to His daughters. Your social status doesn't matter. God even pours His Spirit out upon the slaves. This power is for everyone.

What is God nudging you to do? He has already given you the power to do it. What dreams are inside you? His power is with you to fulfill them. Now is not the time to give up or give in. Step out, and let God's anointing hit you square between the eyes. Now is the time to proclaim His Word to all nations so they might become saved before Christ comes again. God will help you succeed in this endeavor.

Have a blessed day!

Ears and Eyes

Proverbs 20:12:

The hearing ear and the seeing eye—the LORD made them both.

The abilities to hear and see are wonders within themselves that God gave us to experience, enjoy, and engage the world around us. However, how two people can hear or see the same thing and perceive two different stories is amazing. For example, two different teachers may observe a misbehaving child. One may see an irritating menace while another may see a hurting cry for attention. How each responds to the child will be completely different, although they both witnessed the same thing.

What one person hears or sees may differ from what another hears or sees, yet God made them both. Some people have the ability to see the big picture of things, while others notice minute details. Separately, they work in a bubble that never lets them see God's complete picture. Together, however, they can connect pieces of the beautiful puzzle God has given us as His perfect plan.

If the teacher who sees a hurting child will begin to show love to the child and earn his trust, she can open a door for new behavior. The two teachers working together can make a huge difference in the life of that child with one ministering to the emotional need and the other teaching behavior modification. Likewise, it takes the local church to minister to the body of Christ and evangelize the world around us.

What has God shown you? How has He tuned your ears to hear and crafted your eyes to see? Who has He brought to work alongside you? God created the hearing ear and the seeing eye. Follow what He teaches you through them, and carefully consider what He is showing others. Put your pieces together and look to see a bigger picture of what God is doing in your world.

Have a blessed day!

From Experiences to Ministry

Luke 19:26-27:

I tell you, that to everyone who has, more will be given; and from the one who does not have, even what he does have will be taken away. But bring here these enemies of mine, who did not want me to rule over them, and slaughter them in my presence.

These are the last words recorded in the parable of the 10 minas or the 10 talents, where a certain master gave his servants gifts and expected an increase when he returned. As the story goes, two servants used their gifts and multiplied. One servant buried his for fear of losing it. The master was very displeased with the one who buried his gift and took it away from him, giving it to the one who had increased the most.

The point to this parable is that when God blesses us, He expects increase. We should all be using the unique gifts God has given us to further His kingdom. The gifts He has given us include not only our spiritual gifts, but also our life experiences.

Widowhood is a very difficult road to travel, as we have all learned. What makes this road bearable and even a blessing at times is the love of Christ, and that love is what we need to share with others. We do so simply by telling what He has done for us. Every time we share what God has revealed to us or what He has answered in prayer, we are sharing His love for us. We are all living, breathing, walking testimonies of the grace of God, and there are many out there who are struggling to understand just how one lives, breathes, and walks as a widow. We have the answer: Christ, not us. Without Him, none of us would be standing, either.

Today, I encourage you to simply tell one person what Christ has done for you. By doing so, you are sharing His love and giving hope. Your testimony is a ministry that makes the Savior irresistible!

Have a blessed day!

Jump on Board, or Get Out of the Way!

Acts 13:44-47:

The following Sabbath almost the whole town assembled to hear the message of the Lord. But when the Jews saw the crowds, they were filled with jealousy and began to oppose what Paul was saying by insulting him. Then Paul and Barnabas boldly said, "It was necessary that God's message be spoken to you first. But since you reject it, and consider yourselves unworthy of eternal life, we now turn to the Gentiles! For this is what the Lord has commanded us: I have appointed you as a light for the Gentiles, to bring salvation to the ends of the earth.

This passage reflects Paul's normal pattern: he boldly preached in synagogues first when he entered an area. He loved the Jewish people and desperately wanted them to receive the gospel of Christ. Paul knew that he was sent to spread this news to the Gentiles because the Jews had rejected it. Jewish leaders, who hated Gentiles, wanted to control the way people entered God's kingdom. In efforts to control what they thought was godly, they rejected their long awaited Messiah.

We will always encounter people who desire to control. Like the Jewish leaders in this passage, they will miss the boat altogether and forfeit the blessing of God's promise if they try to decide, manipulate, or determine what only God could do. His blessings come through submission to His authority.

God does not consult us or any other religious group when He decides to act. He merely invites us to join Him in His plan. We may participate with Him, but He still drives the vehicle! God's plan of salvation would spread throughout the earth whether the Jewish leaders participated or not. Trying to stop a move of God is like trying to stop a freight train at full speed. You need to either jump on board or get out of the way. Standing in front of a fast moving train is sure to bring your eminent demise.

If God has called you to do something, don't worry about what others may think. Notice that the Jews opposed Paul and Barnabas out of jealousy, which is always accompanied by a need to control. These Jews desired what Paul and Barnabas had attracted—the crowds. Do you want to be popular, or do you want to be powerful?

Paul followed the orders of his Commander and continued to preach the gospel wherever God would lead him, regardless of what kind of trouble he encountered. He was a rebel with a cause. I am amazed how his teaching and the letters he wrote, some even from prison, are still available for us today. God intended His message through Paul to be known, and He still works through Paul's message every time we read the Scriptures. That is the power of a mighty freight train known as the Bible.

Today, consider what God is telling you to do. Since He has invited you to work in a part of His great plan of evangelizing this world, jump on board with all your might, or get out of the way! You will never be able to control a move of God, but you can participate in its power. Just beware: as Paul learned well, it can be a bumpy ride.

Have a blessed day!

Magnificent Works and Profound Thoughts

Psalm 92:5:

How magnificent are Your works, LORD, how profound Your thoughts!

When seeing a problem, we are often faced with the question, "What should I do?" In wanting to serve God, we often seek to perform those works to which we feel we are called or can contribute in some way. In fact, we can run ourselves ragged trying to do things that we feel need to be done. Our works, however, should not be our focus.

The psalmist here turned his focus appropriately. He began to notice the works of God. He can do what no man can do, and when He steps in to do a work in our lives, the result is magnificent.

We all design plans for ourselves that fall through in some way or another. Many times, God just has a better idea. His thoughts are certainly profound.

When life doesn't happen the way we planned, or if we encounter a setback or disappointment, we should turn to gaze upon God and see that His works are magnificent, and His thoughts about our lives are profound. He can do what we could never dream or even imagine if we will but submit to His plan for us.

Today, take some time to ponder the magnificent things God has done in your life. Where has He stepped in to do a work you could never do? When has He surprised you with something greater than you expected? What do you need Him to do now that you have worked yourself to death to try to accomplish but cannot? Ask for and expect His magnificent work and His profound thoughts in your life again. He is just waiting for you to turn it all over to Him.

Have a blessed day!

Mourning for What God Has Rejected

1 Samuel 16:1:

The LORD said to Samuel, "How long are you going to mourn for Saul, since I have rejected him as king over Israel? Fill your horn with oil and go. I am sending you to Jesse of Bethlehem because I have selected a king from his sons."

Samuel mourned the fact that God had rejected Saul as king. He loved Saul and the nation of Israel. His heart was broken when God rejected Saul. God did not, however reject Israel. His hand of favor was still upon them. However, He would no longer work through Saul as their leader.

God asked Samuel an important question. "How long will you mourn for Saul, since I have rejected him?" Do you ever find yourself mourning over something or someone that used to be in your life? God, however, is no longer working through that same venue, yet you still long for days past.

I often see this same mind set in fellow Christians. Obviously the Spirit is not moving and no life is left in a particular area of ministry. However, some people refuse to move to a new place because they remember what used to be and long for it to be that way again. They seem to think that if they just try harder, they will see God move there again. Samuel's mourning did not move God. God moved Samuel to anoint a new king. Any move of God is not dependent upon our self-effort. When He moves, we are wise to move with Him.

Have you sensed God's anointing leave some area of your life? Are you mourning something that used to be? You cannot work to get it back. Just as God did not reject Israel, He has not rejected you. You simply need to move with Him. He may just be directing you to focus your talents in a different area. Ask Him to lead you to the place where His anointing for you is alive and active.

God knew Saul would sin against Him before He ever anointed Saul as king. He also knew He was preparing David in the lineage of His own Son. Both were crucial to His plan. God knows what He has destined for your life, as well. Saul refused to let go of what God had taken away, and it cost him his sanity, his life, and his kingdom in the end. If God is no longer in it, let it go and accept the new direction He is leading. He is still moving and working among His people.

Have a blessed day!

Number Your Days

Psalm 90:12:

Teach us to number our days carefully so that we may develop wisdom in our hearts.

Procrastination is, perhaps, the biggest destroyer of dreams we encounter. If we put off for tomorrow what we know to do today, we delay the time for fulfillment and success. If the Devil can't talk you out of your dream, he will try to destroy it through delay. If we procrastinate long enough, we may very well wake up one day to find the opportunity gone.

We must learn to number our days and make the most of our opportunities. In doing so, we make progress toward God-given goals and dreams. We must learn to move with intentionality. We don't fulfill our purpose on earth by accident. We need a vision, a plan, and action. Otherwise, all we will ever do is daydream of potential and possibilities that never materialize because we procrastinate and never take a step of faith. To number our days carefully and make the most of the opportunities we have is wisdom.

What dream is inside your heart? Find a way to take a step toward it. What has God given you to do? Pick it up and begin to do it with diligence. If you are not moving toward your dream, you are running from it. Today is the time to number your days, change direction, and begin living the life God intended for you and placed inside your heart. Realize that procrastination may be convenient, but it is your enemy. Begin living life with intentionality, and watch your dreams materialize as you make one step after another in faith.

Have a blessed day!

Reaping What We Sow

2 Corinthians 9:6-7:

Remember this: the person who sows sparingly will also reap sparingly, and the person who sows generously will also reap generously. Each person should do as he has decided in his heart—not out of regret or out of necessity, for God loves a cheerful giver.

What Paul is trying to explain here is that when we give, whether it be money, time, goods, or deeds, it should be because our heart wants to do those things. That is the motive God desires and loves. We should never give because we feel obligated or because we are trying to receive something in return. We should always give because our hearts desire to give. That is true generosity. Those who sow generously will reap generously. Generosity is rooted in love.

People who are not generous have a love problem. The more you love someone, the more generous you will be. This is the cheerful giver that God desires us to be. When you really love someone and have the generosity to show it, it will be heaped right back on you.

Be generous to someone today. Someone needs to know that you care. Whether you sow seeds of money, time, a good deed, or even a compliment doesn't matter. Watch to see what comes back to you.

Have a blessed day!

Significance and Sacrifice

Luke 21:1-4:

He looked up and saw the rich dropping their offerings into the temple treasury. He also saw a poor widow dropping in two tiny coins. "I tell you the truth," He said. "This poor widow has put in more than all of them. For all these people have put in gifts out of their surplus, but she out of her poverty has put in all she had to live on."

God notices sacrifice. When people put their offerings in the temple treasury, large amounts of coins would make a loud noise as they clanged against the metal receptacles. To notice the big givers and to be impressed with them was easy. The two coins this widow contributed hardly made a sound and went unnoticed by the masses. Hers, however, is the offering Jesus recognized as greater than the rest. Hers was not just a gift; it was a sacrifice. She trusted all she had to God.

Many of us fall into the error of trying to find our significance from others. Those who made loud noises as they gave their offering seemed important in the temple. Certainly, they were recognized and respected by the majority of the people. This widow, however, would have hardly been noticed. Her lowly and humble state would have little to offer and nothing to impress. They could certainly function without her little, pitiful contribution.

The fact that she is a widow is significant here. Widows had no one to care for them, no one to defend them, no one to speak for them. In many ways, they were a liability. Certainly, no one wanted to walk in their shoes or to be like them. They were the humble and lowly of society. They certainly had no surplus from which to impress. Jesus recognized her gift as a sacrifice. Her gift revealed her total dependence and trust in God.

Those who have much often seek to impress others with what they have. They want to be viewed as important or successful in another's eyes. God is not impressed with the gifts of our surplus. He desires the humble heart of sacrifice that relies totally upon Him and finds significance in being in a right relationship with Him.

God is not looking for a big gift from our surplus. He wants the sacrifice of a heart fully devoted to Him. That is the heart that finds true significance and can live life to the fullest.

As widows, our lives may not be as whole as they once were. That does not mean we are not significant to God. Never be ashamed when your gift is a sacrifice. While it may not impress others, it has God's full attention. What more could we ask?

Have a blessed day!

What the Father is Doing

John 5:19-20:

Then Jesus replied, "I assure you: The Son is not able to do anything on His own, but only what He sees the Father doing. For whatever the Father does, the Son also does these things in the same way. For the Father loves the Son and shows Him everything He is doing, and He will show Him greater works than these so that you will be amazed.

Jesus did only what He saw the Father doing. This means that every time He healed, He first saw the Father healing. Every miracle He performed, He saw it first in the Father. Jesus was moved with compassion for hurting people. He first saw it in His Father. He taught like no one had ever taught before because He first heard it from the Father. He allowed the Father to teach Him and to enable Him before He gave it to the people.

We cannot give anyone else what we have not first received from the Father. We simply cannot give what we do not have. If we are going to have compassion for others, we must first receive it from the Father. If we are going to teach, we must first be taught. God, however, will give us whatever we need to reach those He has called us to reach.

Paul instructs us to comfort others with the same comfort with which we received (2 Cor. 1:4). Wherever God has comforted us, He plans to use us to comfort others. He expects us to give only what He has equipped us to give. First Corinthians 10:13 tells us that no temptation has overtaken us except what is common to humanity. That means that if you went through something difficult and overcame it by God's grace, others are struggling with the same thing now and desperately need that same grace. You are called to help them find it.

If you have ever wondered where God is calling you to serve, just look closely at your struggles. They are a roadmap to your calling. God gives you grace to overcome in areas to equip you to help others who are struggling in that same area. What have you seen the Father doing in your life? Do that same thing for someone else, or, better yet, point them to Jesus, with whom all things are possible. What is the Father doing in your life now? Watch carefully. You may soon be called to repeat it.

Have a blessed day!

Works of Righteousness

James 2:14-20:

What good is it, my brothers, if someone says he has faith, but does not have works? Can his faith save him? If a brother or sister is without clothes and lacks daily food, and one of you says to them, "Go in peace, keep warm, and eat well, but you don't give them what the body needs, what good is it? In the same way faith, if it doesn't have works, is dead by itself. But someone will say, "You have faith, and I have works." Show me your faith without works, and I will show you faith from my works. You believe that God is one; you do well. The demons also believe—and they shudder. Foolish man! Are you willing to learn that faith without works is useless?"

According to James, faith and works operate together. When we have faith, works follow as a natural outflowing of that faith. Works are the evidence that faith exists. Works without faith tries to earn what cannot be earned. Faith alone is dead without works. The two must cooperate.

Remember the story from Matthew 15 of a Canaanite mother who cried out for mercy and was denied. She knelt before Christ in full submission and worship, yet she was still rejected. Finally, she pressed through in faith just waiting for whatever crumb of grace might fall. She displayed the works of persistence. Her faith in Christ was solid and sound. She knew He could help her. She stayed the course and continued to appeal to Him until He granted her healing for her daughter. She did what she knew to be right, even in the midst of offense and rejection. This is how her faith was displayed.

While the Canaanite woman could never earn grace, works of righteousness stemmed from her faith. She could die to herself and put all personal feelings aside in order to appeal to grace. This is where we have difficulty. We have no trouble doing good deeds in order to help someone or to feel better about ourselves, but it is much more difficult to persist in faith when we are rejected, insulted, offended, and outright denied. Personal feelings often stand in our way of obtaining the grace we need.

Today, make the determination to press through with works of righteousness when things don't go your way. Keep appealing to Christ in an attitude of submission and worship when you don't get your way. Sooner or later, a crumb will fall.

Have a blessed day!

Made a Servant by Grace

Paul states from prison in Ephesians 3:7:

I was made a servant of this gospel by the gift of God's grace that was given to me by the working of His power.

Paul sees himself as a servant of the gospel of Christ. He sees servanthood as a gift of God's grace, and he received it by the working of God's power. In other words, God looked upon Paul with grace and made him a servant. Paul did nothing in his own merit to receive this gift of grace. All was done through God's power.

Paul continues in verses 8-9:

This grace was given to me—the least of all the saints!—to proclaim to the Gentiles the incalculable riches of the Messiah, and to shed light for all about the administration of the mystery hidden for ages in God who created all things.

Paul sees himself as the least worthy among all the saints. Perhaps, this is because he sought with diligence to kill followers of Christ before his conversion. The fact that God would bless him with such grace seems unfathomable to him. He sees his mission as that of proclaiming the gospel of Jesus Christ to the Gentiles and to reveal God's plan of salvation for the whole world.

Paul desired to share the grace he had experienced with the world. God's plan was for all people to come to know Him through Jesus Christ. Paul had this revelation, and he wanted to share it.

God has made you a servant by His grace. He has equipped you to serve Him in some way. By His grace you were saved, by His grace you are blessed, and by His grace you are able to serve Him. Give God what you have today, and share the grace He has given you with someone else. You were bound by your old way of life, but true freedom comes by being God's servant through grace.

Have a blessed day!

Your Life – An Object Lesson

Ephesians 3:10-13:

This is so that God's multi-faceted wisdom may now be made known through the church to the rulers and authorities in the heavens. This is according to the purpose of the ages, which He made in the Messiah, Jesus our Lord, in whom we have boldness, access, and confidence through faith in Him. So then I ask you not to be discouraged over my afflictions on your behalf, for they are your glory.

God's grace upon the church teaches a lesson of His wisdom to the rulers and authorities in the heavens. Wow! We are object lessons to rulers and authorities in heavenly places. This reminds me of Job. Everything that happened to him was a result of God's teaching the Devil a lesson. He knew what He had placed in Job and was confident in the man he had created. The Devil doubted him and sought to destroy the righteous man God created. God allowed the Devil to make his case and proved him wrong in the end. All the loss Job had to encounter as a result of being an object lesson was restored to him. In the end, his blessings far outweighed his suffering.

We have access to God through faith in Christ. This access is power: power to bring God's will into the earth, power to set His kingdom above the rule of the prince and powers of this age. In other words, God gives us power to live above our earthly circumstances and the things that ensnare us.

Paul saw his afflictions—imprisonment—as a tactic of the Devil to discourage and defeat him. By the grace that was alive in him through Christ Jesus, these very afflictions would minister to others who would come to know Christ and bring more of God's kingdom into this earth to defeat the power of the Devil. The Ephesians were the beneficiaries.

Paul knew that God would take the very tool the enemy used against him and turn it into a channel of grace to win others. Paul wrote his finest works from prison. Perhaps, he had the time to think, pray, and hear more clearly from God. While the Devil thought Paul was bound, God was hard at work in that prison cell. We are beneficiaries today when we read the book of Ephesians. Paul may be long gone, but the work God did in that cell still lives.

Your life is being watched by those in the heavenly realms, as well as by those around you. Someone is learning something just by watching you. Let them see the grace of God at work in you, and display the heart of a grateful servant. Allow your afflictions to work in your favor by simply submitting to God's authority over them. You have access to the very throne of God, which gives you power to overcome.

Have a blessed day!

The Power that Works in You

Ephesians 3: 14-19:

For this reason I bow my knees before the Father from whom every family in heaven and on earth is named. I pray that He may grant you, according to the riches of His glory, to be strengthened with power through His Spirit in the inner man, and that the Messiah may dwell in your hearts through faith. I pray that you, being rooted and firmly

established in love, may be able to comprehend with all the saints what is the length and width, height and depth of God's love, and to know the Messiah's love that surpasses knowledge, so you may be filled with all the fullness of God.

Paul seemed to know that trials would be woven into the fabric of the Christian life. He prays for power to strengthen us in the inner man and that Christ may dwell in our hearts through faith. Indeed, it is the inner person—the spirit—that is strengthened through trials. You see how strong a person really is on the inside when they face difficult things on the outside.

Paul also prayed that we will be able to understand just how great God's love is for us. When we go through trials, it may seem as if God does not love us or that He is angry with us for some reason. What we need is a greater vision or understanding of His love, which is much greater than we realize. The more we understand this, the easier our struggles and burdens are to bear. In realizing His great love for us, our empty lives become full.

Verses 20-21:

Now to Him who is able to do above and beyond all that we ask or think—according to the power that works in you—to Him be glory in the church and in Christ Jesus to all generations, forever and ever. Amen.

The power mentioned here is the power of the Holy Spirit. What we need is not more of the Holy Spirit; The Holy Spirit needs more of us. The more we submit to His power in our lives, the more powerful our lives will become. As we die to ourselves and our fleshly nature, the more the Holy Spirit is able to work through us. When that power is alive and effective, God is able to do above and beyond all that we ask or think. Through this power, His glory is reflected in the church and becomes a light to all generations.

Many of us are in a position where we cannot handle the trials of life in our own strength. We need the power of God at work in us to live above these circumstances. What He needs is more of us for that power to become alive and effective. Consider your life. What object lesson could the Devil be learning right now? Would he sense victory or defeat in his schemes?

Pray, as Paul did, to be strengthened in your inner man and to comprehend the magnitude of God's great love for you. Nothing would give me greater satisfaction than to see the Devil's schemes against me used to destroy his work in my life and to bring glory to God! That is what God did on the cross, and that is what He desires to do in our lives!

Have a blessed day!

Your Life is a Letter

2 Corinthians 3:2-3:

You yourselves are our letter, written on our hearts, recognized and read by everyone, since it is plain that you are Christ's letter, produced by us, not written with ink but with the Spirit of the living God; not on stone tablets but on tablets that are hearts of flesh.

I can't help but think William Faulkner must have studied writing under Paul. Faulkner's use of improper run-on sentences will drive the language arts teacher nuts! You have to ignore some things to understand the meaning of both writers. The theologian in me, however, is humbled by this passage. Your life is a letter. What does it say?

In our daily lives, people around us are judging what it means to be a Christian by the things we do and say. How do our lives compare with the Word of God? Do others see faith that is alive and active or doubt that drags us down? Are we plainly Christ's letter, or do we look like we were written in some foreign language or odd code? Would an unbeliever be attracted to Christ in us or turned off by the hypocrite he sees? Would another Christian be challenged to live more closely by the word or satisfied to find justification in *little* sins?

Frankly, by looking at my own life, I am extremely grateful that God gave us His Word in print! The Bible is His standard, and I am but a poor representative. If I am the only Bible others may ever read, I'm afraid they won't get the full story! Just as the movie is never as good as the book, so our lives portrayed before the world are never as good as the real Word. We are not the standard. We are poor reflections, at best.

Movies that do well at the box office often have a sequel, and the story continues. Regardless of what people may have read from our lives in the past, our stories continue. We are still a work in progress, and we can make changes today to live closer to God's Word. People can see how

God changes us if we are willing to change. What will others read from your life today?

Have a blessed day!

Your Trumpet Sound

1 Corinthians 14:8:

In fact, if the trumpet makes an unclear sound, who will prepare for battle?

In the Old Testament, the trumpet call signaled the call to battle. When Jesus returns, His coming will be announced by a trumpet. He is not coming as a tiny baby to save the world at that point; He is coming as a mighty warrior to take charge!

The trumpet makes an unclear sound when it is blown by an inexperienced player. One must learn the art of trumpet playing in order to play clearly. (I know this well because my child has tried to learn to play the trumpet. It sounds like a dying goose with no instruction!) No one wants to follow someone into battle who is inexperienced, just as no one really enjoys listening to an inexperienced trumpet player. Public performance requires private practice.

In this passage, Paul is speaking to the Corinthians on the matter of maturity. They were fascinated with spiritual gifts, especially the lesser gift of tongues. Paul stressed to them that having this gift is wonderful, but unless they spoke intelligibly to others, the gift was meaningless. No one would understand what they said. They were to eagerly seek the greater gifts, such as prophecy, which actually helped edify and develop other believers (1 Cor. 12:31).

God has given everyone a gift in which to serve Him. Our responsibility is to use that gift and to develop it so we can build each other up in the faith. He never gave anyone a gift just so they could feel special or say they could do something unique. He equipped us so we can edify others.

How clearly does your trumpet sound today? We all have to begin somewhere. We develop our gifts by using them. If you are unsure of where God has gifted you, many spiritual gift resources are available in Christian bookstores, online, or in a library that can help you discover where God created you to serve. I highly encourage you to find that place because that is where you will be truly satisfied. If you do know your spiritual gift, find time to use it. Help build someone else with a word of encouragement, explain something God has shown you in Scripture, help a friend who has a big project, take on a community project, or maybe just listen to a friend who is hurting. All of these things display a spiritual gift in action. You will walk away feeling a sense of purpose, peaceful, and productive. I just did.

Have a blessed day!

God's Work in You

Philippians 2:13:

For it is God who is working in you, enabling you both to will and to act for His good purpose.

Do you realize that God is working in you? When you suddenly change your bad attitude to a good one because you realize it is futile otherwise, God has done a work. If a verse of Scripture has new meaning to you, God just paid you a visit. When you change your mind on something because you gained more insight into the situation, God has been working. If you now desire to do something good that you would have never attempted before out of fear, God has been working. He has been changing your heart and your desire to bring it in line with His own.

God does not force His will upon us. He knows what to do to make us desire to do His will, and He empowers us to do it. He created us, and He knows just what it takes to make us run like a well-oiled machine! He fills us with the oil of His Holy Spirit and speaks to us in ways we understand.

We are all a work in progress, and God works from the inside out. We may not outwardly see what is happening, but God is actively working on the inside. Eventually, what He is doing will work its way out. Be patient with yourself and with others. God knows how to work all things together for our good and how to bring His will into being. Where we are unwilling,

He knows how to make us willing! This is both a promise and a warning. Whether we are as gentle as a lamb or as stubborn as a donkey, we will eventually fulfill our purpose. Some just require more discipline than others. Which will you be?

Have a blessed day!

No Fear

2 Timothy 1:7:

For God has not given us a spirit of fearfulness, but one of power, love, and sound judgment.

Most everyone I know struggles with some type of fear. Fear is the source of worry, indecisiveness, inactivity, perfectionism, self-righteousness, and many other characteristics that make us less than what God created us to be. Fear paralyzes us. Fear is a tranquilizer the Devil shoots at us to keep us from doing what God intends for us to do.

Notice carefully the things God gives us. First, He gives us power. This is not power in our own strength. He gives us His power to work through us. He is greater than any evil source known to man; the Devil knows God's power is no match for him. His only hope of overcoming God's power is to stop it before it ever goes into action. The Devil cannot stop God's resource of power to us. He can only prevent us from recognizing it and using it, and he does that through fear.

The second provision mentioned that God gives us is love. God's love for us is perfect and whole. We can trust it completely. 1 John 4:18 explains that perfect love casts out fear. When we truly believe just how much God really loves us, we are able to overcome fear and do what God has called us to do. In fact, His love drives us to respond to Him, rather than to other voices. Fear is an emotion, and you cannot trust it. God is love, which is not an emotion but a truth. We must learn to live by truth and not driven by emotions.

Finally, God gives us sound judgment. In anything He calls us to do, He gives us the wisdom to carry it forth. James 1:5 tells us that all we need to do is ask to receive wisdom from God. I recently watched a

Christian do something that was very unwise. For the life of me, I could not understand why he would jeopardize so much by doing what he did. To me, he didn't have the sense God promised a Billy goat in the matter! I finally realized that he did what he did because he lacked sound judgment. In fact, God was not involved in the situation at all! Because he lacked sound judgment, he lost his ministry. Indeed, when we follow the leading of the Devil, we will fear what we shouldn't and have no fear of that which we should. As Proverbs reiterates to us, the fear of God is the beginning of wisdom.

Today, make a decision to look fear in the face and use the power God has given you. Believe in the undying and unfailing love He has for you, knowing that He has given you sound judgment. Don't let the Devil rob you of your high calling or your God-given dream. God wants the very best for you, and He is bringing you opportunities that will lead you to the good things He has for you.

Have a blessed day!

Ask

Psalm 2:7-8:

I will declare the LORD's decree: He said to Me, "You are My Son; today I have become Your Father. Ask of Me, and I will make the nations Your inheritance and the ends of the earth Your possession."

These verses are speaking of Christ. The Father decreed that the Son should ask of Him. He didn't just give the Son all things. The Son was to ask. Upon asking, the Father would grant the nations as His inheritance and the ends of the earth as His possession. All He had to do was ask.

When we pray, we are to pray in Jesus's name because our relationship with the Father is through faith in the shed blood of Jesus Christ. His finished work on the cross enables us to enter the throne room of grace and boldly ask for anything in His name.

James 4:2-3:

You desire and do not have. You murder and covet and cannot obtain. You fight and war. You do not have because you do not ask. You ask and don't receive because you ask wrongly, so that you may spend it on your desires for pleasure.

In this passage, James explains further why we don't have what we want: because we do not ask. We fall into strife with others when our needs are not met, and we often blame them for our lack when God is the only one who can meet our need. All we have to do is ask.

At other times, we ask God for something, but we ask with the wrong motive. He always sees our hearts, even when we can't fully see what is there. To ask wrongly here is to ask for things that feed the sinful desires of the flesh. God will not grant those things because they work in direct opposition to His will for us and to our overall well-being. God creates desire and longing in us that reflect His perfect will for us. These desires draw us closer to Him because we cannot fulfill them on our own. They display His glory and His grace through us. These are the desires we can bring boldly before His throne of grace and expect Him to answer. We must be dependent upon Him to grant them.

What need or desire do you have today? Is it in accordance to God's Word? Would the fulfillment of it bring glory to God? If so, bring it boldly before the throne of grace in Jesus's name, and ask the Father for it today. If He expected the Son to ask, He surely expects us to ask. He has promised the nations for our inheritance and the ends of the earth as our possession in Christ. That means there is nothing He will not do for you that conforms to His will. Ask and receive so that your joy may be complete!

Have a blessed day!

Go Boldly Before the Throne

Hebrews 4:15-16:

For we do not have a high priest who is unable to sympathize with our weaknesses, but One who has been tested in every way as we are, yet without sin. Therefore, let us approach the throne of grace with boldness, so that we may receive mercy and find grace to help us at the proper time.

Jesus is our great high priest before the Father, and He was tempted in every way we are. Unlike us, however, He was victorious over temptation. He never fell into sin or its bondage, yet He paid the penalty for our sins. Because He was tempted, He understands completely how we succumb to our weakness. His victory is our hope. Because He overcame and paid the price for us, we can come boldly before the Father to receive grace for the empty places in our lives. Because Jesus was victorious, we can overcome the sin that ensnares us.

Marred in our own sin, we could never come before the Father and ask Him for anything. Since we have all failed, we would have no hope before God without Jesus's sacrifice. When He died, God imputed our sins upon Jesus and gave us His righteousness in return. That righteousness allows us to ask God for anything with boldness! Wherever we have fallen, we find grace to overcome. We can ask for grace to triumph over any weakness and have confidence that God will grant that request. We can ask God to fill any need in our lives and have assurance that He will meet all our needs according to His riches in glory and not according to our own merit.

Don't take your high priest for granted or underestimate His power. He sits at the right hand of God interceding for you and making you righteous before Him. What do you need? Go boldly before the throne of grace and ask. Where have you struggled with sin? Go boldly before God's throne and ask for grace to overcome that sin. What desire or dream is still unfulfilled? Go boldly before the throne of grace and ask God to fulfill the dream He has given you. Even if you have asked before, ask again. Keep on asking until you receive the breakthrough you need. Delay is not denial; it just means God has more to teach you or show you before you receive your answer.

Have a blessed day!

Effective Prayer

1 John 5:14-15:

Now this is the confidence we have before Him: whenever we ask anything according to his will, He hears us. And if we know that He hears whatever we ask, we know that we have what we have asked Him for.

The key to effective prayer is praying according to God's will. While it may be hard at times to know exactly what God's will is in a situation, there are times when His will is evident according to Scripture. When we pray for those things we know are God's will, we have assurance that He will answer.

John continues his instruction on this passage in verses 16-17 by giving an example. When we see a brother in Christ sinning, we should pray for him, and God will give him life. When we pray for God to awaken the brother to his sin and to draw him back to God, we are praying according to God's will. God longs to forgive and grant grace. We can pray for a fellow Christian to turn from sin with confidence because that is God's will.

Do you have a loved one who is trapped in sin? This is not God's will, and you can pray with full confidence for God to draw him or her back to Him. Do you know someone who needs to be comforted by God's grace? You can pray with full assurance that God will comfort those who mourn. Instead of talking to others about how bad the situation is, talk to God about how great His power is to resolve the situation and bring new life. Anytime we see something that is clearly not God's will, we should pray and ask God to work in the matter according to His will. Just think of what God might do in our lives if we prayed His will over every wrong thing we encounter. We would see His power at work in our world and witness miracles on a regular basis.

Have a blessed day!

Pray at All Times

Ephesians 6:18:

With every prayer and request, pray at all times in the Spirit, and stay alert in this, with all perseverance and intercession for all the saints.

We certainly live in a time of both spiritual and physical warfare. That is why it is so important to pray. There are times when it seems hopeless, and we lose heart to pray. We think this must just be God's will for us. Paul instructs us here, however, to pray at all times. This is even more important when things seem hopeless.

As Christians, we are not without hope. Our hope is in Christ. If God raised Him from the dead, He can work miracles in our lives, too! Prayer is our connection with God. As Paul instructs here, we are to pray with perseverance until we get the breakthrough we need.

Paul also instructs us to pray for others. That is intercession. Loved ones who have fallen into sin or friends who have become ill are like soldiers who are down in the battle. We need to intercede in prayer for them. We may not be able to do one thing for their situation, but we can pray.

Ephesians 6:12:

For our battle is not against flesh and blood, but against the rulers, authorities, against the world powers of this darkness, against the spiritual forces of evil in the heavens.

To come against problems in the physical realm, we must first come against them in the spiritual realm. We do this on our knees in prayer. I'm speaking figuratively. I know some of you have trouble getting on your knees. I can still get on my knees, but it is getting harder to get up. I don't think God cares about our posture as much as He does our heart and our willingness to communicate with Him, even if all hope seems lost. Prayer energizes our forces in the spiritual realm and ultimately changes things in the physical realm.

Make today a day of prayer wherever you are. Praying makes you a mighty warrior, and the Devil wants to stop you by making you feel hopeless. Pray anyway—it is your ultimate weapon against him.

Have a blessed day!

Searching with All Your Heart

Jeremiah 29:12-14:

You will call to Me and come and pray to Me, and I will listen to you. You will seek Me and find Me when you search for Me with all your heart. I will be found by you—the LORD's declaration—and I will restore your fortunes and gather you from all the nations and places where I

banished you—the LORD's declaration. I will restore you to the place I deported you from.

If God declares a thing, you can count on it; He does not make empty promises! Notice what God declares in these verses: We will find Him when we seek Him with all our heart, and He will restore our fortunes and gather us from the places where He has banished us. When we turn to God and seek Him completely, He gives us full restoration.

As a widow, you have suffered loss. This loss has most likely affected all of your relationships, your finances, your time, and your hope for the future. God intends to restore every bit of that! When we turn to Him completely, He can take us from that place of loss and begin to build back into our lives, restoring us to a full place.

This day marks the anniversary of my husband's death in 2005. Since that day, God has led me through seminary, changed my career, established PHOEBE Ministries, and given me new friendships I would have possibly never had encountered, otherwise. Each day He seems to add a little more as I look to Him. I can honestly say that He is still restoring me to new life in this journey.

Psalm 130: 5-6:

I wait for the LORD; I wait, and put my hope in His word. I wait for the LORD more than watchmen for the morning - more than watchmen for the morning.

Hope is the eager expectation of good. With hope comes a wait. They always seem to travel hand in hand, and I'm convinced they must be marriage partners; you never see one without the other. Faith takes hold of hope and leads us into the promise. If we lose hope, we tend to lose faith.

God has good planned for our future, even though we have encountered loss. We find these good things by seeking Him in prayer. Seek and find those good things He has for you today by bringing your whole heart before Him. Find hope, healing, and restoration in knowing He already has it all worked out for you.

Have a blessed day!

Pressing Through

Matthew 9:22:

But Jesus turned and saw her. "Have courage, daughter," He said. "Your faith has made you well." And the woman was made well from that moment.

The woman with the issue of blood had to press through the crowd to get to Jesus. She had been isolated, rejected, and declared unclean for 12 years. Her whole social status was affected by her infirmity. She could have no relationship with a husband nor have children. Her family was affected. She was alone. She had exhausted all efforts to be healed from doctors and had nowhere else to go. Then, she heard about a man who had healed others and had the power to heal her, too. But with such a huge crowd around Him, how could she get to Him? She was in an unclean state. She would be turned back and shunned. Under Jewish law, she had no hope to get to Him. If only she could get close enough to just touch the hem of His garment, maybe some of His power would touch her, in return.

She could have shrunk back in hopelessness and lingered in depression, but she didn't. She plowed right through the crowd and pressed through to get to Jesus. Her hope was bigger than her fear of being rejected. Her hope was greater than her social status. Her hope, accompanied by her need, pressed through to get where she needed to be.

Jesus assured this woman. She need not fear He would punish her for being unclean. Her willingness to press through had enabled faith to grab hold of hope and lead her to her healing! Her faith in action drew power from Jesus!

Satan will do all he can to cause us to lose hope because he knows that if we do, our faith is destroyed. We have nothing with which to lay hold of Jesus's power. Refuse to give up hope; when the Devil attacks you and tries to convince you that all is hopeless, keep pressing through! Don't let what someone else thinks rob you of what Jesus has for you. He has promised to restore you, and you can press through with confidence that He who declared it will accomplish it! If you are unclean from sin, it doesn't matter. Jesus paid for that sin when He died on the cross. His redemption is full. Turning your heart toward Him is repentance. Turn to Him and keep pressing through until you touch the hem of His garment.

Today, realize that in Christ, we have hope. Keep pressing through in those areas where you have lack and are in need of an answer. God promises to restore you, and He will do it—His hem may be only a nudge away.

Have a blessed day!

Prayer and Confidence

Why is it we pray sometimes and see nothing happen, yet there are times when we see answers just lining up and waiting to be noticed? Sometimes God seems to be silent; at other times He speaks loudly. I'm convinced that God is always speaking or teaching us something. He has promised never to leave us or forsake us. The question is whether or not we are listening or watching what he is trying to communicate to us.

Psalm 61-7:

LORD, do not rebuke me in Your anger; do not discipline me in Your wrath. Be gracious to me, LORD, for I am weak; heal me, LORD, for my bones are shaking; my whole being is shaken with terror. And You, LORD—how long? Turn, LORD! Rescue me; save me because of Your faithful love. For there is no remembrance of You in death; who can than You in Sheol? I am weary from my groaning; with my tears I dampen my pillow and drench my bed every night. My eyes are swollen from grief; they grow old because of all my enemies.

We find a strong prayer in this Psalm. The psalmist poured his heart out to God and expressed his anguish. He was clearly not a happy person and appealed to God's mercy and grace. He realized his weak and lowly position and understood he could not help himself. These words express a prayer of deep groaning and sorrow. The Psalm, however, takes a different turn beginning in verse 8, and we see a shift in the mood, altogether.

Verses 8-10:

Depart from me, all evildoers, for the LORD has heard the sound of my weeping. The LORD has heard my plea for help; the LORD accepts my prayer. All my enemies will be ashamed and shake with terror; they will turn back and suddenly be disgraced.

The Psalm begins with weeping and sorrow and ends with total confidence in an answer from God. David is the psalmist here, and he cries out to God, pouring all his emotions, fears, needs, and concerns to a loving Father. David got all of this out of him, then he had confidence that God would answer. This is exactly what we need to do. When difficulty and sorrow hit us, we need to just cry it all out to God, and have faith that He will answer. When we recognize our weak and helpless condition before an Almighty God, we become ready to submit to His plan. God can then work His plan into our lives.

In verses 8-10, nothing appears to have changed in David's situation. He addressed his attackers with a warning that God WILL help him, and they needed to be afraid—very afraid. Intense prayer moved David from fear to faith.

Today, cry out to God with all your concerns, and rest assured that He will handle every one of them. He does hear us when we cry out to Him in total dependence. Be confident that God is working on your behalf.

Have a blessed day!

AUGUST 8

The Privilege of Prayer

Isaiah 56:6-8:

And the foreigners who convert to the LORD, minister to Him, love the LORD's name, and are His servants, all who keep the Sabbath without desecrating it, and who hold firmly to My covenant—I will bring them to My holy mountain and let them rejoice in My house of prayer. Their burnt offerings and sacrifices will be acceptable on My altar, for My house will be called a house of prayer for all nations. This is the declaration of the LORD God, who gathers the dispersed of Israel; "I will gather to them still others besides those already gathered."

While Israel was God's chosen nation and chosen people, He always planned for Gentiles to be a part of His kingdom. Even under the law, He provided for foreigners to convert to Hebrew belief and worship Him. God always accepted Gentiles, even though religious leaders looked down upon them and often didn't accept them.

In this passage, we see that God allowed Gentiles, foreigners, the privilege of prayer. God desired for unworthy, unchosen Gentiles who dared seek Him the opportunity to commune with Him in prayer. They could praise His name, thank Him, and even ask Him for things. By accepting their burnt offerings and sacrifices, He was offering forgiveness. These foreigners could have a relationship with God the Father under the law.

Today, another sacrifice has been made. We no longer need to bring burnt offerings and sacrifices. Foreigners may come to God through the shed blood of Jesus Christ and have the privilege of prayer. God does not exclude anyone from the privilege of prayer based upon their nationality.

Under the law (old covenant) and under grace (new covenant), a sacrifice is still needed for the privilege of prayer to be effective. If we have accepted the sacrifice of the finished work of Christ on the cross, we have the privilege of prayer. If we are trying to have relationship with God some other way, our prayers are not accepted.

We are so very blessed and fortunate to be living under God's new covenant of grace! God saves us and blesses us through His grace by faith in Jesus. We don't have to earn the right to be accepted. We don't have to work for our salvation or for God to bless us. We have the privilege of prayer with the Father!

In this passage, God also promised to gather together others who worshiped Him. Fellowship with others who have the privilege of prayer is essential to our well-being. God created us for fellowship and to live in the community of fellowship. He gives us each other as a blessing and to build each other up. This way, we know we are not excluded and that we are accepted.

God has given us to each other. Rejoice in that privilege today. May we be women known for taking advantage of the privilege of prayer, and may God continue to work His mighty and glorious plan into our lives.

Have a blessed day!

The LORD Accepts My Prayer

Psalm 6:9:

The LORD has heard my plea for help; the LORD accepts my prayer.

I'm constantly amazed at just how much God answers prayer when I totally surrender a matter to Him! It seems the longer I hold on to a matter and try to force or find an answer myself, the more God lets me wait. We must learn to ask and surrender to see the LORD's response.

God hears us when we pray. He doesn't ignore us or turn a deaf ear to us. He wants us to ask of Him and to completely trust Him with the answer. Ask in full confidence, then wait in full expectation. God acts on behalf of those who wait for Him.

Is something heavy on your heart? Do you have a great need? Are you worried over your future? Cry out to God, and know that He accepts your prayer. Surrender that matter to Him, and rest in full, assurance that He is acting in your favor. You can't control it anyway, so just give it to Him. Then stand back in amazement at what He will do with it.

Have a blessed day!

Prayer as Incense

Revelation 5:8:

When He took the scroll, the four living creatures and the 24 elders fell down before the Lamb. Each one had a harp and gold bowls filled with incense, which are the prayers of the saints.

Unless we journal, most of us probably forget about prayers we prayed long ago. God, however, doesn't. He stores them as incense—a sweet smelling aroma. He places them in gold bowls as something precious to obtain.

Many of my prayers are laden with need, requests, and tears. Others are quick, short, and to the point. Some are filled with praise and thanksgiving. God cherishes them all. They are expressions of our hearts to Him.

Don't ever think your prayers are meaningless or ineffective. God doesn't always give us a view into His plans or what He is doing behind the scenes. Those prayers get to Him through the shed blood of His Son, and they are precious to Him. So, take time to pray today. Pray for yourself and for one another. Our prayers move God and change us.

Have a blessed day!

A Confident Heart

Psalm 57:7:

My heart is confident, God, my heart is confident. I will sing; I will sing praises.

Not only did David pray well, but he was an excellent song writer and musician. This man after God's own heart looked for ways to verbally express his heart to God. This verse is believed to be part of a song David wrote while he was hiding in a cave from Saul.

If I were hiding in a cave from a mighty king who was seeking to kill me, I imagine I would be terrified. Yet, David declared his heart to be confident before God. Instead of sinking into doubt, worry, and depression, David chose to praise God in song. God chose to record the song for all of us to enjoy throughout the ages and into eternity in His living Word. Now, that is what I call a real record deal!

In times of trouble, we can have a heart that is confident before God. Choose to praise Him in those times, and don't let the Devil get a foothold in your mind. Doubt and worry are the Devil's praise. Choose who you will entertain today.

Have a blessed day!

Your Praise is Beautiful

Psalm 33:1:

Rejoice in the LORD, you righteous ones; praise from the upright is beautiful.

God finds beauty in your praise! Just meditate on that for a moment. When God sees you worshiping Him and giving praise to His name, He sees you as beautiful!

We must remember the only way we can be truly righteous is through the righteousness of Christ. When God sees us as a partaker of the blood of Christ in worship, He beholds us as beautiful creations. He doesn't see all the mistakes we've made and the places where we have failed. He doesn't see our outfit, our hairdo, our makeup, or even our dazzling jewelry. He sees the righteousness of Christ and our offering of praise, and He is blessed by our beauty.

Take advantage of your chances to enter into both individual and corporate worship, and become a beautiful sight of praise to God. Rejoice in the LORD, dear one! Your praise to Him is beautiful!

Have a blessed day!

Time to Praise

Psalm 103:1-5:

My soul, praise the LORD, and all that is within me, praise His holy name. My soul, praise the LORD, and do not forget all His benefits. He forgives all your sin; He heals all your diseases. He redeems your life from the Pit; He crowns you with faithful love and compassion. He satisfies you with goodness; your youth is renewed like the eagle.

When things are difficult, it is easy to sit and complain about everything. We also can easily fall into depression and self-pity. While things may hurt, praise is always the best response. The Devil won't stay where the name of God is praised! Praise is one way we have to resist the Devil when he tries to drag us into those self-defeating emotions that wear us down.

Praise helps us remember the goodness of God and to look forward to seeing God's glory revealed in our lives again. Praising God also sends a message to the Devil that you do not believe his lies. He wants you to believe your situation is hopeless and that things will never get better. God, however, is always at work for your good.

The best thing we can do today is to just praise the name of Jesus and watch the Devil flee from our emotions and our circumstances. Determine today to make your mouth one of praise instead of a mouth of complaint. If you hurt, carry that directly to God. No one else can really help you anyway. Just remember that God truly cares for you and is working things out for your benefit and His glory, and praise Him for it. Praise exercises your faith. Without faith, it is impossible to please God.

Have a blessed day!

Praise in the Assembly

Psalm 149:1:

Hallelujah! Sing to the LORD a new song, His praise in the assembly of the godly.

Never underestimate the value or the power that comes from corporate worship. We can all worship God privately in our homes and be blessed, but there is something about corporate worship that pleases God and blesses us in the process. When God's people come together to worship Him and magnify Him, He takes notice.

God dwells in the praises of His people. When we gather to worship Him, we experience His presence in a way like no other. In His presence, we find peace, understanding, and encouragement to continue in the way He has planned for us. We need to experience His presence and become revived, refreshed, and renewed.

I get tired of singing the same old songs over and over. When routine becomes dreadful, we find ourselves in a rut. No one wants to live in a rut of despair. Learn to sing a new song to God and believe Him for something new. Stretch your faith to believe God for changes to the ruts you create for yourself. There is no better place to sing a new song to God than in the assembly of corporate worship with other believers.

Encounter the living God as you sing a new song of praise to Him, and seek His presence in the midst of the praises of other believers. Look and listen for the special word He has just for you. He is alive, and you can encounter Him today. Hallelujah!

Have a blessed day!

The Power of Rejoicing

Nehemiah 8:10:

Then he said to them, "Go and eat what is rich, drink what is sweet, and send portions to those who have nothing prepared, since today is holy to our LORD. Do not grieve, because your strength comes from rejoicing in the LORD."

After Nehemiah completed the wall of Jerusalem, the people gathered around Ezra for the reading of the law. They began to weep and mourn as he read because they realized their sin. That is what the law does: it reveals our sin in the light of a perfect God. No one can measure up to His standards. By breaking only one, you break the entire law and are guilty.

While the Israelites realized and repented of their sins, Ezra told them not to grieve because their strength comes from rejoicing in the LORD. He ordered a time of rejoicing. This reminds me of the prodigal son in the New Testament. While he returned to the father in sorrow, the father planned a feast of rejoicing because the son he lost had returned.

The Israelites of Nehemiah's day had to offer a sacrifice to atone for their sins. This sacrifice would provide a temporary atonement. Today, we live under a new covenant of grace, which provides permanent atonement. Our strength comes from turning to God from sin and rejoicing in the finished work of Calvary. Because of Jesus's sacrifice, we no longer have to make our own sacrifice for sin.

Today, rejoice in the finished work of Christ for you and begin to see your strength renewed. Let the past be the past, and look forward to a new day in Christ. Grieving will sap you of energy and strength, but rejoicing will refresh, renew, and revive you. Because of Christ, we all have reason to rejoice.

Have a blessed day!

Praise Brings Power

2 Timothy 4:18:

The LORD will rescue me from every evil work and will bring me safely into His heavenly kingdom. To Him be the glory forever and ever! Amen.

Have you ever felt like you needed to be rescued? I feel that way quite often. Rest assured that your Rescuer is alert and watching over you.

Paul got into much trouble simply by preaching the gospel of Jesus Christ. By doing exactly what God wanted him to do, he landed in prison many times. Eventually, it cost him his life. Regardless of how much the enemy tried to stop his efforts, God continuously delivered him. The enemy's goal was to silence Paul. By killing him, however, the letters he wrote became more effective in their ability to reach people with the gospel of Christ. Indeed, the evil the Devil schemed to destroy Paul ultimately spread the gospel to multitudes! Virtually every Christian knows who Paul was and what he preached. Even many who are not Christians know who he is. His words and message are forever alive in the Bible and proclaiming the message of salvation through Jesus Christ.

If the Devil is trying to destroy something in you, it is only because it is a threat to him. The LORD will rescue you from every evil work. What God has placed in you, the Devil cannot steal. God can raise or resurrect it in a whole new way that destroys the Devil's stronghold forever. Wherever the Devil is at work in your life, a testimony of God's grace and His glory is waiting.

If you feel the heat of the Devil's schemes today, know that your Rescuer is alert. Give Him praise and honor today, just as Paul did. Paul had an eager expectation of God's goodness in the midst of his trials. The same

God who rescued Paul will bring you safely into His heavenly kingdom, too. Praise brings power. Your Knight in shining armor is with you. Look to Him and glorify His name.

Have a blessed day!

Praise, Fruitfulness, and War

Zechariah 10:3-5:

My anger burns against the shepherd, so I will punish the leaders. For the LORD of Hosts has tended His flock, the house of Judah; He will make them like his majestic steed in battle. From them will come the cornerstone, from them the tent peg, from them the battle bow, from them every ruler. Together they will be like the warriors in battle trampling down the mud of the streets. They will fight because the LORD is with them, and they will put horsemen to shame.

Prior to this, God's people had looked to idols and diviners for guidance. Religious leaders had relied upon the empty dreams and comfort spoken by these false gods, and there was no one to properly lead God's people. Therefore, God brought judgment upon these leaders. The term *LORD of Hosts* depicts God as a warrior or judge. Here, He protected the house of Judah, which means *praise.* Indeed, God, alone, is worthy of all praise, and He will not share it will a false god who speaks lies.

From those who praise Him, He will build a mighty army. Jesus was born from the tribe of Judah. God brought forth great things from praise. Praise goes to war, and God fights alongside. This should be a wake-up call to us all! If we want God to fight for us, we need to embrace praise.

Verses 6-7:

I will strengthen the house of Judah and deliver the house of Joseph. I will restore them because I have compassion on them, and they will be as though I had never rejected them. For I am the LORD their God, and I will answer them. Ephraim will be like a warrior, and their hearts will be glad as if with wine. Their children will see it and be glad; their hearts will rejoice in the LORD.

God promised to strengthen the house of Judah (praise.) He promised deliverance to the house of Joseph. The house of Joseph was restored through Ephraim (fruitfulness). He promised to restore them because He had compassion on them. Rest assured that God sees our desperate situations. He is fully aware of the places where we hurt and have no other hope of healing or restoration other than Him. He has compassion on us, and He moves on our behalf.

God promised to make Ephraim like a warrior and to bring gladness to their hearts. We see the picture of strong men in battle, victorious and undefeated. When God restores us, it is for the purpose of battle, not for self- indulgence. We are in a war, and we must be ready, capable, and willing to fight. When we begin to praise, regardless of our circumstances, He brings us into His fight and strengthens us. He restores us and makes us fruitful, defeating our enemies.

The children of Ephraim learn from their parents. They grow up learning how to praise and fight. What a wonderful legacy to leave to our children and grandchildren, especially in such a day of uncertainty. Today, realize that someone is watching how you handle your difficult situations and is learning from you. Stand up and praise God, regardless of how bad things may seem. Allow Him to strengthen you and make you fruitful and victorious. You have nothing to lose from it and absolutely everything to gain.

Have a blessed day!

A Reason to Rejoice

Psalm 122:1:

I rejoiced with those who said to me, "Let us go to the house of the LORD."

I hope you like going to church. This is usually the high point of my week to see all my friends and cohorts in Christ and to be filled with God's Word and fellowship. This experience strengthens me to face each week. If you don't rejoice when it is time to go to church, it may be time to re-evaluate. Perhaps, a change of some sort is needed.

The psalmist rejoiced with others who shared his same feelings. To rejoice with someone means that at least two of you felt the same joy. God does not call us to walk in places alone. He always brings us to places where we can rejoice with others in our journey with Him. In this case, those who rejoiced together enjoyed going to the house of the LORD together. They were excited to hear from God and to be a part of what He was doing.

I hope you feel the same way about your church. At times, I don't know what God is doing, but I'm just glad He lets me be a part of it. He has placed me with great people who edify me, and He is using me in certain avenues to edify others. I feel like I only see a very limited view of what is happening, but at least He has included me in the picture!

If you don't have a church family, I strongly urge you to find a church that is biblically based and supportive of your needs and condition as a widow. God created the church to encourage and edify believers, and He uses the church to minister to those who are hurting in the world. We are fed in the church, and we find our place of ministry there.

Rejoice with those around you today that are a part of the same thing you are. Whether co-workers, neighbors, family members, or fellow church members, you are all called to work together in some aspect. Celebrate one another and the fact that you are not alone.

Have a blessed day!

Worship in Spirit and in Truth

John 4:23-24:

But an hour is coming, and is now here, when true worshipers will worship the Father in spirit and truth. Yes, the Father wants such people to worship Him. God is spirit and those who worship Him must worship in spirit and truth.

In this passage, Jesus addressed the Samaritan woman at the well. She had just tried to start an argument with Jesus about the proper place to worship—the mountain or in Jerusalem. The Samaritans followed their ancestors in worshiping on the mountain, while the Jews taught the proper place to worship was in the temple at Jerusalem. Jesus's response to her dismissed either option. Instead of addressing where to worship, Jesus instructed her how to worship. True worshipers will worship in spirit and in truth.

Notice closely how Jesus began this response. "But an hour is coming, and is now here…" When Jesus came into the earth, worship changed. Wherever Jesus was, the presence of God dwelled within Him. The Jews taught the proper place to worship was the temple in Jerusalem because they believed the presence of God was there when a sacrifice was made for sin. Once God sent His Son, His presence went wherever Jesus did. God's presence left Jesus on the cross when He poured out His wrath upon the sacrifice which bore our sin. When Jesus died, the veil separating the Holy Place from the Holy of Holies, where God dwelled, was torn. This opened access to God's presence to anyone who received Jesus's sacrifice.

Today, you don't have to be on a mountain or in Jerusalem to worship God. All you have to do is believe in the sacrifice Jesus made for you. This is the truth of worship. Receiving this sacrifice is an act of grace from the heavenly Father. He promises to dwell in you through the power of the Holy Spirit when you receive Jesus as your Savior. Therefore, you have the ability to worship Him anytime and anywhere. Going through the motions of a ritual is not true worship. Worship is a response to His love for us. Worship is obedience to His commands. Worship is praising Him for who He is and what He has already done for us.

His Word tells us not to forsake the gathering of ourselves together (Heb. 10:25). When we come together in corporate worship, our hearts are encouraged and strengthened. Private worship is possible any day of the week, but you have limited opportunities for corporate worship each week. Take advantage of them. You don't *have* to go to church to worship God. You *get* to go to church to worship God and to fellowship with others who want to worship Him, as well. Let God strengthen and encourage you today through other believers.

Have a blessed day!

Your Freewill Offering

Psalm 54:6-7:

I will sacrifice a freewill offering to You. I will praise Your name, LORD, because it is good. For He has delivered me from every trouble, and my eye has looked down on my enemies.

In this Psalm, David remembers how God has delivered him in the past, and he chooses to worship God. In the preceding verses, he cried out for deliverance from his enemies. Here, he remembers how God has delivered him in the past, and he trusts in God's faithfulness toward him.

The freewill offering was a burnt offering totally consumed on the altar and offered smoke that rose to heaven as a sweet fragrance to God. This required a previous sin offering to atone for sin, and the burnt offering was a statement that the individual stood in a covenant of grace with God. By making such an offering, David was stating that he stood in the grace of God, who had been faithful to him, in trusting that God would deliver him from his enemies.

Today, we who are Christians stand in the grace of God because of what Jesus has already done on the cross for us. No other sacrifice must be made for us to stand in God's grace! Our freewill offering is simple praise to God for His faithfulness to us. When we praise Him for what He has done for us, it rises as a pleasing fragrance to God and places us in a state where we acknowledge His grace is both sufficient and effective to meet our every need.

If you are waiting for God to move on your behalf to answer prayers, offer Him a freewill offering of praise today. Thank Him for the times He has delivered you in the past, and trust in His faithfulness toward you. You stand in a state of grace before Him. God is good, and we can expect to see His goodness manifested in our lives. Praise Him for prior victories and for the victories yet to come.

Have a blessed day!

Clothed with Strength

Psalm 18:32:

God—He clothes me with strength and makes my way perfect.

I am often told that I am a strong woman. Perhaps, in some ways I am, but in other ways, I still feel very weak. I need all the help I can get in some areas! I have a friend who constantly tells me, "I wish I were as strong as you are." Ironically, she is the one who is strong in areas where I feel weak, and she doesn't see herself as a strong person.

This verse reveals to us the secret of strength. We don't obtain it by our own means; God clothes us with strength.

I remember when my son, Samuel, was a baby. He had so many clothes that he couldn't possibly wear them all! I would dress him, take a picture, then change him and take another picture. He couldn't clothe himself, and he would wear anything I put on him. Our strength comes in the same way. We can't clothe ourselves with it. God clothes us with strength much as we would clothe a baby.

The secret to obtaining strength comes in resting in the Father's lap. When we submit to His plan and humble ourselves before Him, He clothes us with the strength we need for the task He has placed before us. When we choose to learn from Him, rather than resist Him, He clothes us with the strength to grow. People who see us as strong are merely recognizing the growth we've obtained through the strength with which God has clothed us.

God makes our way perfect. We do not have to be perfect. He knows just how and when we will fail, and He makes the path to fit our failures. When we stumble off the main path, He will provide a side road to lead us to His predetermined destination. This reminds me of the words to a song I've come to love and appreciate - *God blessed the broken road and led me straight to you.*

As you worship the Lord today, allow Him to clothe you with strength. Submit fully to Him, and open your heart and mind to learn from Him. Rest assured that He will make your way perfect. Even if you have blown it, He will provide another route for you to have exactly what He planned for you. He is a loving Father, and He wants the very best for you. Trust Him as He clothes you with the strength you need to grow.

Have a blessed day!

The Secret to Inner Strength

Psalm 73:25-26:

Whom do I have in heaven but You? And I desire nothing on earth but You. My flesh and my heart may fail, but God is the strength of my heart, my portion forever.

God wants to be first place in our hearts. He made us for His glory, and He is our rightful priority. When we place anything else before Him, we set ourselves up for failure. We can do nothing without God, but in Christ, we can do all things (John 15:5, Phil. 4:13). Our faith must be placed firmly in Him as a Person. When our faith is in Him, nothing is impossible (Matt. 17:20). He goes to work on our behalf and strengthens our hearts with confidence. He gives us inner strength.

Proverbs 21:25:

Strength and honor are her clothing, and she can laugh at the time to come.

When God strengthens your heart, you begin to wear that strength as a garment. People sense it because you carry the presence of God with you. We live in very uncertain times, and we desperately need the strength that only God can give us. This strength has the power to overcome strongholds, build faith, and move mountains. This strength reveals the glory of God in the earth because it is His power working in us.

The secret to obtaining this strength is to become completely dependent upon God by placing your trust in Him. Who do we have in heaven but Him? We need no one in heaven but Him! To desire nothing but Him is to have all the power of earth and heaven on your side and fighting for you. And if God be for you, who can be against you (Rom. 8:31)?

Have a blessed day!

Limited Strength, Open Door

Revelation 3:8:

I know your works. Because you have limited strength, have kept My word, and have not denied My name, look, I have placed before you and open door that no one is able to close.

You are not the only one aware of your limitations. God knows them and will open doors for you in spite of them. He will do for you what you are not able to do for yourself! When He opens a door, no one can close it. You simply have to be willing to walk through it.

Sometimes, we become so accustomed to rejection that we don't know how to act when we are faced with full acceptance. We become afraid that if we try to walk through the open door, it will slam in our face. This is not true with God. At other times, we fear what is on the other side of the door because we have become comfortable on the outside. God knows how to make us uncomfortable enough to want to walk through any door He opens.

Expect God to open doors for you. He knows we are not strong enough to climb every mountain in front of us, so He graciously opens doors for us that take us exactly where we need to be much quicker than if we had tried to find our way on our own. He will do this simply because we serve Him, honor Him, believe Him, acknowledge Him, and depend upon Him. Watch for an open door today, and be willing to walk through it.

Have a blessed day!

Strength Training

Philippians 2:13:

For it is God who is working in you, enabling you both to will and to act for His good purpose.

God does not tear His people down, nor does He set us up for failure. He is constantly enabling, developing, and training His people. Trust the work He is doing in you. Know that if you fall, God will be faithful to pick you up, brush you off, and put you right back in the game. He has not given up on you, so don't give up on yourself or on Him.

Too many of us live defeated lives because we depend upon our own strength. We place ourselves in a box where we feel comfortable, and we won't even try to do anything outside that box because we know we don't have the natural strength or ability to step outside. If we never attempt to get outside that box, however, we will never grow beyond our current strength. What is worse, if we don't use the strength we have, we will soon lose it. We need to exercise our strength to maintain it; strength must be challenged in order to grow. Know that if God is working in you, He is enabling you to do what He has called you to do. He is working on both your ability and your will to move in your purpose.

Don't let your limitations define you. Know beyond a shadow of a doubt that God is working in you. With Him, all things are possible! You have a purpose, and the enemy would love nothing more than to see you come up one yard short of your dream and live with regret the rest of your life. God's purpose is for you to cross the finish line. Trust what He is doing in your life, and allow Him to develop you. Your victory is waiting.

Have a blessed day!

When I am Weak, I am Strong

2 Corinthians 12:10:

So because of Christ, I am pleased in weakness, in insults, in catastrophes, in persecutions, and in pressures. For when I am weak, then I am strong.

I have to admit that I am not yet at a place where I am pleased in difficult times or situations. I feel the frustrations of life far too often. Paul encourages us in this verse that God's power resides in us during the times when we feel weak. He reminds us that we cannot overcome in our own power, but we must rely upon God.

While I can certainly be a fighter, much of the time I feel weak, frustrated, and overwhelmed at the pressures and responsibilities of widowhood. This is where I must rely upon God's power to be strong. When we cry out to Him in those places where we cannot help ourselves, He comes roaring into the heavenly realms to take care of those spiritual forces that are trying to destroy us, much like a mama bear defends her cub. We need only call on Him and trust Him in the matter.

We will never realize all the battles God has fought for us until we reach heaven. I'm convinced we will be absolutely amazed and humbled when we see just how much He has intervened on our behalf without our even knowing it. God's power in our lives is not dependent upon our feelings; rather, it is determined by our relationship with Him through Christ. While we may feel weak and even appear weak to the world, we are children of God Almighty, who works in us and for us to accomplish His purpose and bring Him glory.

If you feel weak today, rest assured that God is strong in that area. Submit it to Him. Regard your trials and pressures as opportunities for God to show Himself strong on your behalf. His power is made perfect in your weakness. Hallelujah! Let the weak say, "I am strong."

Have a blessed day!

August 26

Justice or Power?

Job 42:10:

After Job had prayed for his friends, the LORD restored his prosperity and doubled his previous possessions.

Luke 23:34:

Then Jesus said, "Father, forgive them, because they do not know what they are doing."

Job's friends spoke wrongly against him. Jesus's friends betrayed Him, and His own people crucified Him. Job was a man who walked blameless before the LORD, yet calamity struck him as one who had been cursed. Jesus never sinned, yet He died the cruel death of a hardened criminal. In both men we see a pattern of unfairness, injustice, and what God requires when such things happen to us.

God instructed Job to pray for his friends that had wrongly accused him. They were to make sacrifices, and Job was to act as the priest who presented their requests to God. Jesus interceded for His accusers while still on the cross, making a way for their repentance through Him. When others hurt us, we are to pray for God to forgive their sins. When we do, it releases the power of God to work in our lives. Both Job and Jesus experienced God's power after they prayed for their accusers.

After Job prayed for his friends, God restored his health and his possessions. In fact, God made his later years greater than his former years. After Jesus prayed for His accusers and died, God raised Him from the dead and seated Him at His own right hand so that He now intercedes for all of us. Power flows into our lives from the throne of God when we ask God to forgive those who have wronged us or hurt us in some way.

Do you want justice, or do you want power? Some things will never be made right in this world, but we can still walk in God's power through any situation. You can't change people, but you don't have to live in bondage to anyone. To seek justice is to get even with someone who owes you. To seek God's power is to seek deliverance from their power over you! Give me God's power over justice any day.

Have a blessed day!

Spiritual Exercise

Romans 16:25-27:

Now to Him who has the power to strengthen you according to my gospel and the proclamation of Jesus Christ, according to the revelation of the sacred secret kept silent for long ages, but now revealed and made known through the prophetic Scriptures, according to the command of the eternal God to advance the obedience of faith among all nations— to the only wise God, through Jesus Christ—to Him be the glory forever! Amen.

Now that is a mouthful! The grammar freak in me wants to clean this three-verse sentence up by inserting a period somewhere, but to Paul, this was one complete thought. He is saying that God has the power to strengthen us through the gospel of Jesus Christ. The gospel was once a secret but now revealed through Scripture. As we come to believe, it advances our faith. For whatever it produces in us, Paul gives all glory to God, who is the only wise God through Jesus Christ. You could preach an entire sermon using only one phrase.

The gospel of Christ does strengthen us. In fact, the greater the revelation we have of Christ, the stronger we are. We get a deeper revelation of Christ by studying the Word of God. When we meditate on His word and apply it to our everyday life, the gospel of Christ takes on new meaning for us daily.

The whole purpose of Scripture is to advance our faith. If we never read it, our faith never grows. If we are content merely to listen to our pastor preach from it once or twice a week but never dig into it for ourselves, we will advance only as far as our pastor can preach.

I admit that I am very envious of some of my cohorts who work out religiously. They have perfectly toned bodies and can't wait for beach season. I, on the other hand, dread putting on a swim suit because it is obvious I have NOT worked out in a few years. These women, however, have spent much time in the gym and are now sporting the results. If I want to look like them, I need to spend some time in the gym doing what they have done, too.

Meditating on God's Word is a spiritual work-out. This strengthens our inner selves and prepares us to wage war against the Devil. Meditating on God's Word gives us faith to reach for God's promises. Personally, I could spend hours in the Bible and never realize how much time has passed because I find it so refreshing. I only wish I found physical exercise so appealing!

Spend some time in God's Word today. Meditate on a favorite verse to see how it comes alive in your life. Watch for God to speak to you about that verse as you go through your day. Give Him the glory for the revelation He gives you, and watch your faith and your joy increase!

Have a blessed day!

Finding Strength in God

In 1 Samuel 29, we find that David and his men had been rejected by the Philistine army and had returned to Ziklag. In 1 Samuel 30, David returned to Ziklag to find the village burned and women and children taken by the Amalekites, who were descendants of Esau and enemies of Israel. To make matters worse, David's own men were thinking of stoning him at this point because they were hurt and angry at losing their families. If David hadn't taken them into battle, they could have been there to defend their homes. Just who is David's friend at this point?

1 Samuel 30:6:

David was in a difficult position because the troops talked about stoning him, for they were all very bitter over the loss of their sons and daughters. But David found strength in the LORD his God.

David turned to the One person he knew would never desert him or turn against him. As a young shepherd boy, he had been accustomed to loneliness and depending upon God to guide him. As a result, God worked supernaturally through David to conquer real enemies. Here he learned not to fear battle because he knew God was on his side.

There may be times when things hit us from every side and literally exhaust us. Just when we discover great loss, we can't even grieve because those who should be comforting us are thinking about stoning us out of their own sense of loss. In those times, we must follow David's example and find strength in the LORD our God.

David did not react immediately or try to find a solution on his own. Neither did he try to defend himself against his own men. He sought the LORD for guidance.

Verses 7-8:

David said to Abiathar the priest, son of Ahimelech, "Bring me the ephod." So Abiathar brought it to him, and David asked the LORD: "Should I pursue these raiders? Will I overtake them?" The LORD replied to him, "Pursue them, for you will certainly overtake them and rescue the people."

David was willing to pursue his enemy to take what had been stolen from him, but he sought the LORD's guidance first. He knew that unless God was with him, he would not succeed. He sought direction and followed God's word. God cleared the way for David's victory.

Sometimes we need to surrender and accept our losses, and sometimes we need to fight and regain what is rightfully ours. Also, we may need to continue to fight, even though we are physically, mentally, emotionally, and spiritually exhausted. We must look to God for guidance in distinguishing the difference. We are certain to lose if we engage in the wrong action, but our victory is assured if we pursue the right one. Be willing to fight or surrender, whichever He may lead you to do. Your victory waits at the other end. David's crown was very near—so is yours.

Have a blessed day!

Ascribe Power to God

Psalm 68:34:

Ascribe power to God. His majesty is over Israel, His power among the clouds.

To ascribe means to recognize something as the source. We need to recognize that God is the source of power. He reigns over Israel and the church, and His power hovers above us everywhere. When we recognize God as the source of all power, we must realize that we are not the source.

When we think of walking in power, we often picture that power in ourselves. To walk in God's power means that God works His power through us. He is the originator and the navigator; we are simply the conduit. We do not control or manipulate His power in any way. As we walk forth in obedience, God wields His power through us.

To consider the opposite, we must understand that when we do not walk in obedience, we operate without God's power. We might as well have a dead battery as we experience the results of unfruitful and unproductive lives. We need to spend some time recharging in His Word and redirecting our walk to the pathway of power through obedience.

Recognize God as the source of power in your life today. If you have some dry, barren places, submit them to God, and do whatever He shows you to do. He has the power to change any situation, but He will work it through you as you follow Him. His power is all above you in the clouds. He has not forgotten you or abandoned you. He merely wants you to ascribe power to Him and allow Him to work through you. Determine to become a conduit through which He can do mighty works.

Have a blessed day!

Your Strong High Priest

Hebrews 7:26:

For this is the kind of high priest we need: holy, innocent, undefiled, separated from sinners, and exalted above the heavens.

This verse describes a very strong high priest—one who can go before God's throne with boldness, confidence, and great favor. Unlike earthly high priests, this high priest does not need to offer a sacrifice to God for his own sins in order to be accepted before the throne: He is fully accepted and favored. This high priest does not have to worry about the sins of His people being too much to present to God because He has already made the perfect sacrifice for them. He can go before the Father completely undefiled and present requests for His people, who are also blameless before the Father in Him. If this high priest is for you, no one can be against you.

Jesus is our strong high priest, and in Him we can go boldly before the throne of God! While we may have fallen many times and are completely unworthy in our own merit, we have a strong advocate before the Father in Christ. He is the best attorney you will ever find, and all you have to do is admit your guilt and turn to Him.

This same strong high priest brings mercy and grace from the throne room of God. You receive mercy to pardon your sin and grace to help you overcome in the future. Make your requests known to God through Christ. He will give you complete victory in every situation. He is the one worthy, holy, innocent, undefiled, sinless, and exalted high priest, and He has already paid the price for you to enter the throne room boldly and with confidence. Nothing is hopeless as long as He is your high priest.

The best part is that today He is sitting at the right hand of the Father making intercession for you. He is already working on your behalf today, even though you may not yet be fully awake. You are His priority before the Father. Make Him your priority as you begin your day.

Have a blessed day!

If the LORD Had Not Been My Help

Psalm 94:17:

If the LORD had not been my help, I would soon rest in the silence of death.

Have you ever come through a difficult time only to look back and see where God's hand was there with you all along? There are just times when we must go through things in order to see a different view from the other side. When we look back, we see where God's hand guided and protected us, even though we didn't understand things at the beginning of our journey. If the LORD had not been my help through many things, I would certainly have been silenced by death. Instead, He has allowed me to live to tell my story.

As widows, we've all encountered this sense of realizing the LORD's help. If He had not brought us through many difficult days, we would have lost hope and given up on life. Because of His help, however, we have found the strength, hope, encouragement, and even vision to live again.

God knows and understands the difficulty of each heartache, difficulty, trial, and unrealized dream we must face. He never makes us face them alone. He alone is the force that brings us through those times and enables us to flourish and prosper after loss has devastated our dreams. Know that He is with you, and fully rely upon His help—the help that is often invisible to our physical eyes. If it were not for the LORD's help, we would have never come this far; with the LORD's help again, we will go even farther. Take time to thank Him for helping you to this point, and trust where He is leading you today.

Have a blessed day!

A God Like No Other

Micah 7:18:

Who is a God like You, removing iniquity and passing over rebellion for the remnant of His inheritance? He does not hold on to His anger forever, because He delights in faithful love.

How wonderful to know that God cannot stay mad at us! I can stay mad for a long time, but that is a part of my human frailty. The nature of God is not to remain angry at His children; He looks over offenses just so He can love us—that is His delight.

Any other god we may serve demands from us. If we serve money, it will demand we become a slave to it. If we serve self, we find she is never pleased. If we serve others, they will always want more from us. God, however, longs to give us Himself. He longs to give us the desires of our hearts and to make us whole. When we serve Him, we are fulfilled, rather than depleted. He frees us from the bondage that other gods have invoked upon us.

Take time to worship the God like no other today. He delights in His love for us and not in anger toward us. He is faithful to us even when we are not to Him. Give Him praise today.

Have a blessed day!

Consider the Work of God

Ecclesiastes 6:13:

Consider the work of God; for who can straighten out what He has made crooked?

Man spends too much time trying to change things, circumstances, and people to suit his own desires. He would be much happier if he would simply accept things the way God made them and less stressed because they don't accommodate him. God made things and people to suit His own purposes and not ours.

A fish was made to swim. If we try to make it climb a tree, we shouldn't consider the fish a failure when it doesn't happen. We need to learn to trust that God put the fish in the water for a reason. Other people were not created to make us happy, either; they were created to bring God glory. The sooner we realize this and accept it, the happier and less frustrated we will be.

Whatever or whomever God has allowed in your life that frustrates you is there for a reason. Your purpose is not to change that thing or that person but to accept it and to seek God's guidance on how to respond to it. If change is needed, God will do the changing. Your job is to stay in prayer and to obey what He shows you.

We must also remember that God is the judge over sin. If God says it is wrong, it is wrong. Regardless of how we may try to dress it up or justify it, we cannot make sin right. God does not judge by majority rule or by political correctness. He judges by what He has established as good. Just because a political party accepts it does not mean God will tolerate it! Trying to change public opinion regarding outright, blatant sin will only create factions and stir up conflict on both sides. Sin is neither pretty nor acceptable in God's eyes, and He will judge it. We must, however, let Him be the judge.

When Jesus came into this world, He upset a religious and political system that served itself. This system tried to control the people with heavy rules and regulations. Jesus, however, displayed a power through healings and miracles that the system could not deny. When the system could not change Him, they killed Him. Their actions never changed what was right or what was wrong, but the power of God raised Him from the dead! Today, His sacrifice has the power to forgive sin and transform a sinner into a saint. That is what His sacrifice was made to do. We need to stop trying to change people and simply point them to Jesus. Consider the work of God, and realize you can't do His job. Your job is to accept, love, surrender the matter to God, obey, and trust. God always does His job.

Have a blessed day!

My Redeemer Lives

When my husband died, I was so much in shock that I could not eat, sleep, or think clearly. Someone else had to plan his funeral. When I was asked about music, I wasn't even sure what music was! The only song that would come to my mind was *I Know My Redeemer Lives*. I didn't know why, but I needed it sung.

At the funeral, Dr. Jim McAfee presented the eulogy. I will never forget his words: "God will redeem the death of Eddie Martin." He had no idea the song *I Know My Redeemer Lives* was about to be sung. At that point, I realized God had planned this funeral, and He was speaking to me.

Job 19:25:

I know that my Redeemer lives, and that in the end He will stand upon the earth.

Although his life was in shambles and turned upside down from loss and illness, Job knew God would have the last word concerning his life. He would not be left to the faulty discretion of others. Job still expected to see the grace and goodness of God in this lifetime, and he did!

The word *redeemer* is often used in Scripture in connection with a widow. *Redeemer* in this passage means, *to be the next of kin and as such to buy back a relative's property or to marry his widow*. According to Hebrew law, women could not inherit property after the death of a husband without a son. This was custom in all ancient near eastern law codes. The next of kin had the right to the property and could buy it back for the widow through marriage. Not anyone could be a redeemer. One must be qualified (next of kin) and willing to act as redeemer.

Job realized he was very much like a widow in his situation. He had no power to act upon his own behalf, and his friends accused him of bringing calamity upon himself. He trusted God would act as his Redeemer and restore what was lost. God, in turn, blessed the latter part of Job's life even more than the first. That is redemption!

I often think back to Dr. Jim McAfee's words, "God will redeem the death of Eddie Martin." I believe PHOEBE Ministries is a part of that redemption, and I praise God for it! God does not waste one heart-ache or one tear that is turned over to His care. He forms it all into something beautiful for His glory and for our good.

Have a blessed day!

The God of Comfort

Isaiah 49:13:

Shout for joy, you heavens! Earth, rejoice! Mountains break into joyful shouts! For the LORD has comforted His people, and will have compassion on His afflicted ones.

In times of sorrow, we can turn to God for comfort. He is a God of compassion, and it does not please Him to see His children suffer: His heart is always toward us. When He comforts His people, there is reason to rejoice. When He expresses compassion, both heaven and earth rejoice!

When we hurt, heaven hurts for us. When we rejoice, heaven rejoices with us. We have a great cheering section we cannot see (Heb. 12:1). Heaven, however, fully understands the benefits and glory of God. Often it takes us longer to realize where and how God is working because we are dependent upon our senses and emotions. We must begin to sense the presence of God with our spiritual man in order to see how God is working in our lives. He considers every sorrow as He weaves His perfect plan into our lives. We simply need to trust and continue to seek Him.

No one or no thing can comfort us, strengthen us, or renew us as God can. When He comforts us, He gives us reason to rejoice as heaven shouts with us and for us. Worship the God of all comfort today. Let Him turn your mourning into rejoicing.

Have a blessed day!

Our Good God

Psalm 145:8:

The LORD is good to everyone; His compassion rests on all He has made.

You do not have to earn God's goodness. He is good to everyone, regardless of whether or not they believe in Him. God is good all the time simply because it is His nature. He has compassion on all He has made, and He longs for unbelievers to come to trust in Him through Jesus Christ. His compassion keeps them from coming to a swift end. We can count on God to be good to us all the time.

That doesn't mean that bad things won't happen. Jesus assured us that in this world we will have tribulation. If bad things are bound to happen because we live in a fallen world, I want to know I'm on God's side and that He has my back.

God is good even to the unbeliever because goodness is His nature. Romans 2:4 explains that God's kindness is intended to lead us to repentance. We often think that when God is good to us, it is because He is rewarding us for something we have done. While God does reward His people, we must remember that His kindness or His goodness is also intended to draw unbelievers to Him.

Has God been good to you lately? If so, praise Him. Have you failed in some area thinking you would be punished only to see God heap a huge blessing your way? If so, turn and praise Him. Do you have loved ones who still need to come to Him? If so, ask God to bless them in a way that will draw them to Him, and praise Him. He is a good God and worthy to be praised.

Have a blessed day!

A Friend of God

John 14:21:

The one who has My commands and keeps them is the one who loves Me. And the one who loves Me will be loved by My Father. I also will love him and will reveal Myself to him.

God gives us His grace to overcome sin, not to continue in it. Anyone who is led by the Holy Spirit will seek the path of holiness and desire to please the Father. Anyone who seeks an excuse or opportunity to serve the flesh is being led by another spirit.

God reveals Himself to those who truly seek to know His commands and keep them. He will use and anoint those He can trust to draw near to Him. Without His anointing, any ministry is in vain.

If we realize and appreciate the grace God has bestowed upon us, we will love Him. If we love Him, we will want to know His commands and how to please Him. If we merely want approval to continue in our sin, we have befriended the wrong spirit and are not a friend of God.

We all need God to reveal Himself to us and through us. Knowing Him and seeing His handiwork in our lives is worth far more than any pleasure a wrong spirit may give us. Choose your friends carefully, especially those who live in the heavenly realm! Determine to be a friend of God, and reject any person, spirit, or desire that would have you pursue an unholy path. You don't want to miss the glory He wants to reveal in you!

Have a blessed day!

Who is Jesus to You?

Mark 8:29:

"But you," He asked them again, "who do you say that I am?" Peter answered him, "You are the Messiah!"

Who is Jesus to you? This is a question we all must settle in our hearts and our minds. What others think doesn't matter. Who do you say Jesus is?

Messiah (Hebrew) or Christ (Greek) means *anointed one.* To be anointed means you have the power from God to do something. Is Jesus just someone who died on a cross over 2000 years ago, or do you recognize Him as the anointed one who has the power to change your situation and your life? To recognize Jesus as the Messiah is to acknowledge His power and authority at work in your life. Otherwise, He is just someone who was crucified unjustly.

At the time Peter recognized Jesus as the Messiah, Jesus had not yet died. He had not risen from the dead. Yet, Peter had seen Jesus perform enough miracles that he knew Jesus was not a mere man. He saw Jesus as the promised Messiah, the anointed one, who had come to save Israel. This same anointed one came to save you, and His power has now been perfected in His death and resurrection. He is not a mere man. Today, He is alive, and His power is still anointed. Who is Jesus to you?

If Jesus is Messiah to you, acknowledge Him for it today. Realize He has the power to change any situation or to deliver you through it. If He is really Lord of your life, His power is with you. You do not serve a weak, incapable god. Trust in His transforming power, and dare to believe Him for a miracle. His power cannot be harnessed or manipulated. Therefore, you must submit to Him. Submit, however, in complete confidence that He is able, anointed, and willing to work in your life and your circumstances. Who do you say Jesus is? He is the One anointed with power to overcome anything the Devil throws at you today!

Have a blessed day!

The Man at God's Right Hand

Psalm 80:17-19:

Let Your hand be with the man at Your right hand, with the son of man You have made strong for Yourself. Then we will not turn away from You; revive us, and we will call on Your name. Restore us, LORD God of Hosts; look on us with favor, and we will be saved.

I'm awestruck at how prophetic the psalmist is in these verses. While this Psalm was written in Old Testament days, it rings with the promise of the New Testament covenant. How could the writer have known such a profound truth unless He was inspired by the Holy Spirit to write such verses? God tells us ahead of time of His wonderful promises to come so we may proclaim them with the spoken word and with song.

The psalmist asks for God's hand to move through the man at His right hand and describes this Man as the Son of Man, who God has made strong for Himself. This is a clear and perfect description of Christ. Jesus referred to Himself as the Son of Man, and Romans 8:34 explains that Jesus now sits at the right hand of God.

The Man at God's right hand has the power to keep us, revive us, and restore us through God's power. So, just what does this Man (Jesus) at God's right hand do? Romans 8:34 reveals this further. Jesus sits at the right hand of the Father to intercede for us! Without this prayer of intercession before the Father, we would perish from our own sin and tactics of self-destruction. As our high priest, Jesus makes intercession for us so the sacrifice of His body will continue to cleanse us!

Take comfort in knowing that Jesus is praying for you today. His prayer for you has the power to revive and restore you. Whatever need you have today is expressed to the Father through Christ if you will but trust in Him and what He has already done for you on the cross. He is your great high priest, and he sits at the right hand of power with the God of the Universe! Expect Him to look upon you with favor!

Have a blessed day!

One Word

John 21:12-13:

"Come and have breakfast," Jesus told them. None of the disciples dared ask him, "Who are You?" because they knew it was the Lord. Jesus came, took the bread, and gave it to them. He did the same with the fish.

After fishing all night, the disciples had caught nothing. The next morning, a man called to them from the shore, instructing them to cast their nets on the right side of the boat. They caught so many fish they were not able to bring the large haul into the shore. This was the second time they had witnessed such a catch, and they knew exactly who had given the instruction; they had no need to ask.

When your efforts are exhausted and unproductive, one word from the Lord is all that you need to change your situation from emptiness to abundance! Notice what Jesus did for the disciples. First He spoke a word to them which required obedience. Then, He blessed their obedience and fed them. He did not leave them empty handed or hungry. They obeyed one simple word, and Jesus did the rest.

If you have an empty area in your life, ask Jesus for one word. If you already hear it, simply obey. Even if you have tried that same thing numerous times before, do it again. He will bless His instruction. He will then feed your hunger and satisfy your real need. You won't have to ask who it is, you will know.

Jesus used this miracle to restore His disciples, especially Peter, into ministry. Know that even if you have failed miserably, Jesus is still willing to bless you and use you. You just need to listen for His instruction and let Him feed you. Realize that He is your source, and apart from Him, you can do nothing. With Him, however, you can do all things.

Have a blessed day!

The Goldsmith

Jeremiah 51:17:

Everyone is stupid and ignorant. Every goldsmith is put to shame by his carved image, for his cast images are a lie; there is no breath in them.

We must remember that we create our own idols. They don't just reach out and take us hostage; they are ours by our choosing. We make them what we want them to be. We are, in effect, goldsmiths to a large degree.

Gold is a precious and valuable metal that can be formed into beautiful adornments, fit for royalty. When we take what is valuable and create things that distract our focus from God to ourselves, we have created an idol. We have given what is valuable— our money, our time, our adoration, our full attention—to an empty image that cannot sustain us. As this verse explains, there is no breath in them. Our idols cannot give us life; rather, they require our energy and our resources.

Where are you using your energy and resources today? Have you given God what is rightfully His? Have you created an idol from something valuable that belongs to God? We must remember what this verse says of goldsmiths who do such things. They are stupid and ignorant! Any god we create will ultimately put us to shame.

We have the privilege of entering into fellowship with the Almighty God of the Universe who will withhold no good thing from us. Why would we waste our energy and resources on other gods? Perhaps it is because other gods entertain us. Boredom has caused many to fall. David is the perfect example. We must be very careful with what we choose to entertain ourselves. The riches of God's kingdom are endless, but we must seek Him first to partake of them. He is of much greater value than any idol we create. Make an effort to tear down any idols you find today, and give your energy and resources to God. Watch His kingdom increase in your life as you do!

Have a great day!

Reflect on What God has Done

Psalm 77:12:

I will reflect on all You have done and meditate on Your actions.

As we remember the devastation of September 11, 2001, we face the sobering fact that we live in a world of uncertainty and chaos. We hear of new disasters every time we turn on the nightly news. Everything seems vulnerable to loss and attack, and there seems to be no safe place anymore. Just how should we face such potentially threatening situations?

Think of all the wonderful things God has done in your life. Focus on His faithfulness to you. Re-direct your attention from the madness of this world to the majesty of your God. There is nothing in this world that we cannot overcome if God is our center. Nothing has ever been certain or secure in this world. To have found security in any earthly system or provision is to have believed a lie of the enemy that it would sustain you. God is greater than anything that can be shaken in this world, and His Word tells us that what can be shaken will be. Rely upon the security of God's love and His faithfulness to you.

To meditate means to think about continually or to ponder the meaning. If you meditate on something, you think it through to the end. Meditate on God's actions toward you, and see how His hand is guiding you. What has He already done for you? How has He protected you? Where has He directed you? Where has He gifted you? All of these are keys to unlocking doors to your destiny. Meditate on God's actions in your life, and find yourself overcoming the paralyzing fear of threat that uncertainty in this world hands you. You were created and ordained to live in this day and at this time for the particular purpose of bringing glory to God. Trust Him to fulfill that purpose in you as you reflect on all He has already accomplished in your life. Your future is brighter than you can imagine!

Have a blessed day!

Remembering Your Ebenezer

1 Samuel 7:12-13:

Afterwards, Samuel took a stone and set it upright between Mizpah and Shen. He named it Ebenezer, explaining, "The LORD has helped us to this point." So the Philistines were subdued and did not invade Israel's territory again. The LORD's hand was against the Philistines all of Samuel's life.

The Philistines were an enemy who tried to steal what rightfully belonged to Israel. In 1 Samuel, God allowed the Philistines to defeat Israel when they tried to fight them in their own strength. As long as the Ark of the Covenant was with them, they were victorious. The Philistines recognized the power in the Ark and stole it. They placed it in their temple with their pagan god, Dagon, and Dagon's head fell off. The Philistines repaired it, only to find both the head and hands broken off the next day. In God's presence, every lesser god must bow. In His presence, other gods are helpless. The power of the Ark had a much different effect on the Philistines than it did on Israel!

In 1 Samuel 7, God gave victory to Israel over the Philistines at Mizpah by throwing them into confusion. Afterwards, Samuel set up a stone of remembrance to state that God had helped them against the Philistines to that point. He called that stone *Ebenezer,* which means *stone of help.*

That we remember when and how God has helped us is important. In whatever battles we may be facing, we should remember that God has helped us to that point. If He has helped us in the past, surely He will help us now. If we take matters into our own hands, we are setting ourselves up for defeat by not trusting in God. Remember what He has done for you in the past, and trust Him to do it for you again.

Today, think back to certain places where God has helped you, and make a stone of remembrance to honor God. Scrapbooking is a wonderful way to do this. I don't have the time or patience to scrapbook, but I admire those who do. Try writing a list of the times God has given you victory, and keep it in front of you. Praise Him and thank Him for what He did for you. Remembering His faithfulness to you in the past increases your faith to believe Him for your future.

Spend some time today remembering the milestones God has helped you reach. Raise up your Ebenezers in praise. Bless the LORD today, and trust Him for what lies ahead.

Have a blessed day!

Hidden in the Messiah

Colossians 3:3-4:

For you have died, and your life is hidden with the Messiah in God. When the Messiah, who is your life, is revealed, then you also will be revealed with him in glory.

We have no life outside of Christ. Those who abandon Him because they are just too busy doing other things eventually run back when things go terribly wrong. God has a perfect plan for each of us, and it is hidden in the Messiah. To find that plan is to seek God. As Jeremiah 29:13 states, "You will seek Me and find Me when you search for Me with all your heart." No one finds God's perfect plan—that good and prosperous plan for their lives—outside of Christ because it is hidden in Him.

You find God's plan for your life by seeking Him—dwelling in His presence. The Messiah is your life, and no man comes to the Father except through Him. He died for you. All He is asking is that you live for Him. He came so that we might have life and have it more abundantly, according to John 10:10.

Are you currently in a desert or a difficult place? Have you felt like God has forgotten you? God has not forgotten you! Christ has not yet revealed Himself in your situation. I'm sure Mary Magdalene felt the same way when she went to the tomb and found Jesus's body missing. Jesus, however, revealed Himself to her in that situation, and she beheld Christ in His glory as He gave her the command to go and tell the brothers. Sooner or later, if you have sought God with all your heart and submitted a matter to Him, Christ will reveal Himself in that situation, and you will be able to see where He has been working all along. In that moment, you will be revealed with Him in glory. Others will see what God has done in you and for you.

Your life is hidden in the Messiah. Dwell in His presence today, and seek Him. When you find Him, you find His plan for you.

Have a blessed day!

Reminding God

Isaiah 62:6-7:

Jerusalem, I have appointed watchmen on your walls; they will never be silent, day or night. You, who remind the LORD, no rest for you! Do not give Him rest until He establishes and makes her Jerusalem the praise of the earth.

God made a promise to restore Jerusalem. She would be a glorious crown and a royal diadem in God's hand. She would no longer be called Deserted or Desolate, but she would be known as *My Delight is in Her.* God promised the land would be married, meaning it would be restored and fruitful.

God appointed watchmen to stand on the walls. Watchmen would stand in high towers and look out over the land to watch for approaching enemies. These towers allowed them to see in every direction and were considered military posts. When they saw danger approaching, they would cry out so the people could be on guard and ready to defend what was rightfully theirs.

The fact that these watchmen were never silent indicates that trouble was always lurking. There was no rest for the watchmen. If they rested, the city could easily fall under attack. The watchmen were to remind the Lord of His promise of restoration until God established Jerusalem and made her the praise of the earth. Jerusalem had many enemies that shivered at the thought of her restoration. The same is true for us. When God is in the process of restoring us, you can bet your bottom dollar the enemy will pull out all the stops and try to attack, halt, or destroy the work God is doing. We need to be like those watchmen and remind the Lord of His promises to us.

God does not forget us or the promises He made to us. When we remind Him, we are speaking out the promises He has made to us in faith that

He will deliver. Speaking in faith resists the temptation to doubt, and the enemy is put to flight.

These verses are often compared to Luke 18:1-8. The persistent widow who suffered injustice at the hands of her neighbor never let the unjust judge forget it. She kept reminding him until he granted her justice. If an unjust judge would grant justice to this persistent widow, how much more will a just, loving, and holy God grant His promises to a persistent widow now?

Nothing is stated here about the watchmen going into battle or giving up their posts. If we try to take the matter into our own hands, God will rest just to let us see that our efforts are futile. He will not share His glory with another! Reminding Him of His promises states our faith and keeps Him working.

If the enemy is trying to steal your peace on a promise God has made to you, remind God of His promise. This is how we fight the Devil and protect our ground, how we guard our hearts and minds from things that set themselves above the knowledge of Christ. Just keep reminding God of His promise, and He will protect what is rightfully yours.

Have a blessed day!

Devouring Fire and a Storm

Psalm 50:3:

Our God is coming; He will not be silent! Devouring fire precedes Him, and a storm rages around Him.

When we pray, we can expect God to answer. We just don't always know or understand His timing or His methods. This verse depicts how God appears as judge. He will defend us in unfair circumstances, although He may not come as we expect or hope.

1 Corinthians 3:13 tells us that each one's work will be judged by fire. Anything that is built on a foundation other than Jesus Christ will be burnt up in the fire. Those who build on the foundation of Christ will receive a reward. Those that build on any other foundation will find their works lost and only their salvation remaining. Before God appears in our situations,

He will send forth His devouring fire to see if the foundation upon which we are building is solid. If we are depending upon anything other than Christ, it will be consumed. If, however, our hope is built on nothing less than Jesus blood and righteousness, we will receive His great reward!

Notice that a storm rages around God. When Jesus was in the boat with His disciples when a storm began to rage, He was at rest because He knew the storm raging around Him must bow to His instruction. When you find yourself in storms, know that God is right there in the midst of them with you. The winds and waves must bow to Him, but storms have a purpose. They reveal how much we can be shaken in our faith. While storms can certainly be frightening and cause much damage, they are the times we are to trust Him the most. Ride out your storm by trusting in the God who dwells in the middle of it, and watch to see how everything bows to His instruction!

God will not allow your case to go unnoticed or unaddressed when you call out to Him. If you see fire devouring everything around you, don't lose hope. God is right behind it. Return to your foundation of Jesus Christ, and depend upon His sacrifice for you. If you find yourself in a storm that has you rocking and reeling, place your trust in God, and just hang on. God is coming into your situation, and He will not be silent!

Have a blessed day!

My Shelter and My Portion

Psalm 142:4-5:

Look to the right and see; no one stand up for me; there is no refuge for me; no one cares about me. I cry to You, LORD; I say, "You are my shelter, my portion in the land of the living."

David certainly felt the loneliness of isolation and the fear of attack. While he could not depend upon others for help, he had the good sense about him to turn to God to meet his needs. He learned to seek refuge in God and to gain strength from Him. When he had no one to meet his physical needs, David sought to strengthen himself spiritually by crying out to God.

God doesn't want us to become co-dependent upon other people to meet our needs. He is our source, and He may allow us to come to a breaking point, where we have nowhere else to turn but to Him. In those times, we can cry out to Him in full assurance that He hears us and cares about us completely. To make demands upon others will only drive them further away. Allow God to fill that void, and find supernatural strength to overcome any enemy you have.

The land of the living refers to this life on earth. While we are still living and breathing, God is our shelter from every storm life brings and our portion for every empty place we encounter. Wherever we have a need, He has a provision. No one else can give you what God has planned for you. Seek Him, and find strength, power, provision, and blessing in His presence. Don't demand from anyone else what only He can give you.

Today, if no one stands up for you or seems to care about you, don't despair—you are in good company. Cry out to God and receive His everlasting love for you. Partake in the grace Christ's blood purchased for you. Come before His throne with boldness and cry out to Him as your shelter and your portion. Revere Him as Lord, and let Him be God to you.

Have a blessed day!

Stop Living Among the Dead

Luke 24:5:

So the women were terrified and bowed down to the ground. "Why are you looking for the living among the dead?" asked the men.

The grave could not hold Jesus Christ. Hallelujah! Resurrection power moved Him from the dead to the living that were on the earth, then to the very right hand of the Father, where He waits to intercede for us until He is instructed to go claim His bride. Christ does not dwell among the dead because He is alive.

We miss the power of God in our lives when we insist upon living among the dead. A dead Savior in the midst of a dead situation brings only grief. We need to look beyond the deadness in our lives to see where God is breathing new life. Sometimes we just have to let things or people go before God can do a new thing. Otherwise, we will continue to mourn when reason to rejoice is just within our reach.

If you cannot find Christ in the midst of your dead situation, begin to look elsewhere. Look for signs of life around you. Ask Jesus to reveal Himself in a whole new way to you. Accept the fact that things are no longer the way they once were or maybe not the way we wish they were, and expect God to do a new thing in your life that will absolutely amaze you!

With power comes the means to transform. Expect to see something new, living, useful, and productive in your life when God's glory is revealed in you. Stop living among the dead, and begin to walk in the power of new life in Christ.

Have a blessed day!

Our Refuge, Our Strength, and Our Helper

Psalm 46:1:

God is our refuge and strength, a helper who is always found in times of trouble.

We will all face times when we have no power nor say about what happens to us. Our future may very well rest in someone else's hands, and they may be hands we do not trust. In these times, however, we have a helper we can trust. In Him, we find a refuge where we can run for comfort and strength to face the battle or trial before us.

Certainly, Daniel, Esther, and Joseph learned these things firsthand. They each had to submit to someone else's decisions about their futures, but God intervened for them all. They learned to trust God and submit to Him so He could work through them. Any authority God places over us must answer to Him for their actions. Therefore, when we submit, God holds the authority responsible for us. We can trust God to care for us when we obey through submission to His command.

God has the power to save us from a bad decision from any authority over us. He is also our refuge, our strength, and our helper when the authority makes a bad decision. Either way, we win!

Have a blessed day!

Heaven is the LORD's

Psalm 115:16:

The heavens are the LORD's, but the earth He has given to the human race.

Heaven is beautiful, orderly, and peaceful. The earth is corrupt, chaotic, and warring. The heavens belong to the LORD, but earth belongs to man. To understand either place, look at the caretaker. Where would you rather live?

Matthew 24:35 tells us that heaven and earth will pass away, but the words of Jesus will never pass away. One day God will create a new heaven and a new earth, and He will be the ruler and caretaker of all. Until then, we must learn to live in a world that is not our home and can never satisfy our true needs.

Jesus died so we might find life with the Father and enter into His kingdom. He taught us to pray, "on earth as it is in heaven." We are to ask God to bring the glory, beauty, and order of heaven into our lives on earth. Through Christ we can live the order of heaven through the chaos of earth. We can have a part of heaven now, even though we are confined to this earth. Those that belong to the earth, however, might think we are strange. The earth may not accommodate or appreciate our desires to follow Christ. The earth, however, can give us no suitable alternative.

When problems arise, learn to pray, "on earth as it is in heaven." Sickness does not exist in heaven; ask God to grant you no sickness on earth. Perfect safety abounds in heaven; ask Him to grant you safety on earth. Truth and love are revealed in heaven; ask Him to reveal truth and love to you on earth. Unity thrives in heaven; ask Him to grant you unity on earth. Ask Him to invade your life on earth so that it resembles heaven. Things may look like the earth on the outside, but heaven can reign on the inside.

Heaven is the Lord's, but you belong to Him. Jesus's kingdom was not of this world, and nothing this world could do to Him could stop Him. This same power lives in you through Him. Heaven can be yours today.

Have a blessed day!

The Source of All Things

Romans 11:36:

For from Him and through Him and to Him are all things. To Him be the glory forever. Amen.

Regardless of how chaotic our world seems right now, God really is in control. We must learn to see all things as coming from God. Even when bad things happen, God can turn it around for our good. He uses all things to mature us and equip us for His purpose.

God is not the source of evil, but He may allow bad things to happen for a reason in our lives. If we never hurt, we cannot relate to those who do and who desperately need to know the love of Christ. When God allows bad things to happen to us, He never leaves us. He loves us through it and reveals Himself in a greater way than we've previously known. He uses those difficult and trying times to draw us closer to Him and to know Him more intimately. Once we have gained victory in our heartache, God leads someone to us who is experiencing the same hurt. We have hope to give because we have overcome, and we can point the hurting to Christ.

May God be glorified in all things in our lives. May others see the glory of God where we have suffered. May we give thanks to God for our many blessings, and may He receive the glory for the good in our lives. May we learn to trust Him as the source of all things and know Him more intimately as a result.

Have a blessed day!

A Bonfire and a Storehouse

Matthew 13:24-30:

He presented another parable to them: "The kingdom of heaven may be compared to a man who sowed good seed in his field. But while people were sleeping, his enemy came, sowed weeds among the wheat, and left. When the plants sprouted and produced grain, then the weeds

also appeared. The landowner's slaves came to him and said, 'Master, didn't you sow good seed in your field? Then where did the weeds come from?' "An enemy did this!" he told them." "So, do you want us to go and gather them up?" the slaves asked him. "No," he said. "When you gather up the weeds, you might also uproot the wheat with them. Let both grow together until the harvest. At harvest time I'll tell the reapers: Gather the weeds first and tie them in bundles to burn them, but store the wheat in my barn."

Harvest is the time when the weeds that have infested our lives are gathered and burned. The enemy is sure to try to sabotage our good works to bring us harm. We may look into a field that is full of wheat and tares, but God waits for both to mature before separating the bad from the good. We may have had to endure some weeds for a season, but they are not permanent—they are destined to be burned. I don't know about you, but I'm anxious for a bonfire!

While God may allow weeds to mature in our lives, only the good is stored for use. God does not allow the weeds to choke out our harvest. He gathers them while they are ripe before He gathers the good wheat. That is why we often see a harvest of weeds before we see our harvest of grain. Notice, too, that He ties the weeds in bundles. God binds what is not useful and unproductive in our lives so the wheat can continue to grow and be harvested. He carefully stores what is good and brings it out to feed others so it may continue to reproduce.

We all have a bonfire and a storehouse awaiting us, and Fall is the time of year to experience them. Bring on a new season, and bring on a harvest!

Have a blessed day!

Jesus Has Conquered the World

John 16:33:

I have told you these things so that in Me you may have peace. You will have suffering in this world. Be courageous! I have conquered the world.

As I read this Scripture, it hit me that Jesus had not yet died. The finished work of the cross was not complete. Yet, He assured His disciples here that He had conquered the world. Just what did He mean?

First, Jesus had conquered the world by not giving into sin. We don't have the power to do that on our own because we were born with a sinful nature. However, His conquering the world offered us hope, and He commanded them to be courageous because of it.

Secondly, the finished work of the cross was a sure thing. Jesus was calling that which was yet to be on earth as if it already were. God had already established it in the heavenly realms and it just needed to be played out on earth.

Jesus promised a life of suffering in this world. He came so we might have peace. While we can't conquer the world, He already has, and grace allows us to benefit from His work.

In whatever trouble you are facing today, know that Jesus came to give you peace in the midst of it. We will just have to go through some things on this earth in order to grow. We can encounter and endure those difficult times with courage, however, knowing that Jesus has already conquered it for us. Lean on His grace today.

Have a blessed day!

Our Protector

Psalm 121:1-8:

I raise my eyes toward the mountains. Where will my help come from? My help comes from the LORD, the Maker of heaven and earth. He will not allow your foot to slip; your Protector will not slumber. Indeed, the Protector of Israel does not slumber or sleep. The LORD protects you; the LORD is a shelter right by your side. The sun will not strike you by day; or the moon by night. The LORD will protect you from all harm; He will protect your life. The LORD will protect your coming and going both now and forever.

A journey requires we move from one place to another. We can count on God's protection when we move from one place to another to worship Him. If, however, we choose to stay in our safe place or comfort zone, we see nothing about God's protection promised. In fact, He often drives us from our safe places and comfort zones in order to get us to journey from one place to another to worship Him. Our efforts of self-protection are in vain.

Have you been avoiding a journey? Is God nudging you to move from one place to another? Are you living in fear of being hurt and missing out on God's very best? He promises to protect you on your journey. He has much more for you than you can imagine. You can lay hold of it only by embarking on the journey and reaching your destination in Him.

Today, meditate on this Psalm, and receive these words into your spirit. Own the fact that God is your Protector, and He will see you through any journey into which He has called you. He has a destination planned for you that you don't want to miss, and He is willing to be your security. Embark upon your journey today!

Have a blessed day!

Shout for Joy!

Psalm 89:12:

North and south - You created them. Tabor and Hermon shout for joy at Your name.

This verse gives us all reason to shout for joy. God created this world, and He is in control, regardless of what the news media depicts these days. You can measure between north and south, while you cannot measure east to west. Our worldly measures may be biased when we consider that God's handiwork is found in both north and south, even though we may see the differences. To be at war with each other is ridiculous when we see that God has blessed each of us according to His purpose.

Tabor and Hermon are mountains in Israel. Tabor means *pain*, while Hermon means *abrupt*. We will all face mountains in this world that seem painful, abrupt, and hard to climb. Tabor and Hermon, however, shout for joy at the name of Jesus. He brings victory to the painful and abrupt situations of life that we face. Our strongest battles against the enemy are often fought on mountains of pain and abrupt blows. God, however, never allows us to go to these mountains alone! He sends us into them knowing that Jesus has already provided the victory for us. Hallelujah! May we shout for joy at His name, too.

Have a blessed day!

Streams of Living Water

John 7:38:

The one who believes in Me, as the Scripture has said, will have streams of living water flow from deep within him.

Jesus told the woman at the well He was living water that would quench her thirst within. When we partake of Him and sit at His feet as Mary did, He begins to pour that living water in us. The closer we draw to Him, the greater our reservoir becomes. Sooner or later, what He has poured inside will overflow into our lives so that others can't help but notice we have been in His presence. When they see this living water, there is hope to quench their thirsts, and they are drawn to that water.

Know for sure that whatever is inside you will come pouring out at some point, so be very careful with what you fill yourself. If you dwell upon negative and depressive thought patterns, those waters will flow from you and affect others. If you fill yourself with God's Word and meditate upon His promises, you will eventually overflow with hope, encouragement, and joy. If your glass is half empty or half full doesn't matter. What matters is what you put inside.

Notice that these waters flow from deep within. Many people try to live in the shallow water, where it is safe. While this may have some benefit at the beach, life is truly found in the deep part of yourself, where you may be hesitant to go. Allow Jesus to fill these dark places and invade your inner being. This is where true transformation begins. He doesn't want just the surface that everyone can see. Jesus wants to be Lord over every part of your being. Let Him fill you with His abundance to overflowing and watch His power work through you.

Have a blessed day!

We Remember Your Name Alone

Isaiah 26:13:

LORD, our God, other lords than You have ruled over us, but we remember Your name alone.

Throughout Israel's years, she fell to worship idols. While she may have allowed other gods to rule, it is the name of the LORD—Yahweh—she remembered when she was in trouble. No one else could deliver her or bless her like He could.

We are really no different as Christians. Many times, we allow things or people to control us. We serve temporary idols that cannot bring us real joy but only a temporary fix. While their allure might be tempting, we quickly forget them when real trouble strikes. They have no power to heal, deliver, or restore. When we need a miracle, we turn to God.

Perhaps the struggle you face today is meant to turn your attention to the one, true, living God—Yahweh. No one can give you peace or restore you the way He can. No one can deliver you or sustain you the way He can. If a miracle is what you need, He is the God who performs miracles every day. Remember His name alone, and let all other distractions go. Look to Him, and know that He has an answer for you. Now is the time to let Him rule in your heart as you surrender completely to Him.

Have a blessed day!

Start an Earthquake

Acts 4:29-31:

"And now, Lord, consider their threats, and grant that Your slaves may speak your message with complete boldness, while You stretch out Your hand for healing, signs, and wonders to be performed through the name of Your holy Servant Jesus."

The early church faced many persecutions. Just before they prayed this prayer, the Jewish religious leaders had restricted them from preaching in the name of Jesus. His miracles threatened their control over the people. In return, the people of the early church prayed for boldness to continue speaking in the name of Jesus.

We certainly live in a time when the name of Jesus is restricted in certain areas. People who want to live according to the desires of their own flesh do not want our gospel. They want to be free to be gods of their own lives and to control what you do with yours. To them, it is okay for Christians to believe in Jesus Christ, but just don't preach that He is the only way. They expect us to be tolerant of those who desire to go another way. We need not only boldness to preach the gospel, we need God's undeniable power to move among us. Those who are anti-Christ will not believe anyway. Those, however, who are desperately seeking truth and answers to the many problems of life need to see God's glory revealed in His people.

People who have come to the end of themselves need to see God's power. They need to look up and find hope outside of themselves and the system of this world. Are they able to see God's power at work in our lives, or are our lives just as pitiful and disparaging as their own? Do we display a victory that we could never win in our own might, or are we as defeated as the addict who just landed in jail? Can you boldly share the gospel of Jesus Christ with someone who is at the end of her rope, or do you doubt God is even willing to work in your own life? If God is going to work in your life, you must first believe that He can and that He will, according to Hebrews 11:6. Activate your faith!

The elders, rulers, and scribes wanted the early Christians to acknowledge the limitations they imposed and to live according to those limitations. The apostles, however, had just seen Jesus rise from the dead, and they knew no limitations. Resurrection power was much greater to them than any limitation the powerless rulers could impose. Your enemy, the Devil, wants you to focus upon the limitations he has imposed upon you. If you live according to his rules, your witness will be limited. It is time to get your eyes off your limitations and focused upon the resurrection power of Christ, knowing what God can do in your life is limitless!

Ask for boldness to speak God's message and for His power to accompany it. We should all use this model of prayer to reach our world for Christ. If you feel a little earthquake today, know that someone just reached the throne of heaven. Start an earthquake at your own house, and change your world.

Have a blessed day!

The Benefits of God's Grace

John 10:10:

A thief comes only to steal and to kill and to destroy. I have come that they may have life and have it in abundance.

When bad things happen, we often think that God is punishing us. We forget that God unleashed the full amount of His anger upon the cross for our sins. Jesus suffered our punishment for all past, present, and future sins. By turning to God when bad things happen, we find grace, not condemnation. He sees us as righteous through the sacrifice of Jesus, regardless of what we have done.

As this verse states, a thief (the Devil) comes to steal, to kill, and to destroy. The works of evil in your life are strictly from the Devil. Jesus, however, came so we might have life and have it in abundance. This word, *life*, in the Greek is derived from a word meaning *beneficence—benefit, good deed done*. Jesus came so we might benefit in life from God's grace.

Wherever the Devil has come in your life to steal, to kill, or to destroy, Jesus came so you could benefit from God's grace. May we find restoration from the works of the Devil. That restoring work is God's grace through Christ.

Have a blessed day!

Remember the Works of the LORD

Psalm 77:11-12:

I will remember the LORD'S works; yes, I will remember Your ancient wonders. I will reflect on all You have done and meditate on Your actions.

In this Psalm, the writer is wondering if God will ever answer his prayer. Has God forgotten him? Is God angry with him? He decides to remember how God has responded in the past. God has performed miracles and wonders. He has displayed His strength among the peoples (v. 14). God has delivered from storms in the past, and He will surely deliver now (v. 17).

Rest assured that God is up to something in your life—He has not forgotten you. While He may not have consulted you on what He is doing, He is still at work in your life. He knows every prayer you have prayed and every tear you have cried, and He is not ignoring you. Yet His silence may test your faith. Remember what He has done for you in the past. Remember His faithfulness and rely upon the God who has promised to never leave you nor forsake you. When you remember His great works and blessings toward you, faith arises to take you to victory. Never forget God's goodness toward you!

Take time today to meditate on all God has done for you in the past. Realize that He who has led you through other storms will surely lead you through this one, too. God has done tremendous things for me over the past few years. He will not leave me hanging now!

Have a blessed day!

I Commit You to God

Acts 20:32:

And now I commit you to God and to the message of His grace, which is able to build you up and to give you an inheritance among all who are sanctified.

Paul addressed the elders of the church at Ephesus with these words from its seaport, Miletus. He had previously caused a stir in Ephesus by preaching the gospel. His message disturbed the business of the silversmiths, who made money from the sale of small replicas of the goddess Artemis (also known as Diana). While he avoided going into Ephesus, he felt a need to encourage those of the faith who had listened to the message of the gospel and had followed Christ.

Paul knew those in the church were surrounded by satanic and worldly influence. Many would become confused and fall away. Some may lose hope and become discouraged in their faith. He told them they would not see him again, but they were to hold true to the message they had believed from him. He had lived a life of integrity before them and had not given anyone cause to doubt his motives or his actions. He warned them that false teachers would arise with false doctrines and to be alert to savage wolves that would join them.

Paul had worked hard to build the church at Ephesus, and he loved the people dearly. He had brought them as far as he could in the faith, but he had to let them go. He had to trust God to carry them further. The same grace which had rescued him on the road to Damascus must now carry his children in the faith.

The Greek word for commit here is *paratithemi*, meaning *to place alongside, to present, or to deposit as a trust or protection.* Paul deposited the Ephesians to God's care as he departed them. At this point, God became responsible for the outcome—Paul could do nothing more.

Do we trust God with the outcome of those we love? I'm reminded of the words of an old hymn, "For I know whom I have believed and am persuaded that He is able to keep that which I've committed to Him against that day." We must be persuaded that God is able to keep our loved ones and to bring them to the fullness of His riches in Christ Jesus. That is something we can never do for them. They must have this relationship with Him themselves. Unless we let them go, they will never learn to trust Him and experience His fullness firsthand. We cannot be the Savior, so we must direct them to Him.

Who do you need to commit to God today? Understand that His love for them is greater than your own, and you can trust them to His care. This is an evil world with many lustful influences, but greater is He that is in you than He that is in the world (1 John 4:4). Paul did it as an example for us.

Just as a good hound dog will diligently run after his prey, you can trust the Hound of Heaven with what is precious to you, too.

Have a blessed day!

Oil in Your Lamp

Matthew 25:1-6:

Then the kingdom of heaven will be like 10 virgins who took lamps and went out to meet the groom. Five of them were foolish and five were sensible. When the foolish took their lamps, they didn't take oil with them. But the sensible ones took oil in their flasks with their lamps. Since the groom was delayed, they all became drowsy and fell asleep. In the middle of the night there was a shout: "Here's the groom! Come out to meet him."

All of the virgins were excited and anxious about the Bridegroom's coming, but only five of them went prepared. Those who were not prepared did not consider the fact that they might have to wait for his appearance. We are like that in our prayer lives many times. When we pray and submit a matter to God, we expect an answer right away. We are not prepared for a wait.

Oil in Scripture represents the Holy Spirit. When we pray, we must be in tune with the Holy Spirit to pray effectively. Prayer—communion with God—and Bible study are essential in developing sensitivity and awareness of the Holy Spirit's presence in our lives. To pray and never seek guidance in God's Word is foolish. Going to meet the bridegroom without oil for our lamps is going in our own strength. Wise virgins keep their lamps (light of their life) filled with oil (Holy Spirit) and take their flasks (Bible) with them. It gives them strength to endure the wait.

In the biblical story, all the virgins fell asleep. The wait is very significant here. We all experience the wait, but we don't all endure it with the same result. Those who came to meet the groom prepared were blessed by the wait. Those who were unprepared and trying to meet him in their own strength missed the opportunity when he came suddenly while they were sleeping.

Verses 7-9:

Then all those virgins got up and trimmed their lamps. But the foolish ones said to the sensible ones, "Give us some of your oil, because our lamps are going out." The sensible ones answered, "No, there won't be enough for us and for you. Go instead to those who sell, and buy oil for yourselves."

Does the sensible virgins' refusal to share appear to be selfish to you? When we receive Christ as Savior, He comes to dwell in us through the Holy Spirit. He illuminates the Word of God for us in a way we can understand it. He leads us as we pray. The Spirit is the mediator that brings us in line with God's will. My oil won't work in your lamp! I can't receive the Holy Spirit for you. I can share with you what He is teaching me—and it may draw us closer to each other—but you must develop your own relationship with the Holy Spirit. We make a mistake of expecting pastors, teachers, or other leaders to do that for us.

Verses 10- 13:

When they had gone to buy some, the groom arrived. Then those who were ready went in with him to the wedding banquet, and the door was shut. Later the rest of the virgins also came and said, "Master, master, open up for us!" But he replied, "I assure you. I do not know you!" Therefore be alert, because you don't know either the day or the hour."

Today, if you find yourself in a waiting mode, dig into the Word of God. Spend time in prayer, seeking God's will. Allow the Holy Spirit to speak to you and bring you in line with God's will. This is how your relationship with Christ is developed. The Spirit is the oil you need to endure the wait. Being prepared is the indicator that you have a relationship with Him and He knows who you are. His wait may be tiring, but when He comes suddenly, you won't miss Him.

Have a blessed day!

Let There Be Light

Genesis 1:3:

Then God said, "Let there be light," and there was light. God saw that the light was good, and God separated the light from the darkness. God called the light "day," and He called the darkness "night." Evening came, and then morning: the first day.

In the midst of darkness, God merely spoke to create light. Then, He separated the light from the darkness into what we know as day and night. Evening preceded morning in determining the first day.

When we go through dark times, we must remember that darkness comes before light. The day is not over until the dawn shines, giving light and sight to what we could not see in the dark. To get through the dark, however, we must trust since we can't see.

Trust is vital to survive this life. We need it in family relationships and in friendships. If trust is violated, that relationship is damaged. A lack of trust means you don't believe someone has your best interest at heart. That person will hurt you or take advantage of you to further his or her own interests. Unfortunately, not everyone can be trusted, and we must use godly discernment in determining who we should hold close to us during pain, grief, or sorrow. Those you can trust are true jewels. These are the relationships you treasure. They nourish you, encourage you, and help you reach the light.

We can always trust that God has our best interests at heart. He loved us so much He did not spare His own Son for us. He is who you need in dark times; He is the only one that can speak light into your situation.

When going through dark times, we must also remember that it is temporary. What is dark today will have light tomorrow. Darkness simply means we cannot see what is there. I once visited a cave, where I experienced a few seconds of total darkness and could not see one thing. Once the light shined, I could see stalagmites and stalactites all around me. Although they were still there in the darkness, I just couldn't see them. We often have to wait for the light.

If you are going through a dark time, trust in the One who always has your best interest at heart. He has the ability to speak light into your situation and show you the way to go when there seems to be no way. He can illuminate your circumstances so you can see the beauty He created just for you that you can't see until morning. Trust Him to get you there. Trust Him to strengthen relationships that walk through the darkness with you. Trust Him to provide what you cannot get for yourself in the dark. Trust Him to bring morning and new perspective—your day is not complete without it.

Finally, realize that night was created for rest. If you find yourself in a situation where all is dark, it is a time for you to rest. You labor and produce in the daylight. Wait for God to refresh and renew you. The strength you gain in the dark will be needed for what He calls you to do in the day.

Have a blessed day!

Liberty to the Captives

Isaiah 61:1:

The Spirit of the LORD God is on me, because the LORD has anointed Me to bring good news to the poor. He has sent me to heal the brokenhearted, to proclaim liberty to the captives, and freedom to the prisoners ….

While we must submit to the governing authorities above us, we have good news in Christ today. God gave both responsibility and authority to government, but He gave access to His throne through Jesus Christ. We cannot trust government to always work in our best interests, but we can always trust God who first established government and sent His Son to die for us. He has a vested interest in us, and He fully intends for His purpose to be fulfilled in our lives. We have liberty in Christ.

Are you brokenhearted today? Has someone made a decision that has hurt you? Jesus came to heal you and to give you liberty so you would not be enslaved by the actions of those who did not act in your best interests. He put you first when He died for you, and because of Him, you can overcome any negative situation imposed upon you by someone else. Just submit the matter to Him.

When people make decisions that hurt us, we have a choice. We can choose to remain poor and captive to their actions, or we can be liberated by faith in Christ. We remain prisoners only if we choose to be prisoners. Embrace the good news of the gospel of Jesus Christ, place your trust in His plan for you, and rejoice in the fact that no weapon formed against you shall prosper! You are His Beloved, and He will withhold no good thing from you.

Have a blessed day!

Precious and Valuable in God's Sight

Psalm 118:15:

The death of His faithful ones is valuable in the LORD's sight. (HCSB)

Precious in the LORD's sight is the death of His saints. (KJV)

Regardless of which version you prefer, God does not take lightly the death of one of His children. He sees each death as something precious and valuable and treats it with great care. He knows the pain it causes, and He is careful to provide everything needed for those who are left to deal with the pain. He times each death carefully, and we can trust that what has happened is in His hands.

So, just how do we deal with the pain of loss? The following verses in Psalm 118 offer such instruction.

Psalm 118: 16-19:

LORD, I am indeed Your servant; I am Your servant, the son of Your female servant. You have loosened my bonds. I will offer You a sacrifice of thanksgiving and will worship the LORD. I will fulfill my vows to the LORD, in the very presence of all His people, in the courts of the LORD's house—within you, Jerusalem. Hallelujah!

The best way to deal with the pain of loss is to totally surrender to God as His servant. God takes care of His people; you are never safer than you are when you are in the center of His will. In His courts, you will find true blessing and direction to fulfill the calling He has for you. If you turn to other things for comfort, they will leave you empty, dry, and still trying to fill a void that only He can fill.

Don't let grief drive you from God. In Him alone, you will find everything you need to live again, love again, and even laugh again. Choose to worship Him in the midst of your sorrow. The loss you suffer is precious and valuable in His sight, and He will not allow you to go through it for nothing! Determine that if you have to suffer the pain, you should gain something of value from it. God will pour His blessings and favor on you in ways you never dreamed!

Have a blessed day!

Our Most Effective Defense

Psalm 141:1-4:

LORD, I call on You; hurry to help me. Listen to my voice when I call on you. May my prayer be set before You as incense, the raising of my hands as the evening offering. LORD, set up a guard for my mouth; keep watch at the door of my lips. Do not let my heart turn to any evil thing or wickedly perform reckless acts with men who commit sin. Do not let me feast in their delicacies.

Have you ever been hurt or offended? Have you ever lost respect for someone because of actions that seemed reckless? David suffered many injustices at the hands of Saul, who had sought to destroy him. Yet, David resolved not to lift a hand against Saul (1 Sam. 24:6). David chose not to offend in return.

This is a hard thing to do. Our natural tendencies are to defend ourselves when we are hurt. As we defend ourselves, we can damage others. David handled his hurt emotions my pouring them out to God in prayer. When God smelled the incense of his wounded soul, He would go to work on David's behalf. Had David turned to evil to defend himself, he would have fallen right into the enemy's trap to give Saul reason to destroy him. By keeping his mouth shut and his hands to himself, He made room for God's vengeance.

The last few verses of this Psalm reveal David's battle strategy. Notice **verses 8-10:**

But my eyes look to You, LORD God. I seek refuge in You; do not let me die. Protect me from the trap they have set for me, and from the snares of the evildoers. Let the wicked fall into their own nets, while I pass safely by.

David was a mighty warrior, but he had sense enough to know when a battle was not his but the LORD's. He sought refuge in God while not giving the enemy valid reason to pursue him. By doing so, he avoided any snare that was sure to make him guilty before Saul. David asked that his enemies fall into their own nets while he walked safely by. Your refusal to defend yourself or to take up someone else's offense will allow you to walk safely through a painful valley while God pursues your enemies.

If you have been hurt or offended, stop talking about it; you are falling into a trap. Pour your hurt feelings out to God, and allow Him to take vengeance on your enemies. Don't risk damaging someone else and being guilty of the same sin for which you are offended. Determine to let the Devil fall into his own net while you walk safely by, untouched and unharmed from the entire situation.

Have a blessed day!

Blessings and Persecutions

Mark 10:29-31:

"I assure you," Jesus said, "there is no one who has left house, brothers or sisters, mother or father, children, or fields because of Me and the gospel, who will not receive 100 times more, now at this time— houses, brothers and sisters, mothers and children, and fields, with persecutions—and eternal life in the age to come, but many who are first will be last, and the last first."

This passage leads us to believe God will bless us in this lifetime when we follow Him. This blessing does not come without loss. Notice that those to whom this promise is given are those who have given up family and homes to follow Christ. This reminds me of people who forsake other religions to follow Christ and are ostracized by their families and friends. God will restore to them 100 times what they sacrificed in order to follow Him.

Verse 30 tells us of something else we are promised. Persecutions come with these blessings. Becoming a Christian does not guarantee us a trouble free life. Becoming a Christian equips us to endure a life of trouble.

Right now I'm in a stage of life where I believe God is showing me how to handle conflict. I don't enjoy this at all, but He has shown me that conflict is necessary at times. Conflict may be God's way of giving us an adventuresome life that enables us to grow. Personally, I prefer other types of adventure, but God doesn't consult me on His plan. Persecutions and conflict are opportunities for us to grow. I relate them to fertilizer, and we all know what that is.

Today, realize that God does bless us as Christians. I cannot deny my own blessings and I treasure them. Blessings, however, may come with persecutions. Spiritual growth is considered a blessing. We need grace to handle the blessings He gives us. Grace is all about Jesus and what He has already done for us. We need to walk in that grace daily, seeking His presence.

Have a blessed day!

Free Does Not Mean Cheap

Romans 4:13-15:

For the promise to Abraham or to his descendants that he would inherit the world was not through the law, but through the righteousness that comes by faith. If those who are of the law are heirs, faith is made empty and the promise is canceled. For the law produces wrath; but where there is no law, there is no transgression.

We cannot make up for any wrong we have done in God's eyes. We can't do any work that will erase our sins, yet many of us wear ourselves out trying to make up for the bad things we have done in our past. Righteousness is a gift given to us by faith in Christ and the work He did on the cross. Any blessing we receive is the result of His righteousness imputed to us, not by our own merit. Any sin we have done in the past or may do in the future is covered once and for all through His sacrifice. We need only to realize God's grace and look to Him. When we fully realize the value of that grace in regards to our own guilt, our lives are changed. We are able to walk in the fullness of what He did for us.

To reject God's grace is to place ourselves under the law, where we face condemnation. If we try to work to make up for our sins, we are placing ourselves under the law. If we place ourselves under the law, there is no need for faith because we have agreed to take care of our sin problem ourselves through works. Faith cannot do its perfect work of granting us the grace we need. Therefore, the law produces wrath and judgment in our lives. By receiving grace, however, we reject the law, and there is no transgression. God does not see our sin because we have embraced His grace.

Reject the urge to live under the law today. Choose to live by God's grace. Whatever need you may have is found in Christ. Embrace the grace that comes through the cross for your sins, and realize you have the righteousness of Jesus Christ. Allow His love for you to transform your mind, and experience the presence of God. Grace is a free gift that came with a very high price.

Have a blessed day!

It is Finished!

John 19:29-30:

A jar full of sour wine was sitting there; so they fixed a sponge full of sour wine on hyssop and held it up to His mouth. When Jesus received the sour wine, He said, "It is finished!" Then bowing His head, He gave up His spirit.

The sour wine is in this passage has great significance. When Jesus said, "It is finished!" He signified He had completed the sacrifice, and God's full measure of wrath had been poured out for our sins. He bowed His head in submission to the Father and gave up His spirit to death, indicating his death was a voluntary act. The purpose of this drink was to prolong life and increase the torture and pain. Jesus took the drink to prolong life then declared it finished and gave up His spirit. The act almost seems to contradict itself.

When the soldiers gave Jesus the sour wine, their intent was to keep the torture coming. Jesus took the wine, but He declared the sacrifice complete. The Devil desired to keep punishing, but Jesus declared it finished! When He willingly gave up His spirit, they could no longer torture Him, and the sacrifice would forever cover the sins of men who believed in Him!

Every sin you have ever committed or ever will commit was judged at the cross. Jesus declared: "It is finished!" When you fully receive this, the sour wine of the Devil can no longer torture you! The Devil can no longer heap guilt and condemnation upon you because Jesus removed it.

If the Devil has been tormenting you with stress, declare it finished today. Give up your spirit to the One who can defeat the Devil in your life. Psalm 46:10 says, "Be still, and know that I am God." The HCSB says, "Stop your fighting—and know that I am God, exalted among the nations, exalted on the earth." Whatever your problem may be today, it is finished in Jesus Christ!

Have a blessed day!

How Hungry are You?

I think this is a question we all face at some point. This question challenges our devotion, motivation, and commitment to our relationship with God. Times of hunger are opportunities to grow in our faith. Many of us, however, are not concerned with spiritual growth. We are comfortable right where we are. God often must make us uncomfortable in order to get us to come closer. He makes us hungry in order to fill us.

Matthew 5:6:

Blessed are those who hunger and thirst for righteousness, because they will be filled.

God fills those who are hungry, not those who are full. If we find ourselves in a place where we just don't hunger for God or for what is right, this is a good indication we are filled with something lesser than the great thing God has for us. While being empty might seem like an undesirable place, it is the best place to be in order to be filled to overflowing from the Father's hand.

Psalm 81:10:

I am Yahweh your God, who brought you up from the land of Egypt. Open your mouth wide, and I will fill it.

When Scripture mentions being brought out of Egypt, often this is a reference to salvation. God saved His people from the bondage of Pharoah in bringing them out of Egypt. Today, He saves us from the bondage of this world by salvation through Jesus Christ. So many Christians want to stop right there. They are perfectly content to be saved and to go no further. God, however, has much more. If we are to grow in our relationship with Him, we must allow Him to feed us. Once a baby is born, he or she needs nurturing from the mother. As long as we are this side of heaven, we need to be fed by the Father and to come closer in our relationship with Him. Therefore, He just might create a hunger within us that cannot be filled unless we come close enough to His hand for Him to fill it.

Today, look at your unfulfilled longings, your burdens, and your unanswered prayers as an invitation to come closer to God. He has every provision you need. He is granting you an opportunity to grow in your faith. Come close, open your mouth, and allow Him to fill it. Only those who hunger and thirst will be filled.

Have a blessed day!

Lighten Your Load

Psalm 33:5

Then I acknowledged my sin to You and did not conceal my iniquity. I said, "I will confess my transgressions to the LORD," and You took away the guilt of my sin. Selah

David was a man after God's own heart. The guilt of sin weighed heavily upon him, and he came to a point where he could bear it no longer. He cried out to God and confessed his sin so that God would forgive him and take away the guilt.

Guilt is a powerful weapon of the enemy that robs us of joy and paralyzes us from doing what God has called us to do. Guilt obligates us to things we cannot handle and gives power to the enemy's agenda for our lives. We need to lighten our loads and allow the Father to free us from feelings that enslave us so we can live the life we were created to live. That scares the daylights out of the Devil!

Some people understand guilt far too well. They may try to control others with it by constantly reminding them of their wrongs or shortcomings. Sadly, guilt prevails in many marriages. One partner tries to control the other through guilt by creating a feeling of obligation. Eventually, obligation breeds resentment, and the marriage falls apart.

David did not try to take away his own guilt; he couldn't, and neither can we. Nothing we can ever do to correct a wrong is enough to take away the feeling of guilt. God must take it away through forgiveness. Thus, we have a tremendous need for grace. Grace heals the wound that guilt inflicts.

Conviction is designed to lead us to God. Once we turn to Him, He forgives us and cleanses us from guilt. Condemnation is the counterfeit tool of the enemy that heaps guilt upon us, making us feel unworthy and obligating us to turn to futile efforts to eliminate the guilt. Conviction turns us to God while condemnation turns us to self. Conviction has the power to take away guilt; condemnation only increases it.

Determine today to not be controlled by guilt. Wherever you find yourself feeling guilty, turn it over to God. Allow Him to remove those feelings. If necessary, forgive yourself. Guilt is a heavy taskmaster that will continue to load you with burdens. Lighten your load, and receive the Father's love for you. His yoke is easy, and His burden is light.

Have a blessed day!

Saved or Crushed?

Psalm 68:20-21:

Our God is a God of salvation, and escape from death belongs to the LORD God. Surely God crushes the heads of His enemies, the hairy head of one who goes on in his guilty acts.

God's desire is for everyone to come to the saving knowledge of Jesus Christ and to respond in submission to His sacrifice to receive grace and forgiveness of sin. Since God is a righteous, just, and holy God, He will punish sin. The wages of sin are death. Therefore, if God does not save you, His judgment will ultimately destroy you.

Jesus came to crush the head of the enemy, as was foretold in Genesis 3:15. Regardless of how badly we have sinned, when we repent and turn to Christ, we receive forgiveness through God's grace—His unmerited favor toward us. We depend upon the sacrifice of Jesus for our salvation and not upon our own good works. To turn to Christ, however, means we turn away from our sin. If we insist upon hanging on to it, we will suffer consequences from the judgment God places upon it.

God judged sin on the cross. To see Jesus on the cross is to see how God feels about sin—it is hideous in His eyes and deserves to be punished. He does not, however, issue us grace so we can continue to sin. Grace is intended to free us from sin. If we insist on hanging on to something we know directly contradicts the Word of God, we will eventually suffer the consequences of judgment God has already placed on that sin. If God has judged it, it is condemned; it will not produce blessing.

God will never bless anything we produce from sin unless it is surrendered to Him. We can never be happy outside His blessing. If a blessing is not from God, it is not worth the pain and suffering it will produce in the long run. When God blesses, He adds no sorrow to it (Prov. 10:22). This richness of His grace is worth everything we surrender to Him! Trust Him to meet every need and void you have. Nothing this world offers is worth the pain it produces nor the sorrow of losing God's best for you. God crushes the heads of His enemies. Whether you are saved or crushed depends upon which God or god you choose to serve.

Have a blessed day!

The Appropriate Response to Loss

2 Samuel 12:19-20:

When David saw that his servants were whispering to each other, he guessed that the baby was dead. So he asked his servants, "Is the baby dead?" "He is dead," they replied. Then David got up from the ground. He washed, anointed himself, changed his clothes, went to the LORD's house, and worshiped. Then he went home and requested something to eat. So they served him food, and he ate.

God denied David's request. David's worst fear came true. David responded with worship, a deliberate choice of his will.

When our hearts are torn apart and we are writhing in anguish, our will is still intact. We may not feel like praising God at that point, but it is the appropriate response. Our worship must never be based upon feeling. This must be the choice of our will. When God takes something precious away from us, the best we can do is to give our all to Him. Turning from Him brings no comfort. In these hard times, we must trust that God is doing something beyond our comprehension and allow Him to minister to us.

Has God failed to answer your prayer? Praise Him. Has He disappointed you in some way? Praise Him. Are you still living with a need unmet? Praise Him. This is the appropriate response. The Devil will try to drag you into self-pity, anger, discouragement, and doubt. All of these things are damaging to your faith, and without faith, it is impossible to please God. When the Devil tempts you with one of these feelings, praise God. This is the best way to resist the Devil; he can't stand to abide where God is being praised!

Verses 24-25:

Then David comforted his wife Bathsheba; he went and slept with her. She gave birth to a son and named him Solomon. The LORD loved him, and He sent a message through Nathan the prophet, who named him Jedidiah, because of the LORD.

God responded to David's worship by restoring his loss. He gave him another son. This child was not born from rebellion, as was the first son. This was a child of restoration. He grew to be the wisest man ever known, and the splendor of his temple has yet to be matched.

We all need this type of restoration when we suffer great loss. Restoration begins with the correct response of praise. Make the deliberate choice of your will to worship God today.

Have a blessed day!

Set Free

Psalm 144:7-8:

Reach down from on high; rescue me from deep water, and set me free from the grasp of foreigners whose mouths speak lies, whose right hands are deceptive.

You have an enemy who seeks to destroy you, and he is called the father of liars in John 8:44. He is a foreigner to the kingdom of God, and he diligently tries to convince you that you cannot trust God. Some of his most faithful warriors are worry, doubt, fear, discouragement, and disappointment. He lies to you about yourself so you cannot see yourself as God sees you. He lies to you about your future, your hopes, and your dreams so you will never have the faith needed to enter your promised land. You have to decide who to believe. The enemy's lies become reality if you choose them. God's promises become reality when you choose to walk in faith.

The enemy's lies will ensnare you. They will flood you with fear and despair and even paralyze you from being able to move further in your Christian walk. When you find yourself in such a position, it is time to pray as David did. Cry out to God to rescue you from the grasp of your lying enemy.

John 8:32:

You will know the truth, and the truth will set you free.

Jesus spoke these words to the Jews when they questioned who He was. Jesus spoke only what the Father instructed Him to speak, and His words were trustworthy. Many believed Him, while others did not. Those who believed and continued in His word were truly His disciples. They received the promise of truth that would set them free. The assumption in contrast is that those who did not believe would continue to be bound by a lie.

If you find yourself bound today by enemy warriors of doubt, worry, unbelief, frustration, loneliness, fear, or any other negative emotion, ask God to give you His truth in the matter. Somewhere you have believed a lie from the enemy to have gained such antagonistic companions. Ask God to rescue you with the truth on the matter. Place your trust in Him to show you that truth. Your faith should be in Him and not in anyone or anything for which you have asked of Him. If He has denied a request, the truth about why He denied you will set you free. If He has granted your request, God will expose the lie to confirm His word to you. By placing your trust in Him you prove you are truly His disciples.

Have a blessed day!

Sweet Victory

2 Chronicles 20:24-26:

When Judah came to a place overlooking the wilderness, they looked toward the multitude, and there were corpses lying on the ground; nobody had escaped. Then Jehoshaphat and his people went to gather the plunder. They found among them an abundance of goods on the bodies and valuable items. So they stripped them until nobody could carry any more. They were gathering the plunder for three days because there was so much. They assembled in the Valley of Beracah on the fourth day, for there they praised the LORD. Therefore, that place is still called the Valley of Beracah today.

This great army threatened to take away every provision God had made to Israel in promise. In turn, God defeated every evil warrior and gave everything they had to Judah. Instead of losing, they gained tremendously.

When God defeats an enemy in our lives, He always gives us the reward that enemy held in his hand. If God overcomes rejection in our lives, He will meet us with acceptance. If He defeats depression, we will inherit joy. If He destroys loneliness, God will grant us companionship. In fact, there will be so much we can't hold it all. For Judah to collect everything took three days. How sweet the victory is when the battle is the LORD's.

Now is the time we cease from living defeated lives. God has already given us everything we need to live victorious lives in Jesus Christ. When the enemy tries to threaten you, turn him over to God. Praise Him for the wonderful, righteous, holy, just, and loving God He is. Then, stand still and watch the salvation of the LORD on your behalf. Great is your victory when He is on your side. Praise Him in your own Valley of Beracah today.

Have a blessed day!

Speak Life

Have you ever been forced to let a dream die? Perhaps, you tried and hoped for years for a particular thing, but it just never materialized. Have you ever felt dead inside and wanted to live again, but you didn't know how? This morning, I have found hope for this seemingly hopeless situation.

Ezekiel 37:1-3:

The hand of the LORD was on me, and He brought me out by His Spirit and set me down in the middle of the valley; it was full of bones. He led me all around them. There were a great many of them on the surface of the valley, and they were very dry. Then He said to me, "Son of man, can these bones live?" I replied, "LORD God, only You know."

When I read these verses, I'm reminded of some churches and even some Christians. Everything is just dead, and they are only going through the motions. They possess no real life or passion inside. You sense death all around because the Holy Spirit is not there. They are dry and ineffective. I have felt that way several times in my own life.

Ezekiel's answer to God's question proves he had no faith in himself to resurrect these bones, but He knew God could. When Ezekiel looked at the deadness of the situation, he knew there was nothing he could do to bring life to the situation. He knew, however, that if God wanted those dry bones to live, they would live. He had the power to resurrect. Ezekiel just didn't realize at that point how God could use him in the situation. He had no answers on His own, but He had faith in God.

Verses 4-10:

He said to me, "Prophesy concerning these bones and say to then: Dry bones, hear the word of the LORD! This is what the LORD God says to these bones: I will cause breath to enter you, and you will live. I will put tendons on you, make flesh grow on you, and cover you with skin. I will put breath in you so that you come to life. Then you will know that I am the LORD." So I prophesied and I had been commanded. While I was prophesying, there was a noise, a rattling sound, and the bones came together, bone to bone. As I looked, tendons appeared on them, flesh grew, and skin covered them, but there was no breath in them. He said to me, "Prophesy to the breath, prophesy, son of man. Say to it: This is what the LORD God says: Breath, come from the four winds and breathe into these slain to that they may live!" So I prophesied as I had been commanded. While I was prophesying, there was a noise, a rattling sound, and the bones came together, bone to bone. As I looked, tendons appeared on them, flesh grew, and skin covered them, but there was no breath in them. He said to me, "Prophesy to the breath, prophesy, son of man. Say to it: This is what the LORD God says: Breath, come from the four winds and breathe into these slain so that they may live!" So I prophesied as He commanded me; the breath entered them, and they came to life and stood on their feet, a vast army.

To prophesy is to proclaim God's word in a particular situation, the ability to see what God is doing in the world and to interpret it. Prophecy is NOT fortune telling or predicting; rather it is recognizing a move of God and encouraging others to move with it. God told Ezekiel to prophesy to the situation. God revealed this valley of dry bones to Ezekiel. Ezekiel had heard God speak specifically to that situation. He knew God desired to move, therefore, he had the ability to prophesy over it.

God told Ezekiel exactly what to say. Ezekiel was to speak life to the dead. God desired to resurrect and recreate. He wanted to give new life to that which had been dead for a long time. He still wants to do these things, and He looks for men and women who have faith that He can do the impossible. Those are the ones who can speak life to the dead. If you don't think God can or will move in a particular situation, you don't have the power to speak life to it. You have given up on yourself and upon God in that matter.

When Ezekiel began to proclaim God's word over the problem, the bones began to take on life! A word from God in due season will always bring life! Ezekiel simply spoke God's word, and God worked to bring the result. Faith entitles us to speak God's word. If we speak the word without faith or without knowing for sure it is what God wants to do, we speak in vain. When we know it is God's will and believe it, there is power when we speak it. That doesn't mean you can speak whatever you want and it will happen. You must know it is God's will. Ezekiel knew God had the power, and God spoke directly to Ezekiel in the matter. He had a gift of faith and an insight into God's exact word, so he could prophesy.

God had Ezekiel call the breath from the four winds—north, south, east, and west. When God is bringing life into His people, He will bring everything needed from every direction! The Holy Spirit begins to move, and you feel it everywhere you turn as His breath enters you, bringing you to life.

God didn't just make one person live again; He re-created a whole army. When He brings life to a situation, many will catch wind of His Spirit and live. The Holy Spirit resonates with others, and an army forms that proclaims His glory!

This morning, take a close look at any dead situations in your life. Begin to pray over these situations and seek God's word over them. You don't have the ability to do anything about them, but deadness in your life will hinder your Christian walk. Ask God to revitalize those areas and to breathe new life into them. Have faith that God can do the impossible and listen closely for His direction. Speak life to them and not death. God can resurrect and re-create even when dreams have been dead for a long time.

Have a blessed day!

Set Apart

Psalm 4:3:

Know that the LORD has set apart the faithful for Himself; the LORD will hear when I call to Him.

God recognizes the faithful among His children: He sets them apart for Himself. They are the ones He chooses for special missions and purposes that require faithfulness. By setting them apart, He also isolates them from destructive things and people in the world. While others may seem to be enjoying life to the fullest, the faithful often find themselves waiting for God's perfect plan to unfold.

To be set apart is to be different or to be outside the group. God doesn't intend for the faithful to be like everyone else. He sees something different and desirable in them, and He sets them apart to display His glory.

If you have ever felt like God has denied something valuable or desirable to you and you just can't understand why, realize that He may have set you apart for a reason greater than yourself. He did this in Sarah, Hannah, Manoah's wife, and in Elizabeth. All of these women greatly desired a child but could not produce one by her own means. God waited until later in life to bless these women with a child because the child He had for them had a purpose greater than they could ever imagine.

Consider their sons. From Sarah came Isaac, through whom God's promise of a chosen people came to Abraham. From Hannah came Samuel, who served as a prophet and the voice of God during the reign of Saul and the life of David. From Manoah's wife came Samson, the man of great strength who brought great fear to the Philistines and kept them from consuming Israel. From Elizabeth came John the Baptist, who prepared the way for Jesus to begin His ministry. All of these men had a special purpose that required godly and dedicated mothers who would raise these sons in the admonition of the Lord. God prepared these faithful women to bring these men forth into the world to fulfill their destinies.

Know today that God is not overlooking your faithfulness; He has set you apart. Whatever hope, dream, or desire that has yet to be fulfilled in your life is awaiting God's timing for a special plan or purpose to unfold. Never consider yourself punished; rather, consider yourself blessed to be found faithful.

Realize, too, that the enemy will attack the faithful. They are a threat to him, and he wants to make void what God has filled with purpose. Once he realizes you have been set apart, he will do everything he can to try to disqualify you. Regardless of what happens, remain faithful to God. He will hear your cry, and He will come to your aid against the enemy's attack. Bring every heartache, every need, every dream, every thought, and every doubt to God, and trust Him to go to battle for you.

If you are among the faithful today, realize you have been set apart. Accept your mission, and rest in God's plan. He will not let you miss it.

Have a blessed day!

Moving Forward

John 5:8-9:

"Get up," Jesus told him, "pick up your bedroll and walk!" Instantly the man got well, picked up his bedroll and started to walk.

This story reflects a man who had been lame for 38 years. He had become dependent upon the help of others and relied upon someone else for his healing. Until something happened or someone helped him, he would continue in his helpless state. Jesus, however, told him to get up, pick up his bedroll, and walk. This command required no help from anyone else.

Jesus first told the man to get up. Jesus commanded him to rise above his circumstances. The man would never walk as long as he lay on the ground. To walk, he had to first get up. Secondly, he had to pick up his bedroll. He was to take his provision with him. He was to pick up what he had. Finally, he was to walk. Unless we first get up and pick up what provision we have, we will not be able to walk, either.

Jesus simply moved this man forward. As long as he waited for someone else to help him or for something to happen, he was stuck in his helpless situation. Jesus had to move him beyond the point of helplessness.

We gain more insight into this story with **verse 14:**

After this, Jesus found him in the temple complex and said to him, "See, you are well. Do not sin anymore, so that something worse doesn't happen to you."

The man's paralyzed condition was due to the sinful condition of the world. Indeed, sin can paralyze us. What he needed was the same thing we need when we fall into sin—a personal encounter with Jesus. Grace enabled this man to walk again. When Jesus told him to get up, it was a sign of forgiveness. His sin would no longer keep him bound. He was released to move forward.

If you feel stuck today, get up. You may not yet know just how you will walk, but get up. You will never walk until you do. Pick up whatever provision God has given you, and move forward. This man was healed instantly. By faith, so will you. Your response takes faith just to get up, faith to pick up your provision, faith to make a step forward. If sin has paralyzed you, look to Jesus for forgiveness. His grace will move you forward.

Have a blessed day!

Moving from Locust to Luxury

Just as sin causes lack and devastation in our lives, repentance brings healing and blessing. All that is required is that we admit our faults to God and turn from our wicked ways to follow Him. The problem most of us have is in recognizing and admitting that our ways are wicked.

Joel 2:25:

I will repay you for the years that the swarming locust ate, the young locus, the destroying locust, and the devouring locust—My great army that I sent against you.

When we insist on remaining in sin, God sends a great army to fight against our sin. We cannot win in our own strength. His army will devour us. When we turn to Him in repentance, He repays us for everything His army took from us. His army is sent only to save us from ourselves. Otherwise, we would destroy ourselves in the process. Unless we do things His way, we can never enter into a blessed and peaceful land.

If there are areas in your life where you feel devoured and ravished, turn to God today. Repent of whatever sins may have led to your demise. God has more for you than lack and emptiness. He will repay you for everything you have lost while learning to turn to Him. You can bask in the luxury of His favor and blessing.

Verses 26-27:

You will have plenty to eat and be satisfied. You will praise the name of Yahweh your God, who has dealt wondrously with you. My people will never again be put to shame. You will know that I am present in Israel and that I am the LORD your God, and there is no other. My people will never again be put to shame.

Have a blessed day!

The God of Rest

Psalm 127:2

In vain you get up early and stay up late, eating food earned by hard work; certainly He gives sleep to the one He loves.

Have you ever looked back on something and wonder, "Just what did I really accomplish by all that hard work?" I've been there many times. This reflects a works-oriented mentality that believes we must strive and work hard to receive God's blessings or His approval. Yet, this verse clearly tells us that God gives sleep to the one He loves. He does not demand performance.

All of our blessings come through grace. If we work for it, we earn it. What we earn can never measure up to that with which God can bless us.

Jealousy comes when someone else receives something we think we deserve. We have worked hard for it in some respect where the person receiving it has not. Jealousy is the product of hard work unrewarded. You have labored in vain, and someone else has reaped the reward. We must remember that with God's blessing comes His glory, not our own. For His glory to be revealed, His work must be evident. We are recipients of His work, His grace, His reward—He is the one who performs. We are the ones who rest in His performance.

Have a blessed day!

Whoever Welcomes One Child

Matthew 18:4:

Therefore, whoever humbles himself like this child—this one is the greatest in the kingdom of heaven. And whoever welcomes one child like this in My name welcomes Me.

When we read this Scripture about Jesus and the little child, we often picture a very sweet, quiet, calm, submissive child, and we agree with His words. What if the child He chose was the one who just knocked three others down while he raced to be the first in line? What if that child was the one who just slapped another child for taking her seat? What if that child was the one who constantly tattles and follows you around while whining and complaining? We don't really know the personality of the child He chose. Therefore, whoever welcomes one child like this—regardless of personality, quirks, flaws, or issues—in My name welcomes Me.

While I love working with children, I have to admit that not all children are easy to love. Some make their own rules and operate by their own agendas. Some children can be bossy and try to control the rest of the group. Others are so shy they get lost in the crowd. As I write this, I think of adults who fit the same description. Children who are hard to love often grow to be adults who are hard to love, as well.

We can correct poor behavior in a child, but we cannot change their God-given personalities. He made them that way for a reason. The best way to reach a seemingly unruly child is to accept him as he is with all his warts and quirks and to love him anyway. When you work with children, you can't just choose the ones who are naturally submissive. You must accept them all. I've learned that they will respond well to those who love them and express that love and approval to them. While I'm not in to catching flies, you really can go much farther with honey than you can with vinegar!

Our job as parents, grandparents, or educators is not to change a child's personality. I often see children with strong personalities scolded for things they really cannot control. A teacher with a controlling personality will not appreciate a child with a loud, boisterous personality. We must remember that God gives children what they will need to survive in this world. Some children will have to fight more than others. Some are created to speak, while others are created to strategize. I am not condoning bad behavior, but I am against breaking a child's spirit. We must all learn to appreciate them the way God made them and try to direct them in the strengths He has given them.

Have a blessed day!

Love and the Law

Romans 13:8-10:

Do not owe anyone anything, except to love one another, for the one who loves another has fulfilled the law. The commandments: Do not commit adultery, do not murder, do not steal, do not covet, and if there is any other commandment—all are summed up by this: Love your neighbor as yourself. Love does no wrong to a neighbor. Love, therefore, is the fulfillment of the law.

Romans 3:23:

For all have sinned and fall short of the glory of God.

Love is the fulfillment of the law, yet no one has ever been able to keep it apart from Jesus Christ. It seems we humans have a love problem when it comes to the law. We are not capable of loving the way we should. If we were, there would have been no need for Christ to die on the cross. Why, then, should we expect to get from another human being what only God can give us?

The ultimate act of love was displayed on the cross. This is how Jesus fulfilled the law. He gave His life for those who did not deserve it and allowed us to benefit from grace. As the Son of God, Jesus did not have a love problem; He was love personified, and the world hated him.

Allow the Lord to fill you with His love as you remember the sacrifice He made for you today. Fully receive the grace He has for you. Only through His grace are we able to love as we are commanded.

Have a blessed day!

He Takes Away the First to Establish the Second

Hebrews 10:8-10:

After He says above, You did not desire or delight in sacrifices and offerings, whole burnt offerings and sin offerings, (which are offered according to the law), He then says, See, I have come to do Your will. He takes away the first to establish the second. By this will, we have been sanctified through the offering of the body of Jesus Christ once and for all.

God never delighted in sacrifices and offerings for sin, which were established in the law as remission for sins. They were only a temporary fix to an eternal problem. These sacrifices and offerings had no power to transform the individual. Continued sacrifices and offerings would always be needed because of man's inability to keep the law.

Jesus came to do God's will. He offered the one perfect sacrifice for sin. His sacrifice has the ability to transform lives because He kept the law in perfection. A goat, a ram, or a bull didn't have the ability to keep the law. They were merely innocent animals. God superseded the first covenant of the law and its requirements for sin and established the second, more perfect covenant of grace through faith in Jesus Christ. We don't have to be perfect according to the law. We simply need to believe on and surrender to the One who was perfect and shed His blood for us.

This second covenant was God's will, what truly pleased Him. This covenant has the ability to sanctify us once and for all. All of our sins—past, present, and future—are covered by the blood of Jesus. No more sacrifice is needed. All of God's judgment for our sins was poured out upon Jesus at the cross. We can do nothing to earn this covenant of grace, God's unmerited favor.

If you are a Christian, you don't have to do anything to make up for past failures. Your sins are already forgiven. You don't have to do anything to earn God's blessing on your life. You already walk in grace. Because Jesus was righteous, you now walk in His righteousness. This righteousness was transferred to you when you believed. When God looks at you, He sees the righteousness of Christ, not your sins and your failures.

You can rejoice today because God's favor rests upon you. You can expect success in your walk because God's favor rests upon you. You can come boldly before His throne of grace and ask for whatever you need because His favor rests upon you. You can expect God to work through you because His favor rests upon you. His covenant of grace is established, firm, and steadfast, within you.

Have a blessed day!

God's Dwelling Place

Psalm 132:13-14:

For the LORD has chosen Zion; He has desired it for His home: "This is My resting place forever; I will make My home here because I have desired it."

David longed to build a house for God to dwell, and he secured all the items necessary for its construction. The actual temple, however, was built by Solomon, a man who knew only peace and not war. God still honored David's desire. The temple which David envisioned became God's glorious dwelling place until David's sons rebelled, and God sent them into captivity.

While Solomon's temple may have been destroyed, God continued to honor David's desire. A future Son of David came into the world as a forever king, and those who follow Him have the privilege of being God's temple. God now dwells in us as a promise to David. He has chosen us for His desired home, and in us He finds His resting place.

What amazes me is that God gave David the very desire to build Him a home. He honored that desire in a way David could never have imagined. God always honors the desires He gives us, even if He doesn't answer the way we expect. While David desired to do something immediately, the temple Solomon built was temporal. God had something eternal in mind. When God doesn't seem to answer immediately or in the way we hope, He is looking at our request from eternity. We can't see that far, so we have to trust.

David did not keep his desire to himself. He expressed that desire to God, and he took steps toward it, even after God told him Solomon would be the one to build the temple. David did what he could to bring that desire to pass. God honored his faith. When God gives us a great desire, we must express it to Him, then take steps to bring it to pass. God honors our faith as we put it into action. In fact, we hear Him speaking back quite often through that action.

Whatever great desire you have, express it to God today. God gave you that desire, and He longs to dwell in you to bring that desire to pass. Once you have expressed the desire, move in the direction toward it. Don't just sit by and hope God will do something, take a step. If you fall, God will pick you right back up to try again. He is with you, and He has desired to make His home with you. Listen as He speaks, and enjoy the two-way communication you were meant to have with the One who lives with and in you.

Have a blessed day!

Blessed by the God of Truth

Isaiah 65:16:

Whoever is blessed in the land will be blessed by the God of truth, and whoever swears in the land will swear by the God of truth. For the former troubles will be forgotten and hidden from My sight.

When God blesses you, He blesses you so completely that your former troubles are forgotten. You have so much new in which to rejoice that you can't concentrate on the old. Only God can bring such a blessing. In this verse, Isaiah proclaims the same promise for Israel that God had already performed for Job. While Job was blameless, Israel had brought trouble on herself through rebellion. God's promise of restoration for Israel after she repented, however, was the same as what He did for Job.

Job suffered tremendous loss and hardship. His health deteriorated before him. All he had left were friends who thought he was being punished and a wife who encouraged him to curse God and die. No one had any hope for him. Job, however, submitted his suffering to God. If it were God's will for him to suffer, so be it. There was nothing he could do about it anyway. If he had sinned, he didn't know how. He just knew and acknowledged that God was in control.

We may experience times in our lives when we don't understand the suffering we are called to endure. Friends may abandon us because they have no hope for us. Family members may encourage us to give up because they have already given up on us. We may have brought the calamity upon ourselves, but if we did we are not sure how. We have to submit such times to God, knowing that He is in control. God puts a time limit on our suffering. One day, we will be free from it and will rejoice again. When God brings us through it and blesses us on the other end of it, that blessing will be so great that we will forget all about how terrible it was and know with all certainty that His hand was at work the entire time. God's blessing is worth the wait.

Place your hope in the God of truth today. Even if your suffering is the result of your own disobedience, God's promise of restoration is the same for those who repent and turn back to Him. He sees every tear and pain you bear and has already declared the end. Rejoice in knowing that whatever He has for you, it is so great that you will forget your current hardship. He has not forgotten you nor forsaken you. He is working His glory in you.

Have a blessed day!

A Promise for Families

Isaiah 59:21:

"As for Me, this is My covenant with them," says the LORD: "My Spirit who is on you, and My words that I have put in your mouth, will not depart from your mouth, or from the mouth of your children, or from the mouth of your children's children, from now on and forever," says the LORD.

God promised in this verse to keep His Spirit and His word with the nation of Israel. We are His children through Jesus Christ, and God sent His Spirit to dwell in everyone who comes to Christ. While we may reject the Holy Spirit's leading at times, He has promised He will never depart from us. His Spirit is with us forever.

Family and lineage are very important to the Jewish culture, as they are to most cultures. God promised that His Spirit would not depart from their families or their lineage. God's promise would not die out within the blood line. God cares about our families. His intention is to increase awareness of Him through our lineage. We are all aware that what we do today will affect our children tomorrow. Know, too, that what you pray today will affect your children tomorrow. What you proclaim by faith will affect your children tomorrow.

The Devil knows the power of the family unit, and that is why he is so actively attacking it today. Too many of us Christians don't understand the promise of the covenant God made in this verse. If His Spirit is always with us, we have the power to call on God, to move in the name of Jesus, and to proclaim by faith God's perfect will for our children and our children's children. We can't control what choices they make, but we can pray and expect the Spirit of God to work in their lives. Prayer is our biggest weapon in spiritual warfare, and I think most of us don't fully understand how powerful it is.

If your children are still at home, pray over them every day. Let them hear your prayers and what you want God to do for them and through them. Let them hear how you want God's very best and perfect will for them. If your children are grown and have moved out of the house, continue to pray for them. Proclaim God's perfect will for their future and let them know you are praying for them. God cares about your family, and He wants to increase awareness of Himself through them. Know that He is working, even if you can't see it right now. Your lineage was meant to be a Christian lineage, and God's Spirit and His word will never depart from them.

Have a blessed day!

Practicing Selah

Psalm 62:5-8:

Rest in God alone, my soul, for my hope comes from Him. He alone is my rock and my salvation, my stronghold; I will not be shaken. My salvation and glory depend on God, my strong rock, my refuge, is in God. Trust in him at all times, you people; pour out your hearts before Him. God is our refuge. Selah

We cannot control the storms of life, but God has complete control of them. We cannot always create the outcome we desire, but God can take any outcome and use it for our benefit. We cannot always avoid certain struggles, but God can see us through them and bring us out victorious on the other end. We must place our hope in Him. He is the strength by which we stand, and if we fall, He is the strength that will help us rise again.

Our hopes are disappointed when we place them in the wrong thing. If we are hoping for extra income and expect it to come through a new job, our hope is in the job. We become disappointed if the new job doesn't happen and lose hope that the additional income will ever manifest. If our hope is in God, that extra income can come from any place He chooses. Our hope must be fully established in Him. If our hope is in God, even when the worst happens, we still have hope to overcome.

The word at the end of the Scripture passage, *selah*, is a musical rest. We can rest knowing that our hope is in God, and He can work in the places we can't. He has complete control over the things we cannot control, and He is on our side. He wants our victory even more than we do. He is intervening for us to make everything work for our benefit and His glory. That is the assurance we have as His child. We can rest in Him as our strength.

If strong to severe storms happen today, rest in God as your strength. Selah. If your desired outcome doesn't happen, rest in God as your strength to overcome. Selah. When you can selah, you will never be shaken by this world because God is your stronghold. Keep holding on to Him. What this world needs is a revelation of selah—you can be an example of one today.

Have a blessed day!

God's Word to a Widow's Heart   •   317

Your Time of Visitation

Luke 19:43-44:

For the days will come on you when your enemies will build an embankment against you, surround you, and hem you in on every side. They will crush you and your children within you to the ground, and they will not leave one stone on another in you, because you did not recognize the time of your visitation.

This is the proclamation Jesus made over Jerusalem as He wept for the city immediately after His triumphal entry. They did not recognize the fact that their Messiah had come, so they were doomed to defeat by the enemy. Salvation was in their midst, but they rejected it. Everlasting peace was theirs for the taking, but pride and jealousy prevented them from entering God's rest. They did not recognize the time of their visitation.

How tragic it is not to recognize your time of visitation. Today, we have an open invitation to dine with Christ at any time. We can sit at His feet and simply learn from Him. We can commune with Him and have close fellowship with Him. We can find victory over every enemy by following Him in obedience. Sadly, many are just too busy to accept the invitation to come and dine. One day, the enemy will build an embankment and surround you on every side. When we don't let Jesus into our busy lives, the enemy will find an open door into our lives, move in, and build a stronghold to defeat us. We must learn to recognize our time of visitation and take time to enjoy God's presence.

Have you ever been in a place where you could not find God? Maybe, He didn't seem to be working in your life at all. Perhaps, the enemy seemed to have control of your life or your family. Think back to the time preceding the battle. Did you take time to fellowship with Christ on a regular basis? Did you sit at His feet and just learn from Him? Many apparent victories of the enemy occur because we did not recognize our time of visitation, and we dismissed Christ for other things.

Don't miss your time of visitation today. We still have the opportunity to sit at His feet and learn from Him. We can still commune with Him and meditate on His word. Spend time with Christ today for it will be your strong defense tomorrow!

Have a blessed day!

Shiloh

1 Samuel 3:21:

The LORD continued to appear in Shiloh, because there He revealed Himself to Samuel by His word. And Samuel's words came to all Israel.

When God spoke to Samuel, He revealed Himself to Samuel. God does the same for us today. When He speaks to us, He reveals a part of His character to us that draws us closer to Him and enables us to know Him more intimately. We can confirm God's voice to us by His word. There we will find Scripture that validates the very part of His nature that speaks to us.

If we are feeling guilty and condemned, God will speak His grace to us. If we are feeling rejected and unloved, God will speak His acceptance and unfailing love to us. If we feel hopeless and that the enemy has triumphed, God will speak to us from His greatness. Whatever our area of need may be, God fills that void with an attribute of His character that overcomes a particular weakness in us.

The Lord continued to appear in Shiloh because there He revealed Himself to Samuel. Shiloh means *tranquil.* God spoke to Samuel in a tranquil place—a safe and peaceful place. We often try to hear from God in the midst of raging storms and chaos. Here we are often tempted to act quickly and irrationally. We fail to hear God speak when there is too much noise and distraction in our lives. God chooses to speak in a tranquil place, where we can be sure it is His voice we are hearing.

Today, seek a quiet, tranquil place to hear from God. Don't let the pressure from trying circumstances dictate your faith. Find yourself a Shiloh, and determine to meet with God daily in that place. You will find He will meet you and reveal more of His amazing character to you to meet every need you have.

Have a blessed day!

Hidden by God

Isaiah 49:2:

He made my words like a sharp sword; He hid me in the shadow of His hand. He made me like a sharpened arrow; He hid me in His quiver.

Isaiah is explaining to Israel his mission from God as a prophet to them. He recognized that God hid him for a special purpose. He was very valuable in God's hand as a sharpened arrow to attack the enemy. God hid him as a weapon.

Isaiah's own words about himself seem somewhat different as we read **verse 4. "But I myself said: I have labored in vain. I have spent my strength for nothing and futility; yet my vindication is with the LORD, and my reward is with my God."** While God was hiding Isaiah in His hand, Isaiah felt like a failure, accomplishing nothing.

Understand that before God sends you out with the purpose for which He created you, He may very well keep you in hiding until your appointed time. Like Isaiah, you must remember that your reward is with God. Any success you receive will come from His hand. Isaiah was an arrow, made to be sharp. God would be the one to send the arrow where it should go. The arrow itself does not hit the target. The one who shoots it does. God has fashioned you for some specific purpose, and He will place you exactly where you need to be to accomplish it.

Today, if you feel like a failure, realize that you are a well-hidden vessel in God's hand. Allow Him to sharpen you and fashion you for His glory. He is working everything out according to His timetable, and He has not forgotten you. He has hidden you in His quiver so the enemy will not steal you. At just the right time, He will hit His target with you. A tool in God's hand is of great value. You may be surprised at just how He will use you when your time has fully come.

Have a blessed day!

Receiving God's Favor

Isaiah 66:2:

My hand made all these things, and so they all came into being. This is the LORD'S declaration. I will look favorably on this kind of person: one who is humble, submissive in spirit, and who trembles at My word.

God created heaven as His throne and earth as His footstool. Who are we to challenge anything He says or does? Sadly, many of us charge through life with our own agendas, feeling angry at God when our plans are supernaturally interrupted. Without God's favor, we can accomplish nothing. With His favor, however, we can do anything He requires us to do.

Some people are determined to do what they want to do, regardless of the cost to others or the warnings they receive. They have their own agenda apart from God, and they are bound and determined to carry out their own plans. Sooner or later they come to realize that the One who created heaven as His throne and earth as His footstool will have the final say in the matter. We must remember that we live on earth, His footstool. We are to humbly bow at His feet.

God is a loving, just, and holy God. He loves His people with an everlasting love. He shows His favor, however, to those who are humble, submissive in spirit, and who tremble at His Word. You can be God's child and not receive His favor. While He still loves you, the love He expresses to you may be for the purpose of drawing you back into His arms, rather than enabling you to run from His plan.

Jonah certainly experienced this type of love when He determined to disobey God and go the opposite direction. God's love landed him in the belly of a big fish, where he could change his mind and his plans about whether or not to obey God. A raging storm finally convinced Jonah that he could not defy God and live in His favor.

God longs to bestow His favor on all of His children. As those who are parents know, some children are just more compliant than others. To bless them is easier because you can trust them with the blessing. God looks for the humble at heart, the submissive in spirit, and those who respect His Word enough to obey what He says. Those are children He can trust to carry out His plans and not their own. He will look upon them with favor and enable them to flourish, even in the midst of adversity.

We all need God's favor; we cannot function in life without it. Today, ask Him for a humble and submissive spirit and the willingness to obey. Set aside your own agendas long enough to hear from Him and follow His directions. If what He is leading you to do seems difficult, realize that He will give you His favor to do it. If heaven is His throne and earth His footstool, you can't really fight Him and expect to win. Your destiny and your happiness depend upon His favor toward you. Fully receive what He has for you, and realize the abundance of His favor. This is well worth your surrender.

Have a blessed day!

Be Willing to Fight!

Nehemiah 4:14:

After I made an inspection, I stood up and said to the nobles, the officials, and the rest of the people, "Don't be afraid of them. Remember the great and awe-inspiring LORD and fight for your countrymen, your sons and daughters, your wives and homes."

Israel's enemies had heard of the progress made in rebuilding the walls of Jerusalem, and they threatened to attack it. Nehemiah stationed people at the vulnerable areas and equipped them with weapons. Then, he told the people to fight. Weapons alone would do no good. The people had to be willing to fight for their country and their families. We must do the same.

God has given us weapons to use in our vulnerable places. One of the biggest weapons in our arsenal is His Word. We must speak it and proclaim it over our country and our families daily. Unless we are willing to wield our swords in battle, the Devil can come in and take what he wants. Pick up your sword and fight!

Determine today to engage in battle. Remember God's faithfulness to you, and claim the territory of family that is rightfully yours. Don't give up on the loved one who has gone astray or the promise that seems all but lost. Get in God's Word and speak it over your situation. Find a Scripture that applies to you, and claim it in victory over your enemy. The enemy only threatened Nehemiah. He never even took one blow, and the wall was rebuilt in only 52 days. Your victory may be closer than you think. God's hand is powerful to save where faith abounds.

Have a blessed day!

God of Peace

Romans 16:20:

The God of peace will soon crush Satan under your feet.

This statement almost seems like an oxymoron. You just don't picture a God of peace crushing someone. This seems too violent. David was known as a warrior king, but he was considered very violent to his enemies. He caused so much bloodshed that God did not want him to be the one to rebuild the temple. Instead, He chose David's son, Solomon, to rebuild it because Solomon was a man of peace. Yet, the God of peace, crushes Satan under our feet! We see both David and Solomon in God here.

John 14:27:

Peace I leave with you. My peace I give to you. I do not give to you as the world gives. Your heart must not be troubled or fearful.

When God grants us peace, it crushes the Devil. Satan is energized and strengthened when we become troubled and fearful. That is when we are vulnerable and more likely to make poor decisions. In fact, stress leads to many addictions, which can be very damaging. When we give in to such addictions, Satan gains a stronghold in creating havoc in our lives. God's peace eliminates worry and stress so we can hear from the Holy Spirit and make better decisions.

A clear indicator that the Holy Spirit is leading a decision is the presence of peace. Worry and panic try to get you to make quick, impulsive decisions that can be damaging. Car dealers learned this years ago. If you have to make a choice very quickly, probably it is not from God. God is patient and kind, longsuffering and gentle.

In whatever decisions you have to make, let peace be your guide. Don't move too hastily. God will not penalize you for taking time to thoroughly think through your options. In fact, He encourages us to count the cost (Luke 14:28). If you don't have peace about a thing, don't do it. My dear friend, Janel, used to say, "If in doubt, don't." We find much wisdom in this.

When God is leading us in a particular direction, He will also give us a desire. He will not make you marry someone to whom you are not attracted, and He will not send you to some foreign country where you don't want to go. If God is calling you, you will want to marry that person, and you will have a desire and a love to minister to the people of that country. God's peace and desire work together.

Take time to worship the God of peace today. Ask His Holy Spirit to guide you, and watch to see how stress dissipates when you focus completely on Christ. He is most worthy of our worship.

Have a blessed day!

God's Faithfulness is Our Peace

Psalm 51:1

Be gracious to me, God, according to Your faithful love; according to Your abundant compassion, blot out my rebellion.

In this verse, we find the words of David as he lamented over his sin. He fully realized he deserved judgment and deeply regretted his sin. He asked God to treat him according to His faithful love toward him and not according to his sin; David asked for grace.

David had committed adultery with Bathsheba, and she became pregnant. He then ordered the death of her husband in battle so he could marry her and hide his sin from the people. He could not, however, hide his sin from God. David was guilty, and he knew it. When Nathan confronted him, he then knew God's judgment was both imminent and deserving. How could he ever be in right standing with God again and lead Israel except through God's grace?

David was wise to cry to God for grace. He appealed to God's love for him, even though he knew he was guilty of sin. We must remember that David suffered consequences from his actions. The child Bathsheba conceived in adultery died. However, God in His faithful love toward David, forgave David for his sin. The child Bathsheba conceived after David repented lived to inherit the throne! Grace follows repentance. We cannot expect God to be gracious to us and to keep our sin. Repentance means we turn from our wrong way of thinking and align our thinking with God's holy standard. When we do, we find God's grace abounding to us out of His faithful love for us!

God is looking for hearts that will turn completely to Him. For those hearts, He has abundant compassion! There is nothing in our lives that He won't forgive. We merely need to turn to Him to receive grace in our sinful situations. Turning to Him, however, means we let go of our sin. Don't expect Him to bless what directly contradicts His Word. Once you let that go and cling to Him, you find a faithful love like you've never imagined just waiting to be gracious to you! David grieved the death of Bathsheba's first son for a little while, but he enjoyed and delighted in Solomon for the rest of his days! The blessings God has for you are worth whatever you let go to turn completely to Him!

The name Solomon means *peaceful.* Through His faithful love toward us, God's grace turns our rebellion into something peaceful! David did not have to work to manipulate, hide, or lie to enjoy the blessing of Solomon. He was birthed in full repentance and was a blessing of grace that David did not deserve. May God make our lives peaceful as we turn completely to Him.

Have a blessed day!

Peace of Mind

Isaiah 26:3:

You will keep in perfect peace the mind that is dependent on you, for it is trusting in You.

Our minds must be kept in peace and dependent upon God. With our minds we trust God. Indeed, most of our battles are fought in our minds. Therefore, we must be careful where we allow our thoughts to linger.

Romans 12:2:

Do not be conformed to this age, but be transformed by the renewing of your mind, so that you may discern what is the good, pleasing, and perfect will of God.

Paul calls for the renewing of our minds from the damage of the world. If we are to be able to distinguish the perfect will of God, we cannot think as the world does. We need a different mindset. According to 1 Corinthians 2:16, all who belong to Christ have the mind of Christ. The closer we come to Him, the more He reveals Himself to us. He calls us into an intimate relationship with Him. The closer we move toward Him, the farther away we move from the world. This renewing of the mind is a deliberate, intentional action requiring faith and trust.

Everything that God allows to come into our lives is an opportunity to increase our faith. These times are invitations to draw closer to Him. That is His perfect will for us. Drawing closer to Christ requires keeping our focus on Him. Distractions from the world will steal our peace and cause us to look at our own inability and weakness. The mind that trusts in Him will be kept in perfect peace.

Most of us have a mind that wants answers. With our mind we ask questions and look for answers. As Christ draws us closer to Him, He bids us to come with questions. Faith trusts God, even though her questions are still unanswered. Faith leaves that question in the hands of the Father and trusts Him without knowing the answer. Faith rests in the Person of Christ, not in the answer.

Take advantage of this time to draw closer to the One who gives you perfect peace. Place your questions in the hands of the Father as you worship Him, and watch the cares of the world fade in comparison.

Have a blessed day!

His Plan, His Peace

John 14:27:

Peace I leave with you. My peace I give to you. I do not give to you as the world gives. Your heart must not be troubled or fearful.

To realize that expectations of doom, failure, or disappointment are not from God has taken me a lifetime. Most of what we fear never comes to pass. We only stress over it to wear out ourselves over nothing. This is how the Devil weakens us in our faith, in our bodies, and in our dreams.

When God speaks to us, He grants us His peace. This is how we can recognize that something is from God. If it is His plan, it is His peace; we can rest in it. He encourages us in the path in which we should go. The Devil sees that promise and tries to do what he can to destroy our peace so we never fully enter into our blessing. His strategy is to defeat us before we are blessed. When God blesses us, the Devil is defeated.

Jesus does not give as the world gives. In this world, you have to work for everything you get. You strive and strive to receive. You compete for a job. You compete on the job. You compete for position. We always experience competition, and those that work the hardest or have the most cunning strategy win. Jesus, however, freely grants His favor to all who seek Him. With His favor comes peace, and He offers it to everyone without competition. The right strategy is to submit to Him and follow where He leads. This will give you peace as His favor goes before you to prepare the way.

Don't let your heart be troubled or fearful today. If it is, somehow you still believe that your success is dependent upon you. If God is calling you to it, He will see you through it! Just follow where He leads, and let His peace permeate your heart. The blessings He has for you are designed to defeat the Devil's schemes in your life—and God will make sure it happens. Strive only to enter His rest, and the peace which passes understanding will be yours.

Have a blessed day!

Peace in the Storm

Isaiah 26:3:

You will keep in perfect peace the mind that is dependent on You, for it is trusting in You.

You have no greater picture of this verse than one sleeping through a raging storm. Perhaps, this is why Jesus was asleep in the boat during the storm that so greatly disturbed the disciples they woke Him to do something about it. Jesus depended completely upon God the Father and trusted in Him for His safety. He did not feel the need to address the storm for Himself; He calmed it for the disciples. He would have been perfectly content to let it rage, knowing He was safe in the Father's care.

Whatever has us worried, upset, or afraid is a storm raging inside us. Others may be completely unaware, but we feel the brunt of the wind as it bashes against our souls. These are places where we need to trust ourselves to the Father's care and rest. Most storms pass quickly, but we can fuel them with anxiety, allowing them to linger far longer than they should. We can minimize or eliminate damage altogether by trusting God in these matters.

When we trust God, we take our hands and minds off a matter and submit the results to Him. We give Him complete authority to handle the situation for us and trust Him with the outcome. He who has the authority also carries the responsibility. Therefore, God moves on our behalf to insure an outcome that will work for our good. If we don't take our hands and minds off the matter, the responsibility remains with us. Trust requires submission and submission invokes responsibility.

Today, trade your cares for perfect peace. Become totally dependent upon God for your safety through the storms over which you have no control anyway. Realize that He loves you with love that always works in your best interest. Rest, and let Him handle the winds for you!

Have a blessed day!

A Prize Worth Seeking

Proverbs 8:17-19:

I love those who love me, and those who search for me find me. With me are riches and honor, lasting wealth and righteousness. My fruit is better than solid gold, and my harvest than pure silver.

God has shown me many times that He does not reveal all of Himself to us at once. To really know God and the beauty of His character, we must seek Him. As He tells us in Matthew 7:6, don't cast your pearls before pigs. They will consume what is precious and valuable without the ability to understand their worth. God withholds certain things from us so that we will seek Him. Our desire must be for Him and not for the slop the world throws at us. As we see here in Proverbs and also in Jeremiah 29:13, He promises us that we will find Him when we seek Him.

Mary Magdalene sought the body of Jesus when she found the rock rolled away from the tomb. The disciples found the empty tomb and ran back to town. Mary stood there weeping and searching. As a result, Mary was the first to experience resurrection power. That is the kind of power we all need to experience, especially when we have encountered great loss. This power requires seeking Christ in your situation until you find Him and running your race until you finish.

I am not a runner, but I envy those who are. They are usually trim and physically fit. They are inspired by marathons and feel great accomplishment in meeting their time and distance goals. They build a strong fellowship with other runners who come alongside them and cheer them on in the race.

We are all running a race in our journey as widows, and we need each other to cheer us on to the finish line. Seeking God keeps our focus on the race and not on the distractions that lay in wait on the sidelines. As He promises in verse 19, His fruit is better than solid gold, and His harvest than pure silver. He is worth the seeking. Keep running—the prize is worth it in the end.

Have a blessed day!

God Has Searched You

Psalm 139:1

LORD, You have searched me and known me.

Do you realize that God has searched you? He has investigated you thoroughly, and He knows every inch of you—every thought, every feeling, and every attitude. He is consciously aware of every fiber of your being. He knows you even better than you know yourself, and He loves you with an undying and faithful love.

As Christians, we seek God. We seek to know His will and to understand His word. We seek direction and His hand of favor. Before we ever seek Him, however, He has already searched us. He knows just how to lead us where He wants us to be.

Take great comfort today in knowing that the Almighty God of the Universe has searched you and has a plan for your life. Nothing you can do—or have done—is a surprise to Him. Nothing can separate you from His love or snatch you from His hand and that is more than enough reason to worship Him today.

Have a blessed day!

When God Speaks

Isaiah 40:4-5:

Every valley will be lifted up, and every hill will be leveled; the uneven ground will become smooth, and the rough places a plain. And the glory of the LORD will appear, and all humanity will see it together, for the mouth of the LORD has spoken.

When God speaks a word over your life, no valley, mountain, hardship, trial, or rough place can prevent the glory of the Lord from being revealed in you and to you. When God is about to reveal His glory, you will find yourself being lifted from your low positions; the hills and mountains that have stood in your way will begin to crumble. The places where you have found it difficult to walk will become smooth, and the rough places that have been hewn you in will become a wide, open plain. God will begin to bless that one little area that you committed completely to Him with excellence, and you will see His glory shine.

God sometimes calls us to walk in hard places, and we have all experienced them. The Devil will try his hardest to convince us to give up by showing us just how deep that valley is or high and steep that mountain is to climb. He will tell us it is hopeless to think we can overcome the obstacles he has set for us and that God does not care if we hurt. The more we look at the terrain in front of us, the more we will succumb to the voice of the enemy and surrender our territory to him. What we absolutely must remember is that there is no valley too deep, no mountain to high, or no hard place too rough that we cannot overcome in God's strength. We must keep our focus on Him and what He can do.

What God wants to do in our lives is to reveal His glory. He does so by first speaking it over us. Whatever God has spoken over you will come to pass, so pay close attention to what His Word says about you. You are His beloved, and He has great plans for you. He plans to prosper you and not to harm you, according to Jeremiah 29:11. He is a restoring God, as is seen in the life of Job. He is a redeeming God, as is seen in the life of Ruth. He is a God who works everything the Devil means for harm in our lives for His purpose and our good, as is seen in the life of Joseph. When you realize that God is in control and look to see what He is doing, you will find those valleys, hills, and rough places becoming smaller and smaller as God's power begins to work in your life. Don't give up; look up!

When God's glory appears, everyone will see it. His glory attracts people to Him. God longs for children who will allow Him to display His glory in them! This means, however, that we will have to face some difficult places in order to see the glory of God. If you find yourself in a place today that seems difficult or even impossible to bear or overcome, this means that God's glory waits to be revealed. Begin to claim every promise you can find in Scripture, and pray God's Word continually over your circumstances. Like Esther, you have been brought to this place for such a time as this. God's word will not return to Him void (Isa. 55:11), and the glory to be revealed is worth every inch of the rough terrain before you (Rom. 8:18). Look up, dear friend. God's glory awaits you.

Have a blessed day!

Discerning God's Will

How can we know the will of God for our lives? Many ask this question in search of answers for direction. If we are truly seeking God, He will not let us miss it.

Romans 12:1-2:

Therefore, brothers, by the mercies of God, I urge you to present your bodies as a living sacrifice, holy and pleasing to God; this is your spiritual worship. Do not be conformed to this age, but be transformed by the renewing of your mind, so that you may discern what is the good, pleasing and perfect will of God.

To know the will of God, we must first dedicate ourselves to Him. As I tell children when I counsel with them, Jesus has to become the boss of your life. Our thinking must be transformed so that we don't think like the world but think like Christ. When our mind is renewed in submission to Christ, we may be able to discern God's perfect will.

Verse 3:

For by the grace given to me, I tell everyone among you not to think of himself more highly than he should think. Instead, think sensibly, as God has distributed a measure of faith to each one.

When we think too highly of ourselves, we are not being sensible according to this verse. Selfish ambitions or desires distort our vision. When life is all about us, God's will becomes clouded with our own wills. Just because we desire it does not mean it is God's will; God gives us faith to believe for that which is His will.

If you are truly seeking to know the will of God for your life, He will show you. He will lead you into it. He will open doors that need to be opened to you. He will give you everything you need, including the faith to believe for it. Faith, however, must be rooted and grounded in the Person of Christ. Faith is trusting Him whether you get what you want or not.

God's will never contradicts His Word. Spend some time today in the Word to renew your minds from the corruption of the world. Being Word-guided rather than world-guided will lead you straight into God's perfect will for your life.

Have a blessed day!

Finding and Following God's Wisdom

Proverbs 8:35-36:

For the one who finds me finds life and obtains favor from the LORD, but the one who sins against me harms himself; all who hate me love death.

Wisdom is speaking in these verses. She calls out to all men to search for her. The book of James promises us God will give us wisdom generously if we only ask. Wisdom, therefore, is not hard to find. For many, however, she can be hard to follow.

Wisdom and the favor of God are linked together. You don't find one without the other. This should prove that prosperity is not necessarily associated with God's favor. Many prosperous people don't adhere to God's wisdom. In fact, many who were once prosperous have fallen because they did something unwise. Prosperity, when flooded with temptation, often rejects wisdom.

The one who sins against wisdom harms himself. When we do something foolish, we are actually sinning against wisdom. Knowing the right thing to do and failing to do it is sin (James 4:17). Rejecting wisdom for fleshly gain is sin. This brings us harm that will eventually lead to death.

The perfect example is smoking. We all know that smoking is bad for us. Rejecting that truth and continuing to smoke harms our bodies. Eventually, if we remain in that habit, we find ourselves sick with cancer. Rejecting wisdom's call now can cause grave consequences later in life. One needs both wisdom and grace to overcome such a sin.

All of us have some area where we are probably not answering wisdom's call. We think that one day we will get wise and get that thing under control. Today is the day to seek God's favor and begin to exercise wisdom in that area. Rejecting wisdom is sin, and we all need God's favor to endure difficult times. Now is the time to get wise.

Have a blessed day!

Listen

Isaiah 48:12:

Listen to Me, Jacob, and Israel, the one called by Me: I am He; I am the first, I am also the last.

God's instruction here is to listen. He is the One who called Israel for His purpose. He had the first word in her calling, and He will have the last. The same is true for our lives.

Somewhere between the "In the beginning God created ..." of Genesis and the "Yes, I am coming soon. Amen, Come, Lord Jesus" of Revelation, we decided to insert our own agendas into God's great purpose and have failed miserably at creating our own perfect world. In fact, pursuing our own agendas will lead us right into bondage, as it did for Israel. We cannot ignore our Creator and fulfill that for which we were created. We will not find fulfillment outside what has the ability to truly satisfy us.

So, how do we know if we are following our own plan or God's plan for our lives? One key indicator is found in the preceding verse to this Scripture. Isaiah 48:11b states, "I will not give My glory to another." When we consider our plans, our actions, our patterns, we must ask ourselves one important question. Who gets the glory from what I am doing? If the answer is anyone other than God, we need to take a step back and listen. Remember God created you for His purpose, so consult Him. Listen for His instruction, and do it. Wait for Him to open doors that no one else can open. Trust His favor to work in ways you cannot. When you find yourself doing things you cannot do in your own strength and walking in places you cannot go by yourself, you will find yourself following God's plan because only He can get the glory from it. You cannot take credit for what has happened.

If you are disappointed because of a missed opportunity or because something didn't go the way you hoped it would, don't lose heart. God had the first word in your life, and He will have the last. What He has declared will come to pass, and nothing can stop it. Listen for what He has declared over you. Listen to what He puts in your heart today. Listen for the new direction He will send you. He has called you, and He will place you exactly where He wants you to be to reflect His glory.

Have a blessed day!

Determine to Hear from God

Habakkuk 2:1:

I will stand on my guard post and station myself on the rampart; and I will keep watch to see what He will speak to me.

At times when it just seems like God is not answering our prayers, we have to make a determination to hear from Him. As Habakkuk learned, God may be speaking, but it just may not be what we want to hear. Are we truly open enough to hear from God regarding a matter in our lives, or are we merely trying to persuade Him to perform for us?

My son recently learned this lesson. He missed some very important information in a class one week because he was busy socializing and not paying attention to what the teacher was saying. We do the same thing with God. While He is at work in one area of our lives, we become too busy in another to listen to Him. As a result, we miss important information, and God has to redirect our focus. Like Habakkuk, we need to station ourselves to pay attention to what He is saying, instead of focusing upon our own agendas.

Are you open and willing to hear from God if He doesn't give you the answer you want? If God denies your request, it is always for your benefit in the long run. He may have something better in mind, or He may be trying to lead you in a direction that will ultimately bring you to what you want. You will never know if you don't listen and follow directions.

Make a determination today to listen to God and follow directions. I often hear my cohort, Vickie Shelton, remind her first grade class to "follow directions first time given!" Just think of all the pitfalls in life we could avoid if we would simply pay attention to God and follow His directions the first time He spoke. We would see so many answered prayers that the world would want what we have. Isn't that the whole reason we are here anyway?

Have a blessed day!

When God Stoops

Psalm 113:5-6:

Who is like the LORD our God—the One enthroned on high, who stoops down to look on the heavens and the earth?

Have you ever considered the fact that God Almighty stoops to consider our poor, pitiful condition? When I work with children, I often stoop to their level so I can better understand them and they can better understand me. My posture lets them know I care about what they have to say and am paying attention. God actually stoops to hear us and to speak to us, as if we were His little children. He cares enough about us to become engaged with us on our level.

When God stoops, we have His full attention. We should most certainly give Him ours. To think the God of the universe desires an audience with us to the point where He would stoop to pay attention is quite humbling. He certainly has more important things to do! Why would we want to deny this audience?

When I stoop to listen to children, I rarely find one who won't talk; most of them give me an earful! On the occasion I do meet a shy one, stooping seems to ease the tension. They feel closer to you when you are willing to reach down to their level.

God is willing to reach down to our level to relate to us. He even sent His Son to live on our level and die on our level so we could live on His. While we will never reach His level of authority or divinity, we can rise above our pitiful conditions on earth and become heaven bound.

Today, remember that God stoops to hear you. He cares about you as a little child. Give Him your full attention, and respond to what He has to say.

Have a blessed day!

Learning to Walk

Psalm 37:23-24:

A man's steps are established by the LORD, and He takes pleasure in his way. Though he falls, he will not be overwhelmed, because the LORD holds his hand.

As humans, we will certainly fall when it comes to walking the Christian life. We are like babies learning to walk and children whose footing is not yet secure. God holds our hand while we are in the learning process, which never ends in this lifetime. God establishes our steps, meaning that He makes them secure and sure. We can rest assured that if we take a wrong path, God will gently direct us to the right one. He is always with us—even when we venture out the wrong way.

Regardless of how long you have been a Christian, you are still learning to walk. That is why God takes us through things we've never before encountered. He is continually establishing our steps so we can successfully walk this journey we know as life in Christ. If you fail a test, He will always give you another chance to pass. He will bring whatever reinforcements you need to help make your steps secure.

Learning to walk can be a frustrating process, but I've rarely seen a little one give up completely. The more we grow, the more we are able to take a sure step. Learning to walk can also be painful. I remember how Samuel kept bruises and knots on his head when he was learning to walk. It didn't take him long because he wasn't afraid to fall! He knew we'd be there to pick him up—and we were. The same is true for us. We cannot be afraid to stumble or fall. God is right there with us. We might wear a bruise for a while, but He will pick us up so we can continue.

Today, know that God is establishing your steps. Don't be afraid to fall, and don't become so frustrated with yourself that you give up. God is holding your hand. He is not disappointed that you are not further along; He takes pleasure in helping you learn to walk. Rely upon His strength, knowing that you are about to walk more surely than you have ever walked before because God is with you.

Have a blessed day!

Is it God, or Is it Me?

Psalm 19:7:

The instruction of the LORD is perfect, reviving the soul; the testimony of the LORD is trustworthy, making the inexperienced wise.

We are comprised of three different forms of life: body, soul, and spirit. We live in a physical body that enables us to operate in a physical world. Our mind, will, and emotions are products of the soul - the part of us that is being transformed. This is where the fleshly nature and the tendency to do evil is housed. Our spirit is that part of us that hears from God. When the Holy Spirit comes to live in us as a follower of Christ, He has the power to direct the soul and the body to do what is right. He convicts the unbeliever of unbelief and confirms the believer of righteousness in Christ.

Since our souls are constantly being renewed by the Holy Spirit, just how can we know if we are hearing from God or wanting to act in the flesh? At times I find it difficult to discern: have I really heard from God on this, or is this just my flesh wanting something to happen? I can't begin to count the number of times I have asked that question.

According to this passage, the instruction of the Lord is perfect. If God tells us something, we can trust it. God's instruction, however, also revives the soul—it does not tear it down or condemn. God's instruction makes the soul want to live again.

If you have ever had an inclination that sucked all the life right out of you and made you want to give up or even die, it is not an instruction from the Lord. If you have ever had an idea that sent you into depression and made you lose hope, it is not an instruction from the Lord. If you have ever had a thought that evoked fear in you to the point where you could not stop worrying, it did not come from God. When you are struggling with the question of whether or not you really heard from God, check how your emotions respond to the word. If it revives you and gives new life, it is from God. If it kills everything in you, it is from the Devil, who comes to steal, kill, and destroy. He will certainly try to kill any life God is breathing in you, so beware!

Don't let your emotions run your life because they can be very deceiving. Submit your mind, your will, and your emotions to God, and stand on what you know to be true. God's instruction or promise to you will never contradict His written Word, because His Word brings life. He is perfect and trustworthy, and His intention is to bring you new life worth fighting every tactic of despair the enemy may throw at you. Is it God, or is it you? Determine which word brings life to you, and you have your answer.

Have a blessed day!

From Hurt and Disappointment to Purpose

Luke 24:44-45:

Then He told them, "These are My words that I spoke to you while I was still with you— that everything written about Me in the Law of Moses, the Prophets, and the Psalms must be fulfilled." Then He opened their minds to understand the Scriptures.

For many people in the world, the Bible may seem hard to understand. Some of it may not make sense at all, especially in the day and time in which we live. Most people today find it to be irrelevant and disregard it, thinking it has no purpose or use for their lives. To understand Scripture, your mind must be opened by God; He is the source of revelation helping us understand the Bible.

Jesus opened the minds of those who were seeking Him. He did not just blanket the entire region with an immediate understanding. He gave it to those who were hurt over losing Him and who had been disappointed in what had happened.

Have you been hurt or disappointed by anything? If so, see it as an opportunity for God to reveal Himself to you. He has done this for me so many times I can't count. In fact, my hurt and disappointment gave me a hunger for His Word. When I finally realized what I was doing wasn't working for me and that I needed help from someone greater than myself, I began asking God for answers. That is when He began opening up the Bible to me like never before. I had read the same stories many times before, but they took on a new meaning after God began revealing Himself to me.

Don't let hurt and disappointment drive you away from God. Turn to Him at these times, and pay attention to what He shows you. Begin to search the Scriptures for answers, and watch what He will unveil to you. He is right smack in the middle of your heartache, just waiting for you to seek Him. You will be so amazed at what He will show you that you can't wait to share it. When you do, you will have spread the gospel and met another person's need. Hurt and disappointment lead you to your purpose in Christ.

Have a blessed day!

When God Gathers

Isaiah 56:7-8:

"I will bring them to My holy mountain and let them rejoice in My house of prayer. Their burnt offerings and sacrifices will be acceptable on My altar, for My house will be called a house of prayer for all nations." This is the declaration of the LORD God, who gathers the dispersed of Israel: "I will gather to them still others besides those already gathered."

God made this promise to foreigners, Gentiles, who converted to worship Him. That includes you and me. Jesus has already paid the price for our sins, so we do not have to provide any other sacrifice. We need to bring only our burdens and lay them down. It is time we begin to honor God's house for what it is: a house of prayer.

Prayer is communication with God—not a dialogue but a two-way conversation. We present our praise, thanksgiving, and requests to God, and He answers back. Do we wait long enough for Him to answer? Do we look for a response from Him in every daily activity? Do we expect Him to answer at all? We must stop taking matters into our own hands and pursuing our own agendas in order to hear from Him. When we do, He promises something else. He will gather others to us.

God wants hearts that will seek Him. What does God want from You? He wants you to enjoy His presence. He wants you to seek to be with Him. He will multiply any life and any small group who will seek to engage Him.

Do you feel left out today? So does God. We are all guilty of becoming so busy that we neglect God and others. This is not something we do deliberately, rather we just become so entangled with the cares of life that we fail to lay them at His feet and commune with Him. We need to take advantage of God's house of prayer and allow Him to set things in order for us. God's house of prayer is a place of rejoicing, a place where we can enjoy His presence and the presence of other believers. Why would we not want to go and participate?

Go before God's throne today, and lay your burdens down. Set aside every care, and accept the peace He gives you. Join with some fellow believers and pray. See how your faith is strengthened by the faith of others. We don't need more activity or more projects; what we need is more time in His presence. When we learn to enjoy Him, He will gather others to us.

Have a blessed day!

The Good Choice

Luke 8:18:

Therefore, take care how you listen. For whoever has, more will be given to him; and whoever does not have, even what he thinks he has will be taken away from him.

We all need to meditate on God's Word! We must be careful how we listen to God. If we take His Word nonchalantly and place our own will above His, we stand to lose anything we already have from Him. We must learn to take Him seriously. After all, do we not want Him to take us seriously?

How would we feel if we approached God with a deep, heartfelt need, and He carelessly brushed it away because it was just inconvenient for Him at the moment? Would we not be heartbroken and hopeless? We might even feel a bit irritated and angry at His seeming disrespect toward us. This may be exactly how He feels when we ignore His Word to us.

Whatever word or revelation God gives us, He expects us to obey. If we do, we may experience blessings in there somewhere for us. If we do not obey, however, this may result in consequences to pay. While we are free to choose, we are not free to choose the consequences of our bad choices.

We need to learn to make good choices, to obey what God tells us to do. We need to heed those nudges from the Holy Spirit to take action. We stand to gain tremendously from obedience but to lose drastically from disobedience. God leaves the choice to us. May He encourage us to make good choices and caution us against bad ones.

Have a blessed day!

God's Good, Pleasing, and Perfect Will

Romans 12:2:

Do not be conformed to this age, but be transformed by the renewing of your mind, so that you may discern what is the good, pleasing, and perfect will of God.

At times, we may feel like God isn't responding or that He is just not working on our behalf. We must remember, however, that God reveals Himself to those who seek Him. If we are trying to handle our problems all on our own, He will let us try until we fall flat on our faces, where we may realize our desperate need for Him and become willing to seek Him out.

Paul instructs us here in Romans 12 not to be conformed to this age. When we become engrossed in worldly confrontations, our problems may seem bigger than our God. Our problems will soon begin to conform us to this world and the world's way of handling things. Paul urges us to be transformed by renewing our minds so we may be able to discern the will of God for our lives. Renewing our minds requires we turn away from the distractions of the world and concentrate on the Word of God.

God's will for us is good, pleasing, and perfect. Many times we avoid trusting a matter to God because we are afraid His will for us will not match our own wills. God's will, however, is not only good for us, it resonates with our spirit and is pleasing to us. God has a way of changing our wills to match His when we fully turn to Him. God is always right in the middle of our situations, just waiting for us to stop long enough to search for Him so He can reveal Himself to us. He is really not that hard to find if we will but seek Him.

If you feed on the garbage of this world, garbage is what you will produce. We must learn to feed on the Word of God and to look for Him in every situation. He is just waiting to direct you into His good, pleasing, and perfect will for you because of His great love for you. Seek Him today, and receive His grace for your every need.

Have a blessed day!

Our Personal God

Psalm 86:11-13:

Teach me Your way, LORD, and I will live by Your truth. Give me an undivided mind to fear Your name. I will praise You with all my heart, Lord my God, and will honor Your name forever. For Your faithful love for me is great and You deliver my life from the depths of Sheol.

I continue to be amazed at the things we can learn from David's prayers. He certainly had a heart for God and knew Him well. Perhaps, all that time alone as a young boy tending sheep drew Him to the company of a faithful God who would never leave Him nor forsake Him. In our times of isolation, we have great opportunity to draw closer to God. Without the distractions of the world, He can gain our full attention.

David knew God's way was truth. He had come to trust in a God who had shown Himself faithful, and David had full confidence in Him. He wanted to live by that truth. David asked for an undivided mind to fear God's name. A mind undivided is a mind that if focused upon God and does not allow anything else to sway it off track.

David vowed to praise God with all his heart. His reference, "Lord my God," is the Hebrew word *Adonai*, meaning *personal God*. David had a personal relationship with the God of Israel, and he would honor His name forever. David recognized God's love for him and knew He would deliver him from any snare the enemy may set before him.

All of these things pose some important questions for us to consider in our own personal relationship with God:

1. Do we really want to live by His truth, or are we living by our own truth?

2. Do we long for an undivided mind to fear God, or are we content with other things that distract our minds?

3. Do we praise God in our hearts because we have a close, personal relationship with Him, or are we simply going through the motions of an organized religion?

4. Do we really believe God loves us enough to rescue us from the depths of *Sheol* (the pit), or do we question just how much He really does love us?

Perhaps, a time of isolation with God would be good for us to hash out these questions in our own lives to see what we really believe to be true about God. Do we see Him as our personal God or as a distant entity? The only way to know Him personally is to spend time with Him. You will be amazed at the ways He will speak to you and the things He will reveal to you in private.

Have a blessed day!

When God Mocks

Proverbs 1:26:

I, in turn, will laugh at your calamity. I will mock when terror strikes you …

The preceding verses to this Scripture depict wisdom's plea to a corrupt people. How many times have we seen people who should have known better fall into a trap set by the enemy, and we wonder how that happened? It happened because those people did not listen to the loud voice of wisdom that cried out to them.

When we fail to listen to the voice of wisdom, we find ourselves paying the high price of sin. At that point, we hear the laughing and mocking on the inside. No one ever falls into a trap of sin without warning. We simply ignore its plea and choose to follow the voice of our lustful flesh.

In general, if you have to hide to do it, it is not from God. He will never lead you to something where you have to hide your actions for fear of shame. Shame is the Devil's trademark, and we are wise to flee anything that threatens its entrance into our lives.

We have all fallen into traps of the enemy. Whether it is an inappropriate relationship, a gossip session, or the need to hide how much money you charged on your credit card last month, failing to heed the voice of wisdom brings dire consequences. If we find ourselves in such a position, we need to turn to the God of grace and truth. We must first be truthful about our weakness and ask the God of grace to help us overcome. The Holy Spirit guides you in wisdom. Don't reject Him. Lust seeks to meet a legitimate need in an illegitimate way, but God has a better plan—and wisdom will lead you to it.

Have a blessed day!

When God's Glory Departs

1 Samuel 5:21-22:

She named the boy Ichabod, saying, "The glory has departed from Israel," referring to the capture of the ark of God and to the deaths of her father-in-law and her husband. "The glory has departed from Israel," she said, "because the ark of God has been captured."

God's glory resides in His presence. As Christians, we have the indwelling Holy Spirit in us to lead us into His presence. If, however, we listen to another voice and fall into sin, we forfeit the glory of God.

When Eli the priest heard the news that his two sons were killed in battle and that the Philistines had stolen the Ark of the Covenant, he fell over dead. His pregnant daughter-in-law immediately went into labor and gave birth to a son. This birth, however, caused her death.

Do not expect God to glorify anything where His presence does not exist! Seek His presence first, and His glory will follow. Anything we try to glorify on our own will stink to high heaven, and everyone will know God is not in it. If God is not in it, you don't want it!

Have a blessed day!

Again I Say, "Look Up!"

Luke 9:59-62:

Then He said to another, "Follow Me." "Lord," he said, "first let me go bury my father." But He told him, "Let the dead bury their own dead, but you go and spread the news of the kingdom of God." Another also said, "I will follow You, Lord, but first let me go and say good-bye to those at my house." But Jesus said to him, "No one who puts his hand to the plow and looks back is fit for the kingdom of God."

What the two men asked to do in these verses seems entirely reasonable and responsible. Jesus, however, wanted these two men to make Him their priority. Jesus's remarks to the first man were a command to put the past behind him and to move forward in His plan. For the second, Jesus was asking the man to trust his household to Him. If God calls a man or a woman to move forward in life or in ministry, He will provide what is necessary for that household. Unless we are willing to trust those closest to us to His care, we are not yet fit to minister in the kingdom of God.

Jesus was not encouraging either of these men to abandon responsibility. He was asking them to trust Him. To do so, they would have to look up. They would have to trust God to care for that which they held dear while they moved forward in His plan. We must do the same.

Do you feel stuck? I certainly have. To move forward, we must look up and trust God—trust Him to do what we can't. Believe Him for answers to your prayers. Our answers cannot be found in the past nor within us. We must look up and trust His moving in our lives. Pay attention to where your heart is leading you. Both of these men wanted to follow Jesus. They just felt obligated in other places. Jesus encouraged them to trust Him with their obligations, and we can trust Him with ours.

Have a blessed day!

God's Supply

Philippians 4:19:

And my God will supply all your needs according to His riches in glory in Christ Jesus.

Most of you have probably heard this verse and have committed it to memory. This is a promise upon which we can stand. Paul made this proclamation to the Philippians for their support of him while he was in prison. Because they had met his needs, he was sure God would meet theirs.

The Philippians were willing to share with Paul in his hardship. We often rejoice with others when they rejoice, but it may seem more difficult to mourn with them when they are hurting. We've all experienced the loss or absence of friendships during difficult times. While the church at Philippi could not rescue Paul from his situation, they could aid him. We may not be able to change a friend's circumstances during a difficult time, but there may be something we can do to help her through it.

Paul was confident that because the Philippians had aided him, God would meet their needs. To have a need means to lack in some area where you have no ability to help yourself. For those areas where we have no resource, no provision, no answer within our own means, God has an endless supply of riches from which to pull to bless us in Christ Jesus. We may have no earthly idea how a need can be met, but God has answers waiting that we could never imagine.

Today, let your demand reach for God's supply. Trust Him with every area where you need an answer. Don't be limited by your own abilities or resources. Turn your need over to Him, and trust His grace to provide from His riches in glory in Christ Jesus! I love the next verse:

Philippians 4:20:

Now to our God and Father be glory forever and ever. Amen!

When God meets your need, He is glorified. If you had all the answers all the time, God would not be glorified in your life. The very fact that you have a need means that God wants to be glorified in your life, and He is working toward that end. If you have a need, rejoice that God is working in you. Expect an answer from Him that will make heads turn and take notice. Most importantly, thank Him and give Him the glory.

Have a blessed day!

Entering into God's Rest

Psalm 95: 8-11:

Do not harden your hearts as at Meribah, as on that day at Massah in the wilderness where your fathers tested Me; they tried Me, though they had seen what I did. For 40 years I was disgusted with that generation; I said, "They are a people whose hearts go astray; they do not know My ways." So I swore in My anger, "They will not enter My rest."

The psalmist is describing the children of Israel as they wandered in the wilderness for 40 years. They refused to believe He would bring them in to the land He promised to give them. This unbelief disgusted God, and He swore they would not enter His rest.

When we enter God's rest, we submit the matter to Him and allow Him to go to work on our behalf. We cease our self-efforts and depend upon Him. He is responsible for the results. Even though God had just parted the waters of the Red Sea for them to cross over and destroyed Pharaoh's army behind them, they still did not believe God would take them into the Promised Land.

Meribah was the place where the people complained about having no water, and God allowed Moses to strike the rock so they would have water. Meribah means *striving*. God's promises come to us when we stop striving to make them happen and rest in assurance that He is working the matter for our good. God doesn't want us to strive; He wants us to thrive in a natural outflow from our relationship with Him. When we give a matter to Him, we need to let it go and trust. That is entering into His rest. Until we do, God remains silent and inactive in the matter.

The first principle of Management 101 is a simple, common sense rule. He who has the authority also has the responsibility. Authority and responsibility go hand-in-hand. You cannot have one without the other. Many times, we want to give God the responsibility of meeting our needs, but we fail to give Him the authority to do so. All it takes is one word from His mouth to change your situation, but He will remain silent without the authority to work. At other times, we may give Him the authority in a matter, but we don't trust Him to be responsible, so we try to help Him out. He will let you strive as long as you want while He waits for you to believe Him before He moves.

If you want God to intervene in your life, enter into His rest. Submit the matter to Him, and allow Him to work. Give Him the authority, and trust Him with the responsibility. Just think of all He has done for you in the past. Learn from the ways He has worked for you before. Will He surely not work for you again?

Have a blessed day!

Get a Revelation

John 14:21:

The one who has My commands and keeps them is the one who loves Me. And the one who loves Me will be loved by My Father. I also will love him and will reveal Myself to him.

Sometimes, things that happen in this world just don't make sense. Why do bad things happen to good people? Why do we encounter hurt and betrayal? Why do loved ones have to die at an early age? There are just too many *why* questions to count and no apparent answers.

Will we choose to love God and keep His commands even if something bad happens? Will we choose love for Him over love for ourselves? Some things in this world will never make sense to us. Until Christ reveals Himself to us in the midst of the circumstance, we won't understand. Remember that He reveals Himself to those who love Him.

This is exactly what happened to Mary Magdalene at the tomb. She loved Jesus deeply and was seeking to care for His body after death. All her earthly hopes and dreams died with Him, but she still loved Him enough to seek Him to care for His dead body. As a result, Jesus revealed Himself to her. He was right in the midst of her anguish, but she thought He was the gardener. She would never have recognized Him if He had not revealed Himself to her. (John 20)

When the *why* questions attack us, we need for Christ to reveal Himself to us. In fact, our greatest need in the midst of trials is to have a revelation of Christ. Such revelations are personal; others often may not see or understand. Christ revealed Himself to Mary Magdalene by calling her by name. No one else was there. The revelation was for her and her alone at that time. His instruction to her was to tell others that He was alive.

If you are facing difficult circumstances that don't make sense, ask Jesus to reveal Himself to you today. Take time to look for Him. Ask Him to call you by name so you clearly recognize where He is. He is greater than any difficulty you face. The reasons why really don't matter in His presence. Your real need is not for an answer to your problem; it is for a revelation of Christ.

Have a blessed day!

Leaving the Past Behind

Philippians 3:12-14:

Not that I have already reached the goal or am already fully mature, but I make every effort to take hold of it because I also have been taken hold of by Christ Jesus. Brothers, I do not consider myself to have taken hold of it. But one thing I do: forgetting what is behind and reaching forward to what is ahead, I pursue as my goal the prize promised by God's heavenly call in Christ Jesus.

If we are going to move forward in life and reach the goals God has for us, we must leave the past behind. To try to hang on to it, regardless of how wonderful it may have been, is to stifle our maturity. We actually go backwards. There comes a time when we just have to let some things go and lighten our load for us to move forward.

Sometimes we can easily let some things go. Feelings of bitterness, unforgiveness, or resentment are better taken to the dump with the rest of the trash from our lives. Personal belongings that are no longer of any use to us other than recalling memories, however, may be hard to let go.

Wouldn't those things be more productive in someone else's hands who would really use them?

What is behind us may be painful, or it may be full of happy memories. To move toward the prize God has for us requires we let go and stretch forward. We might just need to be convinced we have a prize waiting for us.

Jeremiah 29:11:

For I know the plans I have for you—this is the LORD's declaration—plans for your welfare, not for disaster, to give you a future and a hope.

God has wonderful plans for our lives. He has a call for every one of us. A plan, however, is just an idea until we put action to it. The first step may be to put the past behind us and be willing to move forward. Moving forward requires seeking God's direction and following it without the baggage of the past.

Where is your past hiding? Are you holding on to anything that might hinder you from moving forward? Are you convinced you have a future and a hope in Christ? Eventually, you'll get sick of looking at the mess and decide to move forward. Our prize is the call God has on our lives. Now is the time we stretch forth and pursue it!

Have a blessed day!

The Rest of the Story

Ecclesiastes 6:8:

The end of a matter is better than its beginning; a patient spirit is better than a proud spirit.

This verse emphasizes the importance of waiting on God. God works on behalf of those who wait patiently for Him and does not let them be put to shame. When God does a work in our lives, everyone notices it, and God is glorified. Indeed, the end of a matter is much better than the beginning.

We miss God's very best for us when we become impatient and try to take matters into our own hands. We could never do what God can do, and it is always wise to wait on Him. To try to set a time limit on God is unwise. After all, He is the creator, not the creation.

A proud spirit wants to boast in itself. This spirit is never patient and often has a point to prove. God will not share His glory with another, so a proud spirit means we often have to wait until humility can grow. When humility grows in complete dependence on God, we find grace for our need.

Paul Harvey used to set us up for a story by building up the problem, then he told *the rest of the story* after a break. The *rest of the story* of our lives is in God's hands. The key word here is *rest.* When we come to completely trust God in a matter, we will find rest. When we accept the fact that He always gives us His best and that we will not be disappointed, we can rest, knowing that He is at work. In God's own timing, we will experience *the rest of the story,* which will be much better than its beginning!

Today, dear friend, is the day of rest. Trust all your cares to God, and just spend time praising Him today! He has His very best planned for you, and if you are waiting for Him, He won't let you miss it!

Have a blessed day!

Something of Value

Psalm 105:37:

Then He brought Israel out with silver and gold, and no one among them stumbled.

This verse refers to the way in which God brought the children of Israel out of Egyptian bondage. They were not empty handed. They had something of value! Not one of them stumbled, meaning that they were all able to walk away. No one was too burdened by the weight of what they had to carry, and no one was lame!

If God has delivered you from a sinful past or brought you through a difficult time, He made sure you came out of that experience with something of value! Matthew 11:28 instructs us to bring our burdens to Christ, and He will give us rest. In Him we can walk in victory over a sinful past or a time of loss and have something of value to share with others that will lead them into victory. What you learn from your past is of extreme value in the destiny to which God is taking you!

While it may seem like a long journey from bondage to your promised land, do not be like the Israelites who took their gold to make a golden calf in the wilderness while Moses was meeting with God. Their impatience caused them to create a counterfeit to worship, proving they were more comfortable with the practices of Egypt than they were with the God who had just delivered them from bondage. Waiting upon the Lord is essential to the fulfillment of His plan and promises to us. Failing to wait upon Him will cause us to waste our gold.

Today, consider the gold and silver you have acquired from your own deliverance. What have you learned from your past mistakes or losses? How can these things help you going forward? Who is about to experience the same mistakes or loss and needs encouragement from you? Use your valuables wisely and give them back to God, who can multiply them in ways you never imagined. You will not stumble; you will find your destiny.

Have a blessed day!

The Need for Wisdom

1 Kings 3:7-9:

"LORD my God, You have now made Your servant king in my father David's place. Yet I am just a youth with no experience in leadership. Your servant is among Your people You have chosen, a people too numerous to be numbered or counted. So give Your servant an obedient heart to judge Your people and to discern between good and evil. For who is able to judge this great people of Yours?"

These verses reveal Solomon's request for wisdom from God. You do not see the word *wisdom* used. He asked for an obedient *heart* to judge God's people and the ability to discern between good and evil. Therein lies the definition of wisdom.

Wisdom means different things to different people. For some, it is the ability to acquire wealth or to be successful. For others, it is acquiring knowledge. Some consider it to be crafty or cunning. Wisdom, however, is none of those things. Wisdom is simply the ability to determine right from wrong and the willingness to do the right thing. We live in a time when wisdom is rare but desperately needed.

Isaiah 5:20:

Woe to those who call evil good and good evil, who substitute darkness for light and light for darkness, who substitute bitter for sweet and sweet for bitter.

We certainly live in a day when people call evil good and good evil. We see it saturating the arts and literature. We observe it every day in the news. We are bombarded by it in politics. If you are not grounded in the Word of God, it can be very difficult to discern good from evil in our society. Evil is praised and good is condemned. According to Isaiah 5:20, woe be to this generation! If we cannot determine good from evil, we are bound to face severe consequences.

God gladly honored Solomon's request for wisdom and gave him blessings beyond what he asked. Just as evil brings consequences, doing good brings blessing. Wisdom will help us discern the two. James 1:5 assures us that all we have to do is ask God, and He will gladly give us wisdom. With such a promise before us, why aren't we asking more? Perhaps, we need wisdom to ask for wisdom!

We live in a day when it is vitally important that we know the Word of God. In the Bible He has given us everything we need to know. Through daily prayer and devotion time, He can guide us to the Scriptures we need and speak His truth through them. Determine to be a woman of the Word, and seek wisdom. Don't let the world tell you what is right and wrong. God's Word is the standard, and by that we will be judged.

Have a blessed day!

Today's Shield, Tomorrow's Success

Proverbs 2:7:

He stores up success for the upright; He is a shield for those who live with integrity.

When we store up things, we are saving something for tomorrow. We don't use all we have for today. If God stores up success for the upright, it means He doesn't give us every success today.

When we follow Him in obedience, we may not always see the reward right away. He may choose to store it up for us to have at a moment when we most need it. Every act of obedience brings reward, but we may just have to receive that reward by faith.

Living with integrity does not mean we are perfect, rather it means we are not deceitful, and we try to do the right thing in a matter. God protects a person with integrity so that integrity will be honored. While the deceitful fall from the darts of the enemy, God is a shield to those who walk uprightly and live honestly.

If you are living faithfully for God and following Him in obedience, rest assured that success is stored up for you. You need not fear failure, disgrace, despair, or destruction. God is your shield against anything the enemy may throw at you to try to steal what God has promised you. If God is for you, no one can stand against you.

Have a blessed day!

DECEMBER 2

God's Pleasure

Have you ever really thought about the things that make you happy? What are the things you enjoy doing most? Where do you find real pleasure in life?

I love studying God's Word and finding fresh insight into my daily life. I also love working with children and the perspective they give me at times. Life can seem so much more simple through their eyes.

Psalm 149:4:

For the LORD takes pleasure in His people; He adorns the humble with salvation.

We should be humbled to realize that God finds pleasure in us. He enjoys listening to our prayers and speaking to us through His Holy Spirit. He delights to bless us and to guide us through our battles to victory. Of all the marvelous things God could do with His time and resources, His delight is in us.

Psalm 145:9:

The LORD is good to everyone; His compassion rests on all He has made.

I'm amazed at those who seem so angry with God that they even deny His existence. He loves even them and is good to them. If He is good to those who hate Him, how much more will He be good to those who love Him? We can count on His goodness toward us because it is His nature.

Psalm 147:11

The LORD values those who fear Him, those who put their hope in His faithful love.

Remember today that God values you. You mean something to Him. He takes pleasure in you, and He desires to be good to you. Rest and rejoice in this. You can count on His Word and His love toward you.

Have a blessed day!

The LORD Shines Over You

Isaiah 60:1-2:

Arise, shine, for your light has come, and the glory of the LORD shines over you. For look, darkness covers the earth, and total darkness the peoples; but the LORD will shine over you, and His glory will appear over you.

These words are not a command. God is not instructing us to do anything here. He is making a proclamation, just as He did when He spoke the earth into being.

Today, God says over you, "Arise, shine, for your light has come, and the glory of the LORD shines over you!" He has said that this shall be true of you, and His Word will not return to Him void! Praise God!

God's plan for your life, His proclamation, His prophetic word, and His destiny for you is that He will shine over you, and His glory will appear over you! God's Word is true, and anything that contradicts it is a lie. This gives us all reason to rest in Him and to praise Him today!

Arise and praise the God who shines over you today! You have reason to rejoice in the midst of a dark world. Let Him shine through you today.

Have a blessed day!

Reflections of My Grandmother

My precious maternal grandmother died in 1999 after a battle with cancer. She was a short, round, Pentecostal lady who wore her long hair up in a bun. She always wore a dress and carried her black leather purse wherever she went. Her purse was sacred ground, and none of us dared touch it! When she attended my college graduation, then Vice-President George Bush was the guest speaker. She had to check her purse through security and fought the security guard for trying to take her purse to place it on the conveyor belt. When Mr. Bush ran for President, her comment was, "Don't vote for that George Bush. He will try to steal your pocket book!"

In thinking about my grandmother and her viewpoint on things, it is easy for me to see how our perspectives often derive from our personal experiences. We form opinions on things based upon how things affect us. For us to get a bigger picture often can be difficult unless we are willing to look outside ourselves.

Isaiah 55:8-9:

"For My thoughts are not your thoughts, and your ways are not My ways." This is the LORD's declaration. "For as heaven is higher than earth, so My ways are higher than your ways, and My thoughts than your thoughts."

When things seem difficult or unfair, we often need a new perspective. This is why seeking God during trials is so important. We need to look higher to find our answers. Our limited view from an earthly or fleshly perspective taints our judgment. We have to trust the One who knows the beginning from the end and is working all things for our good because we love Him and are called according to His purpose.

George Bush was never my grandmother's enemy. She just didn't understand the process of security and was uncomfortable submitting to it not knowing what would happen to her purse. When we face difficulties and hardships, it may be nothing more than God's temporary process to assure our safety in some matters. God is certainly not trying to steal our pocket books or to cause us any harm. Instead of turning against Him in uncertain times, we are wise to turn to Him to get that higher perspective we need. Trust has tremendous benefits.

Dare to ask God to give you greater understanding in the matters that concern you. Ask for the big picture instead of getting frustrated or discouraged with your small, limited view. He can open doors and give you opportunities you never imagined simply because you were willing to look up higher and seek Him on the matter. You can't contain Him in a box, and He doesn't want you to stay in one, either. Trust in the God who loves you and whose ways and thoughts are higher than your own.

Have a great day!

Blue Iris

Ecclesiastes 7:10:

Don't say, "Why were the former days better than these?" For it is not wise of you to ask this.

To long for former days is to live in the past. God has a plan for your present, and He wants you to experience it. There is certainly nothing wrong in remembering good things about the past, but we can't go back there. We will never be effective or productive if we long for the past. Most people are happy when they feel effective and productive, so accepting the present and moving forward is our key to finding those happy times again.

We see this truth portrayed in the grief cycle. We go through stages of shock, denial, deep loss or utter devastation, which lead to acceptance. If we fail to accept the loss, we go right back through the cycle again. We don't grow from the experience until we accept the situation and move forward. Those who try to live in the past are refusing to accept the loss. They are stuck.

Do you remember Lot's wife? She looked back on Sodom and Gomorrah and longed for the life she was losing, even though it was marked with terrible sin. God was rescuing her to a place where she could be free and flourish again, but she disobeyed God, looked back, and was turned to a pillar of salt. She could go no further in God's plan for her. She lost her family, and they lost her.

If you still feel your loss and long for the days of the past, make a conscious decision today to look forward. Heed the words of Solomon, and stop asking, "Why?" You lay hold of God's inheritance for you by faith, moving forward one day at a time. Good days are waiting for you, but you have to live them by accepting the present and looking forward to the future with earnest and eager expectation. The symbol of PHOEBE Ministries is a blue iris because it represents faith and hope, which is an eager expectation of good. Expect God to be good to you on your journey as a widow, and watch faith and hope rise up in you. You will be amazed at what wonderful things He will allow in your life when you do!

Have a blessed day!

From Garbage to Nobility

Psalm 113:7:

He raises the poor from the dust and lifts the needy from the garbage pile in order to seat them with nobles—with the nobles of His people.

This verse paints a picture of the church. God has raised the poor from the dust and lifted the needy from the garbage of this world through Christ and has seated us in heavenly places among the nobles of His people. Had He not lifted us, we would have continued to search through garbage for our very existence.

In God's eyes, the poor child is no different from the rich child: they all have a seat at His table. His desire is for the poor and needy to come and dine at His feast, which is open to all who believe in Him. His blessings are not reserved only for the rich or for those who have learned to follow Him. His goodness is available to all His children, and there is no need to rummage through the garbage of this world in order to be filled.

Where are you poor and needy today? God loves you the same as He does those who seem to be rich in your area of need. His plan for you is always to lift you higher. He doesn't send us to the garbage heap. We choose to go there. Accept His invitation today to dine with Him, and enjoy the blessings of His nobles. Christ has already paid the price for you.

Have a blessed day!

Repent

Matthew 3:2:

"Repent, because the kingdom of heaven has come near!"

This was the cry of John the Baptist as he preached through the Wilderness of Judea. His message, however, is as current today as it was then. We all need to repent because the kingdom of heaven has come near to us.

To repent means to change your mind. You turn away from your sin because you change your thinking on why you do it. You realize it is wrong, and you decide to live differently.

Many of us confuse repentance with confession. To confess something is to admit wrongdoing. If you confess wrongdoing and return to do it again, you have not repented. You may have admitted you have a problem, but you have not truly felt the remorse for the sin and determined not to go there again. To confess a sin and return to it is like trying to have your cake and eat it, too. While the temptation is before you, you enjoy the indulgence too much to refrain. In this case, the sin is your friend instead of God.

We all have a past, and most of us have done things in the past we regret. While the blood of Jesus covers our past, present, and future sins, it does not pave the road for us to continue in them. His blood was shed so we might become victorious over our sins! We do this by repenting. We repent, Jesus forgives us, and we turn away from our sins because of His grace.

When your past is still operating in your present, it is not your past; it is your pattern. A pattern will not be broken without repentance. Change your mind about your destructive patterns. Break free from the chains that bind you. Recognize your true enemy and make friends with God. The kingdom of heaven is near to us today. All we have to do is repent to enter in.

Have a blessed day!

Out of the Mouths of Babes

Psalm 8:2:

Because of Your adversaries, You have established a stronghold from the mouths of children and nursing infants to silence the enemy and the avenger. (HCSB)

Out of the mouths of babes and nursing infants
You have ordained strength,
Because of Your enemies,
That You may silence the enemy and the avenger. (KJV)

When a baby coos, he is singing praises to God. He is displaying the handiwork of a magnificent Creator who brings forth new life. This praise is strong enough to silence the enemy! I love how the Holman Christian Standard Bible describes it as a stronghold. When we picture the Devil as a roaring lion roaming the earth just seeking whom he may devour, it is difficult to think of a nursing baby as a strong weapon against such a vicious predator. In fact, our natural instincts are to protect the baby from the lion. This is why the angels rejoiced to bring the good news of the Savior's birth to the shepherds in Bethlehem. His young voice was already silencing the enemy and the avenger on our behalf.

If a tiny baby's cooing is strong enough to silence the enemy, just think of what our voices can do when we sing praises to God! In praise we have power that we cannot possibly fathom, or we would be singing to the top of our lungs every day. In whatever you are facing, stop speaking to the problem and start praising God. Your praise is a stronghold against the Devil's schemes.

When the Devil starts screaming at you, sing to him. Sing of God's greatness and His everlasting love toward you. When you are feeling overwhelmed or burdened, sing praises to God over the matter. Nothing is impossible with God, and He has promised to work all things out for our good. We can praise Him in everything just knowing that He has our backs. There is power in your praise, so choose today to be powerful, rather than pitiful. If you feel like you just don't have it in you to praise, or if you have forgotten how, volunteer to babysit. Learn from a newborn. An infant has no care in the world and is totally dependent upon those who care for him. He has no choice but to trust, and he does it with praise on his lips! How powerful we would all be if we could simply respond the same way!

Have a blessed day!

On the Outside Looking In

Joshua 2:24:

They told Joshua, "The LORD has handed over the entire land to us. Everyone who lives in the land is also panicking because of us."

Before the children of Israel entered into the Promised Land, they encountered the walls of Jericho. To take their promise from God, they had to defeat the enemy inhabitants on the other side. These inhabitants were numerous, strong, and very intimidating. Israel was afraid.

While on the outside looking in, the children of Israel had no idea that these enemy inhabitants were equally afraid of them because Jericho had seen how God had made them victorious over other enemies. In fact, they were terrified of Israel. The very fact that they were panicking was proof that God had already handed the victory to Israel. Remember God's famous words to Joshua in chapter one: "Be strong and courageous." Where fear abides, defeat is imminent. To be victorious takes courage.

Where in your life do you feel like you are on the outside looking in? That is your point of insecurity. Obviously, there is something on the inside you desire, but fear has kept you on the outside. Realize that God is with you and for you. You are a much greater threat to your enemy than he is to you. Be strong and courageous. Go take your land!

Have a blessed day!

Ruling Over the Enemy

Isaiah 14:1-2:

For the LORD will have compassion on Jacob and will choose Israel again. He will settle them on their own land. The foreigner will join them and be united with the house of Jacob. The nations will escort Israel and bring it to its homeland. Then the house of Israel will possess them as male and female slaves in the LORD's land. They will make captives of their captors and will rule over their oppressors.

While this is a prophecy we will see fulfilled in the end times, it also presents a picture of how God restores His people. Jacob (deceiver) was the given name for Israel, meaning *he will rule as God.* There are times when we return to our old character and follow fleshly ways. When we turn to God, He has compassion on us, just as He did on Israel. His desire is to give us victory over our enemies.

The foreigner is also a picture of the Gentile church. While God chose Israel, the Gentiles more readily received the message of the gospel and followed Christ. Both Jew and Gentile will be united as God's people.

God will bring Israel into her homeland and give the nations to her as her slaves. Today, the world tries to influence God's people with its ungodly character and morally corrupt ideology. God's people, however, are destined to own the world. The Devil is the prince of this world. He knows his rightful place is under our feet, so he tries to take authority over us. He is an illegitimate ruler.

God intends for His people to rule over their oppressors. Whoever or whatever has tried to rule over you will one day serve at your feet. Whether it be the need to please people, insecurity, low self-esteem, rejection, addiction, co-dependency, depression, or any unhealthy habit, God intends for you to rule over it.

You may be thinking that you just don't have the power to conquer your enemy. You are correct. In and of yourself, you cannot defeat this kind of enemy. You will rule over him once he is placed at your feet.

Psalm 110:1:

The LORD declared to my lord: "Sit at My right hand until I make Your enemies Your footstool."

In this verse, LORD is the Hebrew word *YHWH*, or Yahweh and refers to *God the Father*. The word *lord* is the word *Adonai*, meaning *master* and refers to *God the Son*. The Father is speaking to the Son and tells Him to sit at His right hand until He makes His enemies His footstool. God the Father is doing a work of making the enemies bow to Jesus. Jesus is simply to rest at the Father's hand. We are in Christ Jesus. Therefore, this command is also for us. God tells us to rest while He makes our enemies our footstool.

If you have tormentors who are raging against you, look to God the Father. Turn them over to Him, and rest. Trust Him to deliver them to your feet. When God gives you authority over something, nothing can take it away. You can only give it away. Take dominion over your enemies by trusting and resting in God.

Have a blessed day!

The Gift that Opens Doors

Proverbs 18:16:

A gift opens doors for a man and brings him before the great.

When we read this verse, we often think of the talents or spiritual gifts God gives to men as the gift that opens doors for him. Such gifts certainly do open doors. Let us not forget, however, that God's greatest gift to all mankind is His Son. He is the gift that brings men before the Greatest of all and gives us access to the very throne room of God. No greater door could be opened for us.

Not only does the gift of God's Son give us access to the throne, it also gives us favor with God. There is no position, provision, or promotion that

God's favor cannot grant. There is no conflict, confusion, or contest His favor cannot overcome.

During this season of celebration, let us not forget that the gift of God's Son brings us before the Great! He is given to us by the Father, and He is our access to the Father's favor. We have nothing of our own merit. All we have has been granted to us by the Father. Make this season a time to remember and fully receive His gift to us. He is truly all we will ever need!

Have a blessed day!

Good News

Isaiah 52:7:

How beautiful on the mountains are the feet of the herald, who proclaims peace, who brings news of good things, who proclaims salvation, who says to Zion, "Your God reigns!"

We have such bad news in the world today. All you have to do is turn on the news to hear more of tragedies, dangers lurking, dismal predictions for the economy, and hurting people all around us. Don't you just wish you could hear some really good news that would excite you beyond measure and lift your spirits to wonder again?

Jesus was born at such a time. He came into a dark world that had heard no prophetic voice in some 400 years. Rome controlled the government, and an ungodly and illegitimate ruler sat on David's throne. The Jewish religious system was in a mess because Herod had appointed his own priests, and the religious leaders were profiting from the sins of the people. That situation certainly bears great similarity to the day in which we live! Yet, Jesus came at such a time as this. Today, He is alive and well and ready to come into our dark world, as well.

We have the good news of salvation that is found only in Jesus Christ. We know the One who is the giver of all good things and brings peace to His people. Others should look at us and know beyond the shadow of a doubt that our God reigns.

Today, I ask you to consider, "What does your life reflect about your God?" Are others able to see the living Christ at work, or are you as dismal as the TV news? Can God's glory be seen in you, or are you lost in defeat and settling for less than you know life can be? If you are to proclaim the good news of Jesus Christ today, you must first believe He is your good news. Exalt His name in the midst of your dark situations, and watch to see the light He brings. Turn completely to Him, and trust Him to reveal His glory in your heartache. Dare to be the beautiful living example of how God can transform a life, and share your good news wherever you go. Jesus came into a dark world; we can reflect His light into our dark world. Take every opportunity to let your light shine.

Have a blessed day!

Birth from a Stump

Isaiah 11:1-2:

Then a shoot will grow from the stump of Jesse, and a branch from his roots will bear fruit. The Spirit of the LORD will rest on Him— a Spirit of wisdom and understanding, a Spirit of counsel and strength, a Spirit of knowledge and of the fear of the LORD.

If a shoot grows from a stump, this means a tree was cut down. This is an indication of the condition of Israel at the time of Jesus's birth. While they were under Roman rule, longing for their restoration as an independent nation, there was still some hope alive that God would restore them to their rightful position through His promised Messiah. From this branch came the new life of a baby.

This reminds me of some roses I have growing in my back yard. I love roses, and several years ago, my late husband made me a rose garden. I planted many kinds of beautiful species and had some climbing roses growing in the back. As hard as I tried to care for them, I could not control the blackspot fungus that kept damaging them. We finally learned that the mulch we were using was causing it. Since they were so badly damaged, I decided to till up the garden. While that worked to clear out most of the bushes, some of the climbing roses refused to die. They still sprout up in the spring.

There was still life in the stump of Jesse that refused to die, and God birthed His Son through that shoot. God answers faith that refuses to die. Jesus was born in a dark place at a dark time bringing light to the world. One spark of hope can accomplish great things when the Spirit of God rests upon it.

The Spirit of God is a Spirit of wisdom and understanding, a Spirit of counsel and strength, a Spirit of knowledge and of the fear of the Lord. Notice that it is NOT described as the Spirit of power and might. This Spirit works in the soul—the mind, will, and emotions—of people. Jesus was a man mighty on the inside because God's Spirit rested upon Him.

Isaiah 11:10:

On that day the root of Jesse will stand as a banner for the peoples. The nations will seek Him, and His resting place will be glorious.

Eventually, all nations will seek this Messiah for the rest He gives. People are dying from stress every day. They desperately need the Spirit of the Lord on the inside that only Jesus can give. Ironically, the season of Messiah's birth is one of the most stressful times of year. While rushing to get things done and depleting finances to try to please everyone, we lose sight of the very reason we celebrate. The root of Jesse, born in a lowly stable with the Spirit of God resting on Him, provides a glorious resting place for us all.

God still births new life out of our stumps, and He brings rest to those who seek Him and have hope in Him. Have a faith that refuses to die, and find rest in the root of Jesse. Such rest is glorious!

Have a blessed day!

From Disgrace to Delight

Luke 1:25:

"The Lord has done this for me. He has looked with favor in these days to take away my disgrace among the people."

These are the words of Elizabeth concerning her pregnancy. She was beyond child bearing years, and she obviously felt the social disgrace associated with barrenness. While she was loved as a wife and was an honorable, God-fearing woman, she still bore shame from not being able to bear a child.

Elizabeth's disgrace did not reside with God but among the people. She was *less than* in social circles. People assumed something must be wrong with her in God's eyes since she did not have a child. Barrenness was often believed to be a curse from God. God, however, removed her disgrace and the wrong assumption of people by granting her a son in her old age. He made her fruitful in the days she could not bear fruit on her own. This was an obvious sign of God's favor upon her, and no one would be able to argue this sign of His pleasure.

You cannot steal or manipulate the blessing of favor. This blessing resonates with everyone who sees it, and it testifies to the presence, power, and purpose of God. God's favor blesses us and brings Him glory. Elizabeth received such a blessing at a time when she thought it was too late for her, proving that God's favor can rest upon us at any time in our lives. This reminds us that it is never too late for God to bless us and take away any social disgrace!

Elizabeth gave birth to no ordinary son. He was John the Baptist, the forerunner of Christ who prepared the way for His earthly ministry. Everyone knew he was a special child because of the details of his birth. This gave credibility to his message, and those who followed him were able to receive the message of Christ. God always anoints what He ordains, and He stamps it with authenticity.

Is there a place in your life where you feel disgraced? One touch of God's favor can change all that, but you cannot manipulate it or expect Him to bless what you have done in the flesh. When God's favor rests upon you, your blessing is authentic and full of grace. Take your disgraceful places to Him, and ask Him to grant you His favor. Ask Him to reveal His glory in you. We were created to bring Him glory, and He delights to extend favor to those who are fully His.

Have a blessed day!

The Value of a Gift

Isaiah 9:6:

For a child will be born for us, a son will be given to us, and the government will be on His shoulders. He will be named Wonderful Counselor, Mighty God, Eternal Father, Prince of Peace.

Here we find the promise of no ordinary child. This child is the solution to all of our problems. He is endowed with power from God to resolve all the bad things of this world. His name is Wonderful Counselor, meaning He can perform miracles and give wisdom in all situations. He is Mighty God, full of strength and ultimate power and authority. He is Eternal Father, meaning He lives forever. He is Prince of Peace, bringing end to all wars. He is Jesus. Why in this world would we not want to know Him?

Notice that a child was born *for* us. Usually in Scripture where you find a child born, it notes the child was born *to* someone. This child was given as a sacrifice from our heavenly Father for our benefit. All things are possible through Him, and our redemption is found in Him. God could give no greater gift than His own Son and relationship with Him through that Son. Why would we reject such a gift?

We reject what we do not value. Those who reject Christ do not understand His value and have foolishly discounted Him to follow their own path, which will always lead them to a *less than* life of unfulfilled dreams and unmet needs. A pig has no use for pearls and will reject them for mud and slop. What you value reveals what you are.

A child was born for you. God gave His only Son to you. He values you more than you value yourself, and He gave you the very best He had. This is a love worth noticing, worth having, and worth cherishing.

Have a blessed day!

A Light Has Dawned

Isaiah 9:2:

The people walking in darkness have seen a great light; on those living in the land of darkness, a light has dawned.

Jesus was born during a very dark time in Israel's history. God had not spoken through the prophets in over 400 years. They were living under Roman rule and yearning for independence as a nation. God's covenant before them was the law, which merely exposed their sins. The law did nothing to redeem them from their sin. Religious leaders took advantage of this to control the people through tradition. There was no hope for them to ever get beyond their miserable state.

The birth of the Messiah, however, was a promise that had not yet been fulfilled. The coming Messiah would free them from their current bondage and bring new life full of hope, freedom, and abundance. The birth of Jesus was the light that broke the darkness of this era. Few had the privilege to see it firsthand.

While we may be living in darkness, we have one advantage over Israel during the time of Jesus's birth. We live under a new covenant of grace because of His finished work on the cross! What Jesus came to do brought light to Israel, but what He has already done brings light to us. Because of His sacrifice, we have hope. We can depend upon a grace that has the power to raise the dead! To experience this grace, we need only to keep our eyes on Jesus. He is our light for the dark path we follow in this world. When we don't know which direction to take because it all seems dark, He shines a light to direct our next step. When one door shuts, His grace opens a window of encouragement.

Isaiah 64:4:

From ancient times no one has heard, no one has listened, no eye has seen any God except You, who acts on behalf of the one who waits for Him.

If your world seems dark, focus upon Jesus, and wait for His light. Walking in the dark may cause you to fall. He goes before us, making sure we are on a good path. Wait for Him to lead you down that good path. He always has and always will act on your behalf.

Have a blessed day!

The Glory of the Lord Shone Around Them

Luke 2:8-9:

In the same region, shepherds were staying out in the fields and keeping watch at night over their flock. Then an angel of the Lord stood before them, and the glory of the Lord shone around them, and they were terrified.

Shepherds were among the lowly of society. They were humble, hard-working, men who were considered common. They had no claim to fame or royalty. They were simply ordinary citizens. These certain shepherds were just minding their own business one blessed night when an angel appeared and brought an astounding message to them. Why them?

Shepherds were trained to care for sheep, which were merely dumb animals who often wandered into danger to wild predators. In many ways, sheep are similar to humans in that we carelessly wander into the traps of the Devil without any recognition of his schemes or devices. Without someone to look over us, we would be little more than dumb sheep ourselves.

We often compare pastors to shepherds today. Most earn meager salaries and are often wearied with the cares, concerns, and problems their sheep create within the church. While they serve an honorable and vital service to society, they are often ridiculed or disrespected by unbelievers. Like shepherds of old, they are only human and are subject to failure themselves. To such men, however, an angel appeared.

While going about your day just minding your own business, remember that the news of the Savior came to simple, common, ordinary, hard-working men who were in the midst of doing what they were supposed to do. God has good news for you: He wants you to experience His glory, just as those shepherds did! Jesus came for you, and we live in a day of His grace, where anything is possible for those who believe in Him! God's glory can be terrifying because of its greatness and humbling because of its power. His glory, however, is not reserved for the elite. He freely grants it to those who have a heart for Him.

Have a blessed day!

Good News of Great Joy for All

Luke 2:10-12:

But the angel said to them, "Don't be afraid, for look, I proclaim to you good news of great joy that will be for all the people: today a Savior, who is Messiah the Lord, was born for you in the city of David. This will be the sign for you: you will find a baby wrapped snugly in cloth and lying in a feeding trough."

The angel had news of great joy for everyone, but the shepherds heard it first! They even received direction of where to find the baby and a description so they would recognize Him. Would they be faithful to search for Him? Would they spread the news?

Jesus certainly came for all people in the world, but not everyone finds Him. Those of us who have been given the privilege of clear direction and understanding need to lead others to Him. While we may never encounter a personal visit from an angel in this lifetime, we can certainly experience the presence of Jesus and spread the news of His coming.

Who in your life needs to know about the miracle of Christ? Who is still working in the dark and needing hope? The angel intended for the shepherds to spread the news, and God intends for His children to do the same. Don't be afraid to share the good news of great joy that Christ has come into the world. While some may not believe you, others are desperately looking for a glimmer of hope. Jesus is more than just a glimmer. He is our blessed hope and our sure salvation.

Have a blessed day!

Peace and Favor

Luke 2:13-14:

Suddenly there was a multitude of the heavenly host with the angel, praising God and saying: Glory to God in the highest heaven, and peace on earth to people He favors!

The angel was not alone in his proclamation to the shepherds. A heavenly host appeared with him, bearing witness to God's Word. When God speaks to us, He often gives other witnesses to His Word to us. We might read it in Scripture and later hear a sermon preached on that very thing. We may hear the same verse repeated elsewhere during the day. A friend may say something that confirms what we read earlier. God bears witness to His Word in many ways, but in this instance, a multitude of the heavenly host appeared with the angel to praise God. This was a message the shepherds could not deny or forget; they had to act upon it.

The angels were proclaiming glory to God and peace on earth to people He favors. Indeed, the glory of God will bring peace to those God favors. If we are in Christ, He gives us His peace, and God favors those who are in Christ. In a world where chaos, uncertainty, and extreme wickedness abound, God's peace and favor are blessings that transform our lives and sustain us through difficult times. How fitting it is that upon the birth of Christ, the angels sang of peace on earth to those God favors.

This peace and favor can be yours today. If you don't know Christ as Savior, now is the time to start walking in the peace and divine favor of a new life. If you are already a Christian, start speaking His peace to your trying situations, and believe His favor is upon you to do whatever you are called to do. Peace and favor are part of God's gift to us in Christ. Don't trade them for the lesser things of worry and strife. The angels thought they were reason to sing. You should, too!

Have a blessed day!

Go Straight to Bethlehem

Luke 2:15-16:

When the angels had left them and returned to heaven the shepherds said to one another, "Let's go straight to Bethlehem and see what has happened, which the Lord has made known to us." They hurried off and found both Mary and Joseph, and the baby who was lying in the feeding trough.

On an ordinary night, to an ordinary people, news of the extraordinary appeared. The shepherds knew they had to go right away to Bethlehem. They also knew God had made the proclamation known to them. They didn't worry about the sheep. They went straight to Bethlehem to find the baby. They had known of the promise from ancestors who believed for centuries, but they would see the fulfillment.

When they acted upon the news, they found exactly what the angels said they would find—Mary, Joseph, and the baby in the feeding trough. God promised it centuries earlier. The angels proclaimed the time was now. The shepherds saw the evidence after they acted upon it.

In our own lives, God may promise something that doesn't materialize right away. We often have to wait long periods of time before we see that thing happen, and many of us even give up hope. Then one day in the midst of our ordinary lives, God sends word that His miracle has happened or is about to happen. Will we believe Him and go where He leads or shrink back in disbelief? Those shepherds would have lived lives of regret if they had disregarded the message. Christ would have still come for the world, but they would not have been able to participate in the glorious arrival. Don't let disbelief hinder you from experiencing the miracles of God in your own life. He still works in extraordinary ways for and through ordinary people, including you.

Move straight into what God has told you to do today. Even if you have experienced failure in the past, God will bring about exactly what He has promised! Don't let regret ruin your destiny. Run straight to your Bethlehem to see what God says is true!

Have a blessed day!

Celebration and Meditation

Luke 2:17-20:

After seeing them, they reported the message they were told about this child, and all who heard it were amazed at what the shepherds said to them. But Mary was treasuring up all these things in her heart and meditating on them. The shepherds returned, glorifying and praising God for all they had seen and heard, just as they had been told.

The shepherds acted in faith and saw the evidence of the promise. They were so excited they couldn't help but share the good news. Mary, however, enjoyed the moment. She knew she had participated in God's divine plan and treasured every moment in her heart.

We often expect the shouting, excitement, and praise of the great moments of our lives, and there is a time and place for that. These miracle moments, however, are also times to realize that we are partakers with the Divine in His plan. Moments of reverence and awe are appropriate, as well.

Don't miss a thing of what God has planned for you. Take time to praise Him and celebrate the goodness He pours into your life, but also take time to meditate on what you see Him doing in and through you. Christ gives us the opportunity for both celebration and reflection. Your relationship with God is multi-dimensional, and your purpose is multi-faceted. Being a partaker in God's divine plan is too awesome an experience to rush or ignore. Cherish every moment, and praise Him for it!

Have a blessed day!

Return with Joy

Luke 2:20:

The shepherds returned, glorifying and praising God for all they had seen and heard, just as they had been told.

The shepherds went back to their fields and their lives as changed men. The dullness and boredom of their ordinary routine caved to shouts of glory and praise to God. We don't know what happened to these men afterward, but their experience left them feeling joyous and blessed. They had learned to take God at His word and that when you least expect it, you can experience a blessing so great that it takes your breath away.

God is always working in our lives, even when we can't see Him, hear Him, or feel Him. At some point, He will alert you to what He has been doing, and you can choose to go where He tells you or remain where you are in disbelief. God will not lie to you or set you up for false hope and disappointment. He is doing something praiseworthy in your life that you don't want to miss. Your experience with Him will reveal God's glory and draw you to praise. Your alternative is to remain in your dullness and nothingness and wish something would happen.

Believe God's word to you and act on it. Praise Him for the miracles you have already experienced. Know that He is working in the midst of your nothingness.

Have a blessed day!

A Gift Worthy of Worship

Matthew 2:9-11:

After hearing the king, they went on their way. And there it was—the star they had seen in the east! It led them until it came and stopped above the place where the child was. When they saw the star, they were overjoyed beyond measure. Entering the house, they saw the child with Mary His mother, and falling to their knees, they worshiped Him.

Then they opened their treasures and presented Him with gifts: gold, frankincense, and myrrh.

Jesus was worshiped by lowly, Jewish shepherds and wealthy, educated Gentiles. He came as Savior to every race and every class of people. Even as a baby, He is worthy of all our praise, and one day, every knee shall bow and acknowledge Him as Lord (Phil. 2:10-11).

The wise men were diligent in their search for Jesus. They recognized His significance with the rising star and knew it was a sign in the heavens of divine deity on earth. Notice that they were "overjoyed beyond measure" when they found Him. Upon finding Jesus, they immediately fell at their feet in worship. This is the appropriate response.

As a part of their worship, the wise men gave Jesus gifts from their treasures. Gold, frankincense, and myrrh were gifts suitable for a king. Gold was used as money and was also as a metal to create ornate objects normally found in palaces or temples. Frankincense was incense normally used in the temples at the altar for sacrifice. When a sacrifice was made, the incense was burned as a pleasing aroma. Myrrh was a vegetable often used in embalming oil and in holy anointing oil. Gold represented His deity. Frankincense indicated the sacrifice He would make. Myrrh pointed to both His death and the anointing of His ministry. Although they were Gentile by birth, the wise men believed in the purpose of Jesus, and they chose to worship Him.

The best gift you can possibly give this Christmas is to give Jesus your worship. Believe in His purpose as these wise men did, and diligently seek Him. Give Him the best you have, and trust His purpose in your life will be fulfilled. He is God's gift to us; we should honor Him as Lord, recognize the sacrifice He made, and realize the resurrection power that lives in Him is ours through faith. He is a gift worthy of worship.

Have a blessed day!

Joseph's Heart

Matthew 1:18-19:

The birth of Jesus Christ came about this way: After His mother Mary had been engaged to Joseph, it was discovered before they came together that she was pregnant by the Holy Spirit. So her husband Joseph being a righteous man, and not wanting to disgrace her publicly, decided to divorce her secretly.

These verses explain why it is important we understand Joseph's point of view in this birth. He had a major role to play, and what he did would affect history. Joseph and Mary were betrothed to be married. In those days, this was a legal procedure. Marriages were usually arranged, and couples were betrothed or engaged through law before they were actually married. They did not live together or engage in intimacy until they were married. The betrothal period was a legally binding courtship. To end it required divorce.

Under Mosaic law, a Hebrew man was not to marry a woman who was not a virgin unless she was a widow. Since Mary was betrothed to Joseph and was pregnant, he could have had her stoned. Such an indecent action from a virgin would have been a crime against both her father and her betrothed husband. This was the practice of most cultures that lived around the Hebrew people during that time. Imagine how many young women in our culture would die today.

Joseph cared enough about Mary not to have her stoned. He had decided to divorce her quietly. This shows a tremendous amount of honor and humility on his part. As her betrothed, he honored Mary and would have allowed her to go her own way without requiring anything of her. He was willing to let her out of their agreement. He was also humble enough to not let pride destroy him. He did not seem to care about his reputation or what others would think because he had Mary's best interest at heart. This is the heart a woman can trust!

Mary, however, was still a virgin. There was no reason Joseph could not marry her. He just needed to be informed of the situation, so God sent an angel to speak to him, as well.

Verses 20-25:

But after he had considered these things, an angel of the Lord suddenly appeared to him in a dream, saying, "Joseph, son of David, don't be afraid to take Mary as your wife, because what has been conceived in her is by the Holy Spirit. She will give birth to a son, and you are to name Him Jesus, because He will save His people from their sins." Now all this took place to fulfill what was spoken by the Lord through the prophet: See, the virgin will become pregnant and give birth to a son, and they will name Him Immanuel, which is translated "God is with us." When Joseph got up from sleeping, he did as the Lord's angel had commanded him. He married her but did not know her intimately until she gave birth to a son. And he named Him Jesus.

The angel did some things in this dream that assure Joseph this was an act of God. First, he addressed him as the son of David. People who studied the Old Testament knew that the Messiah would come through David's line, and the angel reminded Joseph of his ancestry. (Mary was also a descendant of David.) Secondly, he quoted Scripture to Joseph. Isaiah 7:14 prophesied the birth of a son born to a virgin who would be called Immanuel. The angel explained to Joseph how the prophecy was being fulfilled through Mary.

Joseph did not question the angel. He merely received the word and immediately obeyed. This is the heart of a man that God can trust! I'm convinced God searches for hearts like Joseph's to use for His divine purposes. These men are rare treasures. God chose him as divinely as He did Mary to parent His Son. Joseph's love for Mary and his willingness to obey God would later prove crucial to Jesus's survival when he was warned in a dream to take Mary and Jesus to Egypt.

We may be women, but we can still have a heart like that of Joseph. May we be women who honor the Word of God and who quickly obey when God speaks. There is no telling how He might use such a heart for His purpose.

Have a blessed day!

Christmas: An Act of Warfare

Isaiah 9:6-7:

For a child will be born for us, a son will be given to us, and the government will be on His shoulders. He will be named Wonderful Counselor, Mighty God, Eternal Father, Prince of Peace. The dominion will be vast, and its prosperity will never end. He will reign on the throne of David and over his kingdom to establish and sustain it with justice and righteousness from now on and forever. The zeal of the LORD of Hosts will accomplish this.

This prophecy of the Savior's birth brings a very strong statement. We are fortunate to recognize this Son given as Jesus. His government can be recognized by the titles given here: Wonderful Counselor, Mighty God, Eternal Father, Prince of Peace. This is a government we can truly trust.

His dominion is proclaimed to be large and prosperous. The kingdom of God is fruitful and growing, bringing many to know Christ. Since God is the source of all true wealth, his kingdom is prosperous.

Jesus came to establish David's throne and sustain it with justice and righteousness. Jesus's sacrifice on the cross satisfies God's demand for justice. When we believe and accept that sacrifice, we are made righteous before God. Jesus not only establishes us in righteousness, He also sustains us through His righteousness!

The zeal of the Lord of Hosts will accomplish this reign. To have zeal is to have passion and purpose. The Lord of Hosts refers to God as a mighty warrior. Out of God's passion and purpose for us, He sent Jesus to proclaim war on the Devil! Jesus is God's mightiest weapon against the enemy!

To look at the birth of a baby as an act of war may be difficult, but that is exactly what Jesus was. Every year we celebrate this birth, and it must make the Devil angry to see Jesus magnified in such a grand and glorious way. No wonder he has tried to distract us with commercialism and schemed to change the name of the event altogether!

The birth of Jesus was predestined. Although the Devil tried to stop it and harmed many in the process, the zeal of the Lord of Hosts accomplished it. The Devil continually tries to attack the reign of Christ and all His benefits in the lives of Christians, but the work of the cross sustains us. The Devil will continue to fight against this kingdom until he is defeated and thrown into the lake of fire, but the zeal of the Lord of Hosts has other plans. He will accomplish all He has sent His Son to accomplish because of His zeal— His great passion and purpose—for us!

As you celebrate Christmas with your loved ones, remember that this whole event was an act of warfare. This precious baby was born to defeat your greatest enemy, and the zeal of the Lord of Hosts is with you. Why would we ever want to take Christ out of Christmas?

Have a blessed day!

Out of Egypt

Matthew 2:13-15:

After they (wise men) had gone, an angel of the Lord suddenly appeared to Joseph in a dream, saying, "Get up! Take the child and His mother, flee to Egypt, and stay there until I tell you. For Herod is about to search for the child to destroy Him." So he got up, took the child and His mother during the night, and escaped to Egypt. He stayed there until Herod's death, so that what was spoken by the Lord through the prophet might be fulfilled: Out of Egypt I called My Son.

Egypt was not Mary and Joseph's home; it was a temporary place. Egypt represented a history of bondage for the Israelites. God had once rescued them from that awful place. Now, the angel told Joseph to take Jesus and Mary and flee there for safety. Why would God take them back to a painful place for refuge?

God sent them to Egypt to hide from Herod, who was determined to kill the eternal king of Israel. Egypt was a place of safety for them. Herod had no jurisdiction in Egypt, and who would think the Messiah would flee to a place which had such terrible memories for God's chosen people? Remember that Joseph was taken there as a slave, where he rose to power to save his brothers. Egypt was a place of temporary relief from the famine, but the Israelites made a home there and enjoyed the fruit of the land until Pharaoh subjected them to heavy labor. This required a deliverer, which

God provided in Moses—a man from among their own people. Moses was a symbol of Christ. Now, upon the birth of Christ, God sent them back to Egypt to fulfill the prophecy in Hosea 11:1, which declared that God would call His Son out of Egypt. Jesus went back to provide an illustration of what God did for the nation of Israel. Jesus, however, did not become a slave to the surroundings of Egypt. He went there as a free individual, and He left as a free individual. His stay was temporary, as it was intended to be.

Have you ever found yourself going back to a painful place that you thought you'd never see again because God had delivered you? You may have even asked yourself the question, "Why am I here again?" If God takes you back to a place from which He delivered you, His purpose is not to take you back into bondage with it. Rather, it is to enable you to take dominion over it. Your Egypt is a temporary place to hide you from the enemy that wants to destroy you, a place where you are meant to be. Once that enemy is defeated, God will call you back to the place you are called to minister.

The baby Jesus did not defeat Herod. God took his life. In fact, history reveals he probably lived no more than a year after Jesus was born. God is perfectly capable of removing the Herods in your life that are jealous of what God has reserved for you and want to destroy you in hopes of taking the glory that is rightfully God's. Allow Him to take you to a temporary Egypt while He takes care of those rascals for you. Take dominion over the areas that once held you captive, and wait for God to call you back to the place where you belong. Out of Egypt God called His son, and out of Egypt He will call you.

Have a blessed day!

From Egypt to Nazareth

Matthew 2:19-23:

After Herod died, an angel of the Lord suddenly appeared in a dream to Joseph in Egypt, saying, "Get up! Take the child and His mother and go to the land of Israel, because those who sought the child's life are dead." So he got up, took the child and His mother, and entered the land of Israel. But when he heard that Archelaus was ruling over Judea in place of his father Herod, he was afraid to go there. And being warned in a dream,

he withdrew to the region of Galilee. There he went and settled in a town called Nazareth to fulfill what was spoken through the prophets, that He will be called a Nazarene.

God sent Joseph, Mary, and Jesus to Egypt temporarily while He took care of the enemy in Jerusalem. Once that enemy was dead, He told Joseph to bring his family back to Israel. They were not to stay in Egypt, where they were completely safe from the enemy's threats or power. Joseph obeyed.

To leave our comfort zones can be challenging, especially when they are nestled right smack center in a place of bondage. Herod probably died within a year of Jesus's birth. God did not let them stay in Egypt long enough to become slaves to the environment. He knew if they became too comfortable there, they might not want to leave. He called them out of Egypt and back into their own land. He will do the same with us.

Have you ever become comfortable in a place where you knew you didn't belong? You were safe, but your heart longed for another place. This might be an indication that God is calling you out of your comfort zone and into the place He has ordained for you to grow, minister, and fulfill your destiny. Just what prevents us from leaving our own Egypts?

This Scripture reveals the primary reason we hesitate to go into our promised land. When Joseph heard that Archelaus was ruling in Judea in place of his father, Herod, he was afraid to go there. Fear can be a bigger enemy to us that the physical one with power to hurt us. Joseph knew, however, that if God had sent an angel to give him a message, he had better obey its instructions. Those instructions were to go to Israel, not necessarily to Jerusalem. Since Herod's son had come to power, some degree of threat still existed for Jesus. Joseph settled in Nazareth, within Israel but far enough outside Jerusalem that he was not under the enemy's nose. Thus, he fulfilled the prophecy that Jesus would be called a Nazarene.

Where are you afraid to go? What are God's instructions to you? He will not lead you to a place of harm. If He is leading you to Nazareth, don't be afraid of Jerusalem. Let Him take care of any threat. Nazareth will be a place where you can grow until He can safely lead you to Jerusalem. Nazareth is worth leaving your comfort zone. Nazareth is your launching pad to success.

Have a blessed day!

The Herod Throne

Matthew 2:16:

Then Herod, when he saw that he had been outwitted by the wise men, flew into a rage. He gave orders to massacre all the male children in and around Bethlehem who were two years old and under, in keeping with the time he had learned from the wise men.

If you are thinking Herod seems very vain and evil, you are correct! He was also very paranoid and executed his own son, whom he suspected was planning to usurp his throne. Herod made the mistake of believing that his throne made him immortal. He had heard of a coming king that would reign forever, and he foolishly thought that as long as he could keep the throne, he could be that king. He thought he could determine his own destiny, and he sought to destroy anyone who threatened his rule. Sadly, many of us are just like him.

Somehow, our fallen nature as humanity foolishly believes we are immortal. We see this evident in our younger years when we think we have our whole lives in front of us. As long as we are calling the shots as king of our own lives, we think life will never end. We even try to destroy anyone who threatens our kingship. We have all witnessed this attitude in ourselves or in someone we love. This life never changes until it is surrendered to Christ and submitted to His authority. Like Herod, we cannot stop the power of the King of Kings and Lord of Lords from rising, and our only hope of eternal life is found in Him.

Herod probably died within a year of Jesus's birth. Herod was still king when he died, and his throne could not save him. Our own thrones can do no better for us, either.

Does the thought of Jesus's coming cause you to rejoice, or does it threaten you in some way? He is coming again, and we will see more Herod-like activity as this time approaches. Are you willing to give up your throne to receive Him and make Him your king, or do you want to hold on to what you have in fear of losing some idea of power you think you have? We must all be like the wise men who diligently sought Jesus and gave Him their very best. Herods amount to nothing in the end, but the wise are happy as Jesus's subjects.

Have a blessed day!

Not By Bread Alone

Matthew 4:3-4:

Then the tempter approached Him and said, "If You are the Son of God, tell these stones to become bread." But he answered, "It is written: Man must not live on bread alone but on every word that comes from the mouth of God."

The Devil approached Jesus in the wilderness at a time when he was hungry to tempt Him. His body was physically craving food, so the Devil's suggestion of turning stones into bread seemed to meet a need. Jesus's response, however, indicated that He respected the Father's will in meeting His need. He knew God was His source, and any attempt to try to manipulate an answer was falling into the Devil's trap.

Jesus quoted Deuteronomy 8:3 to the Devil: "He humbled you by letting you go hungry; then He gave you manna to eat, which you and your fathers had not known, so that you might learn that man does not live on bread alone but on every word that comes from the mouth of the Lord."

If God is not the source of the thing that will meet your physical need, you don't want it! If the Devil is leading you into it, it will cost you dearly in the long run. Attempting to meet a legitimate need in an illegitimate way is bowing to the Devil, who will always offer you an easy route to meeting a hunger inside you. He may even try to convince you that God is not concerned, and that the only way to satisfy your hunger is to sin. This is how we justify sin to ourselves. In our minds, we have no alternative.

Jesus, however, presented another alternative for us in this temptation. Wait on God! He never denied His hunger because it was real. He relied upon the Word of God to meet that need, and He quoted it back to the Devil when He was tempted. When we are hungry and in need, we will expose what we really believe when we are tempted. Either we will bow to the Devil and meet that need through sin, or we will wait for God to meet it supernaturally, as He did for the Hebrew children in the wilderness with manna from heaven. If we bow to the Devil, we forfeit what God provides—ministry!

After Jesus resisted all of the Devil's temptations in the wilderness, the Devil left Him, and angels came to serve Him. They restored His strength.

This was the beginning of His earthly ministry and exactly what the Devil wanted to steal—Jesus's sinlessness. Had he been successful, we would have no suitable sacrifice for our sin, and the Devil would have inherited our souls.

Every solution to our problem is not a godly solution. While something may be very enticing, if it leads us into sin, we forfeit the ministry God has placed in us. Allow Him to meet your every need, and watch to see how His angels come to serve you. He is concerned about meeting every hungry place you have, and He allowed you to go hungry for a purpose. God revealed His glory through His Son with miracles, signs, and wonders, and He wants to reveal His glory in you as His beloved child. Let Him meet your every need so the world will see His child revealed. You never know who might be depending upon your victory over the Devil to reach their own.

Have a blessed day!

No Compromise

Matthew 4:9-11:

Again, the Devil took Him to a very high mountain and showed Him all the kingdoms of the world and their splendor. And he said to Him, "I will give You all these things if You will fall down and worship me." Then Jesus told him, "Go away, Satan! For it is written: Worship the Lord your God, and serve only Him." Then the Devil left Him, and immediately angels came and began to serve Him.

The Devil took Jesus to a very high mountain. It seems he always comes to tempt us at a high point. He gave Jesus a view of all the kingdoms of the world and told them they could be His instantly if He would only bow down and worship him. We must never lose sight of the vision and purpose God gave us and continue to serve only Him.

If Jesus had bowed down to Satan and inherited the world as the Devil has promised, He would have never had to go to the cross. He would never had to have suffered nor been whipped. But, He would never have defeated Satan and resurrected, either! Compromise may give you what you think you want at an easy price, but it will cost you in the long run. If Jesus had negotiated with the Devil, He would have inherited a world full of sickness, pain, sin, and hopelessness. The Devil comes to steal, kill, and destroy, and to serve him means we enter into his purpose with him. The only world the Devil could have given Jesus was a defeated one. Christ had a greater purpose in serving the Father, and He did not lose sight of it. God gave Him victory over this fallen world and authority over His kingdom.

God wants to bless you, but more importantly than that, He wants you to gain victory over the enemy in your life. You will never gain that full victory if you accept a blessing through compromise and worship the Devil through sin. That blessing may shine and sparkle at first, but you will also inherit all the works of the Devil associated with it. God's glory is never tainted with sin, and it does not come with consequences to pay. Jesus paid it all on the cross!

Worship the Lord your God, and serve only Him. When Jesus took this stand, the Devil left Him. Make this next year a year of no compromise, and watch to see what wonders God will work in you and through you!

Have a blessed day!

God's Last Word to Us

Revelation 22:21:

The grace of the Lord Jesus be with all the saints. Amen.

How interesting to see that the last words of the Bible are a proclamation of grace toward the saints. They are a final reminder that we cannot make it through this life nor have any hope for the next without the grace of our Lord Jesus. Grace is the reason Jesus came. Grace is the means we can have a relationship with a holy God, and it is the one factor that can change any situation in our lives for our good and His glory. We must never underestimate its power or take it for granted. We must cling to it, knowing that we cannot survive without it.

Our children face overwhelming stress in the world today. They must meet academic standards that will actually rank them in the classroom. They must fight peer pressure that encourages unhealthy competition or complete surrender. For those graduating high school or college, hopes of a better life are diminishing with increasing unemployment and poor economic forecasts. Even the best and brightest may seem socially awkward in a world that no longer nourishes the spiritual and emotional development of young people. The grace of the Lord Jesus is the one thing that can distinguish them from the rest. His hand of favor can take them farther than they ever dreamed possible, but many have no concept of this grace or how vital it is to our lives.

We are where we are today by the grace of the Lord Jesus. He has never left us and promised He would be with us until the end of the age. That means that His grace abounds to us. Our young people need this revelation of grace to overcome the battles they must face. If the Devil can cause them to lose hope completely, he will claim them for his very own. Take time to invest in the lives of young people around you. Reassure them of God's love for them and of this wonderful gift of grace He has so lavishly poured upon us. Encourage them in the hope of a living Christ who intercedes for them daily. The grace of the Lord Jesus is with His saints today. May His saints be a living expression of this grace to a world that desperately needs it! Grace is God's last word to us—and should be the one we cherish and proclaim the most.

Have a blessed day!

CPSIA information can be obtained at www.ICGtesting.com
Printed in the USA
LVOW13s0835020314

375595LV00005B/7/P